DESERTIFICATION IN THE WORLD
Adapted from the World Map of Desertification

Deserts are marked in black
Dots outline the limits of the subhumid

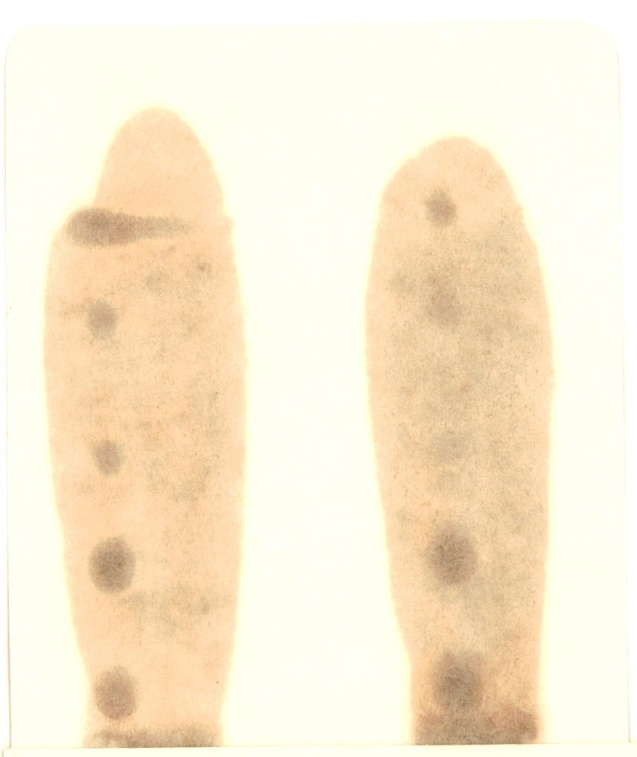

659146

**MARY AND JOHN GRAY
LIBRARY
LAMAR UNIVERSITY
BEAUMONT, TEXAS**

LAND, MAN,
AND SAND

LAND, MAN, AND SAND

Desertification and Its Solution

James Walls

MACMILLAN PUBLISHING CO., INC.
NEW YORK

Collier Macmillan Publishers
LONDON

Copyright © 1980 by Macmillan Publishing Co., Inc.

All rights reserved. No part of this book may be reproduced or transmitted in any form or by any means, electronic or mechanical, including photocopying, recording, or by any information storage and retrieval system, without permission in writing from the Publisher.

Macmillan Publishing Co., Inc.
866 Third Avenue, New York, N. Y. 10022

Collier Macmillan Canada, Ltd.

Library of Congress Catalog Card Number: 79-7852

Printed in the United States of America

printing number

1 2 3 4 5 6 7 8 9 10

Library of Congress Cataloging in Publication Data
Walls, James.
　Land, man, and sand.

　Author uses as point of reference the 15 case studies prepared for the United Nations Conference on Desertification, held in Nairobi, Kenya, August 1977.
　Bibliography: p.
　Includes index.
　1. Desertification.　2. United Nations Conference on Desertification, Nairobi, 1977.　3. Arid regions agriculture.　4. Desertification—Control.　I. United Nations Conference on Desertification, Nairobi, 1977. I. Title.
GB611.W28　　363.3'4　　　　79-7852
ISBN 0-02-699810-6

Permission was granted to quote material from the following sources: on pp. 17, 266, and 267, from Harold E. Dregne, ed., *Arid Lands in Transition* (Washington, D.C.: Publication No. 90, American Association for the Advancement of Science, 1970); on pp. 48 and 167, from René Grousset, *The Empire of the Steppes,* tr. Naomi Walford, copyright © 1970 by Rutgers University, The State University of New Jersey and reprinted by permission of Rutgers University Press; on p. 127, from Jeremy Swift, *Desertization in the Sahel* (unpublished mimeo.); on pp. 131 and 135, from John C. Caldwell, *The Sahelian Drought and Its Implications* (Overseas Liaison Committee, American Council on Education, OLC Paper No. 8, December 1975); and on pp. 260, 264, and 280, from Paulo Freire, *Pedagogy of the Oppressed*, tr. Myra Bergman Ramos (New York: Seabury Press, 1970) and *Education for Critical Consciousness* (New York: Seabury Press, 1973).

The maps were adapted from the case studies by Alexandra Reynolds.

For Margaret Anyango

CONTENTS

Preface ix
1. Nairobi 1
2. Mussayeb 23
3. Turfan 45
4. Gascoyne 59
5. Wushenchao 77
6. Oglat Merteba 91
7. Eghazer and Azawak 117
8. Combarbalá 145
9. Vale 163
10. Luni 179
11. Mona 197
12. Golodnaya Steppe 213
13. Turkmenia 227
14. China 245
15. The Negev 275
16. Turan 293
References 317
Index 323

PREFACE

The United Nations Conference on Desertification was my second such experience. I also worked as a writer and editor for the World Population Conference, held under United Nations auspices in Bucharest, Romania, in 1974. For me, these important events were episodes in an effort to figure out something that has puzzled me since I first started writing for the Peace Corps in 1961 when that organization was new and full of hope. The problem that confused me then—and still does—is why there are so many poor people in a world so filled with riches.

In 17 years I have come to the conclusion that the answer to this puzzle is not to be found in the study of economics. Meanwhile I have passed through three or four different attitudes as to what poverty is and what it means to be poor. Lately, and about time it is, too, I have begun to get a feeling that the reasons for poverty are the same as the reasons for the other disasters and calamities that add so much to the variety and flavor of modern life. The problem of desertification helped me to see that. And that, in turn, has fashioned the way I have approached the subject of desertification, following a suggestion of Tom Wright at Macmillan that the subject might be shaped by the 15 case studies that were prepared for the Conference on Desertification. As I have taken up the case studies, one by one, I have used each as an occasion for discussing desertification in one or another of its more general aspects.

In so doing, I make frequent citations from the case studies, but not always in precisely the words of the original. Here it must be remembered that the case studies are conference documents prepared under pressure and against deadlines. They contain errors of typography, grammar, and syntax, and bursts of fanciful translation which I have not hesitated to correct. Not all of them, but most—they shriek to be repaired. Anyone unhappy with my "improvements" can refer to the originals via the page numbers given with the citations. To avoid footnotes, I have placed the citations in the text by number, as the references are listed in the bibliography in the back of the book.

What I have tried to do is to survey desertification in its status as a world problem, one of a number of such whose solutions might be similar, even interconnected, rather than to analyze it as an exercise in agronomy or soils science. There is no point in duplicating what has already been written on the subject, almost all of which has germinated in the fruitful soil of the earth sciences. Besides, I could not do that properly anyway, having only one professional qualification in those domains—I was raised on a farm. Practically everything I have learned about desertification as the specific problem at issue, I have picked up in the university of work—from professionally qualified colleagues in the Conference Secretariat, from the distinguished researchers who, serving as consultants to the Secretariat, provided the scientific foundations for the Plan of Action to Combat Desertification.

Those who gave of their wisdom to the Conference, and a little of their time to me, included the authors of the component reviews, which were also Conference documents—F. Kenneth Hare of the University of Toronto, Andrew Warren of University College London, Douglas Johnson and Robert W. Kates of Clark University, Worcester, Massachusetts, and Manuel Anaya Garduño of the Escuela Nacional de Agricultura, Chapingo, Mexico. Their ranks also included those passers-by in a stream of visitors who came to Nairobi to work for a time with the Conference Secretariat—Harold Dregne of Texas Tech University, Mohammed Kassas of the University of Cairo, Victor Kovda of Moscow University, Brian Spooner of the University of Pennsylvania, Gilbert White of the University of Colorado, and Oliver Ashford of the World Meteorological Organisation. J.A. Mabbutt of the university of New South Wales, my closest colleague and a member of the Secretariat, was a superb companion on and off safari, an unfailing fount of wisdom.

Nor could one have wished for a more stimulating and congenial atmosphere than that provided by the other members of the Conference Secretariat—Sheila Barker, Hedi Bensallah, Christine Blaine, W.J.Y. Duke, Christopher Dunford, Gaafar Karrar, Maureen Kelly, Christina Macdougal, Ruben Mendez, Bhaskar Menon, Najib Omer, Boris Rozanov, Israr ul-Haq—confined together, as we were, for more than a year in the Nairobi headquarters of the United Nations Environment Programme (UNEP). In immediate charge of this small and valiant troupe was Ralph Townley, a career officer in the United Nations who had performed the same function for the World Population Conference. In charge of all was the Secretary General of the Conference, UNEP's Executive Director, the astute, demanding, no-nonsense Mostafa K. Tolba, a scientist himself, with an international reputation in microbiology. All were brilliant sources of instruction, but none responsible for the the statements to follow, and certainly not for the occasional polemic, and even exaggeration, the pleasures of which are so often denied to those with a professional status to maintain.

LAND, MAN, AND SAND

1
NAIROBI

"Everything known is to be assembled—or created"

FINGERS OF THE SAHARA reach down, stroking the Indian Ocean shore in Somalia, reaching toward that shiny new city, the capital of Kenya. From the restaurant atop the Kenyatta Conference Center, above the site of the United Nations Conference on Desertification, the dry Masai plains can be seen stretching southward to Kajiado and the border with Tanzania. The desert, oddly, is in the other direction, to the north, where the view is green. It lies beyond Mount Kenya, the Aberdares, the forested highlands. Far to the north, where the Nile twists toward the barrier of the Aswan Dam, the great desert is at its widest, measured from south to north. Its length, running the other way, stretches across the full width of north Africa—and beyond. Islands out to sea, those called after Cabo Verde, are sere and brown in a maritime Sahara, not at all the color of their name. In the earth's largest desert, or in most of it, little moves that isn't moved by time or the wind that always blows. Yet to say of its variegated landscapes that they are empty is to signify no lack of brilliant color or wide perspectives, only that they are empty of life, that they lack the basis for life, the water from which life sprang, and it is this deficiency that has made the Sahara a barrier between worlds. People do live in it—a few herdsmen roaming its central mountain ranges, there for the grace of upslope convection, a few others confined to tiny garrisons, those dots on the map, cocooned in isolated oases or on huge disks sprinkled green by water sucked up from deep and ancient aquifers.

There was a time when more people lived in the desert, many more than are there today, their presence attested by their paintings on rocks and in caves. They portrayed themselves as on the hunt, African Apaches in what was once a prairie, pursuing the elephant, among other animals, or performing the harvest dance among their stands of grain. North Africa was wetter then, perhaps as wet (or as dry) as Nebraska is today. The desert Sahara, the place we know, has been that way since at least 3000 B.C., wrung out through processes undoubtedly related to shifts in climatic patterns that embrace the entire earth. As the region dried, it became impenetrable—until Roman times, when the camel came into use and caravans began the transport of gold and slaves, salt, and ivory. Nowadays, old caravan routes congeal into roads. Fingers of pavement probe into emptiness. Crossing the Sahara, scheduled freight service began in the mid-seventies even though in places on the two main routes between the port of Algiers and northern Nigeria there is still no road. In those sections, the route is marked by oil drums or stone cairns, and the lorries fan out to avoid each other's dust. From afar, the Tuareg shade their eyes and watch the clouds raised by the convoys, regiments charging south from Europe.

The passage of the desert surprises the traveler reared on antique movies with their seas-of-sand image of a Sahara ceaselessly trampled by ragged detachments of the French Foreign Legion, those stalwarts who all unwittingly helped the desert expand by their intrusions into old, established patterns of life. Seas of sand—*ergs*, as they call them—are located only here and there amidst rocky plains, jagged mountains, and colored stripes of naked strata. Southward on the journey scraggly plants sometimes pop into view, stringing along those dry water courses where streams flowed in those other days when rain used to fall. Only in certain utterly stark places, as when the traveler is crossing Tanezrouft, "land of thirst," will it be quite clear to him that here at last is the true, the absolute desert where life, to survive, must import an environment.

South fron Tanezrouft, the route heads toward the great bend of the River Niger, toward the adobe palaces of Gao, capital of the medieval Songhai Empire. The traveler crosses no physical boundary—there is nothing definite to tell him so—yet he gradually realizes that he is leaving the desert. Plant life comes ever more into view, occasionally in the striped pattern of *brousse tigrée,* the tiger brush that tells the agronomist that the land has recently experienced degradation. The traveler will begin to encounter people, nomads, herders of camels, walking, riding, resting in the thin shade of isolated acacia trees. The presence of people is his signal that he has left the Sahara and entered the Sahel, that immense rangeland to which the last shreds of summer rainfall penetrate after sweeping northward out of the Gulf of Guinea. This is the rain that drenches jungles on the Guinea shore, becoming ever less as it is carried toward the desert in the summer monsoon, petering out at last into nothing where the Sahel and the Sahara merge. As scanty as the rain may be on the desert's edge where the Tuareg herds his camels, to him the worst thing that can happen is for this thin rain to fail utterly, as it sometimes does, and for drought to strike the Sahel. It is something about which he endlessly speculates, estimating the chances of drought for next year, repeating anecdotes from the last drought, or the one before that.

Three times in this century drought has moved in to smother the Sahel in a seemingly endless *soudure*, soldering lips shut against choking dust. The earliest of these episodes, centering on the year 1913, is remembered by the old people as the worst (36, pp. 19-20). Death by starvation moved over the wide pastureland, but caused little stir in Europe where the colonial masters of Africa were preparing to join in world war. A generation later, the second such war was to speed the end of the colonial order, and that conflict was in full flower when drought appeared again in the Sahel. The third episode, a six-year siege, arrived in 1968 to a world turned upside down. The absence of rain now ravaged political entities called nations where none had existed before. To be sure, the Kingdom of Ghana, medieval Mali, old Songhai, Sahelian empires all, had sprung to life and then fallen, but in a sweep of land that had always been recognized as tribal ground. Now the land and all social relations were altered by the novel rule that all places on earth had to belong to some nation or other.

To this Africa added a second rule, one of its own, whose alternative, so it was alleged, would be chaos. For good or ill, these new nations must keep the same boundaries they had been given as colonies, nor did it matter that these frontiers had been sketched in the chancelleries of Europe by people who were as ecstatic over their heady games as they were ignorant of the continent they were parceling out. The inviolability of colonial boundaries, the only alternative to ceaseless dispute, became a founding stone of the Organization of African Unity whether or not such lines hacked apart former ethnic unities, split natural ecosystems, and paid no attention to such natural divisions as watersheds and mountain crests. The senselessness of boundaries was one of several reasons why four of these new Sahelian nations—Chad, Mali, Niger, Upper Volta—had found their place on the United Nations list of "least developed countries," a category erected to focus development assistance where the need is greatest. Only by contrast could prosperity be attributed to the other two Sahelian countries, Senegal and Mauritania, the latter with its mineral deposits newly discovered in the midst of its desert wastes. Nothing in the new geography provided assurances that these new countries had any of the traits or endowments that countries are supposed to have. They had simply arrived—splat!—on maps, born to the shattering discovery that they were hideously poor. They were merely odd conceptions of that industrial world that had also invented modern poverty. Their citizens needed little time to discover that they, too, were poor, each separately so, quickly informing their governments that poverty is also a state of mind, one which has an overwhelming impact on the state of the soil. But then, so do many of these things—new nationhood, whimsical national boundaries, a lack of system and organization.

A world transformed indeed, and in still other ways. By the time of arrival of the century's third Sahelian drought, television had been invented. International news media, their attention not precisely focused on the Sahel, did not awaken to anything amiss until the drought was in its fourth year. By then, the presence of disaster on an international scale was joined to the appeal of the distantly exotic, a nostalgia for vanishing ways of life, to make what was happening in the Sahel into a television spectacular. Pictures of animal skeletons bleaching on powdery soil, refugee camps, children gaunt with measles and malnutrition were transmitted into the cozy parlors of Europe and America. It was news to most people that there existed such a place as the Sahel, and the region entered their awareness accompanied by a peculiar anxiety. One response was a relief program put together by the United Nations, the United States Agency for International Development, and others that was eventually to transport to the Sahel about $200 million worth of food, fodder, and medical care. Relief, however, failed to allay a sense of unease arising not so much from the evident disaster as from a question it brought to mind. Was the drought an omen of evil for everyone? Did it signal a gathering change in world climate, one that just happened to become obvious first in Africa? Did it mean that the earth as a whole was turning drier?

Climatic change, if that is what it was, could not have been happening at a less convenient moment. For the number of people on earth, the sheer quantity of populations was increasing at a rate never before known in history. How were these people to be fed, their numbers exploding and their vegetable food extracted from that less than 10% of the earth's land surface on which crops are grown? It was a problem already difficult enough, the evidence of its difficulty to be found, so it was said, in the inadequate diets that typify life in the Third World, without the prospect that productive land would be lost, dried up, and turned to waste in a general decline in rainfall. Lands already dry would be the first to go. Television pictures of the Sahel, livestock country even if stricken with drought, might tomorrow look like pictures of the pure Sahara, the great desert having expanded in West Africa, as deserts would grow everywhere if the climate were shifting away from rain.

Although such grim possibilities were brought to public attention by drought in the Sahel, the condition and the fate of arid lands had already been subjected to almost three decades of scrutiny by the new, still blossoming agricultural sciences. These were new sciences because they had to be younger, of course, than their progenitors, the biology and botany that flowered in the nineteenth century and the soils sciences that were only invented a little more than a century ago. In its first infancy, the new agriculture had naturally tended to concentrate its attention on problems arising in rich and humid environments where lush crops spring up to immense market values. It took events—disasters, in fact, such as the American dust bowl of the thirties—to swing the attention of specialists toward those more arid regions where agriculture is thinner in its yields, the term "agriculture" taken here to include the raising of livestock. The aggregate of those thin yields, however, adds up to colossal totals, and all of it placed in danger if, as suggested, aridity, like some cosmic skin disease, had begun an encroachment into damper regions.

It was in 1951 that the Advisory Committee on Arid Zone Research was established within UNESCO and the first coordinated international investigation thereby launched into the problems affecting arid lands. Some 200 desert research institutes, brought to life and activity in 40 countries, have since produced the 30 large volumes of UNESCO's *Arid Zone Research* series. This output was like science in general neutrally descriptive of conditions and processes in quest of the laws that fix limits to life in arid lands and regulate its heartbeat. These expositions were, however, periodically interpolated with warnings intended for the general public but achieving no theatrical success in capturing the public ear. The earth is indeed losing its agriculturally productive land. The evidence for this ominous conclusion had been found in these studies of arid lands. What is worse, the specialists announced, this process so threatening to human welfare has been accelerating in recent years. It has in fact reached startling proportions, with annual losses now estimated at some 58,000 km^2 of once productive land, an aggregate area about the size of the state of West Virginia (32, p. 2).

There are many reasons why land might cease to be biologically productive, some of them provided by purposeful action, as when soil is paved for freeways, used for homes and factories, its surface mined or covered with tailings. Such actions, the public was informed, were but minor irritants compared with another overwhelming reason for the loss of productive land, a reason that had little to do with human intention. Most losses were occurring through a process that the specialists had begun to call "desertification." This was a clumsy neologism that reflected a devotion more to land than to language. Nonetheless, if the coiners of the term were correct, it named a major menace to human welfare—an old problem, in fact, but suddenly threatening in its new dimensions.

The loss of land is a vague concept. In fact, some of the land lost had been barely productive, previously supporting only the thinnest herds of nomadic livestock. Other bits and pieces, however, had been located in irrigation projects and had once figured among the most highly productive agricultural land in the world, at the same time among the most expensively capitalized. Good and bad, all added together, the capitalized value of the land lost was estimated at slightly more than one and a quarter billion dollars per year (32, p. 2). That may be an alarming estimate but neither figures nor warnings attracted much notice until public attention was caught by calamity in the Sahel. As the Australians were to discover and to report in their case study, disaster has that ability. It focuses the attention.

Drought in the Sahel also served as the immediate stimulus to a United Nations call for a world conference on desertification. The debate leading up to this summons was held in the General Assembly's Second Committee, where the rift between rich and poor nations, so evident in recent United Nations proceedings, once again made its appearance. The industrial nations showed themselves generally averse to defining one more global problem whose solution would entangle them in additional financial outlays, the direction in which such definitions inevitably trend. The rich nations, too, had shown themselves to be laggardly capable of dealing with desertification within their own borders. Not that they had brought it to a halt at home, but rather that they had the resources to deal with the problem whenever it became a big enough bother to set off a loud enough outcry.

The resolution calling for a conference was put forward by H.A. Diallo, a member of the United Nations delegation from Upper Volta, a country whose president, General Sangoulé Lamazana, had sought vainly to draw attention to the Sahelian drought from its first year onward. The other Sahelian countries were recorded as sponsors of the resolution. Also appearing as sponsors were countries on the Guinea coast to the south of the Sahel—Dahomey, Ghana, Nigeria, Cameroon—into which the effects of the drought had penetrated along with its refugees. They were joined by all the countries on the Sahara's northern rim—Algeria, Egypt, Libya, Morocco, and Tunisia. Also concerned about the problem, or enough so to appear as sponsors of the resolution, were a number of other African nations—Burundi, Ethiopia, Madagascar, Rwanda, Sudan, Tanzania, Uganda, Zaire. Joining this African phalanx were all the countries of Latin America that face present or potential desertification problems—Argentina, Brazil, Chile, Colombia, Ecuador, Haiti, Mexico, Peru, Venezuela. Add to the list of sponsors some countries of the Arabian Peninsula—Iraq, Jordan, Kuwait, the United Arab Emirates, and Yemen—such countries of Asia as Iran, India, Pakistan, and the Philippines, and, finally, Fiji in the far Pacific, and what message is then revealed? In the full list of 47 sponsoring countries, slightly less than one-third of the entire United Nations membership, only three countries—whose names must also be added—could be classified as "developed." These were Japan, Australia, and the lone European sponsor, Yugoslavia, a country that has sought identification with Third World causes.

Thus it was obvious that those who called for a world conference on desertification were those who wanted financial help to fight it, and just as obvious that those who held back from sponsorship were the countries that would be called on to provide that help. France, the Scandinavian countries, Italy, the Federal Republic of Germany, all spoke up in the discussions to say that while they agreed that desertification was a serious problem, one requiring "an integrated world program in . . . research and development and application of science and technology," as France put it (81, p. 369), none of them were fully convinced of the need for a world conference. France went on to state its views more bluntly:

> The apparently growing practice of claiming that such conferences were the only way of drawing the attention of the international community to important problems casts doubt on the competence of the General Assembly. (81, p. 369)

Since no one has ever claimed that the General Assembly's competence includes more than a tenuous ability to trumpet an issue to world attention, the comment would seem to imply a case of pocketbook fatigue. In any case, on December 17, 1974, and heedless of expressions of loyalty from the rich, the General Assembly passed Resolution 3337 (XXIX) convening in 1977 a United Nations Conference on Desertification. Although they may lack financial wherewithal, the poor countries have the vote, and that for the simple reason that there are more of them, and that, in turn, the bluntest fact about life in the modern world.

The United Nations has been holding world conferences since almost the moment of its birth. The first of them, the 1947 Conference on Trade and Tariffs held in Havana, back in the days when Havana was one of those places where everyone liked to go, embraced one of those same arcane subjects to whose unraveling the old League of Nations used to summon palaces full of diplomats. A quarter century after Havana, almost by surprise, a new kind of world conference was held, and it caught the public imagination in a way that "trade and tariffs" was innately incapable of doing. The United Nations Conference on the Environment, held in Stockholm in 1972, received intensive coverage by a world press that had only recently been instructed that there was an environment to be saved.

Stockholm turned out to be the bellwether of a string of conferences directed toward the resolution of major world problems. Such "problem" conferences were held on population (Bucharest, 1974), food (Rome, 1974), women (Mexico, 1975), cities (Vancouver, 1976), and water (Buenos Aires, 1977). Then was to come the United Nations Conference on Desertification, to convene for two weeks in Nairobi, Kenya, beginning on August 29, 1977. And following that, there was to be a conference on the transfer of technology from rich nations to poor nations to be held in 1979. This series of international meetings had carried matters to a point where holding a United Nations conference on a problem was what defined it as "global" (47).

In their brief course, a certain cynicism had collected around the conferences, giving them a world-weary flavor. "What?" Barbara Ward reported others as exclaiming (*The Economist*, August 13, 1977). "Not *another* world conference!" Such sentiments should not be permitted to camouflage the singular character of those gatherings. Never before in human history have all the nations of the earth, or practically all, gathered together to discuss the important problems, one after the other, facing all mankind. And they are blessed with a certain manner, those conferences, they have a certain style, confident but groping, reflecting the high style of those who attend them, men of knowledge and decision, and the fact, at the same time, that never before in human history has there existed this type of problem, the kind that faces all mankind. The delegates are firm and commanding, seeming to demand the ultimate, while underneath they are prepared to accept anything they can get. These are unique occasions when scholars and scientists, those who know, are brought together with political leaders, men who can act, in an effort to reach and carry through a course of rational action. Together, they embody the world as will and idea, almost as if important people had really paid attention to philosophy.

How many more such conferences there will be has now become a question. The United Nations has been reorganized, with the change symbolized by the appointment of a Director General for Economic Development. The conference on the transfer of technology could be the last of the "problem" series, even though the list of world problems has by no means been exhausted. Energy, for example, or the atmosphere, or even poverty itself remain to be discussed. There is a possibility that the United Nations will take the advice of France—that is, instead of calling for special conferences, the General Assembly will from time to time convert itself into a special forum for the discussion of "global" issues. If that happens, however, it will not be quite the same. It will neither have the same spirit nor give rise to the feelings that accompany an *event*.

The United Nations Conference on Desertification was organized by a small Conference Secretariat settled into the Nairobi headquarters of the United Nations Environment Programme (UNEP) amidst the green, sunlit coffee plantations of Gigiri and within distant view of the lavishly modern tower of the Kenyatta Conference Center, where the conference would ultimately take place. Much of the Secretariat's assignment was occupied with everything involved in "the assessment of all available data and information on desertification and its consequences on the development process of the countries affected." This was to be carried out, and the Secretariat assisted, "through the enlistment of all expertise available." Thus had the General Assembly spoken (80, p. 3).

As its enlistment began, the expertise was prompt to point out that desertification was a peculiar subject, not a subject at all in an independent sense, not in possession of its own university departments. It would have to be structured, this subject, and, in following this advice, the Secretariat was eventually to "enlist" specialists in 19 disciplines by one count, 20 by another. In any case, they included soils science, veterinary science, watershed management, climatology, meteorology, ecology, geography, livestock and range management, anthropology, demography, forestry, biology, botany, economics, political science, sociology, history, agronomy, remote sensing. This was a list to give some indication of how desertification, conceptually, was spread around. Structuring the subject, the experts went on to say, provided the perfect opportunity to add to it, fill gaps and lacunae, settle precisely where the topic stood in the pantheon of human knowledge. Ralph Townley, deputy to the Secretary General of the Conference, passed the message to the Secretariat staff. "Everything known is to be assembled," he said. "Or created."

Creation was indeed to assume first importance. This was because almost nothing had been settled. Even the very word gave rise to heated argument. Many researchers insisted on the older "desertization." Spanish speakers were incensed that *"desertificación"* was coming into use when the perfectly good *"desertización"* was lodged securely in the *Diccionario de la Lengua Española*. Others argued that the older term could not embrace the field because it applied only to anthropogenic events. The General Assembly had used "desertification"—the word was in the very resolution that had convened the Conference—and the United Nations would therefore use it, steamrollering the opposition. In such ways is language shaped.

Whatever the word—and "desertification" it became—no definition for it could be found to which all specialists would agree. H.N. Le Houérou, who had observed the process occurring along the northern edge of the Sahara in conditions of very scanty rainfall, suggested a definition of "desertization" as "a more or less irreversible reduction in vegetation cover ending in the extension of new desert landscapes"(63, p.3). Anders Rapp, noting that desertification could occur even in regions with more than 300 mm of annual rainfall, defined it as "the spread of desert-like conditions in arid or semiarid areas due to man's action or climatic change" (63, p.3). Neither definition gained universal acceptance, although both were everywhere considered useful.

During the first attempt to structure desertification, the subject seemed to cleave naturally into four components, from which Townley conceived a new model of conference documentation. Instead of the blizzard of papers that had characterized previous "problem" conferences, each document devoted to a minuscule aspect of the subject in question, four "component reviews" would be commissioned, each capable of taking a broad, analytic perspective. In this way, the subject came to be constituted out of the four components of climatic change (20), ecological change (22), population and society (23), and technology (21) or the means to combat the problem. The components and other elements in the assembly of knowledge would be summarized in *Desertification: An Overview* (16), written in less technical language for the nonscientist delegates to the Conference. As it turned out, the authors of the component reviews also had ideas as to what "desertification" might mean.

> Warren and Maizels: "A simple and graphic meaning of the word 'desertification' is the development of desert-like landscapes in areas which were once green. Its practical meaning . . . is a sustained decline in the yield of useful crops from a dry area accompanying certain kinds of environmental change, both natural and induced." (22, p.1)
>
> Kates, Johnson, and Haring: "It involves destructive processes in which productive base deteriorates and the social system is imperiled. Unlike drought, which is usually a short-term diminution of available moisture, the physical processes involved in desertification are long-term, chronic and pervasive." (23, p.1)
>
> Anaya Garduño: "Desertification is the impoverishment of arid, semi-arid and some subhumid ecosystems by the impact of man's activities. It is the process of change in these ecosystems that leads to reduced productivity of desirable plants, alterations in the biomass and diversity of life forms, accelerated soil degradation and increased hazards for human occupancy." (21, p.1)

As in other "problem conferences," this one, too, would focus on a Plan of Action, a guide to the world as to how the problem should be confronted and defeated. As has become customary, the principal task of the delegates to the Conference would be to debate and approve a Plan of Action to Combat Desertification. And, as ultimately approved, this Plan of Action would also present a statement on the meaning of the key term.

> Desertification is the diminution or destruction of the biological potential of the land, and can lead ultimately to desert-like conditions. It is an aspect of the widespread deterioration of ecosystems, and has diminished or destroyed the biological potential, i.e. plant and animal production, for multiple use purposes at a time when increased productivity is needed to support growing populations in quest of development. (32, p.7)

Where Rapp had left the cause of desertification open—whether man, the maker of messes, the shiftless, or climate, the endlessly shifting—Anaya Garduño had put the blame squarely on human activities. Could Anaya Garduño be correct—and anxieties over changing climate all be misplaced?

Mostafa K. Tolba, Secretary General of the Conference, consulted with his scientific advisers, and they told him: Man already has sufficient technical knowledge to bring desertification to a halt. This was a powerful statement, rich in significance. Taken as an answer to the preceding question, it, too, placed the blame on man. For if changing climate were the cause of desertification, even the most distinguished of scientific advisers would not have known how to bring it to a halt.

Further research would undoubtedly yield findings that would facilitate the task of combating desertification, his scientist advisers went on to inform Tolba, but there was no need to wait for those findings. Action could be started now on the basis of what man already knows.

But then again, what did man know? To assemble knowledge, it had turned out, was to create it, invent it. How much land was in fact being desertified each year? What types of land were being lost to human use? What would it cost to halt desertification wherever it was occurring, or to rehabilitate land already degraded? There is a practical side to Tolba, the side that drove a microbiologist, and a distinguished one, to become the administrator of an important United Nations agency. It was this side of him that wanted these practical factors specified. He insisted that the Conference be given some idea as to what it all would cost, and most of all, Tolba wanted to demonstrate that repairing damage to the land would be, in modern terminology, cost effective. A set of meetings was organized for the express purpose of bringing economists and financial analysts into working contact with specialists in the earth sciences. The result, as eventually drawn up by Ruben Mendez, a United Nations economist, is a table, *The Costs and Benefits of Combating Desertification*, prepared for the Conference and then revised, with the revised form reprinted on page 14.

Nor was that all that the assertions of his advisers had meant to Tolba. He resolved to come to the Conference with some models of cooperation among nations—transnational projects, as they were to be called—already at some stage of development. If there really was no need to wait, why wait even for the Conference? Delay was expensive—another point on which Tolba had been informed—rehabilitation costs rising exponentially as degradation advanced. The transnational projects would show how governments could join together to contest a menace that pays no attention to national boundaries. Six such projects were eventually selected as both intrinsically worth doing and as potentially capable of gaining the support of the countries involved. They were:

- The monitoring of desertification and related natural resources in arid regions of South America based on satellite imagery supplemented by aerial photography and ground traverses, this project to be developed in Argentina, Bolivia, Chile, and Peru (27).
- A similar monitoring project for arid regions of southwest Asia, involving Afghanistan, India, Iran, and Pakistan (28).
- The stratification of livestock in West Africa, a project that would establish a commercial system in which livestock would be bred in the Sahel and then moved by stages into more humid regions for fattening, finishing and marketing (26).
- The ecological management of deep aquifers underlying the Nubian sandstone formations of northeast Africa and involving Chad, Egypt, Libya, and Sudan, and of other aquifers underlying the Arabian desert and involving seven countries of the Arabian Peninsula (24).
- The establishment of a coherent greenbelt along the northern rim of the Sahara and involving Egypt, Libya, Tunisia, Algeria, and Morocco (25).

The Costs and Benefits of Combating Desertification*

Initial estimates of orders of magnitude of costs and benefits of corrective measures

(1)	(2)	(3)	(4)	(5)	(6)	(7)	(8)	(9)	(10)
	Annual rate of land degradation (000 hectares)[2]	Estimated value ($ per hectare)[3]		Gain		Estimated cost of salvage[4] per hectare $	Total (2 × 7) million $	Net gain per hectare (5) − (7) $	Total net benefits (2) × (9) million $
Type of land[1]		if not salvaged	if salvaged	(4) − (3) per hectare $	(2) × (5) Total million $				
Irrigated	125[5]	200	2,000	1,800	225	850 (250–2,000)	106	950	119
Range	3,200	2	20	18	58	10 (1–50)	32	8	26
Rain-fed Crop	2,500	50	450	400	1,000	100 (50–150)	250	300	750
TOTAL	5,825				1,283		388		895

*A revision of a table prepared for the Conference, basing land values on capitalized values and adjusting unit salvage costs to more realistic levels.

[1] Arid and semi-arid lands only.

[2] Annual rate of land degradation is based on annual rate of change of classes of land to more degraded conditions. The degree of degradation from higher to lower classes of land has been converted to more limited areas assumed to be deteriorating from land yielding highest net return (if salvaged) to land at the point of going out of production (if not salvaged).

[3] In view of difficulties in quantifying social values, these estimates are rough conservative approximations of orders of magnitude of capitalized values. Values are calculated using an assumed net income at half of gross income divided by an assumed opportunity cost of 10%, with a slight adjustment for rangelands to reflect lower opportunity costs. If social factors are included the values would be substantially higher.

[4] Figures within parentheses give ranges of salvage costs. It follows from footnote 2 that cost of salvage is the maximum, equivalent to the cost of reclamation or restoration of practically completely desertified land. Because desertification is a continuous process, the more prudent course of action would be to begin corrective investment as soon as practicable and initially to lands which offer the highest returns to insure continued maximum production.

[5] Due to waterlogging, salinization and, to a lesser extent, alkalinization.

- The establishment of a similar greenbelt along the southern side of the Sahara and involving Senegal, Mali, Niger, Chad, and Sudan (29).

The development of all six projects required 40 signatures by representatives of 29 countries, some countries appearing in more than one project. By the time the Conference convened, more than half of these signatures had been obtained, and the preliminary task of establishing organizational structures for several of the projects had been completed.

The Conference Secretariat, said Resolution 3337 (XXIX), summoning forth a standard principle of conference preparations, should draw on "the resources of the United Nations system, especially those of the United Nations Environment Programme, the Food and Agriculture Organization of the United Nations (FAO), the United Nations Educational, Scientific and Cultural Organization (UNESCO) and the World Meteorological Organization (WMO)" (80, p.2). The specialized agencies such as FAO, UNESCO, or WMO are independent baronies within what is sometimes called, to seal over such separations, the United Nations "family," and the sentiments of the General Assembly have toward them the legal status of exhortations rather than commands. Yet the specialized agencies rarely fail to respond to such appeals, especially when stimulated by the possibilities of creation rather than mere assemblage.

A collaboration among FAO, UNESCO, and WMO yielded the *World Map of Desertification* (17), as specifically requested by the General Assembly (80, p.3). The arid, semiarid, and subhumid regions of the world had already been specified on maps, the classic being the map produced by Peverell Meigs in 1961 for UNESCO's Arid Zone Research Programme. The new map had to transcend the effort of Meigs, showing not only which parts of the world were vulnerable to desertification, but which stood in fact in some imminent danger of being desertified. This required the identification of soil types as well as the use to which the land had been put. At its scale of one to 25 million, the new map indicated whether the desertification hazard was moderate, high or extremely high and provided a reason for the status, whatever it may have been. (A simplified version of the new map appears in the endpapers showing the hazard without the reasons.) The collaborating agencies went on to prepare, on a larger scale, a desertification map of Africa north of the equator, while a similar map of South America was contributed to the Conference by the Mendoza (Argentina) Center for Scientific and Technical Research. Three additional world maps (30) were prepared for the Conference to portray aspects of the desertification problem that attracted the attention and interest of individual researchers.

It was Mohammed Kassas who first suggested that the Conference preparations would do well to include a set of case studies of desertification in action. Tolba seized on the suggestion, having seen the important part that case studies of the environment had played at the Stockholm Conference, which he had attended as leader of the Egyptian delegation. But then Tolba had great confidence in Kassas, a professor of botany at the University of Cairo and an internationally recognized specialist in the vegetation and ecologies of the desert environment. They had been classmates in their student days. In proposing case studies, Kassas, too, was suggesting that the mere assembling of knowledge about desertification would not be enough, that what the Conference would want to know would not necessarily be found in studies already published. It was not so much that the knowledge was not there, somewhere, as that a dynamic and fruitful attitude toward the problem in its own right had yet to be achieved, a perspective in which desertification would be viewed in its entirety, as something more than just a physical problem affecting arid lands. Townley felt this same lack:

> I had just finished reading the 33 papers on problems in arid lands that had been submitted to the UNESCO–UNEP Man and Biosphere Conference held in 1974 in Sfax, Tunisia. Although the problems described all occurred in the developing countries, every paper except one—and that a description of institutions— had been written by a European. That is not meant as a criticism of the papers, which made valuable contributions to the literature on how to deal with degraded lands. But none of the papers contained what our Conference needed—why, in the first place, had desertification occurred at all? How had the process manifested itself? What lessons could be learned that would lead to specific recommendations in the Plan of Action we were just beginning to think about? Worse from our point of view, nothing at all was said about people, and yet they had been telling us for years that the social aspects of desertification are critical.*

The reference to "they," curiously, was to physical scientists, but an exceptional group, those with a broad enough perspective to see the need for social measures and to call for an appropriate con-

*From a conversation in the Century Club, New York City, 16 June, 1978.

tribution to the problem from their colleagues in the social sciences. One of these was Harold Dregne, Professor of Plant and Soil Science at Texas Tech University and chairman of the Committee on Arid Lands of the American Association for the Advancement of Science. According to Dregne (40, p.iii), the need for interdisciplinary cooperation was clear in 1955 at the arid-land symposium held in Albuquerque and Socorro, New Mexico, that "historic event," as he called it, that stimulated interest in the United States in the problems of arid lands. At the 1969 Conference on Arid Lands in a Changing World, held at the University of Arizona under the sponsorship of AAAS and UNESCO, Dregne said:

> Time has demonstrated—not only in arid regions—that the absence of scientific research and technology is not the sole, or even the major, reason for the lack of development. Social and cultural factors, as well as economic conditions, determine the acceptance of new knowledge and practices. (40, p.8)

Professor Dregne was one of those who joined in the effort to define the concept of a case study in desertification. This concept took shape in the opening months of 1975. The studies would adopt an ecological point of view, assessing problem areas as complex systems of interdependent elements, a change in any one of which affects all the others. None of these interdependent factors would be overlooked in the studies, which would contain not only a physical analysis of land and climate but would include also, or so the prospectus went, a demographic, cultural, and economic analysis of the people living in the problem area and of the institutions through which they work the land or use it in other than agricultural ways. The case studies would place problem areas in their historical settings, displaying desertification as a process while unveiling the phenomena through which its advance is manifest. They would discuss the successes achieved and the failures encountered in efforts to combat desertification. They would be more than merely descriptive, and would express a constant search for general principles, "lessons to be learned," as Tolba repeatedly insisted, which would lead directly to recommendations to be included in the draft Plan of Action to Combat Desertification and would provide scientific justification for them.

In a series of informal meetings in Geneva, it was agreed that UNESCO, with its history of experience with the problems of arid lands, would administer the case studies, while the United Nations Development Programme (UNDP) would finance them, and these agreements were eventually formalized. It was Michel Batisse who first proposed a pattern of six case studies, three sets of twins that would make comparisons possible. As UNESCO's Deputy Assistant Director General for Natural Resources and Environmental Sciences, Batisse had been closely associated with his agency's pioneering arid-land investigations. His proposal was accepted, agreement by the governments concerned was sought and obtained, and the six United Nations case studies were carried out in accordance with the Batisse schemata:*

Desertification occurring in a dryland region with cold-season rainfall:

- The region of Combarbalá, Chile (1)
- The Oglat Merteba Test Zone, Tunisia (4)

Desertification occurring in a dryland region with warm-season rainfall:

- Luni Development Block, India (3)
- The Eghazer and Azawak, Niger (6)

Desertification affecting irrigation projects:

- The Greater Mussayeb Project, Iraq (2)
- Mona Reclamation Experimental Project, Pakistan (5)

In the resolution convening the Conference, the General Assembly expressed its increasing concern with the need to transfer technology to the developing world, by which is meant not so much the transfer of equipment and apparatus as the local development of a technological outlook. The resolution insisted that action against desertification should include "the building-up of the indigenous and autonomous science and technology capacity in the area concerned" (80, p.3). The phrasing was not too graceful, but the intent was clear, and the case studies could be taken as an opportunity to escape the Sfax syndrome and work directly with developing-world specialists and researchers.

*For complicated and uninteresting reasons, UNESCO was unable to act as executing agency for the case study set in Chile. For that one study, the Inter-American Development Bank served as executing agency.

Contributions to all six studies would inevitably—and productively—be made by FAO, WMO, and, of course, UNESCO, the executing agent. On the ground, however, much of the work was directed and carried out by indigenous institutions, and studies were to be undertaken by local scientists. In just these six studies, without taking account of associated case studies, mention is made of 33 indigenous institutions, including government departments with a scientific capacity, and of 51 scientists associated with those institutions. A review of the case studies provides no grounds for distinguishing, on a basis of quality, the scientific work carried out by developing-world institutions from those carried out in what is sometimes improperly distinguished as the technological world.

Another traveler to Geneva to participate in the structuring of the case studies was Harold F. Heady, Professor of Range Management at the University of California, Berkeley, whose enthusiasm for what could be learned from these exercises reinforced the Secretariat's conviction of their value. Heady also said that he had been involved in a program of rangeland rehabilitation in southeastern Oregon. This program, he continued, could readily be written up to conform to the case study prospectus. He could present it as an American contribution to the Conference after obtaining the agreement of the U.S. government that it would be given official status.

This was the seed from which nine additional case studies, including Heady's, eventually germinated. Six governments agreed to submit them, with China submitting three and the USSR two. These nine "associated case studies," as they came to be called, were placed in varied settings which, in addition to southeastern Oregon (13), included: Australia's Gascoyne basin (7), Turfan oasis (8), Wushenchao Commune (9) and general desert reclamation (10) in China, Iran's Turan Project (11), reclamation in the Israeli Negev (12), and the Golodnaya Steppe (15) and Turkmenia (14) projects in the USSR.

The associated case studies did not always cleave strictly to the case study concept as it had been elaborated in the Geneva conversations. But then in all senses neither did the six studies sponsored by the United Nations. Carried out by physical scientists, who have worked on without a response to their call for an appropriate contribution from the social sciences, the case studies did not achieve a successful analysis anywhere of the social and cultural elements in desertification, although all of them make reference to those elements. The Chinese attribute their successes entirely to political and cultural factors, but their analysis, which may be correct, affects many readers as lacking subtlety, rigidly strapped in blind sloganeering. The most conscientious attempt at social analysis, exposing its deficiencies by the very effort, was made in one of the associated case studies, that of Iran.

With the addition of the associated case studies, the concept was extended to five continents even if the representation remains lopsided. In the developing world, it is Latin America that could use more attention, while Asia, in proportion, is overrepresented. Still, the additional studies introduce a range of conditions that go far beyond what the United Nations was able to consider with its six original studies. So, too, the associated case studies extend the catalogue of techniques successfully applied in campaigns scattered around the world to save productive land from degradation and ultimate destruction. If there is a difference in tone between the two sets of studies, it is the difference between the student, grinding away at his courses, and the successful man of the world. The United Nations studies remain strictly studies and are thereby touched with an air of pessimism. The associated case studies tend to be success stories. They radiate the optimism that comes from triumph.

Whether the global attack contained in the Plan of Action to Combat Desertification, as approved by the Conference, will ever be carried out as written remained a question one year after the Conference had adjourned. That is something that, in a way, was expected. No plan of action is ever carried out precisely as proposed, and for a time following a conference when it seems that little or nothing will be done, a sense of discouragement sets in that tolls a somber counterpoint to the heady enthusiasm prevailing at the Conference itself. Yet plans of action are intended as no more than broad guides, perhaps no more than as exhortations to the world. The conference always serves as a great stimulus to science and learning, and eventually, surprisingly, to action also. They do awaken the world and bring their subject strongly to mind. Five years after Stockholm, a great deal had been done about the environment in all parts of the world, even if there were many to say that this was still not enough.

The loss of productive land is an obvious menace to human welfare. It is blatant, lacking the subtleties of other problems. Time will tell what the world ultimately does about this fundamental problem. Meanwhile, we have the case studies. They should raise our spirits.

They paint pictures for us—the associated case studies especially—of fat cattle grazing on what had once been shifting sands, of vineyards thriving in rocky wildernesses, of fruits and vegetables, even flowers, blossoming in what had once been the salty wastes of abandoned irrigation schemes. No matter what the world eventually does, the case studies show that desertification can be stopped, that the scientists advising Tolba were correct, that degraded land can be reclaimed if mankind refuses to continue to conspire through inaction in its own destruction.

2
MUSSAYEB

"To break with feudal society'

GOING NORTH from Hillah on the Iraqi State Railway, on the right, almost immediately, the excavations of Babylon come into view. The Hillah River, flowing beside the ruins, was once the main channel of the Euphrates, the wide river which has now shifted to the west among the many channels between Mussayeb and Samawah far downstream. Much of this region was swamp during the great days of the Abbasid Caliphate.

Perhaps it is strange that there is no city today where the Ishtar Gate and 17.6 km of walls mark out where Babylon used to be. Cities are located where they are for good reasons, and if something happens to them, they will be rebuilt in the same place, like Tokyo after the earthquake. Babylon was an important city for 2,000 years, at times the most important city in the world, also the largest. It was so big that it inspired Aristotle to one of his rare bursts of humor. "For it is said that when Babylon was captured, a considerable part of the city was not aware of it three days later." (34, p.183) Nothing remains of all that but these digs and ruins through which nomadic herdsmen guide flocks or in which sporadic crops are planted, using *nirin* irrigation, as described in the case study.

> The *nirin* system is based on a natural lowering of the water table during periods in which the land was left fallow. Salts accumulated near the surface were washed down by the rains. Normal practice was to cultivate during one winter season, leaving the land fallow over two succeeding summer seasons. (2, p.4)

Here in the hot, flat plain of the two rivers, cultivation requires that some style of irrigation be employed. The mean annual rainfall

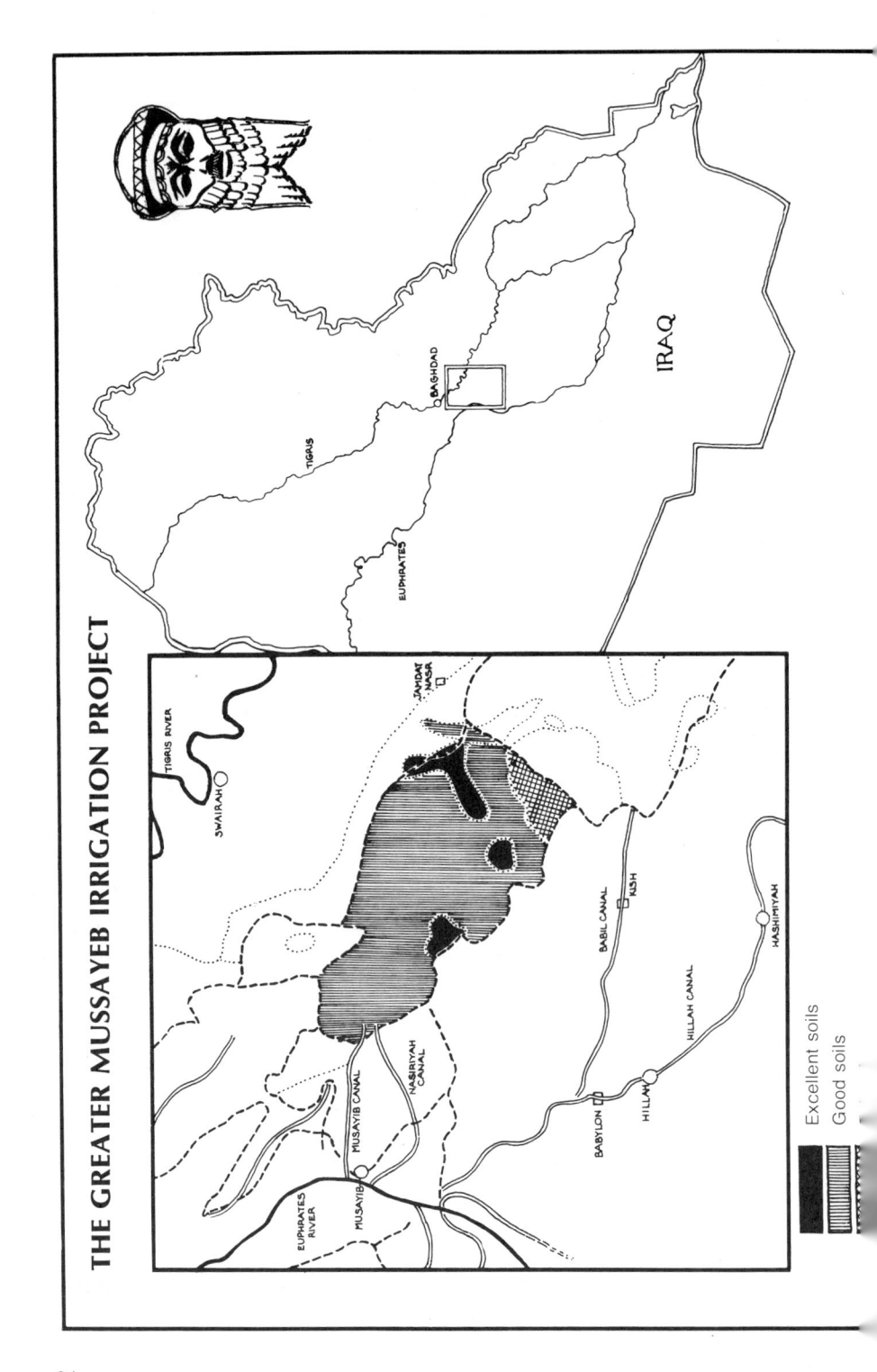

THE GREATER MUSSAYEB IRRIGATION PROJECT

Excellent soils
Good soils

at Babylon is only about 120 mm, no more than the rainfall in the northern Sahel at the edge of the desert. Yet if irrigation can be brought to arid regions such as this, where the land lies warm under uninterrupted sunshine, it becomes the most intensely productive agricultural system to be carried out in the open air. Irrigated agriculture, the financial foundation of Babylon, made Mesopotamia the center of the world. Now Babylon is no more, and the center of the world is somewhere else—around the Atlantic, or in Moscow or Tokyo, anywhere but in this dry, sun-drenched plain where the land has been so hard on man, destroying this great city and all the hopes that once were embodied in it. But is that true? Or is it the other way around? Perhaps it is a man who has been hard on the land. The case study says:

> Soil conditions . . . in most of the Mesopotamian Plain have been shaped by centuries of irrigation. . . . Traces of ancient ditches, scattered pottery, and *tells* (abandoned villages) . . . testify to the successive growth and decline of early city-states. The disappearance of these communities may well have been connected with a progressive salinization of the surrounding lands resulting from over-irrigation. (2, p.3)

In this antique land, however, improper irrigation techniques were by no means confined to ancient history.

> Over-irrigation of these lands was continued until very recently by the sheikhs, feudal lords who commanded large work forces. Selecting arable lands for the cultivation of wheat and barley, the sheikhs irrigated soil through ditches dug to the Tigris or Euphrates. When canal silting and increased soil salinity eventually reduced the productivity of the land, the sheikhs would move their tribes to other areas and the process would begin again. (2, p.3)

The new nation of Iraq, established in the breakup of the Ottoman Empire following World War I, was interested to know how much of its land had been ruined by such practices—or was still being ruined. A commission, appointed to make a survey, delivered its report in 1950.

> It was estimated that approximately 60% of Iraq's agricultural land—most of which lies in the lower Mesopotamian Plain—had been seriously affected by salinity. As a result, 20% to 30% had been entirely abandoned, and each year an additional 1% was being lost. (2, p.3)

This was a loss to ponder as the train continues northward to leave the ruins of Babylon behind. What could be more destructive of national welfare than a nagging, persistent disappearance of the means of producing the very food that nourishes the nation's citizens? The railroad encounters the Euphrates just below the Hindiya Barrage, a dam constructed in 1913 to divert the river's waters back into the old Hillah channel. Of course, still pondering the matter, one notes that Iraq has oil and therefore possesses the financial means to do something about its desiccating agriculture. This country may no longer be the center of the world, but it is no Sahel either, helpless in the face of drought. Iraq is capable of agglomerating funds wherewith to build great works of rehabilitation. A few kilometers beyond the Hindiya Barrage, where the railroad leaves the Euphrates to cut across the waist of Iraq to Bagdad on the Tigris, the train crosses a bridge over the Greater Mussayeb Canal. This artificial channel takes Euphrates water to the Greater Mussayeb Project. Initiated in 1953 on an 83,710-hectare South Carolina–shaped section of land "between the rivers" or, to use the Greek word, in Mesopotamia, this project was the first national response to the gloomy findings in the commission's report.

> The decision to establish the Greater Mussayeb Project was prompted by a number of considerations. Primarily it was an attempt to reverse the desertification process in the lower Mesopotamian Plain. At the same time, it was an effort to intensify crop production, replacing the traditional *nirin* system with modern practices of reclamation and drainage. . . . Finally, the project was a conscious effort to break with traditional feudal society. Distribution of land to local landless farmers and the organization of work on a cooperative basis give this project an unquestionable social as well as technical and economic interest. (2, p.4)

"Modern practices of reclamation and drainage." A canal from the Euphrates. Yes, indeed, Greater Mussayeb was a complex irrigation project developed not too far from those stringy, intermittent watercourses in Khuzistan where, some have suggested, irrigation was first invented. Once discovered, this new, more demanding style of growing food went on to establish new ways of life, to germinate and yield new harvests of custom that ancient man the hunter, the berry picker, would scarcely have understood. What a leap of the imagination it had meant—here and in other places, in far China or in savage Peru, where irrigation had probably been invented all over again—to realize that half-naked earth, soil that had never produced much of anything, would explode with seas of shimmering grain if only fresh water were brought to it.

Where the land is flat and level, as it is in the region of the two rivers, an irrigation project might consist of doing no more than the sheikhs had done, cutting a ditch to lead water away from a river. The flow would then be turned off by blocking the ditch wth a gob of earth. The problem in this sort of operation is to develop a gradient so that water will flow onto the fields.

Since rivers run between banks, irrigation water can be lifted out of them, as by the Egyptian *shadoof*, a simple, counterbalanced bucket. Somewhat more complicated is the Persian wheel around which buckets descend to be filled, thence to rise and automatically to tip and spill their contents into a sloping trough.

To achieve a gradient, a canal might be excavated to some distance upstream—or far upstream, if the natural gradient is slight. Or the level of the river can be raised by throwing a dam across it, a monument such as the Hindiya Barrage, with canals leading away from the reservoir backed up behind it. Downstream from either system, the barrage or the long canal tapping upstream water, a complicated network of canals will be constructed, or—as in the past—might gradually evolve along with the evolving civilization that it supports. Organization and skill are then required to maintain the system as well as to operate it—to direct the precisely proper amount of water into each field and to make sure that adequate drainage prevents waterlogging and succeeds in leaching away the salts and alkalies that might otherwise accumulate on or near the surface of the soil. According to one theory, called by some the hydraulic hypothesis (84, p.152ff), the organizational requirements of complicated irrigation systems made up the needs that gave birth to civilization itself, everywhere it has appeared. Irrigation was undoubtedly the activity that called forth civilization here in Iraq, the first civilization ever to be seen, rearing lofty ziggurats out of this hot, flat, unprepossessing plain. It was irrigation that may very well have conjured up the other original civilizations too, those in the Indus Valley where the inhabitants still live off irrigation, along the dangerously unreliable Yellow River, in Peru, in Yucatan. Of course it was irrigation that created Egypt, whose fortunes rested on the automatic and annual bath provided by the rising of the Nile, but it may have been travelers from the two rivers who first taught the Egyptians how to write. For Mesopotamia was the earliest to write, there where feudal sheikhs, even in modern times, injected salt into defenseless soil.

The first domestication of plants and animals, that achievement now called the neolithic revolution, took place, so far as present evidence indicates, in the Zagros-Taurus mountain system, in those jagged, contorted ranges created by the tectonic collision of Arabia with Asia. Here on the frontier between Iraq and Iran and in the Anatolian highlands of modern Turkey, those seeds were planted which contained in them, as if in embryo, the Babylon of hanging gardens, Hadrians's Rome, Paris of the Enlightenment. In these adjacent regions, the wild progenitors of wheat and barley flourished—and indeed still flourish—in stands dense enough to confine humanity to a sedentary life style even before domestication when man became tied for the first time to a plot, his new prison. Cereal grains were the instrument that did this to people, bringing the beginning of the end to three million years of wandering, and it was probably at the edge of their natural habitat, where wild stands would be thin, that artificial cultivation would first have been attempted. It would have been in a site like that at Ali Kosh, down from the mountains in the hot plain of Khuzistan where, after draining the central Zagros, the sluggish Karun River winds into the Shott el-Arab, the combined mouth of the Tigris-Euphrates. At the lowest level of Ali Kosh, digging into the Bus Mordeh phase (7500-6750 B.C.), bits of cultivated wheat and barley were found. These few carbonized grains of *Triticum boeoticum*, *T. monococcum* (einkorn), and *T. dicoccum* (emmer), recovered by the flotation method, are among the earliest samples of cultivated plants yet found, distinguishable from their wild ancestors by the genetic changes that follow domestication. Overshadowed by the edge of the Iranian plateau, Ali Kosh receives an annual average of 300 mm of winter rainfall, barely enough for the "dry farming" of cereals and a reason why the site may have been chosen by goat-herding pastoralists as a place in which to try to get a crop.

Farther north in the Zagros, at the village site of Zawi Chemi and the associated Shanidar cave, a few bits of something perhaps midway between wild and domestic cereal grains would take the origins of agriculture back close to 9000 B.C. In the cave at Shanidar, the bones of a domesticated sheep (*Ovis orientalis*) were found. This and other early connections between the first domesticated plants, wheat and barley, and the first domesticated animals, sheep and goats—except, of course, for the ubiquitous dog—indicate that farming and herding were born together, beginning at birth the endless stimulation of their continuing mutual interchange.

To find the origins of agriculture in what has become this remote corner of the globe is not to deny that it may have been invented independently elsewhere. The debate between diffusionists, arguing for one center of invention, and those who would say that invention anywhere is proof that invention elsewhere is possible is as old as archaeology and need not be settled here. Present evidence would indicate however, that the cultivation of maize was born independently in America. Perhaps, too, southeast Asia witnessed another independent emergence of agriculture before 7000 B.C., and if there are these, there may be still others.

An impression lingers that paleolithic ways of life had little impact on the natural environment. Populations were meager than, and our Acheulian, even Mousterian, ancestors are thought of as blending into ecosystems, animals among many others. It is technology that wreaks havoc with nature, and yet the genus *Homo* had technology from its earliest appearance. There must have been occasions when fires escaped control, especially those flames set to stampede large game over cliffs. Men of the old stone age hunted numbers of species to extinction, thereby altering ecosystems by removing from them key elements. The annihilation of the American pachyderms, for example, all except the elusive, jungle-hidden tapir, must have had far-reaching environmental effects.

Nevertheless, the impact of economies based on hunting and gathering was probably benign when compared with the heavy effects neolithic man must have begun to exert by the invention and development of farming and herding. Intrusions into nature would not be evident all at once, to be sure, when farming methods may at first have consisted of broadcasting seed on untilled ground and then, with farmers still ignorant of fertilizer, moving on when the soil began to give out. If desertification by man can be said to have taken hold with the agricultural revolution that marks the end of the mesolithic, most of the damage was at first probably done by pastoralists and their livestock. These early herdsmen have been accused of desertifying the route to be taken across Asia in subsequent epochs by the Silk Road, as they moved with their flocks in the direction of China, destroying natural pastures on the way, overgrazing them to extinction (77, p.67ff).

That same plain of Khuzistan slanting down from the foot of the Zagros to the torrid gulf at whose edge the gigantic oil refinery at Abadan is the modern world's monument, this arid, aluvial landscape, today so remote from the central ganglions of human life, once nourished Elam, a civilization as ancient as Egypt's. Susa was here, the capital of an Achaemenid Empire that extended from Greece to the Ganges. And Tepe Sabz also, only a few kilometers removed from Ali Kosh, one of several sites in Khuzistan that give evidence that this was where irrigation was first practiced, its techniques applied as early as 5500 B.C. Sites formerly inhabited, their remains at least, are aligned along dry stream beds where water once coursed and from which it was drawn off by hacking a simple breach in the natural levees that embanked the surface flows. Traces of what once were dwellings follow these ancient wadis away from the mountains and their accompanying rainfall, downslope into ever more arid conditions, into regions where the rain is not enough for dry farming, where, in order to live, the inhabitants would have had to practice irrigation. Yet even back up the slope, under the blessing of somewhat heavier rain, irrigation would still have been practiced as insurance against the sour circumstance that the rain was erratic, as it always is in arid regions.

A little more than 2,000 years later but close by—just across the marches of the Tigris in the lower Mesopotamian floodplain—that first recorded civilization burst forth suddenly, as it seemed, its presence attested by archaeologists at level four at Warka, the Erech of the epic hero, Gilgamesh, and at the site far upstream called Jamdat Nasr. This was Sumeria, with its baked-brick construction, its walled cities centered on temples raised to skyscraper heights, where history begins with the emergence of writing. Coming from no one knows where, speaking a language whose affinities have not yet been traced, the Sumerians are as mysterious as the statues they made of their gods, with their lozenge eyes staring into nothing—or resting their vision after checking the readings on their countless water gauges.

For there is no mystery as to how the Sumerians made their living and accumulated wealth. They founded their city-state civilization on irrigation techniques that have since come to be applied throughout the world. The network of irrigation canals that supported a densely flourishing agriculture in a region with less than 200 mm of annual rainfall required a skill in expert management that must have developed in a long evolution. Drainage problems are critical in a landscape as flat as that of lower Sumeria. When effective drainage cannot be achieved—and this is the commonest affliction of large irrigation schemes even today—then the soil will become waterlogged. This was the curse and affliction of Sumeria. In the cool Mesopotamian winter when evaporation is low, water collected on the surface of Sumerian fields. In the heat of summer, the water evaporated, leaving behind a residue of salts. Good irrigation practice demands a refined allocation of water, assigning to each field the precise amount needed for plant growth. Usually this will be enough to insure that potentially harmful salts are washed away, but in certain situations, it will not be enough, and an additional amount of water, called the "leaching requirement," will have to be sent across the fields, dissolving surface salts and carrying them into the soil below the root zone. When drainage is poor, as might be the case where the gradient is minimal, even the application of additional water will fail to clear the salts from the surface.

But if all goes well, good soils in warm, rainless environments exhibit their lush productivity in a yield of two harvests in the year gathered into bins and barns without worrying about when the rain will fall. Blessed rain, that gift of erratic nature, nourisher of the earth, with its unpredictable habits, arriving too late so that plants haven't time enough in which to mature, or sweeping in too soon, spotting the tomatoes, bloating the grapes left on the vines. Irrigation is plagued with no such worries as it works the soil to its maximum capacity. Continual harvesting means a constant removal of nutrients from the soil, but these can be restored by fallow or fertilizer, or by rotating nitrogen-fixing legumes with another crop. The Sumerians may have manured their fields by pasturing their livestock on the stubble of the harvests.

The skilled management required by Sumerian irrigation, or any other system so large, called forth the social stratification that ever since has typified civilized life. Class differences were strengthened by the circumstance that the land with highest productivity was limited in extent because it was irrigated and therefore could be monopolized. Their completed system of locks and dams struck the Sumerians as so marvelous that they attributed their construction to the god Ninurta. This was an attribution that supported the monopoly of the best irrigated plots by the temples, whose bureaucracies were directed by priest-managers and whose echelons of personnel included the scribes who maintained the production records and the skilled workmen who operated the mills and breweries which also belonged to the temple, or who handled the livestock recorded as the property of an institution that resembled the corporations of Rockefeller Center as much as it was reminiscent of St. Patrick's across the street. Sumerian history was a long chronicle of disputes over water rights, of miniwars over which cities could use which canals and where the boundary stones were to be placed separating irrigated fields.

That the main Sumerian crop was barley, the most salt-tolerant of the important cereals, is an indication that the Sumerian irrigation works had chronic problems of waterlogging and salination, as was to be expected in the sluggish drainage of the lower Euphrates, today a region of swamps inhabited by the so-called Marsh Arabs. It was probably salt that brought Sumeria to the point of internal collapse, laying the first civilization open to the invasions of the many other peoples, practically all the world, who were still barbarians. In the twenty-fourth century B.C. the Semitic peoples make their entrance into history under the leadership of the legendary Sargon of Akkad, who united the city-states of Sumeria into a kind of empire. This was a dominion that was to last less than a century before it, too, was overwhelmed by the Guti, wild men from the high Zagros. Apparently, the rulers of Akkad had proved incapable of taking care of their major problem, the salting and anaerobia that had facilitated their own apprenticeship in civilization. History has usually been written in reverse, attributing to invasion the destruction of settled means of production. But in Sumerian times, it was doubtless the irrigation system that collapsed first, the once productive fields slicked with salt, crumbling a system of defenses that no longer had so much to defend. And when invasion came, it would complete the wreckage of physical structures that had long since ceased to receive proper maintenance. Complex irrigation networks require the political order that comes with stable societies for the maintenance of dams, canals, locks, and outlets. They also require an answer to drainage problems, which, in the end, became insuperable for the Sumerians. As the centuries passed, the lands that had made Sumeria prosperous became permanently degraded, sinking into the condition in which they are still to be found today, more than 4,000 years later. In the land of the two rivers, civilization retreated northward away from the Gulf, in the direction of a slowly steepening gradient that diminished the menace of waterlogging, toward Babylon first, then to Nineveh, to Seleucia of the Macedonians and Ctesiphon of Sassanid Persia, to Bagdad of the Abbasids, the city of a thousand and one nights, today the capital of modern Iraq. Sumeria, Sargon, the Gutian invasion—yesterday's shadows and stirrings out of the first written transcripts bring mankind onto the stage of history locked in implacable conflict with a relentless enemy. In the twentieth century, this enemy was to receive the name "desertification."

As the degradation of its soil subverted Sumeria's economic foundations and opened the land to invasion, climatic change may simultaneously have been pressing Sumeria's Semitic conquerors to move out of the heart of Arabia. The hither Orient entered the Bronze Age around 3000 B.C. together with a shift toward aridity that gradually dried up those Arabian grasslands on which Semitic herdsmen had pastured their flocks. Desert peoples, abandoning the nomadic life, had been infiltrating the cities of Sumeria for centuries before Sargon made his overwhelming appearance. Climatic interpretations of history have been criticized for reducing human beings to automatons who, unable to do anything about climate, can only react to natural forces in a sequence of events that seems to make no allowance for the play of free human will. The nomadic herdsman, on the other hand, must be credited with the drive to abandon pastures afflicted with drought and with intelligence enough to take control of sophisiticated cities. Sometimes history has been written as if Sargon's conquest and the Gutian invasion were mere expressions of human yearning. The crude, unlettered nomad stares out of the desert in envy of metropolitan delights. That may indeed have been the attitude. In the endless interplay between mind and nature, drought pushed the nomad from behind in the direction of satisfying his longings. But it was waterlogging and salination that, in the end, made it possible for him to sip his wine in hanging gardens.

The arrival of the Mongols in Mesopotamia in 1258 A.D. provides another illustration of the interchange that endlessly operates between the fall of rain, its comings and goings, and the fertile human imagination. Their numbers increased by a long succession of years with good rainfall, these invincible pastoralists rode out of the Gobi steppes to conquer their known world under the inspiration of a vision that in many ways was the opposite of the dream that had inspired Sargon. The Mongols were appalled and alienated by cities, as they were by the arts of cultivation, and they were lured onward, ever farther, by the entrancing image of a world converted to pasture in which men could wander wild and free with none required to submit to the confinements of city life or the degrading toil of raising a crop. The last of the Abbasids, al-Musta'sim, refused Hulagu's order to dismantle Bagdad. The city was thereupon sacked and destroyed as part of a utopian effort to revert Mesopotamia to the prairie and pasture that it had been 5,000 years before. Iraq'arabi never recovered from Hulagu's massacre of 800,000 persons, who included the operators and managers of the irrigation system, which promptly drifted toward disintegration (76, pp.42–43). The fabulous city of Sheherezade became a country town, a sheep town. Iraq became sheep country, fulfilling Mongolian desires, except for small bits of it that continued to be irrigated by the *nirin* system, or by vagrant feudal sheikhs.

It was in the wasp waist of Iraq, where the Tigris and Euphrates approach each other before moving apart again to embrace ancient Sumeria in their southward flow, that the modern government decided to initiate the work of rehabilitation with a carefully engineered irrigation project. The task of undoing the work of the Mongols would begin in this inland isthmus that for four millennia had been an important center of human life. The project, Greater Mussayeb, would squat atop one of the places where civilization was born. The mound of Jamdat Nasr, one of the two sites that mark that parturition, humps upward on the project's eastern edge. Although this region is not quite true desert by the strict definition applied by the specialists at UNESCO who elaborated the new World Map of Desertification, it is extremely arid, occupying a climatic condition sometimes called subdesert. Its mere 120 mm of annual rainfall is overmatched by an evapotranspiration of 1972 mm, as measured at Bagdad, not far away, by the Penman method, to give a dryness ratio of 16.4. This means that the blatant energy pouring down in the almost constant sunshine is enough to evaporate the little bit of rain that falls 16.4 times over. Or, to put it another way, 16.4 times as much rain would have to fall to avoid a chronic moisture deficit, although somewhat less rain than that would in fact avoid a deficit since increased rainfall would mean increased cloudiness and, in the interconnections of these matters, less sunshine to evaporate more water. Such niceties are properly forgotten in a situation in which the true desert of Arabia is only a few kilometers away, over there, on the other side of Euphrates. Here between the rivers summers are scorching, with temperatures exceeding 40°C on more than 100 days. In Greater Mussayeb, as in all lower Mesopotamia, the original vegetation has long since vanished through 50 centuries of hacking away at the wood of arid-land shrubbery in a chronicle interspersed with episodes of salination and overgrazing. Here and there, *nirin* irrigation was practiced on the site before the project moved in, but most of the district had served as a camp for nomadic herdsmen who pastured flocks on succession-al growth, mainly halophytic chenopods forming thickets on an abandoned wasteland.

As the design of the Greater Mussayeb Project got under way, estimates were made of the water requirements of the crops proposed to be grown, figuring that 21,055 hectares would continue under the old *nirin* system while the remaining 62,625 hectares, or most of the project, would become a model of new styles of intensive cultivation yielding both summer and winter harvests. On these terms, water needs were calculated at 686.3 million m^3 in years of normal to low water storage and 855.6 million m^3 in years of exceptional upstream rainfall when a flooding Euphrates would impound enough water to support more intensive cultivation. The intake canals were designed to supply water in the correct amounts, beginning with 40 m^3 sec in the main canal, taking into account an estimated average loss of 35% between the river and the crop. An analysis of soil samples revealed deficiencies in nitrogen, phosphate, and organic matter which would have to be made good by applications of fertilizer. In this portion of treeless Mesopotamia, the watertable was found to lie at 1.5–2.5 meters beneath a surface sloping ever so slightly, with groundwater containing up to 4% salt, or so saline from centuries of alternating cultivation and abandonment that leaching would have to be applied to lower the salts beneath the root zone before the project would be ready for crops. Leaching, calling for an even application of water, could require a considerable amount of land leveling where poor use had pocked the surface with hummocks and holes, not to mention the scattering of ancient *tells*, the low, round hillocks that, like Jamdat Nasr, mark the sites of ancient towns and cities.

Between 1953 and 1956, construction work proceeded on the irrigation network, gouging about 50 km of main canal, 13 branch canals, 7 parallels, and a large number of laterals for a total length of 710 km. It was a system equipped with head regulators, takeoff laterals, farm turnouts, drop structures, and escape structures to assure a sufficient discharge to carry away silt during seasonal periods of low water use. As part of its well conceived design, Greater Mussayeb would incorporate a complete drainage system, a vital element in a landscape where the total gradient was only seven meters over the 40 km from the project's northwest to its southeast corner. Designed with the same care that had been devoted to the intake system, the drainage network would consist of 170 km of main drains, 120 km of branch drains, 370 km of collector drains, and 1,050 km of field collectors, for a total length of 1,710 km. Intake and drainage together determined a division of the area into uniform plots, one-half km in length by one-third km in width, for a total farm area of 16 2/3 hectares, and a total of 2,705 such farm units were designated. Twenty-three villages were planned for eventual construction on the project, each with a school, a health post, and other community facilities. As was evident from its prospectus, Greater Mussayeb would be a complex project integrating agriculture with life's other necessities, and it would be one requiring constant and expert maintenance, in return for which its farmers would be paid in the coin of a new life graced with economic prosperity. Their lives would have been broken free from the shackles of a feudal order. Those assigned land in the project would be assisted to these goals by their participation in multipurpose agricultural cooperative societies which would provide them with supplies, credit, marketing facilities, and a sense of community solidarity. The project was divided into 11 districts and a cooperative association was projected for each one.

In 1956, when the intake and drainage systems approached completion, distribution of the project's 2,705 farms began. Among the many applying for land, allotments were made first to people already living in the project area and then to landless farmers and pastoralists from outside the area who had been attracted into it by the lure of the project itself. According to a report issued just as allotments were getting under way,

> a number of unknown factors existed during the whole or a part of the design stage which prevented very accurate engineering and which certainly will require adjustments in the field, although every effort has been made to reduce the extent of their effects (2, p.29).

The missing data were: water requirements for crops had been estimated in accordance with general theory, but not established experimentally; the size of farms units and the system in terms of which the land had been subdivided had not been settled in advance of construction—whatever dark implications that might have had; a detailed classification of the soil into land types had not been carried out. The missing information concerned only physical factors, although the size of the farms might have had its social ramifications. But physical or social, four years from this moment, when the first allotments went out in the euphoria of a future beckoning with limitless prospects, the Greater Mussayeb Project was in a state of collapse. What had happened? Could this shocking development be attributed to missing data, to failures in design?

> In 1954, the area's population was estimated at 3,000 persons, most of whom had applied for an allotment. By 1956, when the farm units were distributed, population had reached an estimated 5,000–6,000 inhabitants. During land distribution, a number of units were taken up by absentee landlords; the actual farming on these units was carried out by tenant farmers and laborers. As canal deterioration and increased salinity reduced the area's productivity, many settlers left. By 1960 an estimated 55 allottees had abandoned the settlement, and by 1964, only 1,458 allottees remained (out of an original 1,775 farm units distributed). In addition, the number of units retained by outside landholders had dwindled. (2, p.34)

The hopelessness of the situation can be seen in the fact that even absentee landlords abandoned it. Again, what had gone wrong? The engineers and technicians who had worked on the project sought the answer to that question in an inquest into physical conditions. A quick survey revealed that only 31% of the irrigable lands allotted were actually being cultivated.

> This under-utilization of available land caused maintenance in certain portions of the irrigation and drainage network to be neglected. As a result, canals and drains were rapidly clogged with weeds and with suspended and wind-blown silt.... By the beginning of 1960, after only a few years of operation, much of the project's infrastructure was simply breaking down.... Water regulation was seriously impaired. The radial gates to the head regulators had been fitted in the wrong position, so that the heavy silt-laden water of the river's bottom layers—instead of clear surface water—was drawn into the canal system.... Hardly any of the secondary regulators had been properly maintained. In many places, gates were stuck, damaged or out of alignment.... At the canal

> headworks, the river banks in the vicinity of the intake were to be protected by dry stone pitching resting on a filter layer. It was noticed that this pitching, designed to act as a free draining material to keep the subsoil behind it well drained, was disturbed and overgrown with plants and shrubs. . . . The canals had also undergone major deterioration. . . . The maintenance of laterals and sublaterals required silt and weed clearance, but this was either seldom or improperly done. . . . Finally, siltation and weed growth had had disastrous effects on the escape and drainage systems, clogging the main escape structure. The secondary escapes were nearly collapsed. Furthermore, blocked drainage was causing a rise in the watertable of the irrigated sections to a level very near the land surface. (2, pp.30-31)

So the inevitable followed, the waterlogging that ensues on the failure of drainage. The situation seemed unreal, absurd. Had no provision been made for the proper maintenance of canals and drains? Well, yes, maintenance was supposed to have been provided by the new farmers who had received land allotments. Then why were they not providing it, something so clearly connected with their own self-interest? Their rejection of the project's housing might provide a first clue to their strange behavior. By 1959, two of the planned villages had been built—Imam, with 98 houses, and Rashayed, with 77 houses, both communities equipped with a primary school, market, coffeehouse, bathhouse, and clinic.

> The houses were of masonry and consisted of two rooms, each four meters square, and a covered veranda measuring 5.5 × 4 meters. The veranda was closed at the back but left open at the front to allow for added construction; a condition of ownership was that construction be completed by the allottee himself. Thus minimum living space during the initial settlement period was provided, and each allottee would have the possibility of enlarging his house according to his family's needs and tastes. By this time, however (1959), most settlers had already built mud houses on their own farm units, and as these structures were naturally better adapted to the local life style, most of the new construction was left unoccupied. (2, p.35)

"Naturally better adapted," the case study says, indicating that the people who would occupy the project and actually make it work—or fail—had not been consulted on the design of their houses, while the city folk who had developed Greater Mussayeb to present it to the peasants as a gift, the manna of development, falling from heaven, had somehow neglected to take into account the distinctive social needs of rural people in Iraq, that they must have spacious and very private courtyards in which the family centers its social life, that provision must be made whereby the life of the men, in their social mixing and conversations, can be kept separate from that of the women. The failure to consult the people, and the resulting failure of the housing, might appear at first sight to be no more than a waste of building expenses—but no, in the planned ecosystem of Greater Mussayeb, its elements supposed to intertwine, it was a much more serious matter than that. The allottees, as they were called, went off to live in their mud houses, separately and alone, the official housing standing empty in the clusters of haunted villages. And that spelled doom to the planned village life, the basis of the cooperative associations that were to provide credit and marketing facilities, that were intended in fact, to pull allottees out of their feudal past.

> According to the agrarian law of 1958, each allottee was expected to join a multipurpose agricultural cooperative society, providing credit, marketing and supply facilities. The isolation of the farmers' families on their own lands, however, did not foster the growth of the communal and cooperative spirit which the government had hoped for. (2, p.36)

But perhaps the project had made its fundamental error in expecting so much from people so bound in tradition that they refused modern housing when it was offered to them.

> The lands were distributed mostly to pastoral nomads with few savings and very low standards of living. Most of the allottees had very limited experience in farming, and over 95% were illiterate. Malnutrition was common, and child mortality was very high. A good number of allottees had no intention of becoming farmers; some discouraged farmers shortly abandoned their farms. Thus it was obvious that the farmer, with his poor financial and technical means, could not utilize the land satisfactorily. Among those who remained, agriculture became increasingly exploitative, as among semi-nomads. Consequently, fields were in general neglected, and crops were often overgrown with weeds. In addition, idleness among farmers became increasingly common, and much time was spent in the cafes located at the entrance to the project area. In fact, the farmer's lack of motivation to improve his situation was one of the area's main social problems. Social life, incentives, and adequate leadership did not exist. (2 p.36)

Ah, these deceivers, idle loungers in cafés, shiftless people lacking motivation! There was little wonder that Greater Mussayeb had collapsed. But those who had designed it, those whose emotions or ambitions had become entangled in it, were determined to rescue this first assault on what the Mongols had done so long ago. They decided that rehabilitation must be launched, and it was, beginning in 1965, with the course of repair accelerated after 1968, when Iraq's President Ahmad Hassain al-Bakr personally inspected the works and ordered an allocation of funds and authority sufficient to insure its success. If, that is, success could be assured by funds and authority. The scientists returned to Greater Mussayeb to carry out the studies that, as they had already pointed out, should have been completed before the project was originally designed.

Water consumption requirements of different cropping patterns were determined experimentally. Sunshine intensities were registered with a network of recorders to gather data for the determination of a precise evapotranspiration rate, not for nearby Bagdad, but for Mussayeb itself. The hydrophysical properties of the soil were ascertained by the careful classification of soil types and by measuring the texture, permeability, porosity, and infiltration rate of each type. Drainage requirements were thus specified with precision, and a determination was ultimately made to install a dug-in network of tile drains as the most cost-effective system. This ambitious task, perhaps a measure of the ambitions that came to be lodged in Greater Mussayeb itself, and still under construction when the case study was written, will eventually involve a total of 7,858 km of 10-cm field tile drains installed at 1.8–2.0 meters below the surface and equipped with flushing outlets and manholes, plus 775 km of 15–30-cm closed pipe collector drains—all to serve 38,750 hectares of 88% of the area now planned to carry a cropping intensity of 125%, or more than one crop per year. The remaining 12% of the intensive area would now consist of model state farms having a cropping intensity of 170%. A demonstration project showed that salt-affected soil was readily rehabilitated by proper leaching, and leaching requirements were precisely fixed in quantities of good-quality Euphrates river water. The project administration was strengthened. Rehabilitation forged ahead on all fronts. Hummocky land was leveled. Irrigation and drainage networks were cleared of debris and restored to their original depth and design.

But what about all those indolent peasants on whom the project had previously foundered and on whom its ultimate success would depend? A tone of blame crept into the case study when it viewed them wasting their time in cafés. If only they had been college graduates, eager to make that extra dinar for a down payment on a pickup truck. Alas, they were not college graduates. And not only were they not consulted in advance, in all their ignorance, the case study admits a crowning lapse—that they were given no guidance after land had been allotted to them.

> Other factors such as the lack of extension services, an inadequate technical infrastructure and insufficient agricultural machinery also contributed to the initial failure of the project. (2, p.30)

The lack of extension services—a remarkable omission, which "also contributed" to failure. Nomadic pastoralists, most of them illiterate, were allotted irrigation lands without being interviewed in depth enough to determine even whether they were serious about ever becoming farmers. The practice of irrigation was known to require skill and experience, and the complex, modern project of Greater Mussayeb was supposed to have been maintained by the people given lands within its tangle of canals and drains. But no arrangements had been made to give these callow, inexperienced landholders instruction in the complex arts they would need. An "inadequate technical infrastructure" is bureaucratic phraseology signifying that these uninstructed people would receive not even supervision. What happened to them is clear—they were thrown onto the land and then abandoned.

It is easy to be critical of what happened in Iraq in the hindsight in which errors leap out in bold relief. The Mussayeb case study can only be commended for the frankness with which officials and official institutions admitted errors, thus making this study more valuable than a thousand success stories. One can understand, perhaps even sympathize with, the impatience of technicians at seeing their masterpiece destroyed, or their advice ignored by people who, from a narrowly technical perspective, were being handed a better life on a platter and who then responded to this gift with what must have seemed to the technologist to have been a shiftless lack of motivation. But it is right at this point that the realization should have dawned that since it was the allottees who had effected the downfall of Greater Mussayeb, and that since allottees, for all that term, are people, then the collapse of the project must have been for social rather than physical reasons. An awakening to this truth did in fact occur in Iraq. And it is to the credit of those involved in Greater Mussayeb—engineers, agronomists, administrators—all carried by this truth out of their depth, beyond their particular competence, that they came fully to admit that the success of any such massive project depends on paying as much attention to people, with their incalculable requirements, as to physical matters, such as land and water, whose requirements can be determined by mathematics.

> More difficult and urgent than technical matters . . . are the sociological problems. The adoption of a system which relies on the combined presence of special managerial skills, a well organized administration, teams of engineers, researchers, economists, technicians and social workers, and—last but not least—a farmer population receptive to new methods and advice, often means a revolutionary change in life style—for technical personnel as well as for the farmer population. Both groups are required to live for protracted periods on new agricultural settlement areas often cut off from their social and cultural roots and without apparent professional, material, or spiritual compensation. The authors of the study believe that the factors which thus motivate staff members and settlers alike are too little understood.
> Concerning in particular the farmer population, it appears beyond question that a more intensive cultivation of reclaimed areas requires a continued education of the farmer. The establishment of extension services able to explain to the farmer, in his own language, the advantages of alternative methods of land use and to train him in the use of equipment, seeds, fertilizers and pesticides is of particular importance. (2, p.95)

By 1972, the population of a rehabilitated Greater Mussayeb had risen to 32,000 people, and the project had begun to make a substantial contribution to the national economy. But its problems were far from resolved. It had become clear that it would display no overnight success and that maximum productivity, presumably to be accompanied by a prosperous life for the farmers, would be achieved only after a long, continuing, and painful ordeal. For one thing, a competent extension service had still not been organized.

> Until very recently, the administration of the project never had extension officers in sufficient numbers, nor adequate organizational structures to provide an effective extension service to the farmers. No research or demonstrations were done to supplement farm operations. . . .

It is necessary . . . for the government to give greater priority to this service. In particular, the practice of eroding the ranks of extension service personnel so as to meet *ad hoc* needs in other project sections should be discontinued. (2, p.76)

Extension services, then, still have a low priority, but this is no more than typical of a branch of activity which, everywhere in the world, continues to give its major attention to physical matters, rather than to such questions involving people as their state of information. Then again, this may be because extension services often fail to deliver what is asked of them, even when the services themselves are delivered with some enthusiasm. The truth is that illiterate nomads may not be the easiest people in the world to teach. Their minds may not function in quite those channels—as if they were children in elementary school. One's thoughts are drawn back to the Sumerians, wondering whatever happened to them? Scarcely a drop of Sumerian spirit seems to be left in rural Iraq—indeed, in few of the Third World's rural settings—exhibiting the dilution of ancient energies made by ages of time. Or is it time or the crushing course of events that has made such a transformation? Here, where humankind made an original attempt to answer every question, the present inhabitants give every appearance of unconcern with asking even the first question. For instance, why didn't they *demand* instruction when they were thrown into a situation that so obviously required it? No, instead they went off to lounge in the cafés. If that sort of response were only understood, Greater Mussayeb might have no more problems.

3

TURFAN

"Tame the wind! Harness the sand!"

WHERE THE ANTIQUE Silk Road plunged from the glacial heights of the Pamirs into the mountain-rimmed Tarim basin, it evaded the sterile emptiness of the Taklamakan desert by splitting into two. One branch passed from oasis to oasis on that desert's southern rim, a course that edged the colossal rampart of the K'un-lun, the northern wall of Tibet. This is the route Marco Polo took on his three-year journey from Italy to the court of the great Khan in Peking. The merchant of Venice was unimpressed by earth's most awesome mountain landscape, the true spine of Asia. "Nothing here," he said, "worth mentioning in our book" (60, p.82). In fact, he found more to interest him in the northern branch, the route he did not take. "The chief city," he said, "is called Kara-khoja. . . . The people are idolators (Buddhists), but they include Christians of the Nestorian sect and some Saracens. . . . The land produces grain and excellent wine. But in winter the cold here is more intense than is known in any other part of the world" (60, pp.88–89).

This last comment indicates that Marco Polo never went there. For the Turfan depression, in which Kara-khoja was in his day the largest city, is protected from Siberia's wintry blasts, although not completely, as will be seen, by the "Mountains of Heaven," the T'ien-shan range to the north. Yet the Silk Road has never served as one of those regular beaten tracks, and few were the Europeans who visited Turfan before the twentieth-century explorations of Sven Hedin and Aurel Stein revealed to a fascinated western world the remains of an ancient culture, with its Irano–Buddhist sculptures, its bodhisattvas carved to look like Greek gods or painted to resemble Rustam, hero of Persia. What place in the world could have been in fact and history more remote from the distant West than Turfan?

NORTH CHINA

Showing the locations of Turfan, Wushenchao and Tachai and the ancient Silk Road entering China from the northwest.

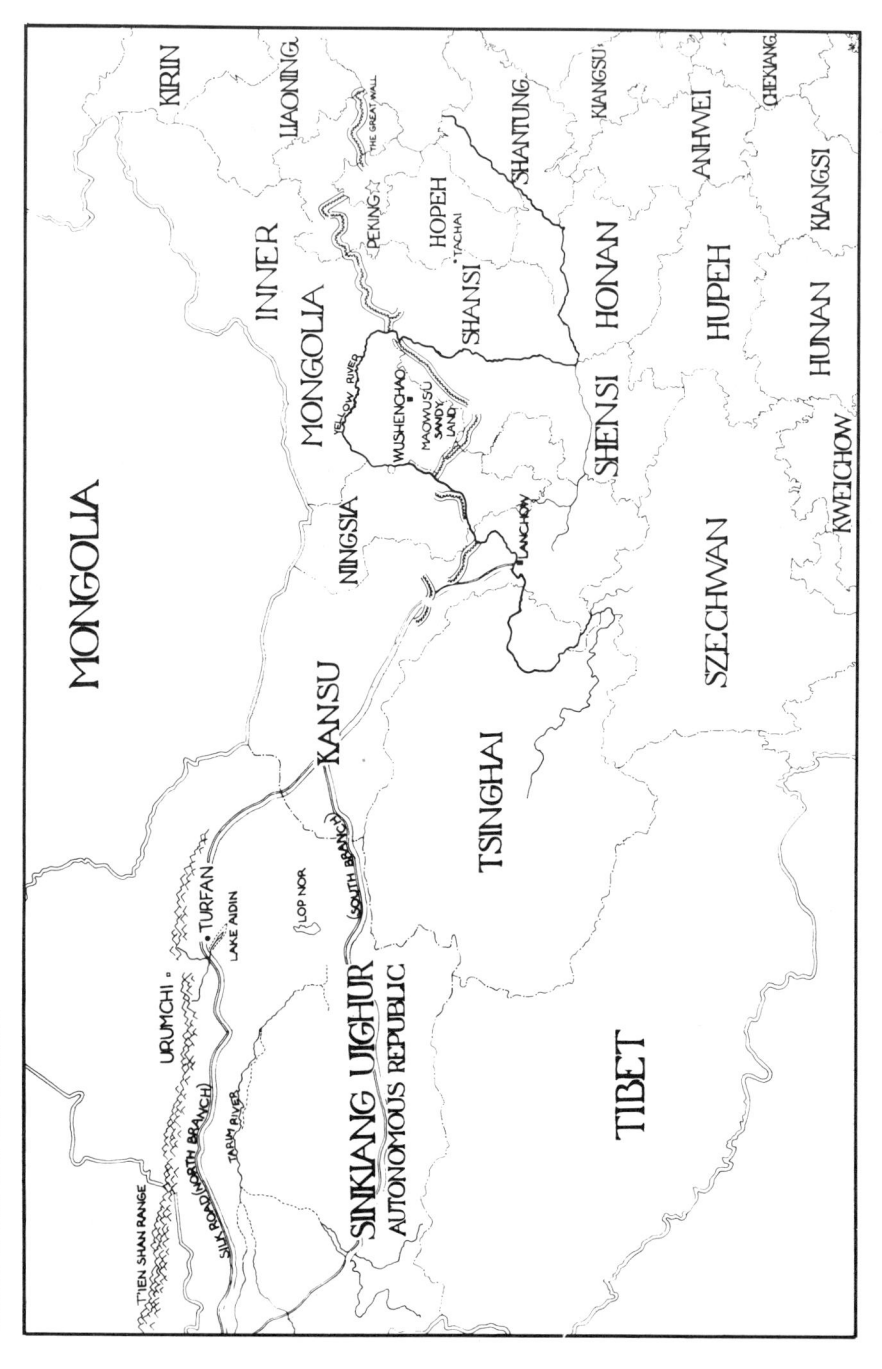

And that, even though it was always a commercial center, a stop on the long highway between East and West, and even though the first inhabitants remembered in the region spoke Indo-European languages, were related to the Scythians of Europe and were anciently reported by the Chinese to have red hair and blue eyes.

Aurel Stein, who made an archaeological dig at Kara-khoja in 1914, provided a vivid description of the desolate, exaggerated landscapes surrounding the green fields of cotton, fruits, and cereals under cultivation at Turfan (70, p.225). To the south lie the jagged barren wastes of the Kuruk-tagh, the "dry mountains" of the Uighur Turks who had once made Turfan their capital, and at their base, there in the very heart of elevated, mountainous Asia, the Turfan depression, sinking at Lake Aidin to 154 meters below sea level. To the north rears up the great wall of the T'ien-shan, snow-covered here in its Bogdo-ula section. Below the snow line, the long boulder-strewn glacis of the mountain range is naked of vegetation as it slopes down to the "flaming mountain," as the Chinese call it—the "hills of fire," in Stein's phrase—a foothill ridge displaying the brilliant reds of exposed minerals. It is from these hills of fire that the people of Turfan get their water.

They have tapped this foothill from a time long forgotten—or so they were doing when they first made an appearance in history. That was in the epoch of the Early Han, around 200 B.C., when the rich oasis was a prize of contention between the forces of Imperial China and the mounted Hsiung-nu archers—"the Huns," as Europe was to call them. The snow melt from the high T'ien-shan emerges in springs of fresh water at the flaming mountain and in artesian springs lower down, toward the lake.

> The T'ien-shan water system has an annual flow of 300 million cubic meters. The subterranean flow in the flood and alluvial plains supplied by the T'ien-shan water system is blocked by the Flaming Mountain and the Salt Mountain, thereby forming a spring-fed water system with an annual flow of 200 million cubic meters. Some 60 to 70 meters underground, along an east-west belt in the Aidin Lake area, exists a water regime which provides artesian irrigation. (8, p.1)

All this is tapped for irrigation through a network of wells and mainly underground canals called the *karez* system. Without irrigation, nothing would grow in Turfan, which is climatically a true desert. Variable, undependable rainfall averages only 16.6 mm a year, less than one inch, while the powerful sun, shining out of cloudless skies, is capable of evaporating 3,003.1 mm of moisture annually. The aridity ratio is therefore 180.9, an index encountered only in the driest portions of the earth, places celebrated for their desolation, such as the Libyan desert or the Empty Quarter of Arabia. It is why Turfan is a desert oasis.

Besides this extreme aridity, Turfan has to cope with violent winds. When the sun heats the bowl of the depression, air rises out of it as in a chimney, creating a shaft of low atmospheric pressure. Other air rushes in to replace what has risen, most of it coming through a pass in the T'ien-shan leading to the northwest and to Urumchi, the capital of Chinese Turkestan, now called the Sinkiang-Uighur Autonomous Region. These powerful northwesterlies, rushing down on Turfan through the wind gorges of the Peiyang River and the Triple Springs, strike the oasis with velocities above 8 on the Beaufort scale (above 55 km per hour) for an average of 36.2 days every year, and above 10 on the scale (above 80 km per hour) for an average of five days every year. Wind so strong picks up the sand that surrounds the oasis, mobilizes it into moving dunes, blankets young growth in sterile grit, or kills plants by abrading them as if with sandpaper. Turfan oasis is constantly at war with the wind. "Tame the wind!" the case study exhorts in its subtitle, adding, "Harness the sand! Transform the Gobi!" Wind and a complex irrigation system mean that life in Turfan is dependent on unremitting and skilled maintenance. The century of political turmoil that preceded the establishment of the present regime in China was damaging to Turfan. When the present government established its authority in the oasis, it found this old capital of the Uighur Turks in pitiful condition. An anonymous scribe depicted conditions as they then were, employing the poetic Chinese manner:

> *When there is no wind*
> *the land is covered with sand.*
> *When the wind blows*
> *your own house can scarcely be seen.*
> *Soft soil is carried away by the wind.*
> *Farms are buried beneath the sand. (8, p.3)*

René Grousset, the historian of Central Asia, exaggerated when he said that the Silk Road in the Tarim basin, "this slender dual thread . . . was strong enough nevertheless to ensure that our planet should consist of a single world and not of two separate ones" (48, p.xxii). One world was hardly created by the occasional exchange of bales of silk for Roman merchandise at a stone tower in the Wakhan, somewhere in the panhandle of Afghanistan, the precise location of which has been lost to memory.

Nonetheless, peering along this old road eastward and westward, one gazes from Turfan to the ends of the earth along a corridor of arid lands stretching all the way across the Old World, from the Gulf of Chihli, an arm of the Pacific, to Mauritania on the Atlantic, and even beyond—to the Cape Verde Islands, arid dots in the midst of a desert sea. This is the largest of the earth's five major dryland complexes as they can be seen displayed on the World Map of Desertification.

The great African–Asian dryland belt is centered on deserts—in the west, on the Sahara, separated from the Mediterranean by narrow strips of fertile land and from the jungles of Guinea and the Congo by the wide belts of the Sahel and Sudan. In northeast Africa, where the Sahara is at its widest, coming in Libya to the very shore of the Mediterranean, the drylands to the south skirt the Ethiopian mountains and flank the Red Sea and Indian Ocean through Somalia, extending southward as far as central Tanzania.

In its central portions, the Afro–Asian drylands have at their core the deserts of Sinai, Arabia, and Iran, whence they sweep broadly across Afghanistan and Pakistan into Rajasthan and central India on the south, into Soviet Central Asia on the north. To the east, finally, drylands spread out from the stark Takla-makan and the true desert portions of the Gobi, extending over the wide plains of Mongolia and north China, with arms reaching northward into Siberia and eastward into Manchuria and all the way to the Pacific shore.

The second of the five major dryland complexes centers on the narrow Namibian desert that hugs the south Atlantic along Africa's southwest shore. Eastward, the purple sands and stark hamadas of Namibia blend into the Kalahari and other arid lands in Botswana and South Africa and on across the water into the climatically related dry southwestern portions of Madagascar.

Another thin coastal desert, the Atacama, is to be found strung along the Andean shore of South America from the southern tip of Ecuador along the full length of Peru and deep into northern Chile, with related dryland extensions from the high plains of Bolivia down the eastern side of the Andes to include eventually all of Patagonia.

Disconnected drylands occupy northeastern Brazil and the Caribbean shore of Colombia and Venezuela, extending offshore to islands such as Curaçao.

A fourth dryland region containing very little true desert, perhaps only Death Valley and a few other small, isolated fragments of hyperaridity, centers on the Mexican state of Sonora, but ranges far across much of the North American West from Saskatchewan and the Dakotas to central Mexico and Yucatan.

The fifth of the great dryland regions composes most of Australia, the driest continent, but one containing no true deserts according to the strict definition applied in preparing the World Map of Desertification. The Australians themselves, at the Conference and elsewhere, declared their opinion that the definition so employed was too stingy, and that the Gibson Desert or the Simpson Desert, in western and central Australia, respectively, were examples among several other antipodal landscapes where desertification is not a problem since these regions, like the Sahara or the Takla-makan, lie outside the need for worry since they can be put to no agricultural use.

The mapmakers might have replied, in agreement with Aurel Stein, that the unused regions of Australia are "'tame deserts.' . . . They may well impress the town dweller . . . with their sense of solitude, emptiness and, let me add, peace." But, Stein goes on to say, such are not "true desert" like "the dune-covered Takla-makan and the wastes of hard salt crust or wind-eroded clay of the Lop desert (where) . . . the absence of moisture bans not only human existence but practically all animal and plant life" (70, p.5).

Of the earth's entire 149,162,000 km^2 of land surface, only about 10 million km^2, or less than 7% of the total, consists of "true desert," with two-thirds of all of it in the Sahara. Another 15 million km^2, or about 10% of the total, is permanently covered with ice, most of it in Antarctica and Greenland. It is curious to note that if the poles were not cold, they would be deserts, since precipitation at the poles—in the form of ice or snow—registers little more than it does in the Sahara, both occupying as they do regions of subsiding air. On a warmer earth, polar agriculture would develop odd practices in response to a weak sun shining 24 hours a day during the summer growing season, and agriculture might have been possible there during the mesozoic when dinosaurs roamed the continents. On the present earth, almost all the land above the Arctic Circle is locked in permafrost, a condition in which the soil moisture is frozen, and discontinuous and sporadic permafrost reaches down into much lower northern latitudes.

The occurrence of desert conditions is only one among a number of circumstances that can balk the use of tropical or temperate-zone land for agricultural purposes, including among those purposes pastoralism, the breeding and raising of livestock. One thinks of mountainous or swampy terrain as preventing agriculture, yet dizzily steep mountain declivities are terraced, put to slash-and-burn cropping, or given over to goats as pasture, and swampy land is drained or otherwise adapted to food production. The commonest barrier to agriculture is poor soil. Plants, whether in the form of crops or as pasture for animals, require soil to grow in—all except for certain weird botanical forms such as algae and lichens. To constitute a home for plants, soil must have certain qualities—of structure, texture, constituent minerals—some would say of the qualities that make it soil, as distinct from an amorphous agglomerate of mineral particles. Soil must contain humus, the organic residue of former growth. It must be located somewhere near the middle of the acid–alkali spectrum if it is to support desirable plant life. It can neither be waterlogged, except for odd plants such as paddy rice, nor bone dry, and it must have a structure that moves the liquid readily through its pores. Nor can it be poisoned by the presence of noxious salts. Good soil—dirt—is one of the unsung treasures of the planet. Without it, animal life is impossible on land, since land animals depend for their nourishment on the plants that soil nurtures. The qualities of soil, the structure and constituents that make it soil, are those very elements that are attacked by the process of desertification. Soil quality can be so degraded by desertification that the land can lose all capacity to support plant life and can pass beyond all practical hope of recovery within a reasonably foreseeable future.

The quality of soil or, more precisely, restrictions in it, is then one of the principal reasons why only 9.3% of the earth's land surface is at present under cultivation. And even of this acreage, only one-half to two-thirds is harvested in any given year. In 1967, a Science Advisory Committee to the President of the United States estimated the amount of land that *could* be cultivated at 7.86 billion acres (61, p.83). This 3.19 billion hectares amounts to 21.4% of the earth's land surface, or well over twice as much land as is now under cultivation. Such assertions have often been made, just as hope has frequently been misplaced when it was lodged in land supposedly capable of being brought under the plow. Sad experience has persistently reinforced the lesson that most of the land that can profitably be cultivated is already under cultivation. The potentialities of new lands can sometimes be tapped only through enormous investments, as in expensive irrigation works. To be sure, such investments are sometimes made, as the case studies prepared by the Soviet Union will show. Increases in food production registered in recent years, however, and required to feed the world's growing populations, have been achieved primarily by increasing the productivity of land already under cultivation rather than by bringing new lands under the plow or hoe. Where new lands have been brought into use, primarily in the developing world, increases in production have not always ensued. Where increases have occurred, they have generally followed the application of modern techniques on new land or old, the massive use of fertilizer, the introduction of the Green Revolution with its high-yield cereal varieties—rice, maize, and wheat.

Seen in that light, from the perspective of modern agricultural methods, the protection of land already under cultivation takes on the highest importance. A philosophy of conservation must also be extended to that additional 15 to 20% of the earth's land surface, up to twice the extension of the world's croplands, that is used as pasture for livestock. These pasturelands, especially those in Asia, contain a sizeable proportion of the land considered by the U.S. President's advisers to be potentially arable, and indeed it can be cultivated if elaborate irrigation projects are constructed for it. Much of the rest of this potential cropland lies under the jungles of the Amazon and Congo river basins, where the presence of lateritic soils in the former at least, has had a history of converting hopeful dreams into agricultural nightmares.

The World Map of Desertification shows that the largest single category of the earth's land surface consists of drylands. To be distinguished from true deserts, the drylands are those arid, semiarid, and subhumid regions that are often associated with deserts and which, because they receive only limited amounts of rain, are particularly vulnerable to desertification. Vast extensions of the world's drylands are today used for nothing at all, and certainly for no agricultural purpose. Other large parts are used very thinly, supporting only the most meager herds or flocks of widely scattered livestock. In other parts of the drylands, animals are raised more intensively.

When their numbers are all added up, it will be seen that the vast bulk of the world's production of meat and hides comes out of regions vulnerable to desertification. So, too, the great staple cereal crops—wheat, barley, millet, maize, and sorghum—are largely the product of rainfed farming techniques carried out in dryland plains or rolling hills, where wind bends the grain like waves crossing an ocean. Wherever irrigation has been introduced, intensive cropping can be practiced, no matter how dry the climate. Europe imports its winter vegetables, and even flowers, from irrigated plots in arid, subdesert, and desert regions of north Africa.

Indeed, everything that man does anywhere, he does also in the vulnerable drylands, home (in 1973) to almost one-sixth of the human race. These varied lands at risk contain mines, industries, parks, roads, pipelines, cities—some of these cities—Cairo, Mexico, or Los Angeles, for example— among the largest in the world. They are the scenes of an uncountable variety of activities, all of which, and not just agriculture alone, influence the onset, the course, and the processes of desertification—or else stand against the process like a protecting wall. They are the regions in which mankind evolved from primate ancestors, in which human beings carried out the neolithic revolution, where they planted their first seeds and tamed those first wild beasts that subsequently formed a symbiosis with human life. It was in arid landscapes, not in green dells or park-like swards, that mankind founded the first civilizations, built the first cities, and learned to read and write. The ancient Silk Road, confined to Asia's vast dryland belt and reaching from classical Antioch at one end to Honan at the other, progresses from one to another of the monuments of vanished powers. At Turfan, in the transition zone between the Takla-makan and the Gobi Desert, the traveler used to mark his passage away from ancient Tokharia, through Uighuristan, and into the Khanate of Jagatai, son of Jenghiz Khan, thence into the Khanate of Kublai, grandson of Jenghiz Khan, host of Marco Polo, and Emperor of China.

"Transform the Gobi!" the call comes from the Turfan case study. The term "gobi" here refers not to the desert but to the type of land from which the desert takes its name. This is land stripped of soil by the wind down to its rocky or gravelly underpinnings. Much of it, including the Gobi Desert to the east of Turfan, was wrenched of its soil cover during the Pleistocene glaciations, when strong temperature gradients generated winds intense enough to have scoured these domains and carried their former soil into the loess lands of the Yellow River, that ultrafertile region in which Chinese civilization germinated, eventually to produce the unexpected, a Communist regime in a once celestial kingdom.

> After the founding of the People's Republic of China, the people of all nationalities of Turfan, under the enlightened leadership of Chairman Mao and the Chinese Communist Party, got organized to combat the wind-sand scourge. Especially since the great proletarian cultural revolution, in the "In agriculture, learn from Tachai" mass movement, adhering to the principle of class struggle and following the party's basic lines of revolution and production, the people of Turfan made outstanding achievements in combating the wind and sand and in transforming the gobi land. (8, p.3)

Yes, that is the way in which the descendants of Lao-tze and Li Po now express themselves. Yet one need not reach far through the political pamphleteering to grasp the conclusion that the Chinese attribute their recent successes in combating their deserts to political rather than to physical changes.

> Before liberation, there were only a few scattered trees around houses. Today there are more than 20,000 mu [1 mu = 1/15 hectare] of land covered with forest, over 1,400 km of protective forest belts, 170,000 mu of contain-sand-cultivate-grass areas, and 70% of the country's farmland is protected by forest networks. (8, p.3)

"Before liberation," the case study goes on to say, water flow in the Turfan irrigation system was down to 13 m^3 a second. Much of what had been cultivated area was damaged by overgrazing and blowing sand, and the oasis perimeter was under siege by advancing dunes. Corrective action involved three principal measures: increase the water supply; stabilize the dunes on the oasis' edge; and control wind velocity and thereby eliminate blowing sand. Under the conditions at Turfan, the last action was the critical one.

The water supply was increased to 30 m^3 a second by constructing new canals. To prevent leakage, these were lined with pebbles mixed with cement. Water came to be delivered through underground channels to limit evaporation on its route to the pit wells from which it was drawn for irrigation.

The entire cropping area was surrounded by grass belts from 300 to 500 meters in width, irrigated by tail-water from cultivation or by water made directly available thanks to the increased supply. Grass belts were planted with native varieties—camel thorn (*Alhagi canescens*), plump maiden (*Karelinia caspica*), and deer horn grass (*Scorzonera divaricata*), and in the lower part of the depression where water is closer to the surface—tamarisk (*Tamarix ramosissima*), reed (*Phragmites communis*), and salt-ear tree (*Halostachys belangeviana*). These plants developed into a bushy cover up to one meter in height, reducing wind velocity at the surface by 49.5% when the cover of camel thorn had reached 85%, as the Turfanese meticulously measured it. The grass belts were protected from grazing and cutting until the cover had reached 60%, after which planned rotational grazing was permitted. The livestock wandering through these restored and bucolic settings present a picture to the decadent westerner far removed from class struggle, but perhaps this, too, is illusion.

While they halt the attack of upwind marching sand dunes, the grass belts are wide enough to cause the wind to drop its load of heavier sand. The lighter particles carried as far as the oasis proper there strike a second barrier, a belt of protective forest which filters out the remaining sand and cuts the velocity of the wind. To plant the quick-growing tree varieties selected for the forest belts, irrigation ditches were first dug. The five-ditch system consists of ditches 1.5 meters wide placed 4.5 meters apart, an arrangement that yields good control of irrigation water, prevents salination and alkalization, and enables water to be used to wash away accumulating sand. Two rows of sand dates (*Elaeagnus angustifolia*) were planted alongside the outermost windward ditch, this being a variety that resists sand and serves as forest-fringe shrubbery during the early stages of growth. Along the middle ditches were planted one row of Sinkiang poplar (*Populus bollean*) and one row of elm (*Ulmus pumila*) and along the leeward ditches one row of Sinkiang poplar and one row of mulberry (*Morus alba*), home of the worm that summoned forth the Silk Road. As the case study said of this pattern of trees:

> This arrangement has the merit of structural stability, and the belt presents at its top an undulating, almost saw-blade-like surface, thus increasing its roughness and adding to its wind-reducing capacity. . . . The five-ditch forest belts at the Five-Star Commune now have an average height of 16 meters, a mighty "Verdant Great Wall" ringing the

oasis. . . . It has been observed that under conditions of medium wind velocity, in areas of one to three multiples of belt height behind the belt, the average wind velocity is only 26.7% of open field velocity and only 29% in areas seven heights behind the belt. (8, p.12)

The cultivated fields within the oasis were further protected by an interior network of narrow forest strips giving the fields a checkerboard appearance. This system received a stern test in April and May of 1975 when Turfan was assaulted by winds above 10 on the Beaufort scale, continuously at one period for 33 hours. Only 4% of the seeded area suffered damage, and that in a section where protective forest strips had not yet been established.

Once the classical area of cultivation had been stabilized and desertification halted in it, the people of Turfan commenced an ambitious program of enlarging the oasis by establishing vineyards on reclaimed gobi land. This project began on a sloping alluvial fan which first required terracing and leveling, after which the soil was soaked to remove a salt pan. Irrigation ditches were then dug five meters apart, and water was introduced again to wash a salt crust out of what would be the root zone of the planned *Vitus vinifera L.* These vines were planted in pits filled with fertilized "guest soil" taken from the farms in the older cultivated areas, the gobi soil, such as it was, lacking a supply of humus. In the first two years of grape cultivation, melons and legumes were grown between the rows of vines both for extra income and to improve soil quality. By the time the case study was being prepared, 19,000 mu (1,267 hectares) of vineyard were growing on what had once been rocky waste, with the grapes, again, checkered with new forest strips to keep down the wind velocity.

Gobi land occupies about 30% of the total area of Turfan county, 14 times the area of the present farmland. The rebuilding of the gobi not only makes full use of its high temperature and its water and soil resources and extends the oasis, but is in itself an effective measure in combating desertification. The successful cultivation of grapes in the gobi . . . represents an important experience for the local people in their development efforts. (8, p.16)

In their new political style, the Chinese say of achievements such as those at Turfan that "the masses are the real heroes." And of course it is true that little can be accomplished unless a spirit is mobi-

lized among the people who actually work the land. Such a spirit has been mobilized at Turfan. It is strong enough to motivate people to carry irrigation water in buckets suspended from poles slung across their shoulders, or to lug "guest soil" in similar fashion in the period before they were rich enough to afford agricultural machinery. Diligence, a willingness to give themselves over to the most grinding toil, have combined among the people of Turfan with high technical competence in combating high winds and shifting sand. "Only socialism can save China," the case study declares (8, p.21). But that is a slogan too broad to tell us what we really want to know. How were technical skills transmitted to the ordinary farmer? How precisely was his enthusiastic cooperation aroused? How is it that Turfan can present such a contrast to the indolence of Greater Mussayeb? Was nothing needed but political stability—under any sort of political order—to unleash the immense possibilities in the Chinese character and culture?

NOTE: A revised romanization of the Chinese language has been promulgated by the government of the People's Republic. In the new system, for example, the name Mao Tse-tung would be transcribed as Mao Zedong. Be that as it may, China's case studies were translated for the United Nations Conference on Desertification, using the older Wade-Giles romanization instead of the Pinyin system approved by the present government of China, which is coming to find ever wider acceptance outside of China. The present text uses the Wade-Giles romanization.

4
GASCOYNE

"Other children in the world attend school"

WESTERN AUSTRALIA—one of the ends of the earth, a third of a continent. The imagination must strain to grasp the monotony of a land whose most striking geographical features are isolation and emptiness, where 2.53 million km² provide a home for only 1,084,400 people (1973 estimate), three-quarters of them tucked into the southwest corner of the province, in and around the cities of Perth and Fremantle, jostling each other in the only tiny portion of this limitless landscape where enough rain falls to produce a crop. The next nearest city to Perth is Adelaide in South Australia, 2,400 km to the east, as if there were no city nearer to Los Angeles than Houston, Texas.

Driving north from Perth on the highway that edges the eastern shore of the Indian Ocean, the land quickly runs out of green. Above Geraldton, wheat land is replaced by sand dunes coming down to the shore of the sea. Some 900 km into the brown north, the sudden reappearance of a few green fields marks the town of Carnarvon with all its 6,500 people. Here, 4.8 km² of irrigated vegetables and bananas, a crop worth $4 million annually, constituted the community's financial mainstay until the establishment of the Texada saltworks on once-dry Lake McLeod, another 50 km up the road. At Carnarvon, the traveler has entered the most arid portion of the world's driest continent, where the inconstant rainfall averages only 200 mm per year. Carnarvon can produce its intensive but tiny harvest because it draws irrigation water from the Gascoyne River, which here enters the sea, in a manner of speaking. For "the upside-down river," as it is called locally, flows beneath the surface of the ground, its winding course marked only by a sandy trail between towering gum trees.

In 1961, however, the Gascoyne River came to the surface, and worse, flooding the town of Carnarvon. Rain, scanty and unreliable, comes to the Gascoyne basin, a sheep range stretching inland from

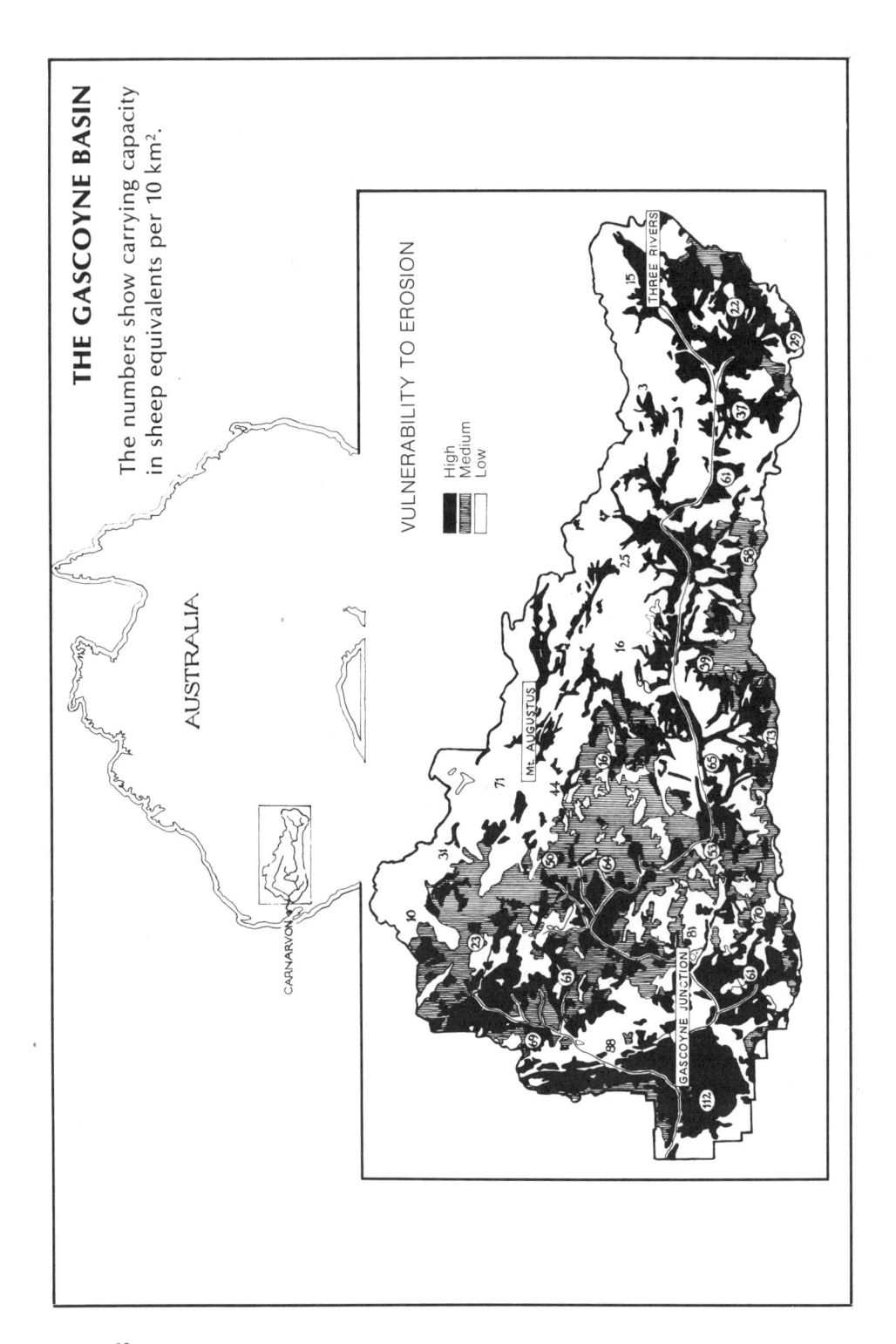

THE GASCOYNE BASIN

The numbers show carrying capacity in sheep equivalents per 10 km².

VULNERABILITY TO EROSION

- High
- Medium
- Low

Carnarvon more than 600 km, mainly as an accompaniment to cyclonic disturbances. In January and February of 1961, summertime in the southern hemisphere, cyclones brought almost 500 mm of rain into the Gascoyne catchment area. In an ideal world, a proper attention to problems would not require catastrophe to precipitate surveys and to organize subsequent corrective measures. In the real world, there is little doubt that

> catastrophes . . . concentrate attention upon a landscape and its people in a way that is seldom achievable by local specialists (7, p. 4).

The local specialists had just found out what drought in the Sahel was later to teach the entire United Nations, if not the world, that catastrophes also have a beneficient function in the interplay of human affairs. What the Carnarvon flood concentrated attention on was erosion in the Gascoyne basin, which in its pristine condition, less than a century earlier, would have been able to absorb a siege of comparable rainfall without flooding—or so the local specialists were convinced. A hasty aerial survey strengthened this assessment, that the basin had indeed undergone extensive erosion. An attempt to interpret aerial photographs failed to yield a precise evaluation because at the photographic scale used (1:40,000), rilling and shallow stripping could not be distinguished from natural runoff. The Western Australia Department of Agriculture decided that a team should go into the basin and check conditions on the ground, and a ground survey was carried out in 1969 and 1970. Published in 1972, the survey reported that 14.9% of the basin was so severely eroded that desertification would become permanent if sections so affected were not removed from grazing. Another 52.4% of the range had suffered some degradation, the report went on to say, and would need careful management if further degradation were to be avoided. Finally, 32.6% of the basin was found to be in acceptable condition, but this happened to be the worst part of the range, hill or shortgrass country of low natural productivity. It had been the least used—that was why it was still undamaged.

The Gascoyne basin made a poor impression on the first Europeans to see it. That was in 1857, when the region was first surveyed. The term "wide open spaces" finds its meaning here in the basin's 64,000 km^2, an unexciting moonscape of low relief, where wide patches of naked earth alternate with mulga shrublands reaching out toward endless horizons. Mulga (*Acacia aneura*) is often associated here with perennial chenopods (*Rhagodia, Enchylaena, Maireana*), while other parts of the range feature saltbush (*Atriplex*) or a short grass-forb pasture, all of which are food for sheep. The first settler was one C.S. Brockman who arrived in 1876. Merino sheep, with their fine wool and adaptability to heat and aridity, were soon imported from regions farther south.

In those days, aboriginal herdsmen came to roam with the sheep like the nomads of other regions of the earth. Today, except for the "doggers," men hired to kill the predatory dingoes, the aboriginals have all departed in the direction of wage labor in the towns. On the subject of "doggers," incidentally, the manager of Bidgemia, one of the Gascoyne basin's largest stations, once said that 20 dingoes, reported to kill sheep for the mere sport of it, would be enough to "run us off the land." If the Gascoyne stations still have to cope with these wild dogs, they are fortunate in having no problem with the rabbits that multiplied with such ferocious geometry in the eastern parts of the continent, where predators were insufficient to restrain this imported menace from eating everything in sight. Western Australia is protected from rabbit invasions from out of the infested east by a 2,000-km rabbit-proof fence running north and south from sea to sea.

By 1971, the Gascoyne basin was occupied by 31 sheep stations, with some of them also running a few head of cattle. Population had reached the grand total of 320 persons, one person for every 200 km^2. A large station, such as Bidgemia, was then running 37,000 sheep and 800 head of cattle on 400,000 hectares (one million acres). This is indeed big country, in which an irritating problem before airplanes and motorbikes came into use was the possibility of losing the flocks when it came time to muster them and bring the sheep to the sheds for their annual shearing.

The Gascoyne pastoralist, surrounded only by his immediate family and his few station hands, is as isolated as a Greenland eskimo. His children attend primary school by radio.

> The socialization of children in these isolated and small family groups is aided by the radio-transceiver communications system; the children talk to their teacher and to other children in the region but at the primary level are difficult to convince that other children in the world attend school. (7, p.17)

Two-way radio is also the medium for medical instruction in case someone gets sick, although the 74 dwellings in the basin, separated one from another by 35 to 70 km, are also serviced by flying doctors and occasional church flying services. Pregnant women find maternity services in Carnarvon or Meekatharra, but many go all the way to Perth to have their babies. Distances are such that if the woman were in Three Rivers Station, her choice of maternity services would be like that of a woman in Iowa deciding whether to have her baby in Indiana or New York City, and if she were to choose the former, it would be a matter of driving almost 700 km (400 miles) on a dirt road. Every year, this tiny population inhabiting the endless monotony of the Gascoyne basin typically channels $2 million worth of wool into Australia's export market.

Isolation and loneliness are natural accompaniments to the fact that the Gascoyne basin is arid. Its 212 to 222 mm of average annual rainfall is erratic and variable in agreement with the general rule that the more arid the conditions, the more variable is the rainfall. Annual evaporation, measured by the standard Australian tank, is between 2,300 and 2,540 mm, yielding an index of aridity which needs only to be combined with the fact that most of the rain falls in the hot months when it evaporates quickly to place the Gascoyne basin right at the edge of true desert conditions. Similar climatic conditions can be found close to the Sahara in the West African Sahel, in the Karoo-Kalahari region in southern Africa, or in the northern Thar desert in India.

> The meteorological systems affecting the Gascoyne basin produce an erratic and unreliable rainfall. . . . In summer . . . cyclonic disturbances move into the area [although] rain-producing cyclones cannot be relied on every year. . . . In winter, the southern anti-cyclone systems reach their northern limit in the Gascoyne area and slightly to the north. . . . Only intense depressions penetrate the basin so that winter rainfall is also unreliable. . . . Evidence of climatic change in terms of past rainfall is not convincing. (7, pp.21-22)

Why is the Gascoyne so dry? How can there be arid regions that extend down to the shore of the sea, that are so close to inexhaustible amounts of water? This question might be expanded into an inquiry about deserts and drylands in general. Why are they where they are? Why do they happen to be located in the regions mentioned when discussing the oasis of Turfan? Why is north Africa so different from North America? Why is there no Chicago in Chad? Why is the hamlet of Carnarvon, so comparably located on its land mass, not the metropolis of San Francisco?

The answer to such questions can be found in whatever it is that creates climate—latitude, access to winds from the oceans, the presence or absence of mountains and other topographical features. It is to be sought in the unraveling of global patterns of atmospheric circulation. Whether or not a region is arid is largely a function of two factors, waves of the air and waves of the earth, atmospheric currents and mountain ranges.

Ultimately, it might be said that arid lands are where they are because the atmosphere, a mixture of gases, obeys the laws of physics by warming up when compressed and cooling down when permitted to expand. As air rises, it enters regions of ever lower pressure exerted by the thinning air around it. Therefore it expands—and cools. Its temperature drops about 1° for every 150 meters of ascent, a cooling known as the dry adiabatic lapse rate—dry because the presence of water vapor changes the rate. Since air always contains some water vapor, the proportion present being termed the "humidity," rising or falling air never cools down or warms up at precisely the dry adiabatic lapse rate. That rate, an ideal schema, is close enough to what really happens, however, to indicate that the change of temperature is substantial whenever air goes up or down.

As rising air cools to a temperature below the dew point, the water vapor in it will begin to condense into droplets, forming on so-called condensation nuclei—tiny bits of dust or pollen or even crystals of salt wind-blown from sea spray—always present in the impure atmosphere. These droplets aggregate into clouds, and clouds will float through the air affecting land only by their shadows, unless events occur which cause the droplets to amass into drops big enough to fall. The amount of rain that falls out of the air on planet earth—100,000 km^3 of water every year—is enough to indicate that the circumstances that create rain are not at all unusual. Indeed, it rains a lot wherever air tends to rise. But, conversely, rain is rare in regions of subsiding air, where reverse processes take place. As air sinks, it becomes compressed, warming up and increasing its capacity to hold uncondensed water vapor. Air descending from altitude will have had its water wrung out of it anyway when it ascended to high altitude in the first place. The clouds vanish in regions of descending air and the sun shines down through skies of brilliant blue.

The presence of wind is a daily reminder that the atmosphere is an engine for transporting the heat of the tropics in the direction of the poles, ever striving to equalize temperatures throughout the globe. Where it is directly overhead, the sun delivers two calories per minute to every square centimeter at the top of the atmosphere, four times the average energy input over the entire globe on which the sun is mostly not directly overhead. One calorie is not much energy—just enough to raise the temperature of one gram of water, 20 teardrops, 1°. But then one square centimeter, about the size of a thumbnail, is not much in the way of area, and the annual energy reaching the earth from the sun, however thinly it may be spread around, adds up to the stupendous total of $5\frac{1}{2} \times 10^{21}$ kilowatts per year, enough to supply human energy needs, at present rates of consumption, for 300,000 years. The rate at which the sun feeds the earth with energy is known as the solar constant, since it varies only minutely in either direction.

Out of this incoming energy, about 34%, the earth's albedo, is reflected back into space enabling astronauts to see man's only home glittering through the darkness of the universe. Much of the rest of it goes into heating the air, with the warming concentrated toward those regions where the sun passes more or less overhead, across the zenith, as it does near the equator. Directly beneath the path of the sun, heated air rises as in a furnace, creating an equatorial girdle of low atmospheric pressure. Out of cloudy, tormented skies cascade down those equatorial downpours that so adversely affected the character of Sadie Thompson and other selected tropical heroines, rain that kept Gauguin and R. L. Stevenson indoors, but also keeps the South Seas green as well as the Amazon and Congo basins and the verdant islands of Indonesia.

On a featureless, untilted, nonrevolving earth heated uniformly around its equator (whatever that would be), air rising from the tropics would come down again 90° of latitude away and flow back on the surface to the heat equator. The inhabitants of such a boring world would experience only a north wind if they lived to the north of the heat equator and a south wind in the antipodes. Because the earth revolves, however, surface winds are prevailingly easterlies in the low latitudes and westerlies in middle latitudes.

On the real earth, air rises from the heat equator also, and just as it does on that imaginary earth, starts off in the direction of the poles. The real earth, however, rotates, giving the tropical air the eastward velocity of 1,600 km per hour with which the planet revolves at the equator. The higher the latitude, the slower the rotation, until the pole is reached where everything turns on one spot, going nowhere, once in 24 hours. Air rushing at high altitude away from the equator and toward the poles gradually finds the earth rotating more slowly beneath it, or—which amounts to the same thing—it acquires a westerly velocity, becoming a high-altitude west wind, a turning of the currents of air which is called the Coriolis force. Where this lateral velocity comes to dominate the poleward motion, at around 30° latitude north and south, the vast currents of high-altitude air, no longer capable of completing their mission and carrying the heat of the tropics all the way to the poles, begin to "feel" the call of the tropics again, summoning them to return and replenish the low-pressure zone created by their own departure. Unable to move backward against themselves, they subside to the surface over a broad region centering more or less on 30° latitude, creating there subtropical girdles of high pressure as sinking air piles up. On the surface, moving back toward the equator, this air is turned by the Coriolis force now working in reverse, driving it in a westerly direction, converting the two converging currents into east winds, those same trade winds that carried Columbus to a landfall in the New World. The two currents merge at the heat equator, where they are heated to rise aloft and start the circle over again. A similar pattern is repeated in higher latitudes, with air rising at around 60° and descending at the poles, which are therefore, paradoxically, deserts, but far outside the regions where desertification is a problem.

So it is that global patterns of air circulation create the great arid regions of the subtropics with their typical high-pressure, fair-weather climates. Thirty degrees north latitude crosses the Sonora Desert of Mexico, the northern part of the Sahara, Arabia, Iran, and Pakistan, beyond which this line runs into the Himalayas and other topographical complications. Thirty degrees south latitude crosses the Atacama and Namibian deserts and all of Australia, entering that continent only a few hundred kilometers south of the Gascoyne basin. The Sahara exhibits certain regularities around its rim, especially on its south side, where regions of gradually increasing rainfall can be shown on maps as parallel stripes. Most arid zones, however, take weird, jagged shapes, indicating that aridity—or moisture—occurs for reasons in addition to those flowing from atmospheric circulation.

Arid zones also occur, for example, in the so-called "rain shadows" in the lee of mountain ranges. Moist air from the Pacific Ocean moves in the prevailing westerlies into the states of Washington and Oregon and into northern California, where, some 200 km inland, it is lifted upward by the Cascade Mountains. As this air rises, its moisture condenses to fall as rain on the dense green forests that blanket the western slopes of the range. Dry air subsides down the far slope, from which one has an eastward vista of semiarid rangelands populated by scrub pine, juniper, and sagebrush.

Most of the dry American West, semiarid country, part of which was called the Great American Desert by European immigrants who had never before encountered anything but green fields and forests, is cattle country because of its relationship to mountain ranges. The Takla-makan to the west of Turfan is ringed by mountain ranges on all sides, while the drylands of Mongolia and north China are separated by mountains and highlands from greener lands to the south, as they lie also at the farthest limit of the movement of maritime air. The Atacama Desert, blocked by the wall of the Andes from easterly air currents, suffers a double handicap in the presence offshore of the cold, north-flowing Humboldt current, which cools any westerly winds which might happen to cross it, causing them to dump their rain offshore. Thus it almost never rains in Lima, whose irrigated parks receive natural moisture only in the form of dew, and coastal rivers rising in Peru's green mountains enter the sea via barren and rocky canyons. The arid lands of western Argentina lie in the subtropical subsidence belt. Farther to the south, arid Patagonia is blocked from moisture-laden westerlies by the southernmost extensions of the Andes Mountains.

So it is that there is nothing freakish about oceanside deserts such as the Atacama or Namibia, the latter with its own Humboldt in the form of the cold Benguela current, or that the most arid portion of Australia, occupying much of the center of the continent, should reach out to include the Gascoyne basin and to come to the very water's edge just above Carnarvon. That such deserts are natural expressions of ordinary phenomena indicates the futility of proposals that would try to change desert climates by flooding interior drainage basins to create large, man-made lakes.

Straddling the line marking 25° south, the Gascoyne basin is not only dry, it is also hot. At Gascoyne Junction, where the road comes up from Carnarvon, January temperatures hover around 40°. Lambs born out on the range in the hot season are doomed; they never live more than a few days. Good ranching practice requires that the rams be put to the ewes at such a time that the lambs will be born during the rainiest and coolest part of the year. This is usually done in December, with a proportion of three to five rams per 100 ewes. Removed from the range for shearing in May or June, rams must be continually imported from the south. They are susceptible to the harsh conditions of the Gascoyne rangeland, with a mortality of around 35% per year, while ewes, survivors of the environment, are better adapted. It has never been easy to run sheep in the harsh conditions prevailing in the Gascoyne country. Besides the constant menace of wild dogs and the sheep blowfly, against which stock are "jetted" with insecticide at shearing time, the rainfall, as in all arid regions, cannot be relied on.

September through December, the southern spring, are usually the driest months in the Gascoyne. Summer cyclones and winter anticyclones bring high winds to the region and a roughly equal amount of scanty rainfall in the two opposite seasons, although rain can arrive any time on the back of sporadic thunderstorms. Variable from one year to another, the skimpy rain is also variable in space, striking one patch of ground but not another. Life in the Gascoyne is dominated by the physical fact that rainfall is so deficient. The dearth of rain and its extreme variability combine with topography, patterns of runoff, and soil types to create a patchwork of microtopographies, a characteristic of most arid regions, with great variations in the densities and types of vegetation they support. Because of eternal variability, the patchwork will not maintain a precisely constant pattern, the pieces of the jigsaw shifting somewhat from year to year.

Desirable perennials string along the wide beds of dry watercourses or clump together on low patches of good soil sheltered from the wind. In places, the soil is salty, producing halophytic pasture; in other places, it is extremely alkaline. Vegetation is spotty, with patches of bare earth between the plants, naked earth dominating the poorer soils and giving the landscape an orange-brown color. Some of the basin consists of highly eroded "badlands" without vegetation of any kind. Sand dunes cover other sections. Annuals, some of them unsuitable for pasture, return each year to certain habitats. As in other arid regions, ephemerals, stored in the soil as seed or spores, will spring up to carpet the ground with color and blossoms depending on where the rain has chanced to fall. Arid pasturelands such as the Gascoyne basin with their jigsaw conformation of microtopographies, call for nomadic styles of grazing. The stock roam from one piece of the puzzle to another among those which supply them with something to eat. Seemingly wandering at random, stock following a nomadic grazing pattern are usually directed on precise routes, often repeated in succeeding seasons, by herdsmen familiar with the most inconspicuous landmarks in a monotonous range and who know when each potential bit of pasture can be expected to come into flower. The same or a similar route, sometimes extending over hundreds of kilometers, will be followed year after year, reflecting ancient experience and hard-won knowledge. Arid pasturelands are very sensitive to grazing pressure. In a region as dry as the Gascoyne, some of the best perennials can regenerate and produce new, young plants only once or twice in a century, in years of very favorable conditions with exceptionally heavy rainfall.

A nomadic grazing pattern is ideally designed to move the stock onward before a given patch of pasture is stripped or trampled beyond its capacity to regenerate, and that patch will be visited again only after regeneration has occurred. Routes are also determined by the location of salt licks and the placement of watering points, whether existing as natural pools in intermittent watercourses or produced artificially by digging down to the watertable. Nomadic pastoralists have been herding stock for the more than 10,000 years since the practice began in the neolithic transformation, and ideal patterns have been achieved that do little or no damage to natural pastures. The traditional nomad is acutely conscious not only of the ever shifting condition of his life-sustaining pastures but also of the number of animals he can herd without using up the most palatable forage. His relation to the pasture can in fact become symbiotic as his herds improve the natural vegetation, bringing not destruction but health to the range. After all, the wild ancestors of his domestic stock were once natural and essential constituents of wild ecosystems. Livestock fertilize the soil with their droppings. Certain plants can regenerate only by passing through digestive tracts to emerge wrapped in a dab of fertilizer. Other seeds are transported onward clinging to shaggy coats and are planted by being trampled into the soil. Nomadic pastoralism is a compendium of tried and tested practices which provide the most efficient way of harvesting the thin and skimpy plant life of arid regions.

Ancient tradition and hard-won knowledge were not, however, brilliantly typical of the development of Australia's enormous wool industry. The rambunctious pioneers who created the epic of opening the outback, established there gigantic sheep stations whose colorful sagas constitute a chronicle as rich as anything from the American West. These rugged individualists often knew little about the finer points of pastoralism, however, and were utterly unfamiliar—and how could it have been otherwise?—with the unprecedented biota of a strange continent. The mammoth industry they developed was geared to an export market and aimed at maximizing profits. In 1967, for instance, Australia pastured 18% of the world's sheep, producing 31% of the world's marketable wool.

Too many sheep, more than the land could sustain, was the almost invariable outcome in all of Australia's pastoral regions. From this arithmetic, the degradation of pastures inevitably followed. The Gascoyne study, triggered by a small flood disaster, was but one of the first of many investigations which revealed the same state of affairs, and out of which, incidentally, Australia's arid lands have become among the best understood in the world. In Western Australia, the Gascoyne study was a pioneer investigation, establishing criteria and procedures used to study other rangelands in the region, as in West Kimberley, eastern Nullarbor, and the Ashburton catchment.

It might seem surprising that a careful and detailed study should be made of the Gascoyne basin which, like most arid regions, has such low agricultural productivity per hectare that the costs of research might be difficult to justify. To be sure, a flood that damaged areas of much higher productivity was the event that set the Gascoyne study in motion, a circumstance "deplored" by the case study authors. Before that, disaster had struck the Gascoyne itself without generating much in the way of alarm or anything connected with scientific deliberation.

Within about 25 years of the first settlement of the basin, its stations were running a total of about 400,000 sheep, or roughly the same numbers on the range that were there when the post-flood survey was made. This is enough to produce an occasional excess of animals for sale. The worldwide economic depression of the 1930s put pressures on the pastoralists, most of whom, like farmers everywhere, were operating in a condition of chronic indebtedness to financial institutions. They responded by increasing the size of their herds so that by 1935, the Gascoyne rangeland, or that half of it on which herding was concentrated, was supporting around 650,000 sheep units, one unit equaling one adult ewe plus lamb. In that year, rainfall amounted to only about 100 mm, half of "normal." This was the first in a succession of drought years, creeping into Australia only a little later than the drought which, in America, converted the high plains into the dust bowl that has since become a nightmare of legend. That worst enemy of the arid-land pastoralist, drought, is as inevitable as it is always unexpected, or so it always seems to be in the drylands where such rainless years are viewed as appallingly bad luck, visitations from hell, or anything but what they truly are—episodes that are normal in regions of scanty and erratic rainfall, the lean years that should be anticipated and prepared for, as the Biblical Joseph instructed Pharaoh.

This was called the "great drought" of 1936, named for its second year, when almost three out of every four sheep perished on the Gascoyne range, and the sheep population crashed down to less than 200,000, and then on down to around 100,000 by 1942, when normal rainfall returned.

What failed in 1936 was not water—wells could still be brought in by digging—but the sensitive pastures already damaged as they were by overgrazing in the previous "good" years. So the stock died not of thirst but of starvation. Following this disaster, pastures were slow to recover. In consequence, sheep numbers were slow to increase, and the previous, and typical, population of about 400,000 had not quite been reestablished when, in the mid-fifties, drought struck again, and sheep numbers crashed back once more to around 100,000. The 1961 rains that flooded Carnarvon were of great benefit to the Gascoyne basin. They revitalized pastures so rapidly that the herds had reached a total of 416,833 sheep units by 1970, the year when their numbers were surveyed by the team carrying out the Gascoyne study. When this study was made public, it was found to contain a recommendation that sheep numbers should be cut almost in half, to 237,290 sheep units, if further deterioration of the Gascoyne rangeland was to be prevented. How had the survey team come to such a conclusion?

This team, sent in to ascertain "ground truth" after the analysis of aerial photographs had proved inadequate, approached its assignment by using vegetation criteria to establish a set of "rangeland types" which could serve as reliable and repeatable mapping units. Range evaluation sites, 280 in all, were marked on the aerial photographs as sites also on which future monitoring would be conducted. Data were taken from each site over the course of six months to determine pasture condition, rangeland potential, and state of erosion. Information was also obtained from more than 4,800 km of vehicle traverse, with the routes also marked on the aerial photographs. It was an approach that led to the identification of 51 rangeland types, distinct topographies, all of which were mapped. On traverse, conditions were recorded as each rangeland type was entered, as it was left behind, and at one-mile (1.6 km) intervals within it, for a total of 2,426 recordings. To eliminate bias, each recording was made by two experienced observers. All information was coded and a computer program prepared that would provide printouts on the condition and potential of each rangeland type on each sheep station. The arid lands of this world have seldom received such meticulous scrutiny. It was on the basis of these procedures that the Gascoyne rangelands were classified finally as severely eroded, moderately eroded, or in acceptable condition.

Vegetation holds soil in place, reduces wind speed at the soil surface, and improves the capacity of the soil to absorb and transport water. Erosion by wind or water, following the destruction of vegetation, blows or wipes away those topmost layers that contain the bulk of the soil's store of nutrients. After erosion has occurred, plants have difficulty in regenerating and thriving in the anemic soils that remain. Water erosion, following rare but torrential thunderstorm downpours, had been particularly destructive to the Gascoyne. Recovery from such damage may take decades—or it may never occur within any reasonable time span, and the land will then have been desertified. In richer, more humid areas, a variety of techniques are regularly applied to repair degradation resulting from erosion. Corrective measures can even be expensive, since this richer land can be counted on to repay whatever they cost. Gullies can be filled in, culverts and drainage works constructed, fertilizer added to exhausted soil, or plowing and reseeding undertaken. Such corrective measures might be feasible on limited plots of the most productive parts of the Gascoyne, but in the broad view of a land that is almost desert, active rehabilitation was considered impractical, never capable of repaying an investment made in a region of such limited productivity, such a low economic return per hectare.

The survey team recommended what it considered to be the only practical procedure for the recovery of the 14.9% of the basin it had classified as severely degraded. This was to revert to a wholly ecological strategy and temporarily abandon those sections, allow no grazing at all, and hope that within some reasonable time—decades, if not generations—the land would recover by itself. From the point of view of economics, even such passive rehabilitation can prove deceptive. It seems to involve a minimum of expenses, but in fact it represents a small annual cost in foregone income that over the years can add up to a substantial total.

The recommendation on the number of sheep that should be allowed to graze the rest of the range—about half of the historic population—was based on an assessment of the carrying capacity of the land. Such assessments are at best a kind of rough and ready calculation, one complicated in the case of the Gascoyne by the partial degradation of much of the range that the stock would be permitted to exploit. In carrying out the assessment, reference was made to American experience.

> In United States rangelands, the management practice of equal levels of use and non-use by herbivores of annual dry-matter production appears to maintain rangeland productivity in the long term. More sophisticated systems have been developed, but these require a stronger data base than exists for the basin. Assuming 50% non-use, dry-matter production levels with median annual rainfall and an annual intake requirement for adult sheep of 450 kg of dry matter, the acceptable stocking rates for each rangeland type can be calculated in sheep per km² or hectares per sheep. (7, p.65)

In other words, as much should be left as is destroyed, with use including amounts trampled and broken as well as amounts eaten. The preferred stocking rates as estimated also included provision for the management of moderately degraded pasture. This would require restrictions on grazing during autumn rains and in the following winter to allow germination of chenopodiaceous shrubs at their preferred temperature of 16°C. This would be a tactic—and such tactics are too often neglected—to make full use of good years to regenerate the dryland pasture.

The publication of the survey report set off a storm among the sheep ranchers of the Gascoyne basin. They were being asked to eliminate from grazing the 9,400 km² that had formerly provided the best pasture and to make an increased management input on the 32,800 km² that would require carefully controlled grazing, and all this while being asked to cut their herds—and their incomes—almost in half. The resentment publicly displayed against the authors of the report provided a graphic illustration of the dangers involved in proposing rehabilitative measures designed without consultation with the people most affected by them. It also reflected the emotional ambience that led to overgrazing in the first place. A casual glance supplies few reasons why the Gascoyne should ever have been overgrazed, with the consequent destruction of pasture, the ranchers' fundamental capital asset. The answer can be found in commercial pressures and a play of economic forces that increasingly placed the station owner at a disadvantage when compared to urban Australia, where he may once have lived.

The pastoralist and his family may be of urban origin themselves. (7, p.15)

From 1970 until April, 1976, the actual number of leases transferred (i.e. stations sold) was 18, but this included one station which was sold three times and four which were sold twice. (7, p.52)

Almost 50% of urban households have two wage earners and combined husband and wife yearly earnings can range from $10,000 to $30,000 with benefits such as sick leave, recreation leave and long service leave paid by the employer. A pastoralist is fortunate to get to this level. (7, p.91)

Thus, desertification may also have resulted from ignorance and inexperience as former city people tried to make the adjustment to the free but hard and lonely life of the sheep stations. And this superimposed on an older, more fundamental ignorance on the part of European immigrants penetrating into a distant world in which the largest life form was a soft-footed marsupial. Nor was there any doubt that the changing owners of sheep stations were as desirous of the good life as anyone else affected by urban values, imported into the Gascoyne, if not with them, then via their transceiver radios. Convinced also that their hard and rugged life entitled them to a standard of living at least as high as that enjoyed by the soft city dweller, the Gascoyne sheep rancher experienced a loss of hope and morale as the natural vagaries of his setting worked in combination with commercial patterns which here, as elsewhere, discriminated against the prime producer and kept him in perpetual hock to the lending institutions.

The government of Western Australia was quick to realize that later was better than never, and that the pastoralists would have to be involved and consulted if the recommendations in the survey report were ever to be carried out and erosion halted in the Gascoyne region. At a meeting held in 1973 in the tiny community of Gascoyne Junction, it was agreed that the general recommendations would be supplemented by a detailed assessment of each of the stations in the basin. This inspection began in 1974, carried out by two assessors who were familiar with the Gascoyne, knew many of the ranchers personally, and had not been involved in the disputed survey. The case study described what then transpired.

The assessors lived and worked in a caravan-office sited near each homestead for the term of the three-day visit. Discussions with the lessee in this office were under more discipline . . . than the free-ranging type which is inevitable in the homestead office, the "territory" of the lessee. The appropriate maps and files were immediately accessible.

Following preliminary discussion on the scope of the inspection, the reasons for it, and the immediate objections of the lessee, the party of three visited all parts of the station in the government vehicle. . . . During this tour, the appropriate rangeland systems were identified and discussed in relation to erosion, production, livestock management procedures used by the lessee, and potential for improvement with *Cenchrus sp.* or deferment to encourage regrowth of edible bushes and scrub species.

After this arduous extension program, the final discurrion sessions in the caravan-office integrated the survey assessments with the tour insights into a property agreement. (7, pp.79-80)

Agreements were achieved with 30 of 31 stations, and an appeal committee was appointed to deal with the final case. The agreements reached did not always involve reductions in sheep numbers as severe as those recommended in the survey report, but that was a small price to pay for an end to resentment on the part of the ranchers, to their feelings that they, the present owners, were unjustly being made to pay for 100 years of previous misuse. Without a change in their attitudes, without obtaining their good will, nothing would have been accomplished in the Gascoyne basin. A plan was made to insure their continued cooperation by establishing "field days" in which all the pastoralists would participate in a combined social event and rangeland assessment exercise. A system of monitoring, by aerial photographs and ground inspection, was established also to provide a continuing check on the status of the Gascoyne range. Monitoring was planned to include the observation of enclosures, fenced sections in which regeneration processes could be observed in the absence of all grazing.

A review of past rainfall patterns for as long as data have been collected provided no indication that the climate in the Gascoyne region was changing—at least on a human time scale. The degradation of the rangeland could not then be attributed to decreasing rainfall. Thus the accusation against man, as agent as well as victim, was reinforced. As the report declared, remnants of climax vegetation, the growth which the land sustained in the absence of human interference, indicated that the degradation of the Gascoyne basin was the result of a European immigration which replaced

> a low level of grazing by small numbers of soft-footed herbivores . . . by a high level of continuous grazing . . . by large numbers of hoofed herbivores (7, pp.97-98).

Directed toward export markets, ranching sought to maximize profits by neglecting to pay the subtle costs of environmental maintenance. Herding was concentrated on the best and most accessible pastures, exactly those rated by the report as most severely damaged, while the more difficult and remote pastures, those rated as in "acceptable" condition, were ignored. Past ranching practices seemed to reflect little understanding that the dryland vegetation, however skimpily it covers the dryland surface, however ragged and unappetizing the plants appear to the human eye, is the fundamental resource on which the entire operation is based. The case study notes that the palatable perennials of Western Australia, those which had drifted into a geriatric condition in the Gascoyne, are very susceptible to grazing while being capable of regeneration perhaps once in a human generation. It is on those rare occasions, years of exceptional rainfall, that control of livestock is imperative as part of an essential strategy that makes optimum use of good years.

The object of all this effort—of the survey, the battle it set off, and the arbitration that settled matters—was to make the range self-sustaining so that flocks of sheep, thinly scattered as always—at an average density of one sheep to from eight to 40 hectares—can continue to graze on this immense and remote rangeland, and preferably without the wild oscillations in their numbers which have characterized the past history of the basin. The alternative is the destruction of all palatable species and invasion and domination by inedible plants which make the great deserts to the east of the Gascoyne useless to man even though their climatic status is not all that different. In Australia, the difference between rangeland and what is called desert is to be found not in rainfall statistics but in the type of vegetation that the land supports. The survey, its report, and the final arbitration, all "fruits of the Carnarvon flood" as the case study admits (7, p.9), resulted in agreements that seem likely to prevent the emergence of a Gascoyne Desert just to the west of the Gibson Desert.

5
WUSHENCHAO

"An enterprise of many facets"

FROM ITS BIRTHPLACE in the snowy ranges of Tsinghai in northeastern Tibet, the Yellow River detours around the great massif of Amne Machin before reaching Lanchow, the capital of Kansu, the northwestern frontier state that contains the westernmost extensions of the Great Wall. Lanchow houses the Lanchow Institute of Glaciology, Cryopedology and Deserts, a principal Chinese center for the study of arid lands. The Institute makes no open intrusion in this case study, however, its authorship attributed only to Wushenchao Commune, Wushen Banner, Inner Mongolia Autonomous Region.

Instead of then heading eastward to the Pacific upon leaving Lanchow, the Yellow River makes another detour far to the north, providing rectangular boundaries to the mile-high Ordos plateau. On this excursion, the river flows through a gap in the Great Wall on its northbound leg and through another as it heads south into Shensi and the cradleland of Chinese civilization. South of the wall is fertile China with its deep loess soil wind-drifted off the high plateaus of Mongolia by the continental northwesterlies that persist even today in picking up sand and mobilizing dunes. North of the wall is an arid pastureland, the ancient homeland of the nomadic Huns against whom the wall was constructed in the first place by Ch'in Shih Huang-ti, the first Emperor of China. The scanty summer rains that reach the distant Ordos are, like rain in the Sahel, the last remnants of a monsoon.

"Monsoon," from the Arabic *mausim*, meaning season, was originally applied to those seasonal winds blowing first from the northeast then from the southwest that propelled the dhows of Arab traders back and forth across the Arabian Sea. Time passed, and the word expanded in usage, coming to be applied to any seasonal onshore wind that springs up from differences in heating between land

and sea. Oceans hoard their heat while land surfaces warm up readily in summer and cool down quickly in winter. The heat of summer causes air to rise over the continents in ascending drafts that leave low pressure at the surface, pulling in air from the cooler, conservative oceans, and moisture-laden maritime air moves inland with its summer rain. Monsoon winds supply summer rain to India, northern Australia, West Africa, and the Gulf Coast of the United States. The Southeast Asia Monsoon sweeps northwestward over China, moving out of the always warm South China Sea, out of the waters around Taiwan, displacing the subtropical arid zone northward to 40° north latitude and beyond. At the commune of Wushenchao, north of the Great Wall on the arid Ordos plateau, annual rainfall averages a mere 377 mm, most of it falling between July and September.

The case study reports that the annual evaporation at Wushenchao adds up to 2,253 mm, or about six times the annual rainfall. The method used to measure evaporation was not specified, and you are led to believe that the measure was made with an open pan kept filled with water. The ratio between rainfall and pan evaporation provides one scale of aridity, a dryness ratio indicating that at Wushenchao, the frequent sunshine provides enough energy each year to evaporate the rain that falls there six times over. Such ratios are developed in order to classify climates. Another kind of index, as crude as it is universally used, simply goes by the amount of rainfall without worrying about ratios. Either way, Wushenchao would be classified by most researchers as *arid*, although unanimous agreement has not yet been reached on the precise use of such terms. In any case, the thin rain of Wushenchao will foster the growth of pasture wherever the soil is good enough. Such regions, as has been seen in the even drier Gascoyne, come to be inhabited by pastoralists who herd stock in nomadic patterns, or some modern variation thereof, to conform with the mixed quality of the pasture and the varieties in soil types and structures that create the land-use mosaics of these arid regions.

Wushenchao lies on the southern border of that wide extension of steppe and savanna, grassland and prairie reaching from Manchuria, close to the Pacific shore, 7,500 km westward to the Danube. Somewhere in the Ukraine, in the western part of this dryland belt, sometime in the fourth millennium B.C., ancestors of the speakers of Indo-European languages domesticated the horse, the "ass of the mountains," as the Sumerians incorrectly called it, an animal used at first exclusively for drayage. It took the people of the steppe and savanna another 2,000 years to learn to ride horseback with any proficiency. But once this skill was acquired, warriors from this heartland of mounted nomadism became the scourge of the civilized peoples on their borders, and military superiority over these marauders from the steppes was not finally achieved until the development of the heavy artillery that Ivan the Terrible used to rid Russia of the Mongols.

The horses that carried the Huns on their raids against Han China have been herded in the Ordos for 2,500 years together with other kinds of animals—sheep, goats, cattle, camels. At the arrival of the modern era, populations have become much denser, both of people and livestock, making a more serious matter out of the political turbulence that has often played havoc with this land. The violent century that preceded the establishment of the present Chinese government ushered desertification across the Ordos pasturelands. When Wushenchao commune was formed, 92 lonely trees constituted the total count on all its 1,600 km^2. Sand dunes, shaped by the inexorable northwesterlies of winter, were marching over former pastures. As the case study described the situation:

> Yellow sand pours down from the sky, and half the grassland lies buried under sand. (9, p. 1)

Exploitative overgrazing and the cutting and removal of woody vegetation had severely damaged a region sensitive to such practices, as all arid regions are. The drier the environment, the more impractical it becomes to repair such damage to the land, one of the facts of economics that has already been encountered in the Gascoyne. Nor is nature quick to effect repairs. Ecosystems on the thin edge of productivity have few options through which to exercise their resiliency. Subhumid, semiarid, arid—the closer the climate comes to desertlike conditions, the more easily the land can be converted into desert. One of the reasons for classifying climates is to get a broad view of the vulnerability of land.

There are, of course, many reasons why one might wish to classify climates—to be able to estimate the expenses of air conditioning, for example. The classifications of value to agriculture attempt to relate climatic parameters—sunshine and seasonality, moisture and wind—to types of vegetation that can be expected to flourish under different conditions. Wet or dry, hot or cold, climates have been classified in one way or another for as long as mankind has talked about them. Modern climatic classifications, however, date from less than a century ago, when the concept of "moisture index" grew out of observations of the amount of moisture available to growing plants. A variety of moisture indexes have been proposed, but all take root in the ratio between the water arriving as rain or dew and the water departing through evaporation and transpiration. Moisture is evaporated by heat, which first raises the liquid to evaporation temperature and then adds the comparatively large amount of energy needed by a liquid to change its state to gas. Evaporation is thus a measure of energy, the incoming energy supplied directly or indirectly by the sun. Cloudy, humid days are those on which rain can be expected to fall, while perfect days for evaporation are the reverse—cloudless, searing, dry, windy. Moisture indexes reflect the climatic conflict between that which wets and that which removes the wet. If precipitation is more than the available energy is capable of evaporating, water is present in surplus. If evaporation potential exceeds precipitation, plants must make up the water deficit by drawing on the deposits of moisture in the soil. Moisture indexes draw the line between humid climates and dry climates at a ratio of one—or sometimes, for convenience, at a ratio of zero, that is, the fraction, precipitation over potential evaporation, minus one.

In a dry climate, the amount of water deficit obviously cannot be discovered by measuring the actual evaporation, which will continue only as long as the limited water supply lasts. No deficit would then appear since precipitation and evaporation would always be equal. What has to be measured is the amount of water that the incoming energy *could* evaporate if the water were only there. This *potential* evaporation is called pan evaporation if it measures the amount lost from an open pan which is prevented from running dry, the amount of water taken up by the air measured in millimeters so that it can be compared with precipitation. In the opinion of some agronomists, however, moisture indexes based on pan evaporation are no better than rough approximations.

Since plant life is what moisture indexes are supposed to relate to, potential *evapotranspiration* is the measurement generally preferred. As perspiration is exuded by animals, so transpiration is exhaled by plants, and evapotranspiration is the combined vaporization from a complex of plants and soil. Ever more precise determinations of evapotranspiration have been pursued, even going so far as to construct a replica of the natural or cropping environment in a container called a transpirometer. The so-called Thornthwaite tank is a veritable garden capable of producing a tiny harvest while yielding also precise data on potential evapotranspiration if nature inside the tank is exactly the same as nature outside the tank, something that can never be exactly guaranteed.

C. W. Thornthwaite was a pioneer in the effort to achieve useful climatic classifications. It was in terms of Thornthwaite's moisture index that Peverell Meigs prepared what has since become the classic map of arid lands. Thornthwaite recognized that the seasons bring periods of water surplus in most climates and other periods of water deficit. Only the most arid climates will be typified by a water deficit in every month of the year. The Thornthwaite moisture index, Im, is featured in the equation $Im = Ih - Ia$, showing that it is equal to the index of yearly aridity, Ia, subtracted from the index of yearly humidity, Ih, or the water deficit (at certain seasons) subtracted from the water surplus (at others). As the index is calculated, $Ih = 100$ times the annual water surplus divided by the annual potential evapotranspiration, while $Ia = 100$ times the annual deficit divided by the annual evapotranspiration. All this turns out to be numerically equal to $100(P/PE - 1)$, in which P stands for annual precipitation and PE stands for annual potential evapotranspiration. And that, in turn, reveals Im to express at its heart the ratio of precipitation to potential evapotranspiration, while failing to display the interesting transpositions taken by these values as the seasons unroll a shifting panorama in which, for example, soil moisture may be exhausted and then recharged. It follows from Thornthwaite's formula that positive solutions to Im indicate a humid climate and negative solutions a dry one.

Thornthwaite used his own moisture index to classify climates ranging from arid ($Im = -66.7$ to -100) to perhumid (superhumid = $+100$ or above). The full development of his system of climatic classification involved not just the concept of available moisture but also that of *effective* moisture. A given amount of rainfall will be more effective for the growth of plants if it falls during the growing season. It will be less effective, on the other hand, if it falls during the hot season when it evaporates quickly. These two factors could conceivably cancel each other by occurring simultaneously. The Gascoyne basin, for example, with its summer monsoon rainfall is more arid than parts of South Australia that have the same annual rainfall but all of it falling in winter. Effectiveness involved the indexing of three additional factors—the incoming energy (called thermal efficiency) and the seasonal variations in both precipitation and energy. Together with *Im*, this makes four factors, all designated by letter codes, so that each separately classified climate ends up with a four-letter designation, and so may be found, by those who are interested, on the map by Peverell Meigs, and on all that map's numerous offspring.

Potential evapotranspiration, although measured in millimeters of moisture, is, as has been indicated, more a measure of energy than of liquid—it is the amount of energy required to evaporate and to set transpiring a given amount of water. Potential evapotranspiration thus pops up not only in Thornthwaite's moisture index but also in his index of thermal efficiency. Since PE is thus joined with precipitation as one of the two key parameters in classifying climates, great care has been taken to develop formulas that will express it accurately, when the desire is to calculate it rather than measure it in a transpirometer. It is never exclusively determined by the amount of incoming energy. It will be greater at higher wind velocity and at lower humidity, two other factors that must be considered in an accurate calculation of potential evapotranspiration. The formula most commonly encountered today, one which takes all such factors into account, is that developed by the English climatologist, H. L. Penman, in 1948. The Penman method is a widely used way of calculating potential evapotranspiration because the parameters employed in the formula are those measured at weather stations as a matter of routine. The formula yields its answer, however, only when multiplied by seasonal constants which are empirically determined for specific areas.

The *radiational index of dryness* is another climatic classifier proposed in 1956 by the Russian climatologist, M. I. Budyko. It is roughly equivalent to potential evapotranspiration divided by precipitation, expressed not in moisture but in energy units. Budyko designated as "desert" anything with an index higher than 3, beyond which many ecosystems produce substantial biomass. Kenneth Hare prefers to restrict the term "desert" to a ratio of at least 10, meaning loosely that potential evapotranspiration is sufficient to gasify ten times the amount of precipitation occurring over some designated time period such as a year (20, p. 13), and an even higher ratio was used to define "hyperarid" on the World Map of Desertification (17, p. 4). The authors of the map inverted Budyko's formula, placing potential evapotranspiration, obtained by the Penman method, in the denominator, so that the more arid the climate, the smaller the fraction. The map was constructed according to these definitions:

hyperarid with an index less than 0.03, *arid* between 0.03 and 0.20, *semiarid* between 0.20 and 0.50, and *subhumid* from 0.50 to 0.75.

In 1968, Mather and Yoshioka found good correlations between vegetation types and climatic conditions—at least in the temperate zone—by employing a moisture index as the abscissa of a graph and potential evapotranspiration as the ordinate (56, p. 126). There is a certain intellectual relish in playing the game of determining those factors in climate which are active in promoting or inhibiting the growth of plants. The resulting classifications, while they may have many important uses, are very broad in their application. This is because in the particular setting, actual plant life is determined by topoedaphic factors—soil quality and the lay of the land—as well as by climate. It is these other factors that turn a region of uniform climate into a mosaic of varied vegetation types and growth responses. Land use can be determined from climatic classifications only in a general way. Particular areas must be examined in all their uniqueness to make out how they will be used.

That is doubtless why the crudest classification system—relating vegetation to nothing more than mean annual rainfall—has persisted in constant use despite all the elaborations of more precise classifications. On the southern side of the Sahara, for example, the boundary of the desert is placed, arbitrarily to some extent, on the line marking 100 mm of average annual rainfall, such lines referred to as *isohyets*, as illustrated by the map on page 119. It may be arbitrary, but such a placement constitutes a definition, as all definitions are to some extent arbitrary.

By this crude method, true desert is defined as having less than 100 mm of annual rainfall, and to this, other definitive characteristics are sometimes added as if conscience required increased precision—a dryness ratio in excess of 10, a region that sometimes experiences no rain at all during a 12-month period. All this constitutes what might be called the stingy definition of "desert," certainly in contrast to Budyko's more expansive use of the term, and such regions feature fields of moving dunes, plains of naked rock, and other vistas of utter desolation even if they are not everywhere totally devoid of life. This is the definition by which the World Map of Desertification shows no deserts in Australia, or in North America either, with the scanty exceptions of such extreme environments as Death Valley.

In the wide region south of the Sahara, with the desert itself designated as *hyperarid*, isohyets neatly fall on lines of latitude, marking strips that cut across the full width of north Africa until they become entangled in the Ethiopian highlands. The strip bordering the desert between 100 mm and 200 mm of average annual rainfall would then be designated as *very arid*, or *subdesert*, terms intending to indicate that the region is so dry that its agricultural potential can be exploited only through nomadic pastoralism, particularly of camels.

The strip between 200 mm and 400 mm then receives the designation of *arid*. This is the true Sahel, a region also suited only to livestock, although in West Africa's arid lands, the stock are humped cattle more often than the sheep that dominate the Gascoyne basin, also with an arid climate. The 400-mm isohyet is the line marking the northern limit of cultivation in West Africa—or what *should* be more or less a northern limit—and the Sudano–Sahelian transition zone between the 400-mm and 600-mm lines, designated as *semiarid*, is a region of mixed pastoralism and cereal production. The trans-African strip of the Sudan (and not necessarily the country of that name, which happens to straddle the strip) is dominated by cereal production, millet and sorghum in West Africa, with the cultivation of groundnuts and cotton increasingly intruding as cash crops. Lying between the 600-mm and 900-mm isohyets is the Sudan proper, designated as *subhumid* (51, pp. 85–86). The humid Guinea coast with its dense tropical forests lies to the south of the Sudan in a region where average annual rainfall exceeds 900 mm.

Such rough distinctions must be sieved through the reality of any particular piece of land. Le Houerou points out, for instance, that the "mist deserts" on the coasts of Peru and Namibia should be defined by only 50 mm of annual rainfall (52, p.18), and that olive trees are cultivated in southern Tunisia in a climate with no more than an average of 150 mm of annual rainfall (52, p.19), less than any part of arid Australia. However they are defined, the drylands of the world, all those productive settings where water income is less than potential water expenditure, amount to 42.5 million km^2, or 28.5% of the earth's total land surface of 149.16 million km^2. So defined by purely climatic criteria, the drylands do not include the true deserts, which are not productive settings, and therefore no longer vulnerable to desertification, and which amount to another 5.85 million km^2. Two-thirds of the 150 members of the United Nations contain lands that are vulnerable to desertification, and it is in this perspective that desertification is seen to be a global problem. Some 628 million people, or 16.3% of the world's population, were estimated to be living in vulnerable drylands in 1973. Seen in that way, also, the problem is global. Out of the total drylands population, 78,546,000 people were then living in places that were currently undergoing desertification.

The 4,000 people living in Wushenchao commune are included, of course, among that portion of the world's population that lives in drylands. By purely climatic standards, they inhabit an *arid* region, suitable only for pastoral activities, but one that is close to that 400-mm isohyet that makes dry farming possible in West Africa. So much might be said in the most general terms, while referring to the possibility that dry farming might be practiced in sustained conditions with less than 400 mm of annual rainfall if the rain arrives in winter, when it would not evaporate so quickly. Wushenchao itself was examined in terms of its varied edaphic settings in an effort to reach more specific conclusions. Although it happens to be situated on the northern edge of the Maowusu sand dunes, which extend southward all the way to the Great Wall, the commune is favored with plentiful supplies of groundwater which can be tapped by both pitwells and artesian wells. This water has made Wushenchao, like Turfan, into an oasis. Unlike Turfan, this oasis remains primarily linked to livestock, the basis of life here since before the Huns, and fodder is a principal crop.

> With stock farming as our major interest, we will develop around it an enterprise of many facets. (9, pp.1-2)

Three major land types were identified at Wushenchao. At the start of the rehabilitation program, shifting sand dunes covered most of the commune's 1,600 km^2. Lakes and alkaline marshes resulting from a high watertable occupied about 10% of the area. The rest consisted of degraded pasture, much of it on low-lying land between dunes. The basic strategy was directed toward enlarging the usable area by stabilizing sand dunes and using groundwater resources to create what are here called *kulun*.

> A *kulun* is a stone wall—or fence—enclosing an area for growing grass, although trees, fodder grains and vegetables can also be grown. This is then transformed into stable, high-yielding grazing grounds which help to overcome deterioration of the pastures and the incursion of sand. (9, p.1)

As at Turfan, dunes were stabilized by means of plantings, first establishing the sand-resistant *Artemisia ordosica* on the lower one-third of the windward slope of crescent-shaped dunes, which at Wushenchao averaged six meters in height. The strong northwesterlies, capable in other circumstances of generating sandstorms, then blow off the tops of the dunes, creating a landscape with undulations. Sand-tolerant willows (*Salix michrostachya*) were placed downwind and in front of the dunes to halt their advance. When plants died, they were promptly replaced to prevent the development of wind gaps. About five years were needed to stabilize moving dunes using this procedure, after which the surface began to show a fragile, crusty structure, soil density was reduced, porosity increased, pedology improved, and nutrient content raised. Other plants (*Corispermum hyssopifolium, Hedysarum mongolicum*) began to grow on the newly created soil.

On land between the dunes where the sand willow was planted, a "three-layer grassland," as they called it there—grass, shrubs, trees—was developed to improve the soil and provide pasture. Pastures were protected by allowing no grazing during the spring growing season and were treated in the best sections by cultivation, including the planting of such high-quality forage as sweet clover. Extensive areas were planted to forest, to sand willow and small-leaf poplar (*Populus simonii*), to cut wind velocities, improve the soil, and eventually to supply timber.

While it was developed with enormous investments of labor, Wushenchao received almost no investments of money. Fertilizers, for example, were not purchased, one deduces from perusing the case study, natural fertilizers being used exclusively, the droppings of the stock, carefully composted, with soils also improved everywhere by judicious plantings. An impression is created as well that the *kulun* is a local invention, making use of local brainpower, enriched as it seems to have been by unforgotten practices stemming from a long tradition. If self-sufficiency is a national policy in a China that accepts no foreign aid, the internal units of the nation, such as Wushenchao commune, display a localized self-sufficiency that reduces outside assistance, technical or financial, to a minimum.

The culminating achievement of Wushenchao is the four-element *kulun*, developed, as the case study indicates, out of years of trials and experiments. Barbed wire, an imported item, has come to be used to surround these productive complexes composed of water-grass-forest-fodder established on marshy land where water resources were ample and available. The first step was to control the water by means of wells—pit wells which are in fact large open reservoirs, sand-drift wells made of 52-cm concrete tubing reaching 20 to 30 meters deep, and artesian wells to tap the deeper groundwater. The next step was to plant forest belts, usually of willows, perpendicular to the wind direction in rows 40 to 50 meters apart. Pasture grasses were cultivated between the trees, whose leaves supplement the supply of fodder. Marshes were filled in with sand taken from nearby dunes, and the resulting soil, become neither sand nor mucky gleysol, was drained, tilled, and fertilized. *Kulun* such as this have created islands of brilliant green in the arid environment of the Ordos plateau. By 1975, Wushenchao commune had transformed 1,000 hectares of sand desert into pasture and another 2,100 hectares of former duneland into *kulun*. The number of cattle had increased from 18,000 head at the start of rehabilitation to more than 80,000 head. Wushenchao claimed that it had reversed the process whereby "as the sand advances, man retreats."

> They built nurseries inside the grass *kulun*, thus overcoming the difficulties involved in bringing seedlings from the outside. They built ponds to raise fish. They raise honeybees and grow vegetables and fruits. They have enriched the life of the people through such activities. (9, p.17)

The *kulun*, especially the four-element *kulun*, is an emerald in the beige setting of the Ordos. A jewel, as portrayed in the case study, it is also a machine whose function is to transform the soil. Manured by the animals that graze it, enriched in nitrogen by legumes, by sweet clover and alfalfa, the soil of the *kulun* improves its texture and structure while increasing its store of nutrients. No resort is made to synthetic fertilizers. As stated in the third of the Chinese case studies:

> The cultivation of green manure crops such as alfalfa, sweet clover, etc., for the amelioration of the soil is an effective means for the reclamation of barren land and the development of agriculture and stock farming. According to the results of an experiment conducted at a certain farm to the southwest of the Kurban-Tungut Desert, the fertility of the soil is greatly enhanced after three years of alfalfa cultivation. Specifically, each mu [1/15 hectare] can accumulate 57.6 catties of nitrogen compounds [one catty = 1⅓ lb. = 604.8 grams], 10.9 catties of phosphorus, and 16.5 catties of potassium—the equivalent of 20,000 catties of animal manure in terms of nutrition. (10, p.36)

That same case study, to be considered below, speaks of the spirit of the Foolish Old Man who removed the mountains. This is an old Chinese fable, often cited by Mao Tse-tung. The Wise Old Man told the Foolish Old Man that he could not possibly remove two mountain peaks using only his hoe. The Foolish Old Man replied: "When I die, my sons will carry on; when they die, there will be my grandsons, and so on to infinity. High as they are, the mountains cannot grow any higher, and with every bit we dig, they will be that much lower. Why can't we clear them away?" (55, p.14). The people of Wushenchao have their own explanation for their accomplishments.

> The great changes that have taken place in the Wushenchao desert have eloquently proved the irrefutable truth of Chairman Mao's teaching that "social wealth is created by the laborers, peasants and laboring intellectuals themselves, and so long as these people grasp their destiny in their own hands, and, following the lines of Marxism and Leninism, face the problems squarely instead of avoiding them, any difficulty in the world can always be solved." (9, p.18)

Without worrying about what Marx, in his London study, would have thought of Wushenchao, let us take the Chinese at their word to see what is involved. Part of China's policy of self-sufficiency includes the production of enough food to provide an adequate diet to all of its more than 800 million inhabitants. So a commune such as Wushenchao, as developed on a model of self-sufficiency, includes the delivery of its production quotas to the state. Indeed, self-sufficiency and production quotas are philosophically intertwined—the one involves the other. Both emerge from the physical labor of the commune members who, like the Foolish Old Man who removed the mountains, cultivate their fields with hoes and transport "guest soil" in baskets slung from poles carried across their shoulders. In the fulfillment of time, their filling of their production quotas yields them benefits from the great world beyond—a station on the railroad, agricultural machinery. To continue with their own explanation:

> In 1964, when Chairman Mao called for "In agriculture, learn from Tachai," the Wushenchao people, under the guidance of Chairman Mao's revolutionary line and adhering to the principle of class struggle and the Party's basic lines of revolution and production, threw them-

selves headlong into the awe-inspiring "Learn from Tachai" movement [see page 246], hitting a new high in the battle against desertification by means of the grass *kulun*. (9, p.1)

"Two initiatives, of the top and the bottom. From the bottom up and from the top down" (64, p.18). These slogans, describing the process of planning in China, indicate an intention, at least, to hearken to the lowly masses as they, in turn, listen to the exalted leadership. What could the masses possibly have to say? In so many places in the contemporary world, it now seems as if the ancient, hard-won knowledge of peasants no longer functions in situations that include heightened population pressures, advanced technology, and distant but dominating markets. To confront such alterations in circumstance, containing as they do factors far beyond the competence of peasants, experts must be consulted for their highly technical solutions.

That is not the view in China, where Mao continually exhorted his retinue to listen to peasant wisdom. This is not to say that he believed this earthy knowledge should always be taken straight. "You know I've proclaimed for a long time," Mao told André Malraux, "that we must teach the masses clearly what we have received from them confusedly" (53, pp.361–62). However the matter is put, the Chinese case studies contain an implicit conviction that the way to combat desertification is to remove obstacles in the way of the peasants' resolving of their immediate problems. Or, to put it another way, those who use the land, heirs of millennial wisdom, know when they are abusing it. They need only to have the pressures removed that prevent them from following their own preferences and from treating the land in ways that will sustain, even enhance, its productivity. Thus the *kulun* was wrought out of peasant lore and experience.

What, then, did Wushenchao require in the way of outside aid, of developmental assistance? To continue to take the Chinese at their word, it required nothing. Or nothing except a stable political order and a certain amount of inspiration. If all this is true, then the lesson of Wushenchao is that once the peasants are galvanized into action, they will transform their world for themselves. They will create a world out of mere brawn and brains. In Mussayeb, in bitter contrast, uninspired and unmotivated peasants could not create a world when it was handed to them as a gift, the fruit of large outside investments.

Thus, to take the Chinese at their word is not to come down on the side of forward-thinking generosity, as some Americans have been conditioned to conceive it. It is rather to agree with the most reactionary appraisal of foreign aid. This is the judgment of those who say that there is no use in giving money to people who can do nothing for themselves—such gifts will simply be wasted—while people who can transform the world for themselves do not need any aid. It is a conclusion that creates such ill-mated bedfellows that there must be something wrong with it.

6
OGLAT MERTEBA

*"The lion, the panther have disappeared;
The moufflon, the hyena are rare"*

SQUEEZED AGAINST the Mediterranean, the northern boundary of the Sahara is abrupt in comparison with the wide stripes through which it merges on its southern side with the soaked forests of Guinea and central Africa. In some places, as along the coast of Libya, the desert comes to the very water's edge. In Africa's far west, in the Maghrib, the ranges of the Atlas stand as walls between the cultivated littoral and the shifting dunes of the pathless *ergs* to the south. In Tunisia, an extension of the Atlas system creates a dorsal ridge that separates the country into two unequal parts. To the north lie cultivated fields, a mere one-fifth of the total, on which the life of the country depends. Here it was that Carthage acquired its eminence based on an agricultural hinterland that was small but rich and, under proper management in Roman times, came to be the breadbasket of the empire.

The four-fifths of the country to the south of its dorsal ridge, along the crest of which the 350-mm isohyet can be traced, is dry, becoming ever drier to the south and southwest as one moves into the sands of the Great Eastern Erg and the salts pans of the Chott Djerid, a hellish, caked landscape occupying a huge depression. In this region, the 100-mm isohyet, marking off the two-fifths of Tunisia that are part of the true desert, runs parallel to the Mediterranean, a mere 100 km or so away. The 200-mm isohyet is actually out over the water, crossing the resort island of Djerba. Between the two lines is the region designated *very arid*, as it is to the south of the Sahara, or *subdesert*, a terrain in which Berbers were herding sheep and goats when the Carthaginians first arrived from the distant Levant, 814 years before Christ.

OGLAT MERTEBA TEST ZONE

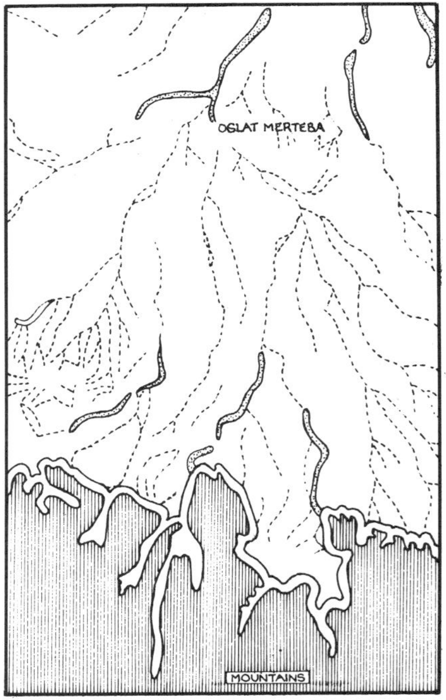

The dotted lines show drainage northward through dry wadis that hold water only after rain.

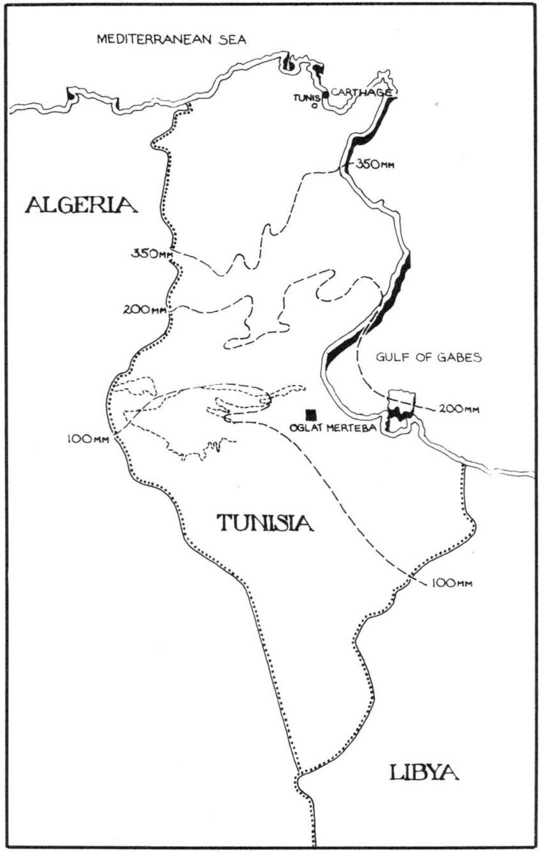

WATER AND ENERGY CYCLES AT THE EARTH'S SURFACE

The sea itself participates in the so-called Mediterranean climate regime of winter rainfall. In the cold season, the water is warmer than the surrounding land, creating a low-pressure zone offshore. Yet the rains that follow are thinned over much of the Mediterranean by the looming presence of the vast desert to the south, with semiarid and subhumid conditions extending across the water to the European shore—to the southernmost parts of Spain, Italy, and Greece. In the dry summers, the hot *sirocco* blows out of the Sahara to make life uncomfortable in southern Europe.

Much of our present understanding of dryland ecosystems comes from research carried out in Tunisia by French scientists working for UNESCO, for the French Office for Scientific and Technical Research (ORSTROM), of the National Center for Scientific Research (CNRS), among still other institutions. It was thus appropriate that the Tunisia case study should be more genuinely a study rather than a description of a program of land amelioration, although such an element was not totally excluded from it. Arising from a collaboration among French and Tunisian scientists—ecologists, agronomists, pedologists, rangeland and livestock management specialists—the study mirrors an effort made to determine the precise causes of desertification in a carefully selected Tunisian landscape, to settle on indicators that would provide quantitative measurements of the advance of desertification, and to decide on techniques whereby the process of degradation could be halted, or even reversed. From a perspective of the physical sciences, the Tunisia case study is virtually a textbook on the subject.

Because of the scientific work long carried out here and in other corners of the Saharan region, Arabic terms for desert formations have crept into the international scientific vocabulary. Thus researchers refer to *ergs* or mobile sand fields arranged in dunes, of *hammadas* or rocky, almost level plains lacking a cover of soil or other fine particles, of *regs* or windblown pavements, of *nebkas* or sand accumulations fixed in place by perennial plants which grow upward as the sand rises around them, of *wadis* or watercourses, usually dry or intermittent, of *tabias* or small embankments with spillways built across wadis to retain runoff, of *jessours* or cultivated areas behind tabias. These terms pop up in discussions about deserts located no matter where.

The test zone selected for the study was a 20,000-hectare rectangle composed of varied but typical Tunisian arid-land ecosystems situated around Oglat Merteba in the center of the very arid region, about midway between the sea and the true desert. Not quite square, the test zone is an interlocking tangle of erosion slopes drained by runoff wadis that lack outlets to the sea. Outside some small bits of good soil—loam, sandy loam, alluvia—the zone features naked limestone, calcareous and gypseous crusts, shifting sand dunes, nebkas stabilized by jujube (*Ziziphus lotus*), and sections stripped to calcareous reg. Most of the soil is starved by aridity, low in nitrogen, potassium, and phosphate and containing a content of organic matter that rarely exceeds 0.5% to 0.6%

Between rocky hillside and deposition surface, 11 ecosystem types were distinguished within the zone which, together with their degraded variants, came to a total of 22 types, each with its characteristic soils and vegetation. The natural vegetation was classified as steppe, scrub, and grass, while each of 50 or so dominant species was distinguished. Much of the steppe features halfa (*Stipa tenacissima*) which supports a small fiber industry. The loamy glacis was once dominated by wormwood (*Artemisia herba-alba*), progressively replaced by *Arthrophytum scoparium*, unpalatable to stock, on overgrazed areas. Sandy plains have a predominance of *Rhantherium suaveolens*, which also provides good woody pasture in the floodout areas. This gives way to the foul-smelling *Aristida pungens* on deep, quickly formed sand accumulations, and to esparto grass (*Lygeum spartum*) where sand overlies a deep gypseous crust. Where flood-out has been cultivated and abandoned, a cover of couch grass (*Cynodon dactylon*) quickly develops. Some tress are ancient and natural inhabitants of the test zone—acacia (*Acacia raddiana Savi*), juniper (*Juniperus Phoenicia L.*), and Aleppo pine (*Pinus halepensis L.*).

This is a harsh land, this skimpy steppe on a thin strip squeezed between the sea, only 50 km to the east, and the desert, a mere 30 km to the west. Yet men have lived here since at least the neolithic, sometimes in more favorable climatic conditions, cultivating wheat and barley and pasturing sheep and goats on scrubby ligneous vegetation so unappetizing in appearance, so marvelously adapted to rainless conditions.

During the past 20,000 years the climate of the Sahara region has probably changed several times, passing through wet periods, called pluvials, and dry periods, or interpluvials. No change of this kind has been recorded during the past 2,000 years, but there seem to have been frequent minor fluctuations. No sign of any trend toward a drier or wetter climate can be detected since the beginning of this century. (4, p.8)

The Carthaginians brought the techniques of arboriculture to this arid clime, and olives, dates, almonds, and figs have been cultivated here ever since in tiny pockets of good soil dampened by runoff. In Roman times, when Tunisia experienced a marked population increase, the test zone was outside the Roman *limes*, the fortifications built against the depredations of the warrior nomads who herded livestock on the steppe that includes Oglat Merteba. The fact is that people have lived here even when population pressures have not forced them out of more favored environments. It is not always easy for the European to understand that some people prefer these savage landscapes, made so by a lack of rain and sculptured by rain when it does chance to fall, often in violent torrents.

Violent downpours are common, capable of reaching 150 mm/hour within the space of five minutes, especially in autumn. They can cause catastrophic floods. (4, p.23)

Recent years have created extreme population pressures in a country in which, as in all of north Africa, the number of people has been increasing at more than 2% per year for the past three decades, the period that has marked the so-called population explosion everywhere in the Third World. If 2% sounds like not so much, it is enough to double the population every 35 years in a geometric progression that with surprising speed reaches devastating numbers. Aware of its population problem, Tunisia was the first country in north Africa to establish a national program of family planning, attempting to make contraception readily available to all.

El Hamma oasis holds the administrative center for Oglat Merteba, and the population of the "El Hamma Delegation" recorded there, ethnically members of the Benizit tribe, went from 32,250 in 1966 to about 41,000 in 1975 despite a considerable emigration in quest of jobs in the cities. Of these, 1,320 people lived in the Oglat Merteba test zone in 1975, an average of 6.6 persons per square kilometer, to which must be added other people who use the area but do not live there. This would seem to be a thin population, and it is, yet it is dense for the resources available—several times as dense, for example, as the population of the comparable climatic zone on the southern side of the Sahara. It is certainly dense enough to put extreme pressures on the fragile ecosystems in Oglat Merteba, and the zone is suffering desertification in the sense that degradation is outstripping recovery. The case study found that one-quarter of the former pastures in the test zone would no longer support livestock and that 12% of once productive land had become unsuitable for any agricultural use.

> The rapid growth of the population has led to unchecked exploitation of the resources. It cannot be denied that the flora and fauna have become impoverished during the past 120 years. The lion, the panther, the ostrich and the antelope have disappeared; the moufflon, the hyena and the gazelle are rare. (4, p.11)

When discussing desertification, the case study authors define the term as it has come to be used by French workers whose findings, the result of research carried out in what was once French Africa, have so enlarged our understanding of the degradation processes affecting productive land. It is the UNESCO tradition of desert research, the tradition of an agency whose home is Paris, the capital of a country whose imagination was captured by the century in which it dominated the Sahara. At the Conference on Desertification, "desertification" was used to refer to any stage in the process leading, finally, to irreversible degradation of once productive land. The UNESCO researchers generally prefer to restrict the word to that final stage, at which biological productivity has been irreversibly destroyed, using "degradation" to refer to the steps in the process. It is in this latter sense that "desertification" is used in the Tunisia case study, with the additional proviso that "irreversible" must be specified. For, as the authors point out, what seems irreversible will be reversed if time enough is available. On a geological time scale, the Sahara itself will one day nourish strawberries—or their remote, succulent descendants—as tectonic processes carry the African continental plate into damper climatic regions. But even with Oglat Merteba staying more or less where it is, in only a few centuries the wind would reseed its desertified portions, provided they were left undisturbed by man. A skimpy covering of perennials would take root in wind veils blown over rocky pavements, and they would begin the work of restoring a more productive soil structure. So it seems that "irreversible" is a notion that requires a time reference. In the Tunisia case study, the time frame selected is 25 years. The authors then propose that land is irreversibly degraded, "desertified" in their definition, if one generation of careful management would do nothing to restore its productivity.

To go then and specify precisely what occurs when land is degraded, eventually to become desertified, just the task these authors have set for themselves, attention must be shifted away from the large-scale perspective in which the atmosphere circulates, determining climate and creating drylands and deserts. The view must use a closer focus, centered on that microclimate that plays around the meeting place of earth and air, including those topmost centimeters in which soil is fertile. In these thin skins worn by continents, events take place that determine the fate of soil, sometimes enriching this substance that nourishes life on land, but sometimes, on the other hand, destroying it, wringing it of its fertility, then blowing or washing it away to leave in its place shifting sand dunes, bare rock, or pebbly plains, the ergs, regs, and hammadas from which life must flee for survival.

Soil was born from rock in ages of geologic time, worked on by algae and lichens, then moved by wind and water, sometimes by gravity, laid down in beds where plants capable of fixing nitrogen could go to work on it, supplying it with organic matter, a store of humus. Water also worked on it, depending on rainfall and runoff, leaching some minerals downward, combining with the wind to create layers in the soil called *horizons*, developing a *profile*, or set of horizons, one atop the other. More highly evolved plants grew in this evolving stuff, thrusting root systems downward into a substance with structure and character, quite different from the original loose aggregate of mineral grains. This stuff, soil, came to vibrate with life —bacteria, insects, and burrowing animals stirred up horizons, sometimes mixing them, as their corpses blended with decaying plant material to be converted into that dark brown colloid called humus, that organic material that serves as food to subsequent generations of plants. Composed of clays, silts, or sands, a classification based on the size of its constituent mineral grains—or made up of a mixture of grain sizes, called loam—soils acquired certain textures, structures, porosities, a pH or position on the acid–alkaline scale, and the other qualities by which they are classified into different types by soils science, a new branch of learning. These are the qualities that dictate—together with climate—that certain plants will thrive in one patch of earth and not in another. Constructed in the course of geologic epochs, fertile soil, the basis of life on land, no more, really, than the dirt beneath our feet, is a treasure beyond price. Endless ages have stocked this stuff with a staggering amount of potential energy in the form of humus, as much as 10^{20} kilocalories, equal to the energy contained in all the plant life aboveground. And that plants contain a colossal amount of energy, inserted into them ultimately by the sun, is evident all around us. Only the most minute portions of plant life need be consumed to support the most energetic efforts of tug-of-war teams, or to enable a horse to plow a field.

The elements contained in rocks of one kind or another include all the chemically active elements occurring naturally in the conditions prevailing on the earth. Plants can ingest all the naturally occurring elements, excepting perhaps only the noble gases, but they *must* have 16 of them, specifically these—carbon, hydrogen, oxygen, nitrogen, phosphorus, potassium, calcium, iron, sulfur, magnesium, manganese, boron, chlorine, copper, zinc, and molybdenum. Absorption of a few of these vital substances can take place through leaves, but for the most part—indeed, almost entirely—essential elements are adsorbed through roots, plants obtaining what they need from soil. Since vegetation is immobile, except for growth, these substances must somehow be brought to the plant—and in a form the roots can use. Most such elements reach the roots dissolved in the moisture that transports them. Plants cannot grow in soil that contains no water, no solvent for nutrient ions. The presence of plants always indicates that the soil contains at least some moisture, which it does, perhaps surprisingly, even in such very arid regions as the extreme Sahel. Soils hoard moisture. The soils of the earth are an enormous moisture bank.

The water so contained, the total store in the earth's land areas, has reached there in the form of rain or dew, ice or snow. Precipitation onto the land is part of a global hydrological cycle regulated by climate. Energy coming in from the sun evaporates water wherever it is to be found on the earth's surface, the greatest part, obviously, from the oceans, thus continuously replenishing the store of water vapor contained in the troposphere, the breathable lowest layer of the atmosphere. Water vapor condenses under certain circumstances and leaves the atmosphere as precipitation, most of it falling as rain back again into the sea. When rain falls on land, different things can happen to it. Some of it immediately evaporates back into the atmosphere again. If it falls on soil, some of it sinks in, to be retained by capillary action. The moisture not held in uppermost horizons percolates downward toward the watertable, where it replenishes the store of groundwater. Some of this will continue to move downward, ever deeper, eventually reaching deep aquifers far beneath the surface where fresh water may be held in storage for thousands of years. Far beneath the scorching surface of the Sahara, enormous fossil aquifers, thousands of square kilometers in extent, testify to downpours that drenched this region 30,000 years ago and earlier at certain moments in the various advances or retreats of the Würm glaciation.

Groundwater moves slowly downslope heading for an outflow, creek, rivulet, river, leaking out of embankments in the form of springs. Water will not penetrate the soil but will flow away on the surface if the soil is already saturated, if the rain is falling faster than the soil can drink it in, or if the soil surface is crusted or contains hardpan. Runoff fills arroyos and wadis when thunderstorm torrents strike arid areas, a frequent form of dryland rainfall that sends flash floods crashing down ordinarily dry watercourses. Whether it cascades down cliffs or seeps slowly through swamps, all the fresh water on the land eventually returns to the sea to complete the hydrological cycle, although "eventually" can sometimes involve a long, long time.

A flow of water through soil's surface layers, dissolving some minerals, precipitating others, hastens the process through which *peds* are formed, those being small clods, glued together in a variety of shapes by natural sugars, whose presence distinguishes structured soil from a loose agglomerate of mineral grains. Plants, too, help structure the soil. Indeed, the relations between plants and soils would have to be taken as the ultimate symbiosis if dwellings, and not merely their inhabitants, were only regarded as alive. Plants dwell in soil. In the process, they build their own dwellings, supplying the soil with the very fertility they require. Humus created from their remains, contained in soil as deep as roots penetrate, is a store of nutrients in the form that coming generations of plants can most easily use. Humus will be concentrated in the uppermost horizons, where plant remains are thickest, and whither inseeping moisture transports that dark brown sludge that constitutes the last will and testament of dead leaves, roots, and branches. As they construct their own habitat, plants hold these precious topmost layers in place, protecting them against assaults by wind and water.

Since soils are enriched by the very plants that thrive in them, dryland soils, with their chronic water deficiencies and skimpy plant cover, tend to be anemic. One of the ten great orders into which all soil types are classified, *aridisols*, the most widely distributed of all orders, are located mainly where the World Map of Desertification shows deserts and drylands to be, occupying in all 18.8% of the earth's land surface or about half the combined area of desert and dryland. The distinguishing mark of aridisols is that their often well developed pedogenic horizons have formed in conditions of low soil moisture. This often results in a calcareous profile, with lime layers, accumulations of salt or gypsum and the presence of lime-cemented hardpans (39, p.419). Aridisols are low in humus, although they can be richly productive if only watered and fertilized.

Aridisols characterize Oglat Merteba, tending to be lithogenic on higher ground and involved in the long process of turning back into rock, something that soils can do. In the lower sections, in the bottoms or at the foot of glacis, the soils tend to be immature sierozems. These light brown or brownish-gray soils are a type of aridisol lacking a clay-accumulation horizon. With a good blocky structure when well developed, sierozems are typical of those aridisols that can be made productive with the touch of water. Like the other soils in Oglat Merteba, they are loaded with calcium compounds which put them on the alkaline side. They are low in humus, as might be expected, with an organic matter content that rarely exceeds 0.6%, and poor in nitrogen, potassium, and phosphate—which is why they should be fertilized if they are to be cultivated.

Originally laid down by wind and water, shifting veils of mineral granules become fixed in place to turn into soil largely through the holding power of plants. If the granules were to remain loose, wind and water would continue to stir them. An earth without plants would be a planet of shifting, unstable landscapes, where colossal dust storms would march across the continents, where rivers would run brown with muck as they carried the remains of eroding land forms out to sea. Plants create their own preferred environment, as well as that of the myriad life forms that depend ultimately on access to plants. Having created an environment, plants sustain it. When the plants are removed, this environment begins to crumble.

Rainfed cultivation always involves the removal of the climax vegetation, the plant life that nature has established over the long years, and involves also the replacement of the climax by preferred and more profitable species, species of vegetation that, given time, nature would eliminate in its urge to return to what it prefers, the climax biota. Departures from the climax, an ecosystem's "natural" order, introduce instabilities which work against a sustained productivity in the desired anticlimax, artificially sustained by man. After a few years of cultivation, the field slashed and burned by a transient farmer will have been exhausted of its store of nutrients and will be abandoned to fallow—to a progression back in the direction of the climax. Moving on to slash and burn another field is one form of agricultural management, as all rainfed farming requires management if productivity is to be sustained. The rules of management, the requirements for successful farming, are embodied in those rich peasant traditions that have developed everywhere in the world where human beings have undertaken the chore of raising crops. New rules of management, extending far beyond anything conceived of by the slash-and-burn farmer or by other traditionalists, have been developed in the contemporary scene by new sciences of agronomy.

When an environment is disturbed with destruction of the climax vegetation and then left alone again, undisturbed, it will move back toward its climax condition through a series of successional stages, each termed a *disclimax*. The speed with which an ecosystem reverts to its climax condition measures its resilience. If severely disrupted, an ecosystem may never regenerate the plant life that constituted its original climax, but may have recourse to other species, a new climax, but a condition that is still "natural" in the sense that it demands no human management, no economic inputs to maintain it. As a general rule, the closer a cultivated successional order is to a climax condition, the less expensive it is to maintain, the more nature itself will supply the elements necessary for sustained productivity. Thus, it was an easy matter for the first farmers when they replaced a climax of wild wheat with domesticated wheat.

All environments exhibit resilience. Increased resilience will usually be associated with higher natural fertility and a greater variety of life forms, factors providing a variety of avenues through which the climax condition can be recovered. In dryland ecosystems, soils are often impoverished and life forms are restricted to species that have special adaptations to arid conditions. Dryland ecosystems are thus especially vulnerable to disturbance. This means that the options open to them are narrowly restricted and that disturbance can easily throw them over a threshold beyond which a former climax cannot be recovered within any reasonable period of time. Such disturbed ecosystems will, if left alone, achieve a new climax, usually marked by a skimpier production of above-ground biomass and a greater proportion of plant species unpalatable to livestock. When that happens it means that desertification has occurred—or at least "degradation," as words are employed by the authors of the Tunisia case study. Such a process can proceed in dryland ecosystems through a succession of climaxes as those ecosystems suffer repeated disturbance, as by intermittent overgrazing, with each climax worse than the last from a human point of view, until that ultimate climax condition is reached in which a sterilized ecosystem displays a naked surface of rock or moving sand dunes.

An environment must be seen for what it is—an ecosystem or group of ecosystems whose elements interact. A soil is bathed in its climate, ingesting energy and precipitation for the use of the life forms that live in it and on it—viruses, bacteria, antibiotic actinomycetes, plants, worms, insects, burrowing animals, burrowing birds, and, on top, livestock and man, to mention only some of them —and giving off heat and moisture again to maintain energy and water balances. An ecosystem that includes fertile soil participates in still other cycles besides those through which flow water and energy. A nitrogen cycle, for example, employs water and bacteria to bring this vital element in usable form to the roots of plants. And so with the other vital elements—phosphorus, potassium, calcium—involved in nutrient cycles in which bacteria work on humus to transform these elements into adsorbable ions. Each separate topoedaphic setting, each a miniature ecosystem in itself, must be seen as a piece of a larger system—a watershed, steppe or savanna, pastureland, cropland—whose elements also interact, affecting one another. A change in any one element contained in the landscape unit affects all the others. The altering of any one element, chemical or otherwise, sends out shock waves that ripple through the larger, embracing systems. The easiest constituent to affect is the plant life. Of the immediate, physical causes of desertification, the commonest is the removal of vegetation. What precisely happens to an arid ecosystem when its vegetation is removed? This is one of the questions that research at Oglat Merteba sought to answer.

Of course, slightly different things happen to the different ecosystem types as they were identified in the test zone. Everywhere, however, the removal of vegetation works effects that hinder the natural processes of seeding and germination among the plants that remain. It establishes new conditions that inhibit the return of vegetation. In a blatant example of positive feedback, stripping the soil acts in the direction of keeping the soil stripped. The immediate effects are worked on the cycles of water and energy.

With its vegetative insulation gone, the soil now responds quickly to heating and cooling, reaching sizzling temperatures on the surface while taking in and storing less energy at depth. Lighter in color than vegetation, naked soil reflects a higher proportion of the incoming light. This change in albedo, warming the air, may affect large-scale climatic conditions if vegetation is sufficiently reduced over a wide enough area, as may happen during drought. Such an effect could not be established in so limited an area as Oglat Merteba, but it has been theorized for extensive regions that a change in their albedo may exert another example of positive feedback by further reducing already scanty rainfall.

Denuded soil is exposed to erosion by wind and water, the two frequently working together. At Oglat Merteba, wind first blows off the "sand veil" that, together with vegetation, protects the surface from the direct blows of raindrops and also reduces runoff. In a typical succession of events, the rare but heavy rains puddle the naked soil, which dries out to a hard crust after the storm has passed and the brilliant sun returns. This "rain beat seal," as the study calls it, hinders water intake the next time it rains, increasing runoff and flooding with their accompanying erosion. As it ingests less water, the soil dries out, and its crust is pounded to powder by the sharp hooves of stock. The powder blows away in the wind which, in lifting off the topsoil, wafts away the horizons richest in nutrients, leaving ever more sterile underlayers until the drama ends with the curtain falling on naked reg or hammada. The soil carried away is, to be sure, deposited somewhere else, but in never as fertile a condition in the new setting as it was in the old. As it drifts in the wind, its precious gobbets of colloid are winnowed out of it.

There are three principal reasons why vegetation is removed from the earth at Oglat Merteba. It occurs with the extension of cultivation into areas that had formerly yielded a sustained product when employed as pasture. Vegetation is consumed in the grazing of herds and flocks. The third reason is to be found in the removal of woody vegetation for fuel and construction. Cultivation has been extended here into areas where, climatically and topographically, it does not belong. Too often grazing had become overgrazing. With the increased demand for wood that comes largely from population increase, woody vegetation is suffering annihilation. Three reasons that make no interference with sustained production when managed with moderation become agents of desertification when carried to excess. They have become the principal agents of desertification, not only in Oglat Merteba, but throughout the world, This is a point so crucial that it is worth quoting the case study at length.

It has been demonstrated that no major climatic change has occurred north of the Sahara since the end of the nineteenth century. *The cause of increasing degradation* must therefore be sought in the growing pressure exerted by man on the natural environment, with its visible manifestation in the shape of more aggressive technology. These phenomena are accentuated by the marked general aridity of the climate and by a rainfall pattern that characteristically varies enormously from one year to another. The main causes are as follows:

The breaking of new ground for cultivation on the steppes is without doubt the principal cause. It is generally accepted that in the arid regions of Tunisia, over 2,700,000 hectares of steppeland have been brought under cultivation during the period from 1890 to 1975. This state of affairs results from the understandable desire of the growing population to increase its immediate income. Fruit trees and cereals, especially in areas where the rainfall is in excess of 200 mm, certainly make it possible—in the early years, before the fertile layer of soil is carried away by erosion—to realize a cash income which is higher than that to be made from pastoralism. In recent years, moreover, the widespread introduction of mechanisation throughout the country has enabled hectare upon hectare of steppeland to be cleared rapidly and with relative ease by means of the disk-harrow. For this reason, and following a series of years of good rainfall, this clearing of ground has progressed at an accelerating rate, even in the zone lying between the 100 mm and 200 mm average annual isohyets.

Overgrazing is another cause of degradation. Because of the increase in human population, there has been no reduction in the average size of the livestock population even though the areas left for grazing have grown progressively smaller with the expansion of cultivation. As well as causing edible species to become rare and encouraging the development of inedible species, overgrazing also leads to a reduction in the plant cover formed by long-lived species and thereby opens the door to degradation processes. Another harmful factor is excessive trampling. In some places the opening up of new watering points for the herds, or the creation of irrigated areas, without regulating the use of the range, has resulted in overgrazing and deterioration of the environment for a radius of 10 km or so all around.

Eradication of woody species. Although less noticeable than the two foregoing causes, this phenomenon is nevertheless very extensive.

> Approximately 1.5 kg of wood per person per day is required for domestic purposes, and this supply comes almost entirely from the vegetation of the steppe. Many of the bushy species producing the most wood have disappeared entirely, and this wood-gathering activity is now directed toward smaller and smaller individual plants and involves an ever-growing number of species. What is more, the plants are often torn up rather than cut. (4, pp.57–58)

Traditionally, cultivation was carried out at Oglat Merteba in the jessours behind earthen dams, intensively applied to tiny areas in ways that resembled gardening. Tree culture has flourished in these small settings, and cereals have been grown for family consumption. Cereal culture, principally of barley but also of hard wheat, has also been carried out on the heaviest soils, the loamy glacis that captures runoff water. In recent years, cereal cultivation—not for consumption but for cash—has been extended to the sandy sierozems, and the traditional swing plow, which spared the bushy perennials, has been replaced by the tractor-drawn disk harrow, which rips up everything. This stirring of the soil breaks its crust and favors the germination of annuals, which tend to thrive with improved water infiltration. Few such annuals make good pasture in the years when the cereal fields are left fallow, nor do they survive long enough to hold the soil in place. After a few years of good rain, harvests decline in areas into which cultivation has been unwisely extended, and abandoned fields are left stripped of their former cover of *Rhantherium suaveolens* and exposed to the work of wind and water.

It is difficult to count moving stock, but it was estimated that about 5,000 head of stock, two-thirds of them sheep and the rest goats, roam the pastures of Oglat Merteba. Since goats can thrive on more degraded pasture, the proportion of goats is increasing. Used for milking, the goat is in any case more of a household animal, and almost every family has some goats. In winter, the animals obtain adequate moisture from forage, but they rarely stray more than 5 to 6 km from watering points in summer, creating locally desertified circles, called *piospheres*, in which trampling and overgrazing have taken place. The animals require no supplementary feed except in drought years, when the stillbirth rate can leap from 20% to 50%. Pastures vary widely in their production of edible biomass, ranging from as low as 50 kg of dry matter per hectare in low-quality, post-harvest stubble to 800 kg per low-lying hectare subject to flooding. Averaging the entire test zone, it was estimated that five hectares can support one sheep in a condition of sustained production. The actual stocking rate is one sheep for every four hectares, but the most degraded ranges, formerly the best, suffer the greatest overstocking.

Rhantherium suaveolens and *Anarrhinum brevifolium* are the most likely plants to be ripped up for fuel, which might be used in home cooking, or in lime kilns, bakery ovens, or *hammam* (Turkish baths). *Calligonum sp.*, once gathered for charcoal, have been collected to extinction in the region, so that charcoal is now made out of *Retama raetam*. Halfa and esparto, with their plaitable fibers, are collected for craft activities. It was calculated that about 750 tons of wood are removed each year from the 20,000 hectares of the test zone. Destructive effects would be much less if the woody vegetation were cut off, leaving roots to regenerate, but, as the case study said, it is more likely to be ripped out, roots and all.

In all seasons, perennials cover 20% to 40% of the ground surface on Oglat Merteba rangelands in good or pristine condition. Rain brings on the growth of annuals, increasing the vegetative cover. It is enough to protect the soil from wind erosion. Soil particles stirred up by sometimes violent winds are deposited around the stalks of perennials. Vegetation cover, in its undisturbed state, is sufficient also to act as a good obstacle to over-rapid runoff, while the roots of the plants reinforce the substratum and encourage water infiltration. The value of the plants, the roles they play in sustaining the environment, are well known to the pastoralists and farmers of southern Tunisia, who have had thousands of years in which to develop techniques for sustained production. They do not require visiting experts to tell them that they are degrading the environment by their overexploitation of its plant life. They are intimately aware of the state of their pastures and croplands.

Like users of land in many places that are undergoing desertification, the pastoralists and farmers of Oglat Merteba are experiencing pressures arising from the overwhelming changes that characterize the contemporary scene in the world and in Tunisia. Two changes in particular have given these people little choice but to apply excessive pressure to the land they use. These are the intrusion of "modern" ways into traditional systems, and the population growth that has been a fateful accompaniment to that intrusion. The case study recognizes how much life has changed "during the past 20 years" in Oglat Merteba.

> The introduction of schooling for all children has resulted in a progressive reduction in nomadism. . . . Once begun, this sedentarization was

reinforced by the establishment of a large number of watering points and by the setting up of dispensaries.

Socio-economic development in general, and improvement in means of communication and information in particular, have brought about the following consequences in addition to a very distinct improvement in the population's standard of living.

- The creation of new demand for foodstuffs, clothing and cultural satisfaction, making it necessary to seek new sources of income as well as to intensify the level of exploitation of land resources.
- The development of emigration, a phenomenon that scarcely existed in these regions before the 1960s.
- The rural exodus, prompted by a desire to find more dependable and better-paid work.
- The introduction and increasingly widespread use of the tractor for plowing and of vans for carrying produce in place of animal traction.

Finally, the growth of population has aggravated the imbalance between the needs of the constantly growing number of people and the production level of an environment that is in the process of becoming degraded. (4, p.101)

This description of transformation and turmoil is not untypical of the way in which situations of socioeconomic change—"development" is the word in common use—are to be found characterized throughout the literature of this so-called development. It is a statement fascinating not so much for what it says as for what it omits, constituting, as it does, a mixture of factual analysis and the value assertions, usually embodied unconsciously, that make up the *modern* attitude. The value content of developmental analysis is so commonplace in the developed world, so taken for granted, that it usually passes quite unnoticed. When it is made explicit, it will be defended as obvious, what any "rational" person would believe, the only hope for the poor world, comparable, in these senses, to the axiom set of a scientific discipline. Poor people, "undeveloped" people, are then often viewed as foolish and misguided, "shiftless," in their frequent resistance to the imposition of these values, imported as they usually are from abroad, together with the experts who pronounce this new testament and the rifles, which, until very recently, provided the ultimate argument in their favor.

In the usually unexamined presuppositions of the modern world, "improvements in the means of communications," the use of agricultural machinery, and "vans . . . in place of animal traction" are all part of that "very distinct improvement in the population's standard of living" by which, as it turns out in the end, independent subsistence farmers and free pastoralists on the three poor continents—and sometimes in other regions, too—have been processed into poor people, dependent on others, and have awakened to find that their old life has become so distasteful, there is nothing to do but flee it, giving rise, in Tunisia, to an emigration "that scarcely existed before." Population growth, that final aggravation, is treated here, also typically, as if it were an unwelcome intrusion into the process of "socioeconomic development in general," and that population should be exploding just as desertification is accelerating is seen as a kind of unlucky coincidence. What is rarely asserted, here or elsewhere, is that this hideous "imbalance" between people and production level is an intrinsic aspect of the disastrous impact of Europe on ancient ways of life.

Cereal cultivation represents a much more profitable use of land, as the case study states, than pasturing sheep and goats on it. The 10% of Oglat Merteba that has been put into cereal production has been yielding (while it lasts) an annual total income of 25,000 dinars (one dinar = $2.38), which can be compared with the 37,000 dinars of total income obtained from livestock production on the remaining 90% of the test zone. It is interesting to note that the 150 hectares of orchard and market gardens cultivated on jessours in conditions of sustained production yielded an annual income of 30,000 dinars. The 750 (metric) tons of wood gathered annually is equal in energy to 12,600 dinars worth of oil. Other economic activities—bee-keeping, milking, crafts—may have been producing an annual income of 16,500 dinars. All this adds up to an average annual income of 97 dinars, or $230, per person in Oglat Merteba. This is an income that provides its own explanation of why cereal production, with its higher rate of return, is expanding into every immediate possibility, however temporary that may be.

The measuring of income in money—indeed, the importation of an entire money and market economy—is little more than a century old at Oglat Merteba and can be dated to the arrival of and penetration by the Europeans with their colonial system. The market economy that encourages cereal crops to be sold for a quick killing, lasting until the land is exhausted or permanently degraded, is based on a technology that supplies the tractor-drawn disk harrow that makes it easy to bring sensitive sierozem soils into cereal production. This is also the technology that manufactures the pins and needles, axes, vans, and transistor radios that helped to convince the subsistence farmer that his traditional way of life suffered from inconveniences and a restricted outlook that money alone is capable of transcending. He was further convinced by his modern government, which kept the colonial system intact as it moved into independence, demanding its taxes in cash rather than in kind, by no means intending to dismantle the modern structures imposed by colonialism. The development experts put the best possible face on all this, calling it the "age of rising expectations."

Among the benefits brought with them by invading, disruptive colonial powers was the science of medicine that had developed in Europe in the nineteenth century when, for the first time, medicine began to exhibit a payoff from the scientific impulses originating three centuries earlier with Vesalius and Harvey. In Europe, the control of contagious disease was taken in stride as another natural development among societies where the germ theory arose as an integral part of an intellectual tradition. Elsewhere, the control of contagion went off like dynamite amidst stable demographic patterns in which disease was taken to be expressive of winds, vapors, and spirits. An import as welcome as it was alien to Third World situations and attitudes, disease control demolished death rates by assuring longer expectations of life at birth. The immunization needle sent those rates on a gradually declining course until the subsequent invention of antibiotics sent them plunging downward in the years after World War II, just as all those former colonies were becoming independent nations. Nothing similar happened to birth rates, enshrined at high levels in traditional societies by the need to compensate for such afflictions as a devastating infant mortality. When death rates dropped out of equilibrium with birth rates, the result was population growth at velocities never before sustained in the history of the human race. Tunisia provides a good example of the course of these demographic events.

In 1844, when the Ottoman Empire attempted a census of its Tunisian dependency, the country was counted as having 950,000 inhabitants (68, p.13). The first effort to take a modern census was made in 1921, when the total population was counted at 1,875,000 persons, admitted to be slightly less than the true total (68, p.18). The crude birth rate was then fluctuating between 46 and 50 per thousand persons per year, in other words, at its traditional level and one typical of a people who are using no means of birth control. The birth rate remained in this region for the next 40 years (or through the next four decennial censuses). The death rate, however, began to drop under the impact of European medicine and French views of law and order. By 1940, the death rate—formerly more or less in balance with the birth rate—had dropped to only half as much, and by 1966, with the assistance of antibiotics, to slightly more than one-third of the birth rate. By then, the population of independent Tunisia was growing at a rate estimated at 2% per year, which meant that by 1976 the country's population was approaching six million and was projected to reach 14 million by the year 2000, a projection assuming no decline in the growth rate. If that should happen, the population will have multiplied 15 times in slightly more than a century and a half.

With its history of conquest by Phoenicians and Romans, Vandals and Arabs, Tunisia has in the past experienced sharp cultural disruptions with their accompanying impact on agricultural practices. The granary of the Romans became under the Arabs that more pastoral order that supported the brilliant civilization of ninth-century Kairouan. Population decline is a common accompaniment to cultural disruption, since disturbance is usually brought about by force of arms. The last major disturbance before the arrival of the French, the tenth-century Fatimid vengeance against rebellious Berbers, converted Tunisia into a cultural backwater after heavy loss of life. The overwhelming cultural dislocation caused by the intrusion of Europe, with its technology and its market economy, was like no other in that one of its elements, advanced medicine, paradoxically produced unprecedented population growth in the midst of disruption. It may contain hidden value judgments, but the case study is clear in indicating that cultural dislocation and population growth are the ultimate causes of desertification in Tunisia. These are social and not physical causes. As such, they require social remedies.

It is interesting that Tunisia was early to recognize the dimensions of its population problem. Pronatalist traditions are notoriously strong is Islam, with its history of reverence for large families. Newly independent Tunisia, however, took its first step toward recovering its demographic equilibrium in 1956 by passing laws against polygamy and in favor of equal rights for women. In 1961, laws against the sale of contraceptives were repealed, and abortion was made legal for women with five or more children. In 1962, discussions with the Population Council and the Ford Foundation led to the establishment of the first family planning program ever to be installed in a Moslem country. In 1964, the legal age for marriage was raised to 17 for women and 20 for men, and a national demographic goal was announced—to reduce the rate of population growth to 1% annually by the year 2000. In 1973, abortion was made legal on request to all women during the first 12 weeks of gestation.

It was perhaps natural that a program so antagonistic to ancient tradition should have been slow to take hold, and a decade was to pass before this family planning program made any visible impact on the birth rate. Then, suddenly in the late seventies, the birth rate began to drop. By 1978, it was approaching an annual rate of 30 per thousand persons, and for the first time, a feeling of optimism developed that Tunisia might attain its announced demographic goal—but with an ultimate population much larger, of course, than the six million of 1977, but much less than the devastating 14 million formerly projected for the year 2000.

Europe, where death control was developed, never grew as rapidly as the countries of the Third World into which that control was extended as one more of those gifts whereby Europe's superiority was demonstrated to backward peoples. In their most rapid period of demographic expansion, European countries rarely exceeded a growth rate of 1% per year, and even that taking place in the midst of unprecedented, unparalleled advantages—an Australia, a New World in which to siphon off excess people, a technology in which death control was a natural part making it possible to support dense populations in comfort, even in luxury. The Third World had no such luck, and the violence of its population growth has shipwrecked all its development hopes. The problem lies only partly in overwhelming absolute numbers, ravaging every natural resource. It consists also in the fact of growth itself, in the need to supply ever more jobs, to build ever more schools, medical dispensaries, dwellings, to duplicate national infrastructures every generation in societies in which nothing is stable, in which the cities are eternally under construction, their streets adrift with abandoned children. The population explosion is a social disaster that complicates every problem confronting the Third World. It is one of the important causes, a social cause, of the worldwide acceleration in the processes of desertification.

The Tunisia case study is under no illusions that solutions to the problem of desertification in Oglat Merteba will not ultimately be social in nature. The physical scientists who prepared the study specified the physical measures needed to halt and reverse the degradation of productive land within the test zone and to maintain the area in a condition of sustained productivity. The extension of cultivation into unsuitable and vulnerable areas is to be discouraged, and plowed-up pastureland is to be converted back into range wherever it has not been irreversibly damaged. Pastoral management procedures are to be introduced to prevent overgrazing and to encourage the germination and growth of the favored fodder species. The destruction of woody vegetation is to be halted by the conversion of industrial ovens, such as those in bakeries, to oil, by a tree-planting program and by consideration of the possibilities of wind and solar energy. A moden design for a pastoral improvement area is included in the case study as an annex.

While the study calls for further research to facilitate the task of combating desertification, Oglat Merteba confirms what the scientist advisers to the Conference on Desertification told Mostafa Tolba, the Secretary General of the Conference. This was that there is no need to wait on research to begin the physical task of halting and reversing the degradation of arid ecosystems. The measures that need to be taken are already known.

The things that need to be done, the physical measures the land requires, are also known already to the farmers and pastoralists who work the land, heirs as they are to ancient traditions of self-sustaining agriculture. This fact is not always clear to visiting consultants, who seem to recognize it in one breath, and in the next suggest that local people need instruction in how to manage their resources. It is natural that physical scientists should think in terms of physical solutions, and suggest the introduction into Oglat Merteba of "pastoral management procedures" instead of turning to social solutions and proposing means whereby social and economic pressures can be removed from local land users so that they can restore the expert pastoral management procedures with which they have long been familiar. For the crucial arena is here—in the application of social and economic remedies. Recognized as this may be by the authors of the study, they are, as might be expected, vague when it comes to social proposals, forced as they are by harsh realities to enter those sloppy realms of thought beyond the boundaries of natural science.

> A mass-education program should be set up, in the schools and universities and among the peasant population. (4, p.111)

Themselves emerging from academic backgrounds, they cannot restrain their yearnings to teach somebody something. What then are peasants, people in general, going to be taught?

> A mass information program should be set up to make the people aware of the problems: Information on plant and animal ecology should be incorporated into educational and cultural programs. Programs for increasing popular awareness should be intensified within the framework of activities carried out by the various committees, organizations, and associations concerned with the problem of desertification. (4, p.108)

But that could not be intended for the people occupying vulnerable land since they are already aware of the problems and understand the local ecology. And the people who are not on the land, whose actions have no effect on endangered ecosystems—what difference does it make what they know? It makes no difference, unless those on the land have to be coerced by an enlightened public opinion into doing what they would already prefer to do if it were only possible. Or it is as if the authors were hoping against hope that the land users do not, after all, know what to do—as if the problem lay there—so that in teaching somebody something, they would find in that a simple solution, one that they are equipped to achieve, to a problem whose roots, instead, penetrate deep into obscure and complex horizons in which standard pedagogy often seems to be useless. This is the pedagogy with an elitist flavor, in which the teacher, filled with knowledge, is superior to his ignorant students. To their great credit, however, regardless of intellectual discomfort, the authors refuse to stop at their educational proposal, where development experts often stop. They suggest other social remedies:

> There is a need to create employment and raise the level of income for the rural population in order to reduce the intensity of exploitation of the environment. This goal can be achieved by setting up an agro-pastoral program and establishing industries compatible with the type of area concerned. (4, p.111)

At first glance this economic prescription might be taken for something as vague as the educational prescription. Fortunately, it is not. The case study provides detailed suggestions for creating employment and raising income levels.

In order to attain these goals, the following actions should be undertaken:

1. The restoration, in an adapted form, of integration between extensive steppic agriculture and intensive oasis agriculture. Oases, in fact, possess very good fodder potential, especially in winter when there is a surplus of irrigation water. The steppe farmers could fulfill the role of *accoucheurs*, while the oasis farmers would do the fattening of the animals. The data available at present show that it is possible to double the weight of lambs raised for slaughter. . . .

2. The introduction of measures for management and improvement of the natural rangelands . . . reduction of overgrazing, for example, by encouraging an increase in the productivity of the herd itself (kilograms of meat per female unit per year) rather than to land area (kilograms of meat per hectare of rangeland per year). The introduction of a productivity bonus would lead to a reduction in the stocking rate. . . . Incentives to convert fallow cereal land back to grazing land . . . limiting the further extension of cereal farming and arboriculture by the introduction of a meat-production bonus . . . encouraging the planting of fodder crops (*Atriplex* and cactus) suited to arid-zone conditions . . . improvement of the genetic potential of the herds by the insertion of tested sires. . . .

3. The fodder potential, and in particular that of byproducts, should be utilized. Common dates and date trimmings, of which it is estimated that more than 35,000 tons are produced; common dates are becoming less and less sought after for human consumption and their use as supplementary feed should be encouraged . . . olive leaves remaining on the cut wood, and olive-oil cakes; it has been calculated that if the leaves produced from the pruning of the olive trees in central and southern Tunisia were used as feed for sheep and goats rather than as fuel, they would . . . meet the energy requirements for the upkeep of over 400,000 head. . . .

4. Far-reaching measures should be undertaken in the domain of soil and water preservation. These measures are designed not only to combat erosion caused by water, but also to create employment. (4, pp.105–108)

Yet it is clear that what the case study has to suggest, and some of the suggestions are obviously superb, are essentially physical measures. Social motivation is needed if these physical measures are ever to be carried out but, in contrast to the detailed description of physical action, the discussion of social motivation is limited to proposing bonuses and other material incentives. The prospect of increased income proved to be insufficient as an incentive capable of generating what specialists would call "rational" action in Greater Mussayeb. The arts of irrigation agriculture, in particular the urge to master them, seemed in Mesopotamia to lie in some dream-like Lethe beyond the lure of economic motivation. Is there any reason to believe that the nomads of Tunisia, also largely illiterate, would be more responsive than those of Iraq?

In making its proposals, the case study bends to the imperatives of economics by recognizing that no remedial measures can be undertaken that damage family incomes, already at an abysmal level. Another problem arises from the expenses needed for remedies that will yield little return in the short term—which is to say, ordinary investment criteria will not support investments in saving land of such limited productivity. The case study thereupon suggests that the aboveground should be rescued by riches drawn from belowground. Resources such as oil, ores, and phosphates should be asked to make a contribution to the low but sustainable productivity of the arid surface. The authors suggest, in short, that in the interests of agriculture, ordinary investment criteria be suspended for mining. This is not to say that such a solution is impossible. It is to indicate that the social and economic solutions to the problems of desertification are intricate and difficult—in Oglat Merteba and elsewhere—and that in this domain, unlike the domain of the physical, present knowledge may not be enough to tell us what to do.

7

EGHAZER AND AZAWAK

"Contrary to the image of the land"

THE TUAREG of the Aïr Mountains remember 1915 as *Awetay wan Mayatta*, "the year of Mayatta," named for a well near Dakoro, 300 km south of the pastures that compose their usual rangeland. That was the final year of drought in the Sahel, in the wide pastures of Niger, the colony of the French, not yet an independent country. To save their herds of livestock, the Aïr Tuareg had led them on the far trek out of the Sahel and down into the region that had come to be called the Sudan, to the well of Mayatta in the more favored savanna below what is normally the 400-mm isohyet. Although the French had moved into Niger 15 years earlier, a last gasp of the great wind of colonial expansion, this long trek was an expression of cultural vitality which the Tuareg had not yet lost and which would carry them into revolt two years later, after the rains had returned.

In 1900 the first military columns occupied Tahoua, but the Kel Dinnik Tuareg did not submit until the end of 1901. The presence of this new authority brought profound changes, not only in society but in spatial organization. The authorities isolated the pastoralists and confined them to the nomadic zone in order to free the agriculturalists from the pastoralists' hold; the nomads were thus deprived of southern markets and cereals which were indispensable to them. Colonization brought with it a partitioning of territory which was completely contrary to the image of the land held by the Tuareg pastoralists.

These restraints, as well as the reduction in the chiefs' power and the creation of new chiefs designed to increase the number of intermediaries, became intolerable to the warriors who tried to free themselves from this new authority by the great revolt of 1917 which mobilized the

EGHAZER and AZAWAK

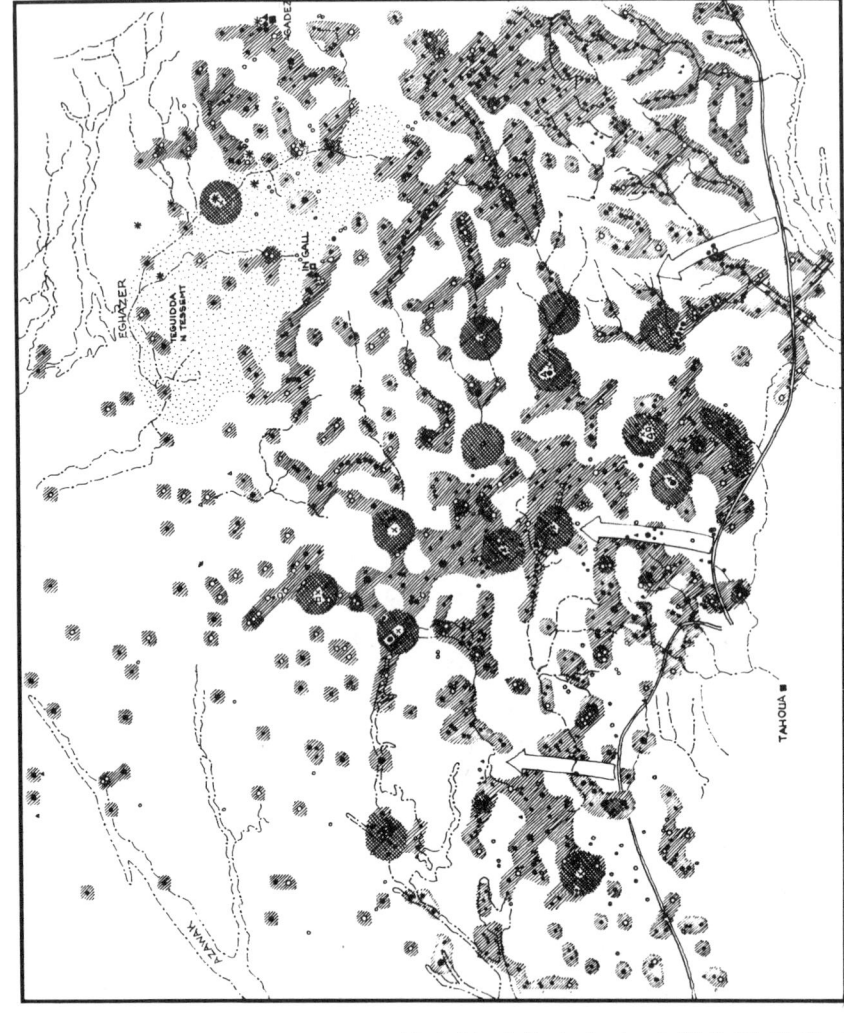

Eghazer is in the northeast corner. Azawak is everything southeast of the wadi Azawak as far as the line, looping over the south, that shows the legal limit of cultivation. The arrows show where cultivation has invaded beyond the legal limit. The dots mark watering points, and the circles show piospheres of desertified ground surrounding the watering points, linking up in large desertified patches.

WEST AFRICA Isohyets in millimeters of rainfall
Eghazer and Azawak form a rectangle in Niger and Mali

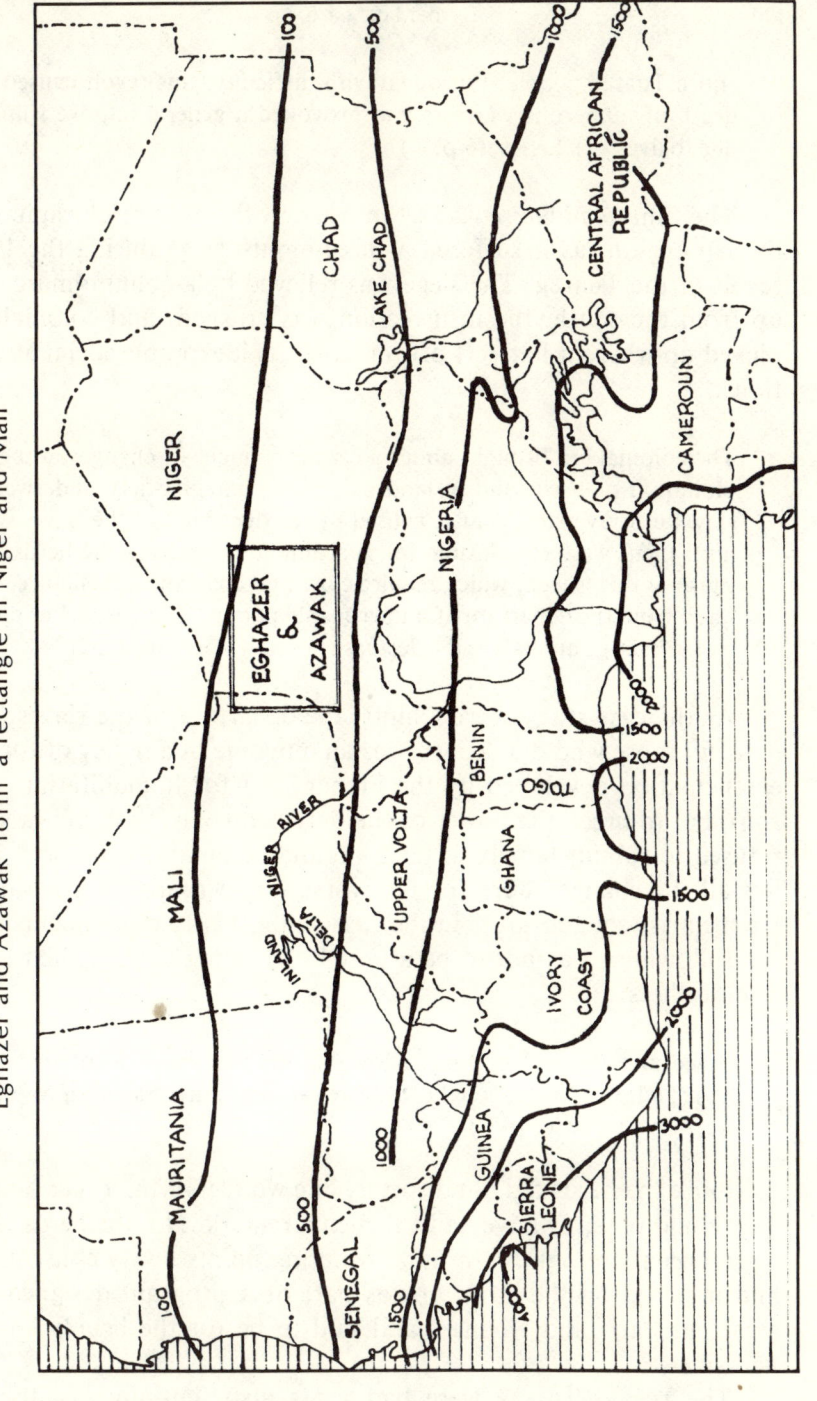

entire Tuareg people. Put down with difficulty, this revolt caused the death of numerous warriors and provoked a general impoverishment due to livestock losses. (6 p.50)

The film *Beau Geste* was set in Agadès, the mud-brick capital of the Aïr region, as it suffered a three-month siege during the 1917 revolt of the Tuareg. The siege was relieved by a column marching up from the south, the insurrection was crushed, and colonialism picked up where it had left off, creating its inexorable social alterations.

> The colonial era brought about a certain number of changes in the exploitation of herds and in land use. . . . Tuareg society underwent a slow but irreversible change caused by the departure of the slaves who, until then, were responsible for guarding and watering the herds. Because of this, sheep, which require close and constant surveillance, suffered from the departure of numerous shepherds. There was thus an increase in large animals and a decrease in small stock. (6, p.52)

As the case study merely hints, the departure of the slaves, the *bouzou*, those who did depart, was an outcome of a policy of forced emancipation developed by the French, not for humanitarian reasons, but to break the power of the only people in West Africa who refused to submit tamely to invasion and colonial domination. But not all the changes were for the worse—or perhaps the specialists from Paris, collaborators in the case study, inserted comments like the following so as not to be accused of turning against their own grandfathers.

> Peace and the end of raids allowed a greater dispersal of men and herds, who no longer sought to cluster around warriors out of a fear of surprise attack. (6, p.52)

Since the herds did not disperse, one wonders what other motive they could possibly have had for such a remark. No, the herds clustered ever more tightly—around watering points newly constructed and imposed on the landscape as part of a program designed far away, in Paris and Niamey, and said to be for the benefit of the herdsmen.

The years 1930–32 were bad years also, but not because of drought or insurrection. This was a time when the desert locust appeared as it always does, suddenly and mysteriously out of its unknown breeding grounds in remote wastelands, to devastate the millet crops, creating famine for herdsmen as well as farmers.

> From 1940 to 1943 a new drought affected the Sahelian zone as a whole, but it was less severe than in 1910–15. (6, p.23)

The great droughts come and go. And the rains were to fail again in 1968. For a complex of reasons, there was no moving south this time to the distant well of Mayatta. As the drought deepened, finally catching the eye of the world, international agencies began to organize programs of relief, establishing refugee camps, one of them right there in the parched Azawak, and a debate began in the far-off United Nations, set off by the Sahelian countries themselves, that was to conclude ultimately in the summoning of an international Conference on Desertification. But the Tuareg, in the eye of disaster, did nothing at all. The case study provides an account of their suicidal fatalism, oddly attributing it to custom rather than to the demoralization that had at last ensued on almost three generations of unremitting assault on their unique culture, on their once wild and free way of life.

> If organized in time, when animals were still strong enough to move, flight to the south appeared to be the most logical course to take; it was a matter of fleeing before the danger and seeking refuge in a more welcoming region which was anyway better watered. This solution was suggested by the government itself, and in September, 1972, a mission, led by the Minister of Nomadic and Saharan Affairs, proposed to the chief of the third group at Tchin Tabaraden that he send his herds to the Gaya region. This region had been spared from the drought, and contacts had officially been made with the inhabitants there. The suggestion was not taken up.
> The reactions of the Wodaabe Fulani and of the Kel Tamasheq [Tuareg] were very different. More recently arrived in the area, the Fulani are much more mobile than the Tuareg; they can without great difficulty leave an area where they have problems. The absence of a centralized chieftancy leads to greater adaptability which is shown by flight from human hostility and from environmental hostility; the drought demonstrated this. Bororo cattle are also much better walkers than those of the Tuareg, and this encourages mobility. The Tuareg are more attached to the area and to the valley which is their natural setting. Their political and social structure tends to unite groups and tribes and creates a rather precise spatial organization in which everyone

has a place. Because of this, they do not leave their country except in final necessity. Thus, all the Fulani left the region; in the most striking case, 68 families registered at In Gall went as far as Cameroon. But the Kel Tamasheq did not leave the area. Some families went off, but only for a short distance. The area remained occupied for the most part by tribes in their traditional setting, with only a few families missing. (6, pp.68-69)

This bizarre piece of anthropological rationalization explains everything except why the Kel Tamasheq did not move south as they did in 1915. In so doing, it suggests that a people whose way of life is based on mobility are not really mobile, and that in the great drought of 1968-73, the "final necessity" had not yet arrived. What this *conte de fées* seems hesitant to suggest is that the Tuareg had lost their defenses against drought, perhaps because the brilliant strategies that had once worked so well against this visitation had been stripped from them by policies for which those who had authorized the study, or their friends, were responsible. In any case, the Tuareg stayed where they were—to be destroyed. In Agadès Province, which includes the plain of the Eghazer, herdsmen lost 88% of 120,000 head of cattle, 80% of 100,000 sheep, 70% of 200,000 goats, and 45% of 100,000 camels.

The 100-mm isohyet, designated as separating the very arid sub-desert from the true Sahara to the north, passes directly across the broad plain of the Eghazer, which occupies a typical peripheral depression at the edge of an ancient massif, that of the Aïr Mountains. In rainier epochs, a river drained the Eghazer after first collecting the runoff from the western slopes of the Aïr. It flowed northwestward into the Azawak, once a considerable stream that bent the direction of the drainage by turning and heading southwestward and south into the River Niger. All this drainage is now fossilized, empty stream beds, dry wadis, scratching a network over the Ioullemmden basin, a vast, monotonous, sedimentary plain which occupies most of the northwestern part of the Republic of Niger and adjacent sections of Mali. The word "Azawak" has been stretched to cover this basin centering on the new town of Tchin Tabaraden, a lonely cluster of mud-brick structures far to the southeast of the ancient riverbed. The arid Azawak is centered in the true Sahel between the 200-mm and 400-mm isohyets, somewhat more favored than the Eghazer but still a region best suited to nomadic pastoralism. Stock losses in the district of Tchin Tabaraden were proportionally less during the great drought but were about the same in absolute numbers since the region supports higher stocking levels.

Like the rest of the Sahel, the Azawak and Eghazer have provided pasture for livestock as far back as memory extends. It is a region of great climatic risk, as represented by the drought and by the extreme variability of rainfall even in good years. It serves as another illustration of the rule that variability increases with aridity. At Agadès, with a mean annual rainfall of 158.0 mm calculated over 53 years, the amount of rain that actually arrives can range from 25% of "normal" (1970) to 182% (1958). At Tahoua, on the southern edge of the study zone, an annual mean of 395.4 mm was determined over 51 years, with variability ranging from 53% (1942) to 154% (1936). Tahoua, with more rain, is at the same time less variable. The season when rain falls is short, lasting in the study area for a mere two months, from about July 15 to September 15. When rain does come, it is irregular.

> Irregular rainfall distribution over time can mean that large annual totals, even above average, may often not be beneficial to the vegetation. Here the idea of "useful rain" should be introduced; that is, the portion of rainfall that has a direct effect on the development of plant cover. In the Sudanian zone, rain that comes too early with too long an interval between each rainfall often obliges the farmers to sow their crops several times. The same is true of the natural Sahelian vegetation; rain which comes too early in the season and is not followed by more triggers the vegetation to germinate and grow, but it cannot survive the subsequent dry spell. If the rains return a month later, vegetation recovery can only come from those species with sufficient reserves and from the germination of a second stock of seeds whose dormancy has not been lifted by the earlier rain. In any case, the vegetation is thereby weakened, stunted and thinned out. (6, p.15)

Yet one must not think of the Sahel any more than of Oglat Merteba, as a place where people raise livestock out of desperation, as though driven there from more favored lands. That nomad, the Kel Tamasheq herdsman, loves his life and the remote country in which he has celebrated it for so long—or loved it before the colonial masters came—as can be seen in his scornful attitude toward farmers and a settled life. He is at home in the immense landscapes of the Azawak and Eghazer. The Sahara, so many of whose landmarks have names in Tamasheq, his language, is where he lives, where he has chosen to make a life. As long as pasture flourishes on its sweeping sandstone plains, northwestern Niger provides excellent conditions in which to herd animals. At altitudes ranging from 600 meters on the south edge of the Ader Mountains, declining slightly to 400 meters at the foot of the distant Aïr, these low plateaus are never too cold, and animals thrive in endless hours of sunshine. In the rainier south, toward the Guinea coast, lush vegetation provides a habitat for the tsetse fly, carrier of the dread trypanosomiasis, that sleeping sickness that is so deadly to livestock and from which the Sahel is mercifully free. Yet the subtropical Sahel is too hot for European breeds of cattle. No whiteface or shorthorns wander its ranges. The Peul, among them the Bororo Fulani, immigrants from the south who have moved into the Azawak only over the past 30 years, herd lyre-horned zebu with a prominent hump and a plain dark coat, much different from the small Azawak zebu kept by the Kel Tamasheq. For the latter, the prestige animal is the camel, found especially in the most arid regions at the desert's edge, grazing on pastures of alwat (*Schouwia thebaica*), which provides fodder as late as March, almost to the end of the long dry winter.

Social factors thus play a role in the choice of animal herded by different nomadic groups. Yet natural factors are not entirely forgotten. In the pastoral strategies developed by nomads on tracks followed here for a thousand years, a variety of animals will usually be herded, each species capable of taking advantage of different portions and products of landscapes, so monotonous at first glance, so varied in microtopography to the trained eye. Sheep and cattle graze while camels and goats browse with only occasional shifts in feeding styles. Goats are notorious for attacking anything digestible. Different stock have different preferences, drawing them by choice to different parts of the pasture and thus making optimum use of a mixed biomass.

Another element in pastoral strategy is provided by ancient relationships with settled farmers. Herdsmen exchange meat, milk products, and hides for the millet and sorghum which tide them over the driest part of the year, the season of *soudure*, when animals are lowest in milk production. When the harvest fails in the south, it has always been a disaster for the north as well. Sometimes the herdsman sells some of his animals to get cash for tobacco, tea, and sugar, for blankets and clothing, for the Kel Tamasheq have never been known as weavers, and their short-haired sheep yield no wool. An ancient custom formerly permitted the nomads to graze their flocks and herds on the stubble from the harvest in exchange for the manure which fertilizes the farmers' fields.

The nomad obtained further protection from an intricate pattern of loans and borrowings, animals moving along the lines drawn by kinship structures, and even occasionally outside them. This was a strategy that was more important in the days before vaccination campaigns eliminated those ancient epizootic afflictions, rinderpest and pleuropneumonia. In those days, when a pastoralist found his herds and flocks reduced by disease, he could restock by calling up old loans he had made, or by effecting new loans to be charged to his account. This network of borrowings constituted a classical insurance scheme in the Sahel, as among other nomadic societies.

Under rainfall regimes that are highly variable in space as well as in time, the essence of the nomad's strategy consists in his mobility, a characteristic also of the wildlife of arid lands. In northern Niger, erratic rain will fall here and not there, on this slope and not on that, filling these rocky basins with fresh runoff and leaving those empty. Long experience has taught the nomad where he has the best chance of obtaining water and pasture—and salt, too, also necessary to stock. The different animals vary in the distance they can graze away from water. Camels with their remarkable adaptations to desert conditions have to be watered only once in six days during the dry season, and with their long legs can browse up to 80 km away from a watering point. Cattle, in contrast, must drink every other day—or, better, every day—during the dry season, and, depending somewhat on type, cannot graze more than half a day's walk away from the well. The rainy season scatters the landscape with pools, but the dry season forces the herds to stick close to the vicinity of rivers or permanent wells. A type of transhumance has prevailed in northern Niger, with nomads from Tchin Tabaraden moving north in the rainy season to the pastures of the Eghazer along routes that remain fairly constant from year to year. In the dry season, the herds have recently been taken to one or another of the new boreholes constructed by the government in Niamey as part of a program intended to open up previously unused parts of the pasture.

The study zone is a large region. It comprises a little over 100,000 km^2 or 10% of the Republic of Niger. With its 6,700 people, Agadès is the metropolis of this region. Some 2,300 other persons classified in 1977 as townspeople were then living in In Gall and in Teguidda-n-Tesemt. The rest of the people in this region are counted as nomads, including those living in the communities of Tchin Tabaraden and Abalak. Some 87,000 of these are Tuaregs identified not racially but culturally, by the fact, among others, that they speak the Tamasheq language. Originally, they were white, as many of them still are in complexion, a part of that wide north African *ethnos* loosely called Berbers, but many of them are now quite dark, the result of intermarriage with other Africans. The rest of the nomadic population consists of 9,600 Arabs who settled in the region at the end of the nineteenth-century with the permission of the Tuareg chiefs, almost the last independent act these chiefs were to make, and 7,600 Fulani, more recent arrivals, new inhabitants who penetrated the Azawak without asking leave of the Kel Tamasheq.

Nomads are not easy to count in a census, and a total population of 113,000 must be taken as an approximation of the demographic situation in the Azawak and the Eghazer in 1977. That less than 3% of Niger's population live on 10% of the national territory is no more than typical of the situation of nomads in all those places in the world in which they still direct the movement of flocks and herds, thinly occupying remote regions whose low productivity is often taken to be sufficient reason why only the most meager investments should be made in them. Roaming with their animals through scrub and grasslands far from the centers of political power, nomads by their very mobility are troublesome to bureaucracies and other forms of systematic administration. In the Sahel, nomads have seen their pastures shrink by recent northward incursions of rainfed cropping. Irrational colonial boundaries were drawn in the chancelleries of Europe by participants in power games utterly ignorant of African realities, and those lines split natural pastures and sliced across ancient nomadic pathways. In the Sahel, as elsewhere, the picturesque nomad finds himself at bay, an unwanted relic of an antique time, better off forgotten, when all of humanity was nomadic. In West Africa, the beginning of the end for the nomad could conceivably be dated back to that epic moment, five centuries ago, when the first caravels from Portugal sailed into the harbors of the Guinea coast to fracture the monopoly formerly enjoyed by the Kel Tamasheq and their nomadic colleagues on trans-Saharan trade. That would have been the beginning of an end, however, that required the colonial era for its final materialization.

Although colonialism often adopted a policy of governing through the medium of compliant local rulers, it never seemed to have occurred to the French to use the Tuareg in this way for all the military dominance exercised by these veiled warriors in the arid Sahel. Undoubtedly, they were not compliant enough. No, their refractory lack of submissiveness made of them naughty children in the eyes of scientific Europe, who found something infantile in anyone who had never seen a test tube, and the discipline mounted to bring the Tuareg into line was intended, first of all, to destroy their power and, secondly, to wreck their culture. In retrospect, it now seems weird that the murder and duplicity that characterized this example of the colonial order, only one among many such, could ever have been regarded as a natural corollary to the "civilizing mission" with its alleged transmission of profound human values. "The Tuareg does not have any more reason to exist than the American Indian," a French commander reported from Agadès. In 1917, lured to the Tanut wells under the pretext of voting for a new chief, Tuareg warriors were subjected by French soldiers to mass slaughter, an event now become the tragic theme of Tamasheq epic. There was no design in any of this—nor in the entire colonization of Niger, so far as that goes, other than to rule for the sake of ruling, and least of all was any thought given to the effects that cultural destruction might have on the sustained productivity of the land.

In the new nations created by the independence movement, the Tuareg found themselves under the control of ethnic groups whom they, in turn, had formerly controlled. A spirit of vengeance against the Kel Tamasheq might have been expected, sharpened by an inheritance of attitudes that new African bureaucrats acquired from the departing French along with the reins of new governments. It was a spirit that in Mali maintained unabated the assaults on Kel Tamasheq culture. But even where such animosity was lacking, as in Niger, the structure of the new situation, nothing more, was all that was needed to perpetuate the disadvantages of a nomadic people who, once the possessor of power, now found itself far away from those new centers in which power, now displayed in the modern manner, had come to be located. Jeremy Swift has commented on the way in which this fact of politics has affected land use in West Africa.

> The French conquest . . . set in motion the transfer of political power from many small competing local sources, based on a fluctuating balance between different traditional organizations, to central bureaucratic organizations which were inevitably less responsive to local conditions, including ecological conditions, than previously locally-based power had been; bureaucratically-appointed people are not subject to local pressures (their constituency is the bureaucracy itself, located in

the national capital) and so can remain unresponsive to the actual needs and conditions of local people and of the environment. Control over many aspects of natural resource use and conservation became vested in the machinery of central government (which however was inadequate to the task of imposing effective environmental conservation measures); meanwhile land users increasingly lost power to make decisions concerning their land. For a number of years they did well out of the increased security, better communications and technical improvements such as new wells. But they were losing ecological and economic flexibility; they were being forced into a market economy, and their own self-help mechanisms were breaking down. (73, p.4)

In independent Niger, intentions toward the Kel Tamasheq were outwardly good. Recognizing that under Sahelian economics, the nomadic style of harvesting arid pastures was the most efficient use that could be made of such thinly productive lands, Niger decided in 1960, just two years after independence, to solve the problem of dry-season water scarcity by digging boreholes that would reach deep groundwater and thereby bring additional pasture into productive use. This was part of a policy intended to increase the size of the herds to the financial benefit of the nation. The boreholes would be lined with cement where necessary and equipped with the pumps required to bring water up from great depth, such as the 690 meters of bore needed to tap the confined continental intercalary aquifer at a site with the appropriate name of Digdiga. To the objection that the boreholes would be expensive, the response was that the pastoralists themselves, whose wealth in flocks and herds would be increased by the increase in water, could afford to help pay for them through the imposition of a use tax, which would also give the herdsmen a sense of responsibility for the borehole project, a feeling that financial participation was, after all, participation of some kind or other. To the objection that the boreholes would cause desertification by the concentration of stock around them during the long dry months, a plan was developed that would fix a maximum stocking rate around each site. This figure was set at 5,000 tropical bovine units, or 10,000 head of all species, on the basis of a usable area of pasture with a radius of 8 km, as far away from water as cattle could graze, to be used for eight dry months of the year.

As the first 15 boreholes came into use between 1961 and 1969, it became suddenly obvious that the objections that had been raised to them were not going to be met. The government finally did not dare to ask for a financial contribution from the pastoralists for the use of the wells, since herdsmen were already resentful, so it was said, believing that their cattle taxes exceeded the imposts required of settled farmers. As for limiting the number of animals around the boreholes, that, too, turned out to be impossible since, so the excuse went, any such limitation would give the appearance of discriminating to the benefit of richer herdsmen or of favoring one ethnic group over another. So in the end no control of stocking rates was exercised as the Fulani extended their northward migrations deep into the Azawak, attracted by the lure of water, pushed from the rear by illegal but nonetheless advancing cultivation. As the government wrung its hands, so to speak, declaring how impossible it had proved to be to give good water to some and refuse it to others, animal densities around the boreholes reached as much as four times the planned density.

This crowding of livestock around the new wells introduced an annual pattern of semistarvation. Before the return of the summer rains—in mid-May at Tahoua, mid-July at Agadès—the pasture around boreholes would be totally consumed, even in good years, to the last leaf and rootlet within the 8–12 km radius imposed by access to water. Trampling by densely packed herds caused changes in the structure and chemical composition of the soil, with consequent changes in vegetation, including the importation of outside varieties via seed contained in animal feces or clinging to the coats of livestock. Concentrations of animals were destructive to trees and woody perennials.

Sometimes, however, concentrations of stock resulted in improvement to the pasture surrounding boreholes, or so the study contended. It is true that trampling can improve the water intake of soil by breaking surface crusts in action that has the effect of plowing and seeding, the seeds drilled into the soil by pounding hooves. The pungent *Cymbopogon proximus* was replaced on dune formations by the preferred dogtown grass (*Aristida mutabilis*), and the latter was occasionally replaced around watering points by denser stands of palatable *Tribulus terrestris* and *Citrullus lanatus*. A higher proportion of annuals, however tasty they may be, results in lowered soil-holding capacity. Nonetheless, reports prepared in the late 1960s were optimistic. According to one agrologist:

> Changes in pasture produced by dry-season grazing last only as long as that grazing continues. Indeed, it has been noted that annual, perennial and native plants have sufficient regenerative power, due to their seeds,

to reappear as soon as the range is deserted for at least one year with good rainfall. The sometimes more spectacular increase in the relative abundance of annual plants from the first year in the most heavily stocked zones, and later in burned areas, is a good reflection of what happens in rangelands, but is too diffuse to be easily measured. Nonetheless, it is an improvement, taking into account the preference of animals for annual forage plants. (6, p.77)

When the question arises if grazing can be managed so as to cause pastures no damage, the answer should emphasize the fact that good pastoral management improves pastures, that proper grazing practices yield better vegetation in both density and quality. The study cites the agrologist Granier:

Non-exploitation encourages litter to accumulate which forms a screen inhibiting the growth of new plants. It also allows an increase in wildlife which attacks the bark of young trees and increases the risk of their dying. (6, p.93)

The ancestors of domestic animals were themselves once wildlife and thus an integral element in the ecosystems that formed their habitats. Once again the point is made that domesticated herbivores improve the pastures they use by promoting the germination and growth of plants. Like the sheep rancher in the Gascoyne, the Sahel pastoralist becomes a part of his habitat. He blends into it, a link in its chains of life. He and his herds belong there; they are not intruders. This vast land, pocked with thorny acacia trees or marked by the occasional monument of a fat baobab, would be worse off without them.

Although stock concentrations were dense around watering points in the years before the drought, much of the dry season pasture remained unused. According to estimates of carrying capacity made locally in the sixties, the rangelands of the Azawak and Eghazer never achieved their full capacity. This was the situation—or at least this was how the situation was perceived—when, in 1968, the summer monsoon developed weakly, bringing poor rainfall to the Sahel and ushering in six years of drought across the full width of Africa. The extent of drought in Niger can be illustrated by rainfall statistics from Agadès, in the arid, northern reaches of the study zone, and at Tahoua, just to the south of the study zone on the line between the arid and the semiarid.

	1968	1969	1970	1971	1972	1973	1974	1975	Normal
Agadès	163.2	80.7	39.7	92.6	73.9	76.3	136.4	130.9	158.0
Tahoua	407.6	317.0	421.7	267.9	266.2	244.9	421.2	421.1	395.4

Neither Agadès nor Tahoua was affected by the first year of the drought which far to the west in Upper Volta was already raising a call for emergency measures. Still, according to Caldwell (36, p.19), Agadès thought of 1968 as a dry year because the rains were badly distributed and came to a halt prematurely. The figures show, as much as anything, the variability of the rainfall. Here and there in the Sahel, despite the overwhelming prevalence of drought, one locality might receive normal or even above-average rainfall, as Tahoua did in the third year of drought. On the other hand, dry conditions persisted somewhat at Agadès even after 1974 when good rain returned to the lands below the Sahara.

During these six lean years, Agadès saw its normal rainfall cut not quite in half, while Tahoua, one of the luckiest places in the region, experienced a decline of only 19%. Caldwell said that "Tahoua was so fortunate that enquiries there about the drought failed to elicit much response" (36, p.19). Elsewhere, the great drought lasted so long and its effects were so devastating that climatologists began to wonder whether or not it represented the opening scene of a long-term trend toward more arid conditions. The period 1931-60, the mean annual rainfall of which determined the location of the isohyets as drawn on the map on page 119, now began to appear as perhaps a favored epoch, wetter than usual, no proper basis for determining mean climatic data. Perhaps that was true of the world as a whole. If estimates of global agricultural possibilities should turn out to have been based on an exceptionally benign era, then they might be ludicrously optimistic.

On the other hand, this had been the third major drought in this century, and good records of temperature and precipitation did not go back as long as a century in West Africa, too short a time out of which to detect a clear trend. The theorists pointed to the position the drought occupied in the pattern of global atmospheric circulation. It had occurred in coordination with something that had taken place—or had failed to take place—off Bermuda. Seated there in the subtropical north Atlantic, a zone of high atmospheric pressure, a part of the subtropical subsidence zone known as the Bermuda High, ordinarily migrates north and south with seasons. As it moves north in summer, as if seeking always to stay at about the same temperature, like a vacationer who prefers Bar Harbor, it permits the intertropical discontinuity on its southern edge to move northward also, and that, in turn, allows the monsoon rain to sweep over the coastline into West Africa.

This Bermuda High, however, had been behaving strangely, lingering in summer too far to the south during the years of drought, blocking the northward movement of the rain-bearing monsoon out of the Gulf of Guinea. Why was it acting that way? Well, for one thing, air in high arctic latitudes had become colder than usual. In fact, the whole northern hemisphere had embarked on a cooling trend beginning about 1945, following 60 years of steadily rising temperatures. The Bermuda High didn't have to move so far north to find itself in its preferred temperature regime. The question then becomes, Why was the northern hemisphere cooling down?

As to that, no one seemed to be quite sure. Perhaps it was because of a recent episode of volcanic eruptions occurring around the world and throwing huge quantities of dust into the air, making sunsets brilliant in New York City while blocking the incoming solar radiation—in which case, the cooling trend would prove to be only temporary, lasting only long enough to allow the dust to settle. Or it was because of the "human volcano," a term devised by University of Wisconsin climatologist Reid Bryson to describe the dust injected into the atmosphere by the ever denser technology of man—in which case the human species would be faced by another of those "critical choices," as they have come to be called. Or perhaps the earth was moving into a new configuration in its orbital relations to the sun, as proposed in a theory elaborated in the 1920s by the Yugoslav astronomer Milutin Milankovitch, a theory revived when it was noticed that its suggestions correspond well with the advances and retreats of recent ice ages. If Milankovitch had the answer, then cooling was perhaps here to stay, for a long time, perhaps long enough to mobilize the glaciers and bring on a new ice age. There is something poetic to be found in the odd fact that one of the first signs of that menacing prospect, if it really were a possibility, would be a prolonged drought in a part of Africa, the Sahel, not too far from the equator.

Amidst this climatic confusion, one thing at least was certain, and that was that the climate had indeed changed in the Sahel during the years in which the drought was in force. Agadès has an aridity index of 0.06, meaning, as previously indicated, that the "normal" precipitation is less than one-sixteenth of what the incoming radiation is capable of evaporating. But during the drought, precipitation was less while potential evapotranspiration was higher because there were fewer cloudy days. In 1972, for example, the aridity index at Agadès was certainly no more than 0.03, while Tahoua, normally 0.16, could hardly have exceeded 0.10 in that year. In other words, in 1972 Agadès had a climate that was typical not of an arid region but of the true Sahara, while Tahoua, instead of occupying the boundary between the arid and the semiarid, was experiencing a fully arid climate. In short, all the isohyets were shifted southward, as shown on the lower map on page 119. While their city remained in the same place, the people of Agadès had been transported into the desert. But then, to take a longer view, the climate is seen to be never the same from any one year to the next. Isohyets dance up and down across the Sahel in a never ending jig. This is the situation to which the nomadic pastoralist of the Sahel is required to adapt himself.

Some of the worst effects of drought could be avoided if only its arrival could somehow be predicted. Successive years of low rainfall are certain to arrive sooner or later in all arid regions, but whether this will be sooner or later is something that not even the most experienced herdsman has any way of telling. If only he had some way of knowing in advance, he could cut the size of his herds in a sensible and systematic way that would maintain good prices for the stock and would provide him with the capital needed to restock upon the return of good weather. Advance knowledge would enable the herdsman to make a fully opportunistic use of his pastures, as he cannot now do. The sad truth is that climate cannot be predicted, not even one year in advance, nor is there any immediate prospect for the development of reliable long-range predictions. Approaches have been made to this distant possibility through the establishment of *teleconnections*—causal relationships between distant phenomena, as between drought in the Sahel and the movement of the Bermuda High. Other attempts to establish a basis for long-range prediction have been made through the modeling of climates. One such model, incidentally, showed that the creation of lakes in the central Sahara made by filling interior drainage basins would have no effect on its desert climate beyond a slight increase in rainfall on the slopes of a distant mountain range. But as for making long-range predictions, no such model has yet been able to handle the colossal number of variables involved so as to faithfully reproduce what happens in the atmosphere of the earth in all its remarkable complexity. And so drought, the enemy, moves in, silently, always unexpected.

All the time the herdsman knows that sooner or later this enemy will arrive, yet the fact of its arrival, when it happens, seems always to affect him as a kind of hideous surprise, a visitation by evil forces. Rapp views drought as the important engine of desertification, each successive drought leaving the land in ever worse condition (63, p.29). The herdsman hesitates to reduce his stock in one dry year—the rains may well return to normal the next year, and he can certainly get his animals through one bad season, even two. By the time the drought is well established, dried-up pastures are being overgrazed to extinction by numbers of stock they could have nourished easily in a good year. In the recent drought in the Sahel, the deep wells and boreholes never ran out of water, although watering points along the exodus routes did dry up. But even if the pastoralist had managed a successful escape to the south, as many of the Fulani herdsman did, he would have found the market for meat in a state of collapse, glutted by everyone trying to sell at once. By 1973 in northern Nigeria, at the end of the escape route, cattle prices had dropped from the usual $60 to $100 per head to as low as $4 (36, p.50). In a way it might be said that nature takes a hand in establishing conditions that will lead to the recovery of drought-stricken pastures after the return of good rain. It does this by the cruel mechanism of annihilating the previous livestock so that fresh plant growth will not be consumed until the vegetation has somewhat recovered. In the worst of the drought, the Azawak and the Eghazer were never emptied of water. What killed stock was the destruction of pasture. Like the sheep in the droughts in the Gascoyne, the animals starved to death.

> After the rainy season of 1972, animals began to die in great numbers. Although pools lasted for a shorter period, thus reducing the length of time that neighboring pastures could be used, groundwater in the study area did not vary to the extent of depriving animals of water. Of the two essentials in the life of the herd, only one, pasture, was missing: Animals died mainly of hunger. (6, p.68)

Livestock was part of an above-ground biomass that a shifting climate made the environment no longer capable of supporting. It is surprising that the destruction of the above-ground biomass did not include more people, even though the drought gave what time may reveal as the *coup de grâce* to the culture of the Tuareg, marking the end of one heroic way of life in sub-Saharan Africa. Not only did the drought kill the Tuareg's beloved animals, it destroyed the structure of his family and his tribe, all winnowed off at last to refugee camps, and on to the ends of the earth.

Yet, as Caldwell said, "The drought publicity hid the vital truth. The real lesson was not how easily man succumbed to the drought, but how tenacious he was in managing his survival" (36, p.26). As the dry years moved on to their 1973 climax, the Niger and Senegal rivers ceased to flood, and the great inland delta of the Niger, the principal focus of Sahelian life, remained dry. Lake Chad broke up into ponds, no longer one coherent body of water. In six countries—Senegal, Mauritania, Mali, Upper Volta, Niger, and Chad—croplands were devastated, with harvests cut to less than half their usual yield. With their tax base annihilated, these six countries, four of them among the poorest in the world—and as such, appearing on the United Nations list of "least developed nations"—were by 1973 approaching a state of economic collapse. Yet the Malthusian impact on the populations of those countries was minimal. That the drought had caused 100,000 deaths became a constant refrain in the media, but there was little basis for asserting such a figure (36, p.24). Starvation is a most difficult malady to measure, since its debilitated victims can always be said to die of something else, and it will be that something else that ends up as a record in the rolls of vital statistics. During the drought, particularly toward its end, there was some upsurge in mortality from contagious diseases—measles and meningitis, particularly—affecting mostly children in the refugee camps. That was plain to be seen, as death by starvation is never so plain to see.

There is no doubt that lives were saved by the establishment of the refugee centers as a part of international relief operations. Many Sahelians simply saved themselves—by eating wild game, severely depleted over the past century, and the seeds, berries, and burrs of wild plants. There were mass migrations in every direction—even Agadès, in the heart of the stricken area, had doubled its tiny population by 1973. A majority headed out of the most arid parts of the Sahel in the direction of those southerly districts where livestock could graze on the stubble of failed crops, and on to the cities where friends or jobs might be found. Along with the price of cattle, the price of night watchmen plummeted in Kano, the metropolis of northern Nigeria. Nor did the streams of migrants stop there, continuing rather on to the great cities on the Guinea coast—Lagos and Ibadan, Dakar and Abidjan—with their promise of industrial employment. Caldwell made the point that

> nomads, like food gatherers and hunters in other parts of the world, are often happier, if forced, to take the leap from their kind of life to urban employment than to farming which is a far more specialized way of life with a mystique all its own. (36, p.29)

Some migrants headed in the other direction, north to the oil fields of Algeria, and on and on, some to Europe, to jobs in Common Market countries.

Many of these wanderers would never return to the rangelands after their conversion from the nomadic life, wild and free, after they had been melted down in the cities into the finally indistinguishable paste of the urban proletariat. Viewed from this perspective, the drought is seen to have brought about a social revolution; at the least, it accelerated a continuing revolution marked by an uninterrupted stream of migrants moving out of the Sahel even in years of good rainfall. And in its urban effects, this drought went somewhat beyond the dumping of refugees into the already overcrowded cities to the south. It generated urban stirrings in the Sahel itself.

Back in the pastures, six years of drought pinpointed those portions of the range most vulnerable to desertification. These lay in general on higher ground, where the roots of trees could no longer strain down to a sinking watertable—*Acacia raddiana, A. ehrenbergiana, A. laeta*—varieties of the acacia tree, and *Balanites aegyptiaca* with its deep root system tended to survive, but the *Commiphora africana* with its wide but shallow root system proved to be most vulnerable, and the plains around Tchin Tabarden and Tassara, as well as the Tegama Plateau region, became littered with dead trees. The effects on the grass cover were even more brutal. Good pasture perennials such as *Cymbopogon proximus, C. giganteus, Andropogon gayanus,* and *Cyperus conglomeratus* had simply vanished over immense areas. A number of annual varieties also disappeared, among them *Blepharis linariifolia* and *Schoenefeldia gracilis*, while *Aristida mutabilis* came close to vanishing. Livestock were reduced to feeding on *Cenchrus*, trying to avoid the burrs, while this genus survived even in areas of extreme water deficit. A measurement made on one pasture that had been producing 1,500 to 2,000 kg of dry matter per hectare before the drought showed a dry-matter production of 360 kg in 1974, with 80% of the surface naked of vegetation. This was said to be typical.

> Desertification does not . . . mean a steady encroachment by the Sahara; it is not a front whose advance can be calculated over the last 40

years. Desertification happens at particular points; *it is patchy, not linear*. (6, p.92)

And where were those patches?

The "centers" which lead to concentric rings of desertification because of the burden they impose on the environment are doubtless inevitable, but they should not be multiplied. Only strict enforcement of legislation can limit the effects of these concentrations and reduce illegal cutting of trees and disorganized sale of wood. (6, p.92)

It is as true in Niger as it is in the rest of the Third World that the destruction of woody vegetation is a major cause of desertification, and that this destruction is most intense in piospheres surrounding population concentrations. In Niger, however, the principal location of those concentric rings of desertification was to be found around the new boreholes, where pastures devastated by starving animals linked up in widening tatters of desertification like holes in a shredded garment. There is a curious reluctance to see this in the case study, which prefers to see desertification centered on human communities, just as there is hesitation to admit that the boreholes were a misapplication of technology made blind by a failure to take an ecological perspective. Perhaps this is because criticism of the boreholes might constitute criticism of the government in Niamey, which authorized the case study, and whose policy it was to drill the boreholes as part of a broader policy seeking to increase the size of the herds and thereby to enhance the nation's wealth, perhaps even improve its balance-of-payments situation by providing meat for export.

Although the new watering points were at first welcomed by the pastoralists of the Azawak, before they discovered that they would demand a hidden price in the form of destructive competition with invading Fulani, there was no question but that this was a technology designed and implanted without advance consultation with the people who would be most affected by it and without obtaining their advance consent to it. As will be seen, this procedure is a very common accompaniment to technological blunders. In Niger, also, it was a procedure that represented a continuation of the high-handed tactics of the colonial power, now transferred to a new, independent government. In addition, it represented a continuity of policy, developed originally by the French in an almost desperate effort to make Niger self-supporting, which is to say, capable of paying the costs of the colonial bureaucracy. It was this policy that demanded that cash crops be grown for export and thus set in motion another major cause of desertification in Niger, the invasion of pastoral areas by cultivation.

In 1961, in legislative action related to its broad arid-lands policy, which included the plans to drill boreholes, the government in Niamey restricted cultivation to the south of the 300-mm isohyet, a line running along the southern edge of the study zone and passing just to the north of Tahoua. Like other well meaning examples of legislative action in Niger, this law, too, proved impossible to enforce. Both subsistence cropping and cash cropping persisted in their advance into the Azawak, reaching to and beyond the 200-mm isohyet to the north of Tchin Tabaraden, first contracting the ancient pastures of the nomadic peoples to the north, then stripping them open to attacks by the processes of desertification, particularly in those areas laid bare by the plow just in time to greet the drought. This incursion, carried out at first in spite of the government, then continued with the connivance of government, so ruined extensive regions that they were no longer useful even for livestock, much less for further cultivation. It was amazing that this invasion of pastures was being permitted at the very time that pastoral herds were being encouraged to expand their numbers.

> Before the drought, the study area had not reached its maximum stocking rate in spite of the very rapid increase in herds. But these figures must be examined carefully: They are of value only where there is balanced pasture use with herds distributed equally throughout the region. However, during the few dry-season months, herds are concentrated around wells and pumping stations. That is why pastoral use of the area is discontinuous in time and space, even in a favorable period like the one that preceded the drought. Although the region as a whole is not overloaded, there are very high concentrations at particular points, as shown by the counts at pumping stations. (6, p.67)

In this odd statement, the "few dry-season months" referred to happen to constitute most of the year, when concentration around watering points is, for livestock, a physiological necessity. As it continues blandly onward, the Niger case study stands in ever more curious contrast to the admirable frankness of the Iraq case study. Here in a red-earth, Saharan dream, the situation is vaporous, ectoplasmic, a fantasy domain in which laws are passed, never to be enforced—legislation against the cutting of trees and other woody vegetation proved also to be unenforceable—in which explanations are supplied out of weird twists given to the facts and in which a stage is carefully set for the drama of destruction, not only of pastures but also of the ancient life of the pastoralists. Piospheres of degradation surrounding boreholes were already linking up when the drought struck against all the apparent anticipations of national policy. Nor could the Tuareg respond, stripped as they had been of all their usual strategies for dealing with drought—this, the heart of the matter, referred to in the case study only in passing reference. Crops were now being grown around the well of Mayatta—illegally, according to a strict interpretation of the law. But that didn't matter. No one wanted desperate pastoralists down there churning up the fields.

Localized overgrazing and unwise extensions of cultivation—both frowned on *de jure* but in fact approved—were not the only practices that were putting excessive pressure on rangelands before the onset of drought. The Tuareg, birth rate estimated at 52 per thousand per year and death rate at 27, were thus showing the high annual growth rate of 2.5%, while the Fulani, birth rate and death rate estimated at 41 and 22 per thousand per year, respectively, were increasing their numbers at an annual rate of 1.9%. The only reason that both peoples were not growing even more rapidly was because of their still comparatively high death rates, but these could be expected to come down as the needles of modern antibiotics were carried ever farther into the arid zones. These rapidly expanding populations were placing ever increasing pressure on the pastures through their continually rising demand for firewood, the commonest reason for the destruction of woody perennials in years of good rainfall. Yet regardless of what disaster happened to be unfolding in Niger, there were those incorrigible optimists who persisted in viewing events as bearing with them an increase in well-being.

> The opening of public works [the boreholes] with free access changed pastoral land use. Self-management of pastures by the nomads themselves no longer worked, and the obvious increase in well being produced by abundant water of good quality was offset by a certain disorder in the destruction of men and herds. (6, p.64)

To find any increase in well-being in something offset by the destruction of men and herds is to take an astoundingly narrow technological perspective. It is also a refusal to see that the two things, abundant water and destruction, are fatally interconnected.

One can conclude, after the recent drought, that desertification becomes apparent particularly through qualitative change in the vegetation. But many of the changes are due to overgrazing and to methods of exploitation which always compound the effects of rainfall shortage. Although man has scarcely any control over climate, he can change the organization of pastoralism and promote rational use of pasture and vegetation in its broadest sense. (6, p.83)

The rational use of pasture and vegetation—this is precisely what must be promoted, as the Conference on Desertification and its scientist advisers repeatedly insisted, if desertification is to be halted on rangelands. Against this bland, almost trivial but undeniably good advice, the case study set in the Azawak and Eghazer fixes some brutal political realities. The pasture and vegetation in those arid regions were already subject to rational use until a succession of political policies encouraged a train of events that culminated in the destruction of the culture and society that had engaged in rational use of the land. The curious tone of the case study gives rise to the suspicion that the continuity of policy in Niger, from the colonialists, operating with the support of advanced technology, to the technologists themselves, replacing the former in the same setting, has all been carried out for no other purpose than to reduce the Kel Tamasheq to that pitiful condition in which they have no choice but to fulfill the yearnings of the technologists and take lessons from them in how to be "rational."

There is no doubt that policy in Niger shows that misapplied technology can be an important cause of desertification. In the case of the Sahel boreholes, technology was applied for national purposes and not for the purposes of the people concerned, an ethical lapse disguised by official pronouncements that the people, after all, were being brought the gift of water, an "obvious increase in well being." The incident serves to illustrate the community development principle, increasingly coming to be recognized, that outside experts are not in a position to tell people what is good for them or to make other value judgments on their behalf. It also illustrates the social axiom that people are the true wealth of a nation and that a cavalier attitude to their welfare, as they alone are capable of conceiving it, is the easiest way to damage the nation. Unfortunately, all these fine lessons are too late for the unique concatenation of traits that once constituted the culture of the Kel Tamasheq.

In 1974, returning rainfall bounced isohyets back northward, and vegetation began to return with the rain, a reminder that the natural resiliency of arid ecosystems should never be underestimated.

> Seeds from annual plants can delay germination until climatic conditions improve. Recent studies in Senegal have shown that seed production on a pasture . . . of the three largest grass formations reaches 30.6 kg per hectare. A third of this annual production (10.3 kg) is eaten on the spot by animals. Another part is scattered by the wind, rain and animals. . . . A small part is destroyed. . . . The remaining seeds (17 kg per hectare) can delay germination for at least two years until the return of better rain. (6, p.81)

And that is what happened also in the Sahel in Niger.

> In the 1975 rainy season, *Schoenefeldia gracilis, Aristida mutabilis* and even *Blepharis linariifolia* began to appear on fine-grained soils. Plants only disappear completely when overgrazing in the rainy season is added to drought, so that seeds are eaten before they fall. . . . When the two phenomena occur together, they cause desertification. (6, p.82)

In stimulating the growth of towns in the Sahel, the drought merely accelerated trends that were already becoming evident. Administrative centers established before the drought became a magnet for nomads who had lost their animals, and a slowly increasing settled population began to attract merchants so that all at once arid northern Niger had half a dozen new towns, some of them converted into markets, with prescribed market days, popping up on the long highway to Algeria. Irrigation in the plain of the Eghazer, dating from the opening of artesian boreholes in 1960, expanded in the wake of the drought, with army units working to train former pastoralists in the complications of irrigation agriculture. Even if most of the Kel Tamasheq preferred the leap to city life, a few decided to see what this new style of farming was all about.

> Some herdsmen on their own initiative sought alternative livelihoods within the area. The Arabs . . . often sold their animals before they died and, with the profits, set up shops in all the centers: Agadès, In Gall, Tofamanir, Abalak, Tchin Tabaraden and even farther south—Tahoua, Dakoro or Maradi. Some Tuareg experimented with agriculture even though they had no tradition of working the land. Others (Kel

Ahaggar, Kel Fadey, Igdalen) started cultivating land around the boreholes of the Eghazer . . . by irrigating gardens of wheat in the winter and millet and sorghum in summer, using seeds from free distributions. In the Tchin Tabaraden region, gardens were made on the edge of pools. The beds were watered by digging channels uphill to shallow basins to which water was carried by hand in buckets. These imperfect solutions were often inadequate to create real independence in food supply. . . . Nevertheless, they show the vitality of the pastoralists, who refused to accept the role of public wards. (6, pp.69-70)

Meanwhile, the government undertook a three-year program (1976-78) to restock the depleted herds. With animals supplied on a delayed repayment basis, this program showed a good chance of achieving its goals of a 100% restoration of predrought populations of goats, 90% of camels, 65% of cattle, and 85% of sheep. But there was more to the program than just this. It also involved the creation of six breeding centers, intended to improve breeds, six weaning stations, and two ranches designed to test experiments in intensive stock raising. Additional programs, a broad rehabilitation of Niger with foreign assistance, were devoted to planting 400 hectares of shade trees around boreholes, the construction of shelterbelts around irrigated plots in the Eghazer and the setting aside of 60,000 hectares of grazing reserve. An ambitious American project, centered on a region near Abalak, is training Nigerians in U.S. techniques and styles of animal production.

Such developments stand in contrast to others not so favorable. As cultivation raced back north of the legal limit as soon as good rainfall returned, so the last pretense of enforcing legal sanctions against it was simply abandoned. The growth of permanent settlements, including craftsmen and artisans, and the expansion of irrigation agriculture were giving rise to increased needs for firewood and placing even heavier pressure on woody vegetation. No consistent approach had been developed against the persistence of localized overgrazing. In short, the factors leading to desertification before the drought were all still present in Niger and were being intensified with the help of rapidly growing populations in a country which, saddled with French traditions that have become obsolete in France, continues to resist the introduction of family planning programs. The present course of events provides few reasons for thinking that the next great drought will not simply be a repetition of disaster in Niger.

The principal reason for this gloomy outlook can be found in the purposeful destruction of a way of life that once managed the arid rangelands of the Azawak and the Eghazer in a tradition that maintained sustained production. It was a life style that had pastured herds in the Sahel for at least a thousand years before the era of colonial intrusions. Once upon a time, when drought threatened the Eghazer, herds were trekked all the way to the well of Mayatta and thereby saved. In the new era of "peace and the end of raids," the nomad, incredibly, seems to be pulling his life together in spite of his demoralization. The collapse of his morale, however, is reflected in the route he is taking, or at least some of them—the once scorned life of the farmer around the pools of Tchin Tabaraden and the artesian boreholes in the Eghazer. That his morale, in the end, seems indestructible, is evident in his taking any route at all. This display of vigor and initiative in the midst of the annihilation of everything the Kel Tamasheq holds dear, his refusal to become a "public ward," displays to the world that the blue-veiled herdsman at the desert's edge is a human being as complex as any other, and that social solutions to desertification problems will not be found except by thinking beyond the slide rule and its technical answers.

8

COMBARBALÁ

"Man alone is responsible"

At Calama, near the great copper mine of Chuquicamata, no drop of rain has ever fallen in the centuries that European man has been there. The Atacama Desert is said to be the driest in the world, squeezed as it is between the desiccating mountains and a rain-wringing ocean current, and its driest part is that bleak, rugged region of northern Chile from which fortunes in copper and nitrates have been extracted. In summer, the southeast Pacific anticyclone lingers 1,000 km offshore, centered over those Juan Fernandez islands on which the shipwrecked Alexander Selkirk provided the model for Robinson Crusoe. In winter, this high-pressure system weakens somewhat and moves west in the direction of Easter Island. This allows frontal systems to reach the long Chilean shore from a southwesterly direction, creating that pattern of climate called Mediterranean—a little rain in a mild winter, drought every summer. The change is gradual as progressively wetter climatic strips are crossed while driving southward from the Atacama along the Pan-American Highway. Even after reaching Santiago, the national capital, the countryside is no better than semiarid. But another 400 km to the south takes the traveler to the city of Concepcion at the mouth of the Bio Bio, a river which for almost four centuries served as a boundary against Spanish colonization farther to the south. German colonists in the nineteenth century finally showed how farms could be carved out of dense forests under rainfall regimes reaching close to 3,000 mm a year. Thus does Chile display a panoply of climates reaching from one extreme to the other. Coming as they did from the more open landscapes of Spain, touched by hot winds from the Sahara, the Iberians didn't care for those wet, somber regions that have since become celebrated as the Lake District.

REGION OF COMBARBALA
NORTH-CENTRAL CHILE

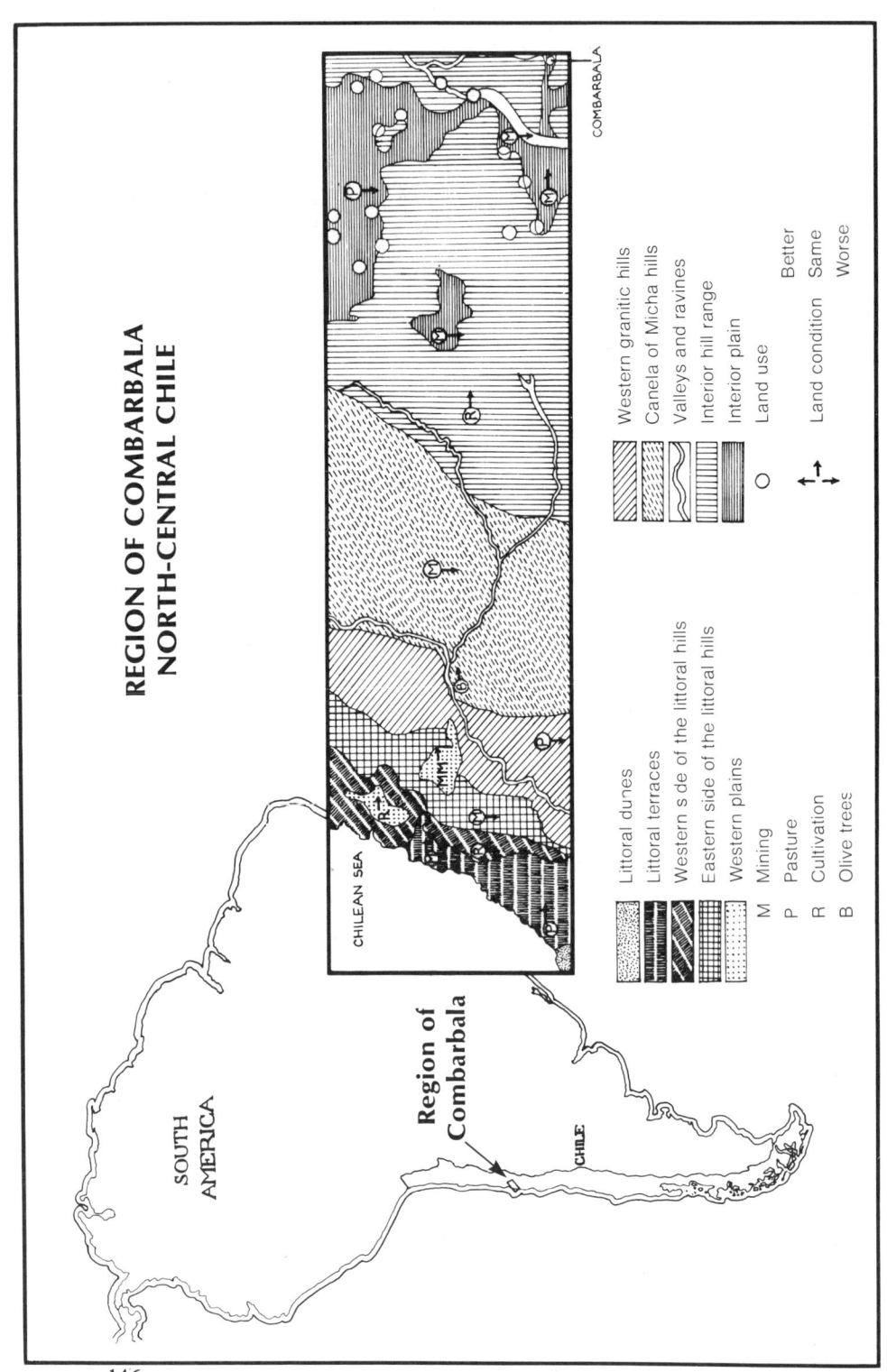

No, the Spaniards preferred the more arid regions where, in the first decades of the seventeenth century, they established cattle ranches, a familiar Iberian enterprise, as far north as Coquimbo, a district lying between the 100-mm and 300-mm isohyets immediately to the south of the desert. This is rugged country, Coquimbo, its coastal hills and intermontane valleys leaping quickly up to the high mountains, the wall of the Andes, in front of which, today, the giant telescopes of Cerro Tololo scan the southern skies. Time has not been kind to the country below the telescopes, a tumbling landscape of small farms and pastures, containing, also, small deposits of rich minerals. The silver and copper which were exploited here even by the Inca civilization after its penetration here in the late fifteenth century, its moment of greatest expansion, have ever since attracted a shifting and shiftless population. Miners are somehow never expected to give heed to practices that conserve the quality of the land. But the farmers and ranchers in the Coquimbo region also paid little attention to good land-use practices. The result was the annihilation of the wildlife, the guanaco and the partridge, and the ravagement of the climax vegetation so utterly that in many places it has become impossible to reconstruct even an idea of what it once must have been. An unlevel landscape where the rain arrives in storms—winter storms here in Coquimbo—is particularly vulnerable to erosion by water, and the lower hillsides have become creased with gullies where, in places, whole mountainsides have been washed away. The soils that remain have been stripped of nutrients and structurally damaged, and agricultural productivity has traced a course of continual decline. In 1961, the Chilean government declared the Coquimbo region to be "a zone of extreme poverty."

UNESCO's arid-lands specialists, accustomed to working in the region of the Sahara and in southwest Asia, had difficulty deciding where to set up a case study in the western hemisphere. Coquimbo's depressing history provided ample grounds for selecting this region as a study site, but when the choice was finally made, it was late in terms of the schedule demanded by the Conference on Desertification. In the final event, the Inter-American Development Bank, rather than UNESCO, became the executing agent for this one investigation, carried out as it was, and admittedly, in somewhat of a hurry.

This case study on desertification had to be carried out in a short period (end of June to September, 1976). It is a multidisciplinary study, with contributions from distinguished Chilean specialists who were already familiar with the region and who had expressed their concerns regarding the problems of this part of the country. (1, p.1)

Specifically, the investigators settled on a rectangle within the larger Coquimbo district, one 72.5 km in length and 20 km wide, running diagonally from the sea at Punta Burros in a northeasterly direction to the town of Combarbalá in the foothills of the Andes. It is a tilted brick of land that the case study calls Combarbalá after its largest community. Located just below the 31st parallel of southern latitude, this chunk of Coquimbo traverses the skinniest part of a *larguirucho* nation, very long and very thin, here a mere 85 km separating the sea from the international boundary on the crest of the mountains. The study zone thus crosses the full gamut of land types up to the base of the Andean wall. The 200-mm isohyet follows the diagonal course of the study zone from the oceanside dunes, over littoral hills and terraces, through narrow western plains, into valleys, ravines, and interior mountains to the interior plains around Combarbalá lying at an altitude of 1,000 meters. The study zone was in part selected because it is a tangle of ecosystems formed by variations in altitude, slope, soil types, drainage, and exposure to sunlight.

Like the Sahel, and possibly for the same large-scale reasons, Coquimbo was also struck by a prolonged drought beginning in 1968. Just as there are those who have said that climate is to blame for the destruction of Sahelian ecosystems, so there are others who contend that progressive climatic desiccation lies at the root of Coquimbo's problems. Conclusions depend partly on how rainfall statistics are handled. Winstanley suggests that mean annual rainfall in the Sahel might have shown a declining trend since the 1930s (51, p.93). To detect any trend at all in the sawtooth ups and downs of mean annual rainfall might be to push the arts of statistics to their limits—or beyond them, since statisticians have not yet reached agreement. In his search for "hidden periodicities", Landsberg, in contrast to Winstanley, points to a vague appearance of short cycles in Sahelian rainfall. Others—Yevjevich, Bunting et al.—say that neither trends nor interannual periodicities can be detected (51, p.94). Meanwhile, back in Coquimbo, Schneider would say that the following data, taken from the weather stations nearest to the study zone, show that rainfall has declined there over the past century (1, p.30).

Place	Years	Mean Annual Rainfall (mm)	%
La Serena on the coast	1869–1964	125.3	
	1871–1900	148.2	100
	1901–30	128.3	86.5
	1930–60	104.7	70.5
Ovalle in the interior	1897–1964	143.0	
	1901–30	152.6	100
	1931–60	125.8	82

A decline in mean annual rainfall in recent years was confirmed by Miller and his associates from a study of tree rings in a stand of *Australocedrus chilensis* near San Felipe, in the somewhat rainier Aconcagua Province to the south of the study zone (1, p.36). By carrying their dendochronology back to the year 1010, Miller et al. disclosed a great many ups and downs in the movement of mean annual rainfall yielding the vague outlines of a possible 100-year cycle but no clear trend toward either wetter or drier conditions. Schneider's trend toward aridity can be fitted into these oscillations.

Of course the climate is changing—in the Sahel, in Combarbalá, on the northern side of the Sahara, in the Gascoyne basin, across northern China, and everywhere else on earth—in the trivial sense that climate is always changing. Tectonic movement inches land masses into other latitudes, just as the movements of the Sahara region have been traced from the south pole to its present position in the northern subtropical high-pressure subsidence zone. In the course of its travels, the Sahara shed the glaciers that once covered it to a depth of several kilometers, passed through storms and calm, suffered tropical downpours during the age of the dinosaurs, when, as the larger Gondwanaland, this continental mass began to shed its edges—South America, India, Australia, Antarctica. That last chunk wandered back again to the South Pole, as we know, carrying with it coal deposits laid down by vanished equatorial forests. Climatic change brought on by tectonic movement becomes evident only on extended time scales—10 million years, 100 million years. This stately parade of continents shifts the currents of the ocean and exerts other effects on climate. The sealing of the Panama connection between the two Americas may have made Europe densely habitable by sending the Gulf Stream off on its present northeasterly course.

The bunching of land masses around an almost enclosed Arctic Ocean may have been the last factor needed to bring on the ice ages of the Pleistocene.

The advances and retreats of the Pleistocene glaciers are clear evidence that enormous changes in global climate can occur at velocities that require no waiting for tectonic movements to work their slow effects. A mere 25,000 years ago, a colder Sahara, affected by less fierce evaporation rates, had finished drinking in the rain that accompanied the advance of glaciers, the liquid which seeped into those enormous aquifers which underlie the sandstones of Nubia. Only 18,000 years ago, two-thirds of North America and almost half of Europe were encased in thick layers of ice. The Magdalenians who painted the portraits of animals on the walls of Dordogne caves hunted reindeer over tundra in what is now France.

The accumulation of such stupendous amounts of ice, lowering the level of the oceans by as much as 100 meters, would seem to have required a lot of time. Only a few years ago, geology was instructing us that the ice had advanced four times during the million years of the Pleistocene, each advance separated from the next by a leisurely 100,000 years of warm, interglacial climate. A saraband of such stately movement fails, however, to fit the rhythm revealed by *Globigerina pachyderma*, a Foraminifera brought up in cores extracted from the seafloor, the twist of whose shell tells whether the water in which it lived was hot or cold. More precise temperature determinations for past eras have combined with improved dating techniques to disclose nine or ten major glacial advances separated by brief interglacials typically lasting a scant 10,000 years. And if it should be the case that the Pleistocene Ice Age has not reached its final end, then the interglacial in which we are living—for that is what it would be, an interruption in prevailing frigidity during which the style of life known as civilization took shape—should just about be over, and the next advance of the ice should be waiting there in the wings all ready to lunge toward New York and Paris as soon as it gets its proper cue.

That we continue to live in the midst of an ice age is evident in the persistence of as much as half of the maximum glaciation still tied up in the ice packs that cover Antarctica, Greenland, and other polar and mountain regions. In the Mesozoic, dinosaurs roamed a planet that was almost everywhere tropical, with an average global temperature higher than 17° C. Ice ages, such as the one we are now living in, are very exceptional episodes, occurring once every 250 million or 300 million years, a periodicity that some researchers have correlated with the rotation of the solar system around the galactic center, although how this cosmic wheel could affect earthly temperatures remains unclear. In any case, that would be only one of several dozen theories put forward to explain why the temperature regime of an earth that is usually much balmier than it is at present is interrupted from time to time by episodes of ice. The attempt to find out why this should happen has even directed attention to the center of the sun.

The output of solar neutrinos detected by Raymond Davis in a tank containing 378,000 liters of cleaning fluid placed 1,478 meters deep in the Homestead Gold Mine near Lead, South Dakota, was less than a fifth of the number expected by theory from the thermonuclear reactions supposed to be taking place at the sun's center. Either present theories of solar energy production are mistaken, or, as a group of English astronomers has suggested, the sun's fires are temporarily banked in a 250-million-year convective cycle that reduces its output at the low ebb by about 5%. This would be more than enough to bring on an ice age. Indeed, Soviet and American physicists have independently proposed that a drop of less than 2% in the energy reaching the earth from he sun would be sufficient to freeze the oceans to the equator. Still another theory would link the prevailing temperature of the earth to sunspot cycles and to the solar storms that distinguish an active from a quiet sun.

A theory which is at present attracting wide support was generally dismissed in the more than a century since it was first suggested—until it was noticed that its proposed periodicities were in reasonable agreement with the course of events described by the latest findings in more precise chronologies. Developed in detail in the 1920s by the Serbian Milutin Milankovitch, this theory, already referred to in discussing the mysterious movements of the Bermuda High, looks to four variations in the earth's orbital and other motions—the precession of the equinoxes, slight changes in the tilt of the earth's axis, variations in the ellipticity of the earth's orbit, the relations between aphelion and the northern summer—to generate a cyclical pattern of northern warming and cooling.

The Milankovitch cycles would work their most pronounced effects only after tectonic migrations had stacked the land masses around the North Pole in a pattern that encourages ice formation. Or around the South Pole—such southern ice ages have in fact occurred. The gradual construction of the present continental design can be seen in the slow decline in global temperatures through the long course of the Tertiary, culminating in a 40,000-year temperature wobble in the last years of Pliocene, a cycle whose ever increasing amplitude blended into the successive ice advances of the Pleistocene.

An explanation of the ice ages achieved by combining the theory of plate tectonics with the Milankovitch cycles is one of those accomplishments of science that suddenly illuminate the mysterious while suggesting the unimaginably disastrous. For the earth is even now swinging into the cold phase of the Milankovitch cycle after a normal interglacial of 10,000 years or so. The global temperature is already well below the maximum reached before 3000 B.C. when warm conditions drew the West African monsoon so deep into the Sahara that people harvested grain in the remote Tibesti mountains in a region depicted in cave paintings to be then teeming with wildlife. If Milankovitch is correct, long-term cooling may already have been responsible for the so-called Little Ice Age of the fifteenth through nineteenth centuries which wiped out the Viking colony in Greenland and promoted ice skating into late spring on the frozen canals of Holland. Oscillations in the general trend are to be expected, and the cooling of the northern hemisphere since the 1940s, to which some have attributed the great drought in the Sahel, would then be merely a resumption of a long-term cooling interrupted by a heat wave somewhat difficult to explain during the preceding 60 years. Yet it was just such an abnormal interruption in a continuing process of world cooling, an intermezzo accompanied by strong monsoon rains and rich harvests, that happened to be taking place while the first systematic network of weather stations was being established around the world, and while the new sciences of soils and agriculture were taking shape. Would it be any wonder then—providing, of course, that all this were true—that these nascent sciences should have embedded in them an overoptimistic view of the world's agricultural potentialities and possibilities? In this sense, the weather itself may have affected the theories that were supposed to describe it, making them ever so slightly balmy.

The new chronology shows that large-scale climatic change can get under way much more rapidly than previously supposed. Cold weather in high latitudes, if it were marking the onset of a new advance of the glaciers, would be accompanied by increasing drought in subtropical grasslands. The retreat of the tree line in the far north and south would precede the advance of tundra and the march of killing frosts ever southward into the great plains of North America, eastern Europe, and Central Asia, and northward into the grasslands of Australia and Argentina. The desert of Patagonia would move toward Paraguay and the arid Kalahari would spread toward the Congo. Long before ice ever moved against Montreal or Stockholm, mankind would find the growing season shrunk to a few summer months everywhere except around the equator, and the climatic vice constricting around arable land would scarcely be compensated by the emergence from the lowering seas of vast salted plains to the east of England or around the Bahamas or across the frigid slopes of a draining Beringia. Once again, genus *Homo* would be confronted with the kind of crisis that may have hastened his evolution in the past. As *Homo sapiens neanderthalensis*, he saw the ice walls of Würm mobilize against Europe, but it was *Homo sapiens sapiens* who pursued the reindeer northward when that ice went into retreat. One wonders who or what will be here to rejoice in—or perhaps to regret—the melting of the next glaciation if the ice should really return.

On the other hand, cooling might have followed from other reasons that have previously been suggested—from real or human volcanoes—and perhaps enough to set the stage for another glacial advance. The decade that began with a publicized drought in the Sahel—and another in Coquimbo, that one ignored by everyone except the people living there—has flowered with dark prophecies, or with at least an awareness of dire possibilities. Yet the fact is that all such grim forebodings are based on theory, some of it elegant and much of it sensible. As for the actual performance of climate, the global temperature has indeed declined in a jagged pattern of ups and downs since the climatic optimum of about 5000 B.C. But as to which way climate is going right now—toward warmer or cooler, drier or wetter—data obtained from climatic observations fail to state. Or, to put it another way, the data fail to point in any particular direction that has attracted widespread scientific support.

Recent years have witnessed an intensifying discussion in the scientific journals, and a certain amount of alarm, over how much of that life-supporting substance, carbon dioxide, is being injected into the atmosphere by the actions of man, and what the effects of that injection will be. By his own activity, man himself enters as a variable into climatic equations which could conceivably overwhelm the Milankovitch effect even if the Milankovitch theory is correct. Carbon dioxide, exhaled by animals and automobiles, flames and factories, and inhaled by vegetation and thus essential to plant life, acts like a greenhouse in the atmosphere by bouncing heat reflected up from the earth's surface back to the surface, warming the troposphere and making the same energy available to the surface once again.

The carbon dioxide content of the atmosphere has risen by 18% since 1850 when the atmospheric reservoir is estimated to have contained 560 billion tons of the stuff, or 268 parts per million (72). That is enough to have caused a rise in global temperature of 0.5° to 0.6°C, which roughly equals the increase recorded between 1880 and 1940. Half of that rise has since been lost in the northern hemisphere in the subsequent episode of cooling, which might possibly indicate that not enough carbon dioxide had yet been added to the atmosphere to dominate the Milankovitch effect. It is now estimated that the carbon dioxide content of the atmosphere as of 1850 will be doubled by sometime early in the next century, primarily through increased burning of fossil fuel. That should be enough to raise the global temperature by an average of 2° or 3°C, which may seem to be a small amount but would in fact be a gigantic increase in the earth's energy budget, quite enough to counter anything that Milankovitch might have had in mind for humanity and to forestall a new mobilization of the ice.

The activities of man may give rise to other effects on climate which are at present not predictable. One such effect would follow from increased admission to the surface of ultraviolet radiation following damage to or the destruction of the stratospheric ozone layer by the excessive release of fluorocarbons from spray cans or by the action of jet engines flying at ozone altitude. Another unassessable element of the future lies in the unknown long-term impact of greatly increased cirrus-cloud formation from jet trails. Foresight is one of the definitive qualities of intellect, and the present existentialist panorama is one of man, the animal gifted by brain, lunging into the future with no clear idea of what the results of his actions will be. It is nonetheless clear that airplanes will not be grounded or highways blocked while man takes the trouble to find out—if he can. It is ironic that the human race may yet save itself from a new ice age by the activity that creates smog, condemned as among the grosser forms of pollution. The chronic smog that in Mexico City makes everyone's eyes water and eternally blocks the view of the tranquil icefields of Popocatepetl may also act to prevent that ice from inching down the mountainside to topple the Pan-American Tower on

Avenida Juarez. Carbon dioxide emissions might warm the earth sufficiently to destroy the nomadic life of the Sahel in a way opposite to the threats that menace it today, by covering it with fields of wheat thriving under a thickened West African monsoon.

The inability to detect a clear direction in shifts of temperature and precipitation means that climatic change cannot be correlated with recent accelerations in desertification. The degradation of the land around Combarbalá has in fact been traced back to the arrival of the Spaniards, and did not begin with any real or theoretical decline in precipitation that might have taken place in this century. Sustained productivity was maintained by the Indian population as far as can be presently determined and in spite of its considerable density—chroniclers estimated that 25,000 Diaguitas were inhabiting the arid and subdesertic districts of Coquimbo in 1535, a number slashed 60% in 10 years, as was typical among American aboriginals, by diseases imported from Europe. The subsequent history of Combarbalá is the history of a *conquistador* mentality with its carefree attitude toward what seemed to be the New World's endless lands, and its conviction that the resources of those lands were inexhaustible. The newcomers imported cattle from Spain and began ranching in Combarbalá while paying comparatively little attention to the ecological requirements of an entirely novel flora and fauna. In the middle of the seventeenth century, vineyards were planted in the region, a time that also saw the beginning of wheat cultivation, with the harvested grain exported to the colonial centers in Peru. That the land was already damaged, even by then, can be seen in the replacement of that era's cattle by goats.

> The decrease in the productive capacity of the ecosystems of the district is not imputable to climate variations. Rainfall records from the zone . . . show that the high variability in annual precipitation constitutes a climatic regularity. . . . A high harvest rate has been the main mechanism causing the successional retrogression of the original ecosystems back to the present state, characterized by original and invasive species of less value. . . . The establishment of annual cultivation (without fallow) and the lack of measures oriented toward keeping productivity at a suitable level, have both finally ended in desertification. (1, pp.100-101)

The same point is restated:

> Droughts, or even a simple decrease in rainfall, have been named as the main factor responsible for the failure of the systems concerned with the production and management of forestry, agrarian and breeding re-

sources. However, it is likely that the present climate conditions are similar to those found by the Spanish colonizers four centuries ago. (1, p.101)

If not climate, then perhaps the omnivorous goats that replaced the cattle of Combarbalá:

> Goats are efficient utilizers of natural resources present in environments like those described in the present work. But neither goats nor grain cultivation is the real cause of the process of desertification. . . . Man alone is responsible for his destructive action upon natural resources. It is necessary to organize man and develop attitudes consistent with sustained conservation management of natural resources; otherwise man's very survival is in peril. It is only a matter of time. (1, p.101)

Man alone is responsible. Anaya Garduño was then correct (see page 12) when he said the same thing in Chapingo's Colegio de Posgraduados, some 6,500 km to the north of Combarbalá. Yes, "desertification" can be defined as the handiwork of man. In Greater Mussayeb, the damage wrought to the soil by salination was assigned to inept irrigation practices, hardly to climate. China attributed the desertification of its arid north to "feudalistic rulers and Kuomintang reactionaries" (8, p.3) and certainly not to any loss of vigor in the Southeast Asia Monsoon. "Evidence of climatic change is not convincing" said the case study on the Gascoyne basin (7, p.22). "No sign of any trend toward a drier or wetter climate" could be found in Oglat Merteba (4, p.8). In Eghazer and the Azawak,

> it should be emphasized that if opinions differ on long-term climate change there has been no decisive proof to show that rainfall is diminishing today. One can here cite hydrologists to the effect that "at present there is no general trend toward the drying up of the Sahelian and tropical zones." Only the irregularity of rainfall, that is the irregular succession of dry years, remains an uncontested feature of the Sahelian climate. (6, p.24)

In Chile's study zone, part of the land was developed as ranches worked by tenants or hired labor. Most of the area, however, developed a type of communal ownership to be found nowhere else in Chile. These *comuneros* maintain small stock, raise some wheat and cumin seed for commercial markets, and cultivate subsistence gardens of fruits and vegetables on small irrigated plots. They are persons described as very individualistic even though the communitarian structure requires cooperative cleaning of drains and canals, construction of animal shelters and social centers, elimination of toxic plants from grazing areas, and distribution of community-owned water resources. One might hope that such a communal pattern might lead to good land-use practices of the kind reported of Chinese communes. Such, however, is not the case, and communal lands have been the most damaged in the region. Why this should be is not clearly stated in the case study, although one gets an impression that communal lands have been overexploited because inheritance has broken family plots into fragments too small to support a family.

> The community itself is the real owner of all arable land, pastureland and places where firewood is collected. But every man having tenure . . . is also the individual owner of a small irrigated area called *hijuela* on the side of the ravines. . . . The right to have land tenure is acquired through inheritance. (1, p.124)
>
> [*Comuneros*] proudly claim descent from the Spanish conquerors in spite of the fact that their present economic situation places them at the bottom of the social scale of the region. An average goat flock in 1965-66 had only 22 animals and the irrigated lands (*hijuelas*) are now generally reduced to a small fraction of a hectare. (1, p.126)

If it is true that the land has been fragmented by inheritance, it must have happened some time ago, since the population of the region has increased only slightly over the past century. The excess of persons generated by a population growth rate of slightly more than 2% per year has given rise to a steady emigration—of men to the mines in the farther north, of women to the servants' quarters of Santiago and Valparaiso. The emigrants are members of *comunero* families, and when the extreme poverty of the Combarbalá area is mentioned, it is the *comunero* who is meant.

Here, as in many places in the world, desertification has resulted from erosion—mainly water erosion, in this case—following overexploitation—overgrazing and the destruction of natural vegetation by clearing fields for cultivation and gathering woody plants for fuel. The case study is at its most expert as it traces in minute detail the course of the degradation that has affected the various ecosystems in the study zone. It relates how the problems of Combarbalá have only been compounded by ill-conceived attempts to reverse the region's declining productivity.

> Portions of the western plains were planted with olive trees (*Olea europea*). . . . [the olive] still now displays a vigorous development, although its cultivation has been given up, due to its low yield as a consequence of the limited water supply. (1, p.83)

The western plains should take a lesson from Tunisia, where olive trees flourish under 150 mm of annual rainfall, an experience that might instruct Combarbalá that its deficiency lies in lack of technique rather than in lack of water.

> A few years ago, the production of roasting chickens was massively introduced because there were temporarily advantageous conditions on the national market. Unfortunately, these centers of production went out of business, abandoned and destroyed soon after their installation. None of the supplies necessary to the business was locally produced; everything came from other areas of the country and even from abroad (imported grains).
>
> Another example of a temporary solution has been the impetus given to the production of cumin seeds. . . . The cultivation has been carried on without any previous explanation of the practices required to preserve the resources. Such cultivation has provided subsistence and even allowed some producers and merchants to grow wealthy, but has resulted in incalculable damage to the soil. (1, pp.134–35)

Like the boreholes of the Azawak, the ill-fated chicken ranches of Combarbalá constituted a misapplication of technology and, for the same reasons, the failure to adopt an ecological viewpoint, as the case study is frank to admit, and a failure to work with the local people at every stage in the development of this plan, as is not so precisely admitted. Chicken farming failed because it demanded more than local ecosystems could provide, the case study reports, but chickenfeed, as one item, might well have been produced locally if the enthusiasm of the *comuneros* had been properly generated and their advice on this subject obtained. Compounding myopia was a lack of extension services.

> Technical assistance to the *comuneros* has in general been insufficient, ill-planned and sporadic. Previous experience has not been taken into account, and an informational phase has not preceded the actual change. However, the mind of the *comunero* is open to technological innovation. (1, p.134)

Similarities are evident with Greater Mussayeb, where one would not exactly say, however, that the mind of the pastoralist is open to technological innovation. One wonders how long this will continue to be true of the *comunero*, as each introduction relapses into failure. Just as pilot projects and successful demonstrations are put forward as essential techniques in the pedagogy that converts traditional people into modern types, so, one supposes, nothing could be more destructive of that sought-after transformation than the spectacle of continual failure. That the mind of the *comunero* is still open may reflect only his confusion, a mental state not conducive to good land-use practices.

Among short-term measures proposed for the rehabilitation of Combarbalá, the case study concentrates on the provision of alternative livelihoods as a means of relieving excessive pressure on the land. The suggestions for new occupations include mining, crafts, secondary industries, and, in general,

> to furnish opportunities for young people to realize their aspirations to do work other than that connected with agriculture and breeding of stock. (1, p.140)

Recommendations for rehabilitation also include a list of long-term measures intended to restore the physical productivity of the land.

- Reorganize the land ownership system, eliminating the excessive partition of the land by assembling the minimal subsistence units into larger units.
- Regenerate ecosystems in these larger units by prolonged exclusion of cultivation and grazing in the most vulnerable areas where erosion is most intense.
- Submit natural meadows to controlled grazing, preventing excessive concentrations of animals and regulating resting periods to preserve and improve the vegetation.
- Consider preservation and improvement of natural vegetation as being of the utmost priority. . . . Under present conditions, no short-term improvement is possible that would raise animal or crop production to economically profitable levels.
- Every program or strategy selected for resolving the problems of the region must be approached in an integrated way, keeping in mind a clear differentiation between the social and even political problems of the population and those related to production efficiency. (1, p. 140)

It is the last recommendation that comes anywhere near the heart of the matter. The steps needed for the physical rehabilitation of a degraded landscape, if rehabilitation is economically feasible, are always comparatively easy to determine, although the case study seems somewhat unimaginative in its physical suggestions, proposing little more than variations on the theme of giving the land a rest. No attack is proposed, for example, on the severe gullying which infests the steep slopes of the study zone. But even resting, no more than resting, the pusillanimous remedy suggested for the Gascoyne basin, involves a loss of income to people described as already among the poorest in the nation. It places the whole expense of rehabilitation on them, although the land has been degraded for four centuries not only by farmers but also by miners and vagrants carrying out patterns of life national in scope. Yet since people cannot be shoved below the subsistence level, the case study suggests that some proportion of them be taken off the land. This would go along with the consolidation of holdings. Those whom consolidation would eject from agricultural life must be supplied with alternative livelihoods, other sources of income.

The case study seems blandly unaware that in proposing to change the land ownership system in Combarbalá, as well as the very owners themselves, it is suggesting nothing less than a social revolution on this maltreated landscape. Not one instruction emerges from the case study as to how such a social transformation is to be effected among fiercely individualistic *comuneros*. An impression is fortified that the people of Combarbalá and vicinity have not been consulted about the list of proposals made in the interests of their well-being. But then, the study seems almost to suggest, why should they be? The proposals are rational and obvious. They are clearly the way to improve local life.

Yet aware, to some extent, of its shortcomings, realizing that its recommendations are too general, and lacking all instruction as to how they might be executed, the document also proposes that "a deeper interdisciplinary study be made of the selected district." Further work is thus proposed for specialists and scientists, those who provided detailed accounts in the case study of the progressive degeneration of plant communities. But this further work does not yet seem to involve the active participation of the people living in Combarbalá. There seems to be a recognition that what is needed in the study zone is less a detailed account of how plant life has passed through the many successions that have ensued on the destruction of the climax vegetation and more of a detailed account of how human life in the region has become degraded. This is on the presumption that "interdisciplinary" implies going beyond the purely physical sciences. If plant successions provide clues to the present possibilities of vegetation, then human successions might open vistas as to how human life might be made brighter amidst Combarbalá's eroded landscapes. But perhaps more study, and ever more study, is not the most effective approach to take after all, even if it should involve social scientists scrutinizing the objects of their branches of learning. Perhaps a program for the amelioration of Combarbalá—and indeed all of Coquimbo—might be developed out of the *comuneros'* own ideas as to how land and life there could be made better. After all, no one is as familiar with this region as its own inhabitants are. To ask them would mean taking a chance, of course—in their own self-interest they might suggest actions that someone besides the people living in this "zone of extreme poverty" might be asked to pay for.

9
VALE

"Laws of the land, court decisions, and the overall public attitude"

THE INCESSANT RAINS of winter and spring that in legend endow the inhabitants of Oregon with webbed feet are blocked as they move inland by the barrier of the Cascade range. Lying in the rain shadow to the east of the mountains is a semiarid, volcanic plateau which becomes progressively more arid as one moves southeastward in the direction of the Great Basin. In the far southeast corner of the state lies Malheur County, whose name suggests the misfortunes of those *voyageurs* from distant French Canada who named nearby Boise, Idaho, after its stands of forest emerging out of drylands. Pine and juniper can be found here and there in the sweeping rangelands of Malheur County, which is larger than the State of Massachusetts and almost identical in boundaries with the Vale District operated by the Bureau of Land Management, a section of the U.S. Department of the Interior with a history of being loved and hated by the cattlemen of the West.

The rolling landscape of Malheur County is broken by canyons, of which the largest is that of the Owyhee River, traversing the long county from south to north before emptying into the Snake. Although its tilted fault-block mountains are typical of Great Basin topography, the Owyhee drainage, along with the east-flowing Malheur River, means that little of Malheur County is actually inside that landlocked drainage system. Its young soils, heavily mixed with volcanic ash and diatomaceous earths, respond well when they get water. A large dam constructed toward the mouth of the Owyhee River provides irrigation to 40,000 hectares of rich farmland, with additional irrigation practiced along the Malheur River and Bully

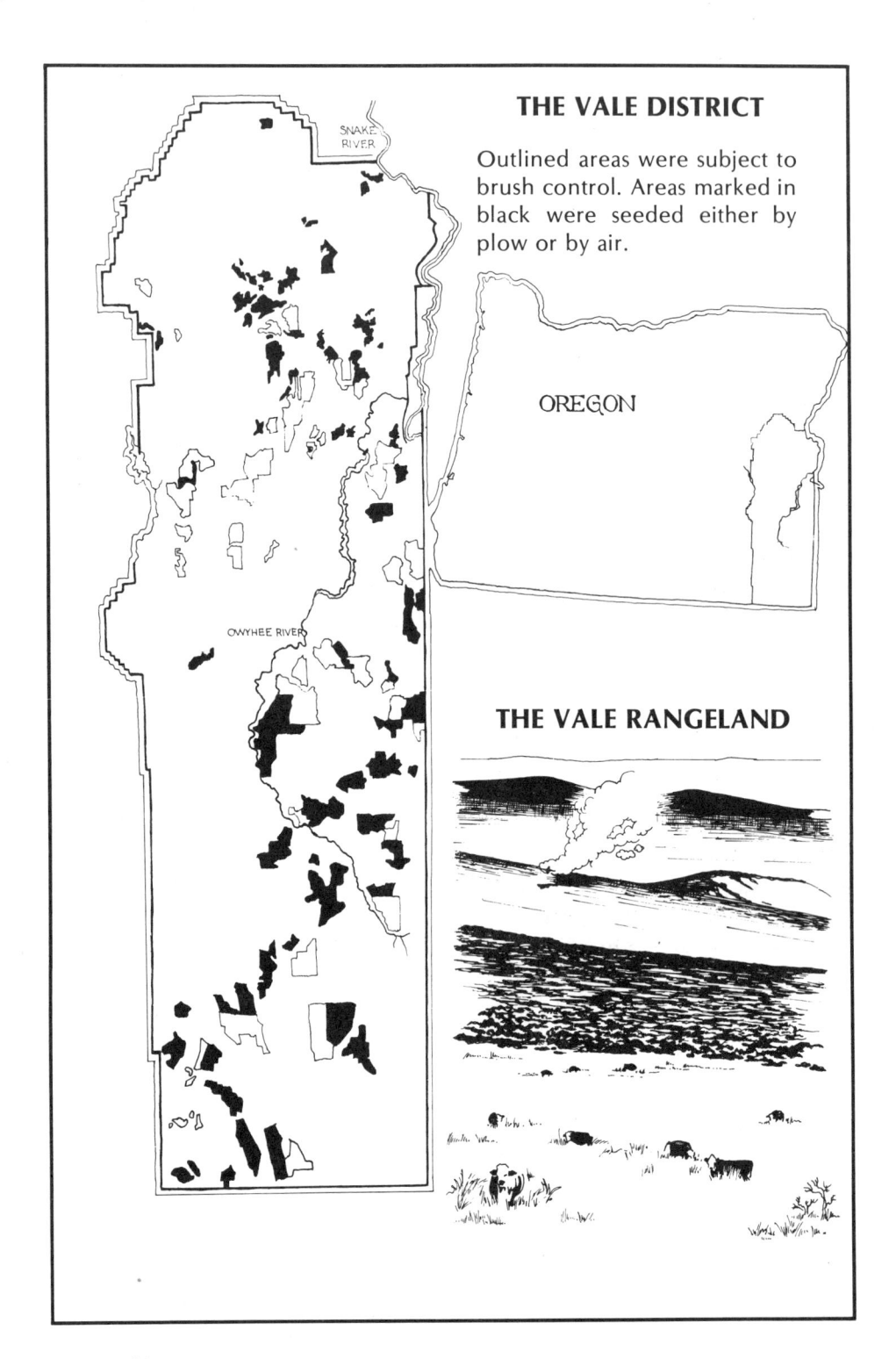

THE VALE DISTRICT

Outlined areas were subject to brush control. Areas marked in black were seeded either by plow or by air.

THE VALE RANGELAND

Creek. An average annual rainfall of from 180 mm to 300 mm, with more rain at higher altitudes, implies that the Vale District, although somewhat more favored than the Gascoyne basin, is not quite wet enough for dry farming. Like the Gascoyne, it has developed into a region of commercial ranching. Here, too, sheep have dominated the range, with large flocks herded into the 1940s by Basque sheepherders based in the small town of Jordan Valley, named not for the biblical site, but for Michael Jordan, who found gold here in 1863. The native vegetation in the Vale District is much superior to what grows in the Gascoyne, and cattle, which do well on it, have in recent years come to dominate the Vale rangelands.

The history of Malheur County is another typical page taken from the epic chronicle of the American West. The Oregon Trail crosses the Snake River in the northeast corner of the district, with most of a flood of immigrants, beginning in 1843, lured onward by the green lands in the Willamette Valley. Some stayed here, however, in this remote corner of the Oregon country, along with the horses and cattle that took the trail with them, establishing the beginnings of a cattle industry originally intended to feed crowds of gold seekers. Raids by Paiute Indians kept settlers to the main roads until 1878, when the Indians were finally conquered, and newer arrivals could settle down to the traditional round of battles among cattlemen, sheepmen, and homesteaders. In this so familiar setting out of the hell-for-leather West, filled with the smell of sagebrush and horseflesh, punctuated by the sounds of gunfire, picturesque cowboys and sheepmen did what they did almost everywhere beyond the 100th meridian. They wrecked the range.

If the longest record of intensive land use can be found in those ancient birthplaces of civilization, such as Greater Mussayeb, the shortest such record is to be found in regions into which European man has most recently penetrated. The Gascoyne basin and the Vale rangeland provide compressed chronicles of destructive land use. Both show that the *conquistador* mentality was not restricted to persons of Iberian descent. Why worry about the land when there is so much of it? This was the private attitude of ranchers, sometimes not so private, among whom sustained productivity, an ethereal concept, was rarely allowed to stand in the way of maximizing short-term profits. And yet these hardy ranchers, creatures of saga and daring whose initiative opened the West, as it opened also the Australian outback, can scarcely be blamed for sharing an attitude that was common to their times. A cavalier view of the land was also the broad public attitude, one which hastened the processes of degradation through institutional mechanisms.

> Livestock overgrazed, miners prospected everywhere, and homesteaders made their own choice of land to plow. They not only did these things, but also were encouraged to do so by the laws of the land, court decisions and the overall public attitude. . . . In effect, political decisions directed social forces to destroy the range vegetation and to retard its recovery because of "crazy quilt" land ownership patterns. It would seem that the public as well as private interests contributed to rangeland deterioration; the Vale District was just a small sample from the whole West. (13, p.25)

So it is man, user of the land, who is once more portrayed as the agent who brings about the destruction of the land. But what about the climate in eastern Oregon? Old-timers used to talk about the days when Malheur Lake, on the other side of the Steens Mountains from Malheur County, had water in it all year around, and when a passenger ferry used to run on Goose Lake, taking people and vehicles from Lakeview, now miles to the north of the water, down to Modoc County in California, in whose tortured lava beds the Modoc suffered the last military defeat to be experienced by Indians in the United States. These memories probably hearken back to an old pluvial which soaked the arid West long before the first European ever saw it and from which its large interior lakes have been drying out ever since. The case study does not bother to elaborate on the climatic history of the Vale rangelands. Yet it is clear that the study finds no grounds to think that temperature or precipitation have changed significantly since 1875, when the range first became saturated with stock. Among past climatic events, mention is made of the catastrophic winter of 1889-90, which annihilated the animals in the region, only to see the rangeland immediately restocked but mostly with sheep brought up from the south. The case study blames the deterioration of the range, not on climatic change, but on overgrazing.

> No doubt exists that cattle, sheep and horses occupied the grazing lands of the Vale District in large numbers for about 60 years beginning in 1875. Little hay or other winter feed was available so the use was yearlong. Grazing on farm-raised feeds and haying increased after the severe winter of 1889-90. Probably range deterioration had reached severe

proportions by 1900. Lack of livestock controls on the public domain until 1934 permitted continued rangeland deterioration and erosion. (13, p.23)

Where atavistic feudal figures are not to be blamed, as they are to be blamed in China and Iraq, then someone else is at fault, some other human being—the Gascoyne sheep rancher, the Arab of Oglat Merteba, the Tuareg of the Azawak, the *comunero* of Combarbalá. Yet to blame acts of man is a new point of view. René Grousset said that the deserts of Central Asia "are like cancerous patches, devouring the grassy belt, on which they have been continually encroaching since protohistoric times" (48, p.xxii). The concept of deserts as cancers may or may not be linked to a feeling that climates are deteriorating. The dryland herdsman or rainfed crop farmer was never prompt to blame himself, at least those of European descent, and however destructive his land-use practices may have been, he was slow to condemn usages that he saw as necessary to his profits or even to his survival. Since degradation doesn't happen all at once, the farmer or herdsman would see good results follow from bad practices for some time before his deeds would catch up with him and harvests and pastures, along with profits, would begin to go into a decline. It would then be his natural impulse to blame the weather, and a kind of folklore of deteriorating climate has collected around many regions where desertification is occurring. People elsewhere have tended to accept the statements of those "who ought to know." The era of a science of climate is new, with all its precise measurements of rainfall, wind, temperature, and humidity, and its universal finding that deterioration of the land has not been accompanied by a corresponding deterioriation in the climate continues to meet the scorn of those old-timers with their stories about how much better conditions were in the good old days.

Yet if the old-timers are wrong and the new science is right, a curious conclusion follows. If it is man who has been creating deserts recently, as he must have been doing, although not so intensively, for long ages past, and if there is no clear evidence that climates have turned drier during the past few thousand years, then deserts must exist in many places where they shouldn't exist—at least as determined by climate. This possibility was recently pursued by the United Nations Environment Programme, an agency which, since its establishment following the Environment Conference, has joined

UNESCO in its concern for the state of the world's drylands. A statement was prepared for UNEP by Mohammed Kassas, professor of botany at the University of Cairo and an internationally recognized specialist in the ecology of arid lands. Kassas quoted Peverell Meigs, maker of the standard map of arid lands, on the extent of drylands and deserts:

> The total area of the world's deserts is 48,350,000 km^2 of which 5,850,000 km^2 are "extremely arid," 21,500,000 km^2 arid and 21,000,000 km^2 semi-arid. This total is equivalent to 36.3% of the earth's surface. (78, p.1)

Although there is a difference in the use of terms, Meigs taking "deserts" to include deserts and drylands, the figures are close to those used by UNESCO, FAO, and WMO in preparing the newer World Map of Desertification. Kassas then went on to say:

> These estimates of desert area are based on climatic data, whereas on the basis of soil and vegetation data, the total area of the world's deserts equals 43% of the earth's surface. The difference is accounted for by the estimated extent of man-made deserts (9,115,000 km^2). (78, p.2)

This is an enormous area to have been ruined by the collective depredations of one species of animal life, by the ape who thinks. It is almost equal in size to the contiguous 48 states of the United States. And if this is true, where are all those desertified places that would not be there if only climate had its way? Some such places consist of broad, coherent chunks of land such as desertified north China, salinized southern Mesopotamia, or the newly created desert covering a strip 150 km wide across the country, Sudan, where acacia trees that used to be found north to Atbara now extend no closer to Khartoum than 60 km to its south. Some of it lies along coastal Mareotis, Cyrenaica, and Tripolitania, where the Romans once practiced a rich arboriculture. Much of it, however, exists as odd patches of desertified land popping out here and there in overgrazed range or in places where arid regions have unwisely been stripped of vegetation in order to plant a crop. It is this patchy advance of desertification, breaking out in sore spots like a skin disease, that typifies the human destruction of once productive land. A changing climate, by shifting an entire bank of isohyets, would cause an advance of the desert—or a retreat—as occurs, one or the other, every year in the

Sahel. The idea of an advancing desert, part of a wide alteration in climate, brings an apocalyptic picture to the mind of newly mobilized sand dunes marching over once productive land in a speeded-up analogue to the advance of glaciers in an ice age. Yet even when climate is the cause, desertification still progresses in patchy fashion, with the most vulnerable patches being the first to go, these linking up with others to create finally the mostly naked landscape of the true desert. This is the way it happened in Sudan where between 1958 and 1975 the desert advanced 90 to 100 km across the width of the country (62, pp.161-162). There, too, blame was placed on the three horsemen of this particular apocalypse—overgrazing, overextension of cultivation, the annihilation of woody vegetation—helped along by drought, of which the most recent manifestation was the same long drought that ravaged West Africa (62, p.155). The end result is the same. It certainly looks as if the desert had simply marched southward across a broad front in fulfillment of that mental image which experts in arid lands are quick to refute. Their aversion to that view links up with their insistence on the anthropogenic character of desertification in modern times. The causes of desertification do not blow out of the deserts. A patchy advance seems more compatible with something in which man has had a hand.

This dreadful work, by which human beings attack the very basis of their material survival, has accelerated in recent years, as previously noted, to an estimated annual loss of 58,000 km^2. To reiterate further, these losses are occurring precisely in an epoch in which man is, so to speak, running a race with himself in a frantic effort to feed an exploding world population. The successes that have characterized this effort so far have mostly resulted from improving the productivity of land already in production rather than from bringing new lands into use. And again, it is no mere coincidence that agricultural productivity is being destroyed by that very population growth whose survival depends on increasing productivity.

As a factor often lurking behind the overexploitation of land, excessive population growth is joined and exacerbated by others, such as the intrusion of market economies into ancient subsistence systems, resulting in new commercial patterns in which too often all else is sacrificed in the interest of maximizing short-term profits. In the Gascoyne basin and on the Vale rangelands, population pressures have not figured in the overexploitation of damaged, maltreated portions of what are industrialized nations of modern times. Low birth rates in these "developed" nations have kept them exempt from the population explosion. In such countries, money and markets have served as the overwhelming influences. The herdsman of the Azawak has been blamed for seeing his wealth in his livestock rather than in the pasture that serves as the foundation for his way of life. Such an accusation, doubtfully but frequently made against all traditional pastoralists, is in fact more applicable to the commercial rancher in America or Australia—or was in the recent past before declining productivity conspired with a resurgence of the ecological viewpoint, temporarily swamped in the western world by the overwhelming triumphs of technology, to batter the *conquistador* mentality into a renewed appreciation of nature. That is what happened in Vale.

Land misuse in the United States led to that theatrical climax of the depression years when the creation of a "dust bowl" in the high plains region made Americans aware that grapes of wrath might be their return for abusing the land. Curtains of grime, creating darkness at noon, were the outcome of an extension of cultivation conducted without windbreaks or other proper land-use measures, when the plow that broke the plains ripped up the buffalo grass (*Buchloë dactyloides*) that had held a thin soil in place. Its effects were felt in all aspects of land use, including grazing. The passage of the Taylor Grazing Act in 1934 marked the end of an era when cattle kings and sheep barons had enjoyed unrestricted rights to make a tragedy of the commons out of the public range. But the Old West died hard under the steady but at first feeble pressure of the new Bureau of Land Management, that at first idealistic branch of government assigned to administer the Taylor Grazing Act. The case study reports on the application of the new law in the Vale District.

> Cattlemen, sheepmen and farmers had been fighting over land for 50 years. Submission to the new law was difficult. Regulations, such as issuance of permits, determinations of grazing capacities, setting of allotment boundaries, improvements to be constructed, formulas to set grazing fees, and other administrative ground rules came into play gradually. (13, p.25)

What the ranchers resisted was the entire concept of having the government tell them how many head of cattle they could run on public land, involving as this did the whole bureaucratic business of grazing permits and grazing fees. The number of cattle permitted to graze would henceforth be determined, and this was very hard to take, by calculations made of the carrying capacity of the range. The remote, romantic cowboy country was not a cultural setting that looked favorably on bureaucratic regulation, on some namby-pamby with a slide rule telling old hands how many head of livestock they could run. The same could be said of almost any rural setting, where people have been accustomed to leading unfettered lives far from the games played in centers of power. Fears of regulation were often justified in those days when distant officeholders or strange international consultants made their first appearance, filled with good will and paternalistic attitudes, to inaugurate programs that as often as not, like the chicken farms of Combarbalá, drifted into immediate collapse. In Vale, the ranchers' darkest premonitions were realized when surveys kept reducing the number of cattle that would be permitted to graze on public lands. In the Soldier Creek unit, for instance, the ranchers argued in 1935, at the first application of the new law, that old established practices indicated that permits should be issued for 77,419 animal-unit-months of grazing, one AUM consisting of one month of grazing by one adult cow plus calf. A full 15 years of meetings, arguments, and rancor that finally resulted in acceptance by the ranchers of 31,000 AUMs on this unit were chronicled by P.O. Foss as "The Battle of Soldier Creek" (13, p.26).

In fairness to the ranchers, it must be said that their attitudes had been shifting along with changes in broad public attitudes in the direction of improved conservation. They were not completely unconcerned about the deterioration of the rangeland vegetation in the Vale District, by the disappearance of such palatable perennials as bluebunch wheatgrass (*Agropyron spicatum*) and Sandberg bluegrass (*Poa secunda*), and their replacement by noxious shrubs and weeds, invading stands of the annual cheatgrass (*Bromus tectorum*), a possible but less palatable forage highly susceptible to range fires, and, worst of all, the gradual spread of vast monocultures of the unpalatable big sagebrush (*Artemisia tridentata*). Already, on their own, the ranchers had begun to improve their grazing practices after the range had reached a low point about 1920, so that successional vegetation was already increasing its cover and reducing erosion when the Taylor Grazing Act came into force. From their side, the ranchers were convinced that the Bureau of Land Management would accomplish nothing and that if the range were eventually to be restored, it would be by their own unaided efforts. Launched in 1962 against this ingrained distrust, the Vale Rehabilitation Program eventually succeeded in changing attitudes so that the district today is practically a model of good cooperation between private interests and public land management. At the same time, there was nothing impersonal, in that sense nothing bureaucratic, in the way this cooperation developed, in personal acquaintance between representatives of public and private interests, in expanding friendships and occasional enmities.

In the settlement of the huge American West, private ownership of land was never established over more than bits and pieces, with vast regions continuing under the ownership of the federal government in the form of national parks and monuments, national forests, and public grazing lands. Since 75% of the Vale District belonged to the federal government, the Bureau of Land Management had the ultimate weapon through which to enforce its will. Yet if rehabilitation had proceeded by simply laying down the law and demanding compliance, it would never have achieved its present results, its future would be precarious, and embittered local interests would have loosed an infection of ill will that would not only have damaged the Vale Rangeland Rehabilitation Program but would have menaced other rehabilitation schemes as well. As in the Gascoyne basin, the cooperation and confidence of the local land users had to be pursued through dense perennial thickets of resentment and mistrust. Unlike the Gascoyne and weak, unimaginative proposals made for Combarbalá, rehabilitation here would try to avoid making the local people pay the bill in loss of income, whether or not that bill would sooner or later have been placed against their account by nature herself.

> Range surveys conducted during the 1950s showed that the range was overobligated to the point that proper use of some areas of the Vale District would require 50% cuts in permitted use. To avoid this reduction by restoring forage production was the principal motive for the Vale program. (13, p.64)

In 1961, just before the program began, the Bureau of Land Management granted permits for 427,476 AUMs on range that the Bureau itself estimated could support only 285,000 AUMs without damage. As the program continued on its course, the Bureau never slashed the number of AUMs to its estimate of the rangeland's true capacity. In 1966, for example 419,567 AUMs were granted against an estimated capacity of 300,000. By that year, rangeland improvement was becoming obvious, and the ranchers were taking a happier attitude toward both the project and the Bureau of Land Management. This was reflected in their acceptance, here and there, of deferred nonuse, of temporary cuts in the number of cattle they would run.

In its discussions with ranchers in Vale, the Bureau had the fortunate example of the rangeland rehabilitation that had just been carried out at the Squaw Butte Experimental Station near Burns, Oregon, just to the west of Malheur County. The station superintendent told the Vale ranchers that AUM permits could be doubled without damage to the sustained productivity of the range if six management practices were employed—the establishment of more watering points to spread the animals around the range, more work on horseback to herd the animals for the same purpose, sagebrush control by spraying, seeding of crested wheatgrass (*Agropyron cristatum* and *A. desertorum*), adjustments in the dates of the opening and closing of grazing on public land, and the provision of winter feed. He said that these practices, put into effect at Squaw Butte, had increased annual per-cow meat production from 70 kg in 1946 to 180 kg in 1960.

But Squaw Butte was a small experimental operation. Vale was a huge region—big enough, in fact, to demonstrate

> a solution to the national problem of depleted and deteriorating public rangelands. It [the project] proposes to do so without seriously impairing the livestock industry and [while] supporting local economies. The Vale District would be a practical demonstration of the government's ability . . . to solve a critical national problem. (13, p.36)

That was what the Bureau of Land Management said when it went to the U.S. Congress in quest of an appropriation to finance the rehabilitation program. Congress agreed, and eventually appropriated about $10 million spent over the eleven-year period from 1962, when the program began, to 1973, when it shifted to a principal emphasis on maintenance.

> Easy passage of the Vale program proposal through Congress resulted from the emergence of several incidental factors. First, the early 1960s marked the end of the bulk of legal action by Federal range users to de-

lay implementation of cuts in permits as a result of adjudication. Second, this period marked a re-emphasis on conservation by the Federal government. (13, p.37)

The proposal didn't say so, but what the Bureau had to do was supply a solution also to a national problem of depleted relations between ranchers and the general public. The ecological awareness that flowered in the 1960s had cast the ranchers as villains in the public view, not only because of their short-term attitudes toward the range, attitudes that in fact had already withered, but also because of their supposedly hostile views about wildlife.

The start toward range rehabilitation before 1962 came as a cooperative effort between the Bureau of Land Management and the permittees—contrary to many stories in the public press which condemned the ranchers for being interested only in range destruction. (13, p.35)

The Bureau had planned to begin the program with a detailed two-year survey of the range to identify sites for treatment. Officials were told by Oregon's Senator Wayne Morse and Congressman Al Ullman, whose district included Vale and who would later go on to become the powerful chairman of the House Ways and Means Committee, that the approach they had planned was not feasible. Vale would have to show immediate results in rangeland improvement if appropriations for it were to continue to move through Congress. Quick results were also desirable if the confidence of the ranchers was to be strengthened. With much trepidation, the Bureau jettisoned its beautiful survey scheme and headed straight for the range with its disk plows, seed drillers, and aerial sprays. Sites hurriedly selected for treatment were not those necessarily showing the greatest deterioration, but rather those that in the opinion of bureau specialists would respond most quickly to measures taken for their improvement. As it turned out, the Bureau experts, already familiar with the range, made effective choices, probably selecting many of the same sites for treatment that a detailed survey would have indicated.

In other words, the rehabilitation of Vale got under way in a very American style, a slambang swinging into action without too much planning and pondering. Such an approach is the reverse of careful science and the bane of researchers in the practical sciences, who foresee possibilities for causing damage instead of improvement by action that is not thought out sufficiently in advance. Sometimes they are right in this attitude, as can be seen in the unproductive olive orchards and abandoned chicken farms of Combarbalá. But in a world of competing claims against funds, money plowed into planning, yielding no immediate material results, must be weighed against that direct application of funds which flowers in new wealth or in the unbeatable demonstration. A correct ecological approach finds its secret in a brilliant methodology rather than in extended surveys, which would have to be carried out in accordance with ecological principles, already decided on, in any case. Vale shows that science, always properly cautious, can be overcautious, and that science is not always justified in its predilection toward extended surveys and continual monitoring. What soils scientists want, in addition to rehabilitation, is the perfect case study, equipped with the full baseline data that a detailed advance survey provides, to be matched against shifts in data that emerge from detailed monitoring.

It must be said, on the other hand, that the endless quest for incontrovertibility in conclusions contains the essence of the scientific procedure that has so rapidly brought these young disciplines—agronomy, soils science, and their allies—to a state of development from which they can propose workable solutions to the physical manifestations of desertificiation, no matter what the setting or the circumstances in which the problem has arisen. The difficulty arises from a kind of benign conflict of interest. The scientists who have discovered these solutions are generally more interested in science itself than in the practical rehabilitation that spins off it, and they will invariably incorporate elements into projects that advance science itself while only coincidentally exerting any particular impact on the problem in question. This is one of the ways in which science maintains its progress and as such might be regarded as a proper part of the bill for rehabilitation—its payoff will pop up in the next problem to be confronted, or the one after that. Sometimes, as at Vale, the bill is examined to see if that part of it must be paid right away. A compromise was made, in spite of the fact that Vale was supposed to serve the nation as an experimental project in rangeland rehabilitation. As matters turned out, the Vale program provided much instruction anyway, arising from what was learned by applying a mixture of treatments to different edaphic settings in this part of the American West. An explicit research element was not totally eliminated.

> Sixty-nine test plots and exclosures, built before and during the early years of the Vale program, played a strong role in site selection and stipulation of treatments. Some of the exclosures continue to provide useful vegetational information. Many areas, alkaline soils for example, on which plot responses to treatment were poor, did not show promise for large-scale success and were cancelled from the projects. Conversely success in plots led to successful projects on areas originally rejected. Test-plot results did not guarantee success. Their use, however, demonstrated the value of pilot tests, a highly important lesson for any rangeland rehabilitation program. (13, p.46)

Spraying, plowing, and seeding, and sometimes fire, were the methods used to eliminate the undesirable big sagebrush and rabbitbrush (*Chrysothamnus spp.*). Although not part of the program, attacks by the *Aroga* moth also thinned some stands of big sagebrush, yet rarely killing more than 10% of a stand. The Lodge brush control project is the case study's example of a spraying operation.

> Three flagmen marked the spray runs, and they used two-way radios and four-wheel-drive vehicles to keep in line. The contractor used two converted TBM torpedo bombers of World War II vintage, each capable of carrying 3,100 liters of spray. He also furnished the spray mixture, consisting of 2.2 lb. acid equivalent 2,4-D in 11 liters of diesel oil per hectare. Each aircraft covered approximately 95 hectares per trip. Each trip involved 20 minutes of flying time from the Homedale airport and 3 minutes for loading. The aircraft flew at an altitude of 15 meters, and spray runs were 58 meters apart. Spray extended over a strip 120 meters wide, giving excellent herbicide overlap. This operation covered 2,630 hectares between 4:45 a.m. and 4:20 p.m. on May 15, 1964, at a cost of $5.20 per hectare. Winds stayed below 16 km per hour; otherwise, the operation would have been halted. Temperature rose from −2°C in the early morning to 18°C in the afternoon. Soil moisture was 12%. The resulting kill of sagebrush was excellent. (13, p.49)

For environmental reasons, the project subsequently replaced the diesel oil herbicide carrier with water, which worked even better provided the applications were precisely timed. Sprayed areas containing dead sagebrush were sometimes burned, sometimes seeded, sometimes both. Plowed areas were invariably seeded, usually with the crested wheatgrass that had thrived so successfully in test plots and at Squaw Butte.

> Contracts required plowing to a depth of 10–15 cm and an estimated 90% kill of brush, which often required two passes over the land.

Rangeland plowing generally commenced in late summer or fall immediately prior to seed-drilling time and at the direction of BLM personnel. Timing of plowing operations was not particularly important as a factor in percentage brush kill, but it may have been critical in preventing brush seedling establishment. Plowing after seed of big sagebrush had matured probably fostered big sagebrush regeneration. Primary factors in the success of plowing operations were degree of rockiness, slope and species of brush. Low sagebrush (*A. arbuscula*) and rabbitbrush resisted plowing. (13, pp.46-47)

Plowing and seeding, using a standard 8 kg of seed per hectare applied with a rangeland drill, cost around $37 per hectare. But no one is going to plow the equivalent of the State of Massachusetts on a budget of $10 million, even at 1970 prices. By 1973, a total of 164 subprojects had applied treatment of one kind or another to 221,780 hectares, or just 10% of the huge Vale District. Yet a survey carried out in 1975 showed that vegetation had improved throughout the whole District, and that erosion had been brought under control almost everywhere, with gullies stabilizing under a brush and grass cover. The most difficult challenges to rehabilitation were those eyesores degraded precisely because they surround population centers, where they persisted as public relations problems under the critical eye of every passing tourist.

That the range improved almost everywhere can be attributed to the superior pasture provided by the treated sections and to the better distribution of livestock which was also a major goal of the program. This was achieved, as suggested, by more herding and riding. It also came about because the district increased the number of its watering points by constructing 583 reservoirs, developing 440 springs, and digging 28 wells, all supported by 860 km of pipeline, opening up new parts of the range to grazing. Livestock control was improved also by 3,200 km of fencing constructed by the program, this equipped with 360 cattle guards.

Focused as it was on rangeland rehabilitation, the Vale program was also concerned with improving wildlife habitat and opening up recreational areas and campgrounds to vacationers, fishermen, and hunters. As an example, the wires on fences were placed so as to contain cattle but not to halt the movement of muledeer and antelope across a range whose general improvement was as good for them as for livestock. Antelope prefer places where brush has been removed and crested wheatgrass planted. Although the number of antelope hunters tripled in the years following the initiation of the Vale program, the population of animals increased 2.6 times. Around 2,500 wild horses roam the Vale rangelands, to the occasional complaint of ranchers who say that the horse populaton is out of control. Bighorn sheep, which had vanished from the region, were reintroduced, and a small flock seemed to be prospering. Reservoirs were stocked with game fish, and nesting sites were constructed despite considerable problems in furnishing some of them with water.

These competing uses of the rangeland were developed with a minimum of conflict with the primary users, the ranchers. Some problems arose because sportsmen left gates open, and gates had to be replaced with cattle guards. A more serious problem emerged out of the use of off-the-road vehicles, which, when operated off the road, have a fatal capacity for generating local erosion. Recreation and the conservation of wildlife serve as reminders that the drylands have many uses besides agriculture, that other uses are also potential sources of desertification, and that the deterioration of dry landscapes is as destructive of other uses as it is of agriculture. An industrialized nation like the United States which can come up with funds enough to run disk plows over arid rangeland can also exercise what seems almost the luxury of maintaining wildlife and constructing campgrounds. No one has yet proposed putting picnic tables anywhere in Oglat Merteba or in the Azawak and Eghazer, where a certain desperate quality to life makes the idea seem ludicrous. Yet the future must eventually offer to lives that are lived everywhere something more gracious than mere survival. Tourism, which has to be managed as carefully as cropping or pastoralism, and even more carefully when it comes to its social impacts, can serve to provide alternative livelihoods in drylands. Care must be exercised to see that the profits from tourism do not leave the touring region, as they do all too often under present arrangements, while the local people are converted from independent yeomen into the servants of spoiled travelers. The long road across the Sahara from Agadès to Algiers will eventually be paved throughout its length. Petrol stations will be placed at regular intervals along it. Sometime after that—we can count on it—the sign "Camping" will show the traveler where he can pitch his tent in the midst of a wide land from which the dome-like huts of the Kel Tamasheq will probably have disappeared.

10

LUNI

"Subjugated, superstitious, illiterate, laden with innumerable taboos"

BEYOND ARABIA, the drylands of the northern subtropics extend eastward following the 30th parallel across Iran and Pakistan. In northwest India, the Aravalli Hills, a low range rising out of the Rann of Cutch, point northeastward to Delhi, a city at the edge of the drylands made into a capital by Moghul invaders who would not have felt at home in humid regions. These newcomers from Mongolia, via arid Central Asia, would be comfortable in Delhi looking northwestward to the semiarid Punjab. Farther to the west, beyond the Aravalli Hills lay—well, not true desert, you have to go as far as Iran for that, to the lunar landscape of the Dasht-i-Kavir—something that here they called the Great Indian Desert.

From Dakar to Delhi stretches the earth's widest swath of unbroken drylands, whence they go on even farther to the east, to be sure, but in a jumbled and confused pattern to the north of the great mountain chains of south Asia, to end, finally, in the grasslands where the Moghuls originally came from. The easternmost portion of the Dakar–Delhi axis has long been the most densely populated of all the earth's arid regions.

> The Indian Desert is unique among the deserts of the world; not a single oasis nor a native cactus breaks the monotony of this vast ocean of sand. By arid-land standards, however, it is quite heavily populated. Average density is 46 persons per square kilometer. . . . It also maintains a livestock population of over 23 million head, as well as a large number of wild animals. (3, p.3)

THE LUNI DEVELOPMENT BLOCK

The case study cites Tod's *Annals and Antiquities of Rajasthan* (Routledge and Kegan Paul, 1929, 1932):

> Tod records that in the year 1212 AD, when a scion of the Rajputs who subsequently founded the ruling dynasty, arrived in the desert, he found the whole region occupied. . . . Jodhpur was colonized by a number of tribes who owed allegiance to a head with a capital at Mandore (10 km from present Jodhpur town) . . . the entire present-day Rajasthan Desert had been colonized by the beginning of the present millennium. . . . The highly adaptive and evolved form of present-day agricultural practices indicates that many centuries of human experience must have gone into its making. (3, p.18)

Here, as in other regions where desertification is occurring, disputes have arisen as to whether the climate is drying out and enlarging the Great Indian Desert. Climatic change has taken place in the distant past—on that the evidence agrees. The most recent of such episodes centered around a time 4,000 years ago when desiccation transformed the Saraswati River, celebrated by the Vedic poets, into the insignificant stream that now loses itself in the sand of Rajasthan. It may have been this episode that spelled finish to the great irrigation civilization of Harappa, the mysterious people who first domesticated cotton, who first tamed the chicken. Or perhaps it was not mere advancing aridity. Perhaps, like the Sumerians, the Harappans succumbed to the weight of sodium spreading the curse of salinization over their irrigated lands. It has been noted that they applied gypsum to their soils, this being a standard treatment for sodium contamination. In any case, no episode of progressive desiccation can be traced in modern times, despite occasional assertions to the contrary. (50, p.25)

What modern times do show without equivocation is a marked acceleration in the density of the already dense populations in India's drylands. This is clearly evident in the Luni Development Block, a 1,989-km^2 chunk of land in western Rajasthan in which desertification processes have been minutely examined by specialists from the Central Arid Zone Research Institute (CAZRI), located in Jodhpur only a few kilometers to the north. Until recently, the population of Luni Block oscillated around a figure of 30,000, kept in check by a high incidence of contagious disease. Modern medicine has learned how to control contagious disease, and the introduction of immunization first, and then antibiotics, produced a population explosion that tripled the number of people in Luni Block in a little more than 70 years. Instead of a traditional density of 16.21 persons per square km (as in 1901), the 1971 population of 95,922 persons congested the district with a density of 48.07 persons per square km without the least sign that this rocketing growth is about to decelerate. The fact of more people has not necessarily meant a corresponding increase in the number of livestock in the mixed cropping–livestock agricultural regime that has characterized this region. That is possibly due to the fact that pastures have degraded and fodder is less readily obtainable. There has been a shift in Luni Block from sheep to goats, to the most destructive of all domestic animals but the genus best able to cope with the degradation of pastures that its omnivorous appetite helps to bring about.

Even the traditional population density was high for a district that gets between 310 mm and 390 mm of annual rainfall, so little that Luni Block, in terms of rainfall alone, should be classified as arid. The scientists at CAZRI would designate 80% of the Block as semiarid in terms of a moisture index calculated by the Penman method. In any case, the traditional patterns of land use are those ordinarily applied to semiarid conditions, which is to say that livelihoods in Luni Block are based on rainfed cropping, employing "dry farming" techniques that typically support populations far denser than those that depend on pastoralism as practiced in the Gascoyne basin, in the Eghazer and Azawak, or in Vale, Oregon. The much higher returns from rainfed cropping explain its destructive extension into regions too arid for its permanent application, whether it is driven there by population pressures, by an excess of people in search of survival, by governments demanding cash crops for export, or by the short-term pressures of market economies which hold out their ceaseless lure of quick money.

Rainfed cropping systems are often blended with the raising of livestock. There are always animals around such farms, raised on fodder crops or on the stubble of harvests where their manure automatically fertilizes the soil—or is used as fuel in woodless regions such as the Luni Block. In a global perspective, larger numbers of animals are reared in the symbiosis of mixed systems than in the monocultures of pure pastoralism. It makes a pattern of land use that goes back to the neolithic origins of agriculture, and it determines the life patterns of the people, so many of them in recent years, who live in Luni Block. The case study provides detailed suggestions as to what those people should be doing to adapt themselves to their new demographic situation. It also devotes some comment to their present practices, unadapted to the demands of a future they have brought on themselves.

> The main activity in the area is rainfed cultivation, accounting for 88% of the area, including fallow lands (12% of the area). The main crops are pearl millet, wheat and sorghum. Yields are low. Agriculture is mainly mixed farming and most households possess sizeable numbers of livestock. Less than 1% of the area is irrigated, the water coming from deep wells. Water for human and animal consumption comes from the village ponds or *nadis* which hold water for between three and six months of the year. (3, p.1)

Rainfed cultivation is nourished by a compendium of techniques for making maximum use of limited rainfall. The soil surface is cultivated, usually with a plow, to enhance water infiltration. This broken surface is kept free of weeds to prevent moisture loss through transpiration. The sowing of seed and its subsequent germination must be carefully timed to occur at a precise point in the rainfall cycle. The crops sown must be drought resistant—such as sorghum, which goes to sleep, as it were, during episodes when moisture is unexpectedly lacking—or drought evasive, such as those crops that come to quick maturity during the short period when rain is falling.

Much of the world's supplies of staple foods, the great grain crops of almost universal use, are all, except for rice, grown in conditions of rainfed farming. They constitute a massive contribution to human welfare and sustenance—to human survival—that is made by drylands vulnerable to desertification. This semiarid and subhumid larder is favored by somewhat more moisture than those almost naked steppes suitable only to pastoralism. In their climax condition, before they were first assaulted by hoes or digging sticks, semiarid regions were preeminently grasslands. Some were pocked here and there by clumps or cover of xerophytic trees and shrubs. Others were unbroken grasslands, like that sea of grass that so caught the American imagination when the descendants of Europeans first entered the great plains. Dry farming is mostly an art of grass. It can thus be traced directly to the origins of agriculture, whose invention, in both the Old World and the New, lay primarily in the discovery of techniques for dealing with grasses.

Grasses grow everywhere, of course, and not just on grasslands. Members of the family *Gramineae* are to be found in Arctic tundra and in the humid tropics. A humble family, grasses are unfavored by spectacular blossoms or impressive size (except for the largest of grasses, the bamboos). Also, they are often a nuisance, popping up even through concrete sidewalks. One is often indifferent to these most important of all plants for mankind, possibly because human beings cannot eat them directly—at least the most prevalent species—and living off the milled and processed products of grass, modern man rarely gives a thought to where his daily bread comes from.

There is something of an ancient symbiosis in the man-grass relationship, one that has only become closer since that distant day when man's ancestors abandoned the trees and the arboreal life, which tied up his hands, in favor of those grassland savannas in which he learned to stand erect and to play musical instruments. Some part of the human intellect must have further developed from the needs of the hunt, that cooperative effort through which evolving humankind enriched his diet by the pursuit of grass eaters. Unable to eat the stalks, human beings eat the seeds, crushed or boiled, and agriculture was first developed to assure the race of men of a constant supply of grass seed. It was a regular and prolific supply of grass seed that converted a vagrant species into a sedentary beast and provided a foundation for the development of ceramics and cities. His wanderings were over when his winter diet consisted of several tons of such seed, gathered at first, cultivated later, eventually to be stored in giant earthenware jars. It is the same substance that still serves as the foundation of the human diet in its multiple modern forms—as wheat, oats, rye, barley, maize, millet, sorghum, and rice. A grass newly cultivated but not for seed, sugar cane has become a major threat to the modern diet.

Much dry farming consists of nothing more than the substitution of some grasses for others, of the elimination of native grasses and their replacement by the sowing of one or another of the domesticated grasses. In Luni Block, where "there is not even a tiny spot," as the case study says, "that does not bear the print of human or livestock activity" (3, p.47), there are problems in trying to determine what the climax vegetation was, or polyclimax, since each separate topoedaphic setting had its own climax. What were the native grasses that were eliminated? A reconstruction has been developed on the basis of what has been found to be growing in certain tiny plots belonging to religious shrines, in which any cutting of vegetation has been traditionally taboo. One notes in passing that here is a taboo that has had a certain scientific value. The various climaxes were then designated in Luni Block by the dominant trees and shrubs rather than grasses—among trees, *Acacia senegal* where the soil has a rocky substratum, *Prosopis cineraria* on the sandy, alluvial plains that make up most of the Block; among shrubs, *Capparis decidua, Zizyphus nummularia*. As for grasses, the successional *Cenchrus biflorus, Eleusine compresa*, and *Aristida spp.* are plowed up and eliminated, to be replaced by *Pennisetum typhoideum* (pearl millet) and other grasses from whose ground-up seeds the chapati bread can be made that sustains life not only here but also in more humid regions of India.

Luni Block is intensely exploited. Besides the grain crops, various pulses are grown (*Vigna radiata, Cyamopsis tetragonoloba,* and *Phaseolus aconitifolius*) as well as sesame seed. Agriculture is supplemented by ancient and traditional habits of food collecting.

> The paucity of water in the desert does not permit vegetable production to meet the requirements of the people. To cope with this shortage in their diet, the people have formed the peculiar habit—luckily restricted to this region—of collecting huge amounts of air-dried seeds and pods of trees and shrubs for the subsequent preparation of curry. The collection and sale of these products have become professions in the desert. Harvests concentrate on seeds of *Acacia senegal*, fruits of *Capparis decidua* and pods of the *Prosopis cineraria*. One can safely state that all the fruits of the *Zizyphus nummularia* growing in inaccessible parts of the desert are harvested for human consumption. Seeds of the grasses *Panicum turgidum, P. antidotale, Cenchrus biflorus, Echinochlos colomum* are mixed with millet for chapati (pancake) preparation, especially during drought years. (3, pp.23-24)

The gathering of firewood is another local industry.

> Most of the villagers . . . procure firewood free from their own fields or from unoccupied lands. The digging of phog (*Calligonum polygonoides*) is a regular vocation and provides employment to a large number of people while making use of camels not otherwise occupied. The digging of roots loosens the soil and accelerates wind erosion. *Prosopis cineraria, Capparis decidua* and *Zizyphus nummularia* are the main victims of this activity. When they are cut at the base levels, the stocks either coppice through root suckers or the above-ground stump gives rise to a new shoot. The trees assume the shape of shrubs or assume prostrate cushioned forms. Large stands of *Anogeissus pendula, Acacia senegal* and *Prosopis juliflora* are cut for making charcoal. . . . All the material used for fencing the crop fields and building houses and villages is drawn from the dwindling desert vegetation. (3, p.22)

The shrubs *Calotropis procera* and *Leptadenia pyrotechna* are cut and left to rot in the monsoon rains, leaving only their long staple fibers from which rope is made. A number of shrubs and trees are topped, sometimes cut to ground level, their leaves sun-dried and stored to be used as concentrated animal feed. The leaves of *Zizyphus nummularia*, a species exploited to the maximum, contain 15 to 18% protein. The red berries of this jujube tree are either eaten or made into syrup. The leaves of *Prosopis cineraria* contain 13 to 15% protein.

The rain that brings life to Luni Block and sprinkles the arid plains of western Rajasthan arrives in the same aerodynamic system that soaks and drenches Assam and the Ganges basin. It is the summer monsoon, and it arrives in June, sometimes accompanied by a clap of thunder that brings dancing in the streets of desert towns. Lasting until September, it is a system of rainfall that dwindles to the northwest, becoming scant beyond the Aravalli Hills, losing ever more force out over the arid plains of the lower Indus in neighboring Pakistan. The timing of the rains in Luni Block, as in all regions of rainfed farming, sets the schedule for the cycles of life. In regions of winter rain, the ground is cultivated after the harvest in late autumn, opening the surface to the intake of water. In Luni Block, the fields are plowed in June, timed to coincide with the arrival of the monsoon. Camels are often hitched to the moldboard plows.

In Luni Block, a thin and stingy environment is exploited for everything it has to give. This is another one of those settings in which land use is the outgrowth of centuries of experience, yielding what the case study calls "age-old and proven local practices" (3, p.51) that make it possible for a region so deprived of rainfall to support such dense populations of men and beasts. It is a complex land-use system that has worked very well for a long time. What is now wrecking this system is the pressure being applied to it by sudden and unprecedented population growth, by the destruction of the culture's demographic equilibrium, increasing the number of people to densities far beyond anything that the system, clever as it is, is capable of accommodating.

> Social values . . . encourage having more and more children. The positive sanctions in the society outnumber the negative ones. Early marriage and the begetting of children are integral parts of the social *ethos* of these people. Any deviation from the established norm is not only looked down upon as grossly aberrant but also as wholly incompatible

with the social fabric of the community. Divorce is a rarity, if not altogether unknown, and widowhood is soon followed by remarriage. While begetting a son is considered essential in order that the family line remain unbroken, a daughter born in the family among several communities which have a system of customary exchange marriage is also held in importance as she has to be given in marriage in exchange for a prospective bride. . . . Coupled with this strong and deep-rooted adherence to the customs of marriage and procreation, improved medical care in recent times has greatly minimized mortality at birth and has prolonged the span of longevity. Family planning has yet to make any inroads into the social life of the population due to its . . . weakness in neglecting cultural variables, creating chains of resistance. (3, p.16)

The population explosion in Luni Block occurred so abruptly that ancient traditions, always somewhat inflexible, have not had time enough to respond. It has summoned in its wake the common causes of desertification—overgrazing, the unwise extension of cultivation, and excessive woodcutting. Cultivation has been extended in two directions, both of which are destructive. It has been carried into the districts with the skimpiest rainfall, those classified officially as "arid," in which productivity rapidly declines while cultivation sets the stage for wind erosion of thin and anemic soils. Also, it has been intensified, slashing the duration of fallow, so that plows come back to the land long before its strength has been restored. At the same time, both practices have reduced the pasture available to stock, thus giving rise to overgrazing without any increase in the number of animals. Overgrazing is brought on, too, by the shift to goats, a species that thrives on degraded pasture, whose increasing presence signals the very deterioration that it helps to promote. As for wood supplies, the case study provides a table showing that in Luni Block the wood situation has become desperate (3, p.22):

Exploitation of Woody Biomass (Metric Tons)		
	1963	1973
Fuel wood requirements	32,703	42,732
Wood for other requirements	1,662	2,338
Total wood produce standing on forest, barren and fallow lands	153,695	81,215

Desertification is hastened in Luni Block by two other causes that sometimes function in other parts of the Third World. Clouds of locusts (*Schistocerca gregaria*) that once swept in with the monsoon clouds to strip the vegetation of its last green leaf seem to have been brought under control through complex campaigns combining aerial sprays with work on the ground. Cyclical plagues of the desert locust (*Locusta migratoria*) have also been brought under control in the Eghazer and Azawak, that other case study area with warm-season rainfall, largely through a United Nations campaign that happened to have been directed by Ralph Townley. Locusts have been a particular threat because the years of especially good rainfall that promote lush pastures and abundant harvests also trigger the hatching cycle of clouds of insects capable of toppling trees by the sheer weight of their massed numbers. Locusts are difficult to control, breeding as they do in the most remote regions out of all human sight, and because they are almost impervious to ordinary insecticides, such as DDT. Insecticides that are effective against them (such as DNC dinitro-orthocresol) are also toxic to man.

A more persistent problem in Luni Block arises from activities by rodents. This menace was described by H. S. Mann, Director of the Indian Council of Agricultural Research.

> Pests join man and his livestock in depleting the vegetative resources of a region. Rodents are an important factor in desertification. Besides maintaining a perpetual pressure on the natural vegetation for their food, because of their burrowing habits, rodents significantly induce soil erosion. . . . Out of 17 species of rodents found [in India's arid regions], ten are of economic importance. In various desert habitats, their number fluctuates from 7.4 to 523 per hectare and their biomass from 435 to 2,641 kg per hectare. Their dietary demands (1,044 kg per hectare) are so insatiable that a resident population of *Meriones hurrianae* during the monsoon can consume the total forage production of an area (1,100 kg per hectare), thus virtually leaving nothing for the livestock. Rodents also ravage the germinating and growing vegetation, feed on seeds, thus lowering the regeneration potential of the vegetation and even debark 20-30% of one- to eight-year-old saplings planted for reforestation of the dunes. The merion gerbils alone are estimated to excavate 61,500 kg of soil per day per square kilometer in cultivated fields during summer, and 1,043,800 kg/day/km^2 in uncultivated areas. (54, p.3)

Gerbils and other rodents loosen the soil to assist the process of wind erosion which acts as a dominant instrument of desertification in regions of rainfed agriculture where fields are stripped of protective vegetation to conserve moisture and to prepare them for sowing a crop of productive domesticated grasses—or herbs, such as groundnuts, or pulses or legumes. Erosion by water also occurs in the Indian Desert, as in other regions of rainfed cropping, but its effects are limited by the flatness of a land on which runoff is slow. Wind erosion is the bane of Luni Block. As the case study says:

> The dominant soil in the Block is light textured. A highly intense arable farming activity for an arid environment and the need to keep the land as clear as possible of natural vegetation so as to conserve moisture and improve the chances for success of a crop in the ensuing rainy season, have led to an induced instability of the soil surface. This situation has interacted with the strong wind regime of the region and accelerated the process of wind erosion. As a result, 26.4% of the area, once a relatively flat plain, has been converted into hummocky plain. The change has been accompanied by a significant loss of soil fertility and a reduced soil thickness over a calcium carbonate concretionary stratum. Human efforts to control the problem through the construction of barrier fences and the plowing back of piled-up sand has so far produced limited success. (3, p.47)

Wind erosion and consumptive rodents are only the most constant of the problems afflicting Luni Block. Improper extension of cultivation in the exteme eastern portion of the Block has interfered with the natural drainage and led to the rise of a saline watertable with the result that 40.3 km^2 of land have become salinized. The destruction of natural vegetation has reduced pasture productivity to what the case study estimates is only 10 to 15% of its potential. The specialists at CAZRI who prepared the case study see the inhabitants of Luni Block as the agents of its destruction.

> By and large, the people have remained subjugated, superstitious, illiterate, caste and faction ridden, traditionalist, and laden with innumerable taboos. The adoption of newer agricultural and other developmental technologies, family planning measures, etc. have made only small leadway. (3, p.5)

An example of such attitudes can be found in their treatment of cattle, by implication irrational, in a region suffering from a forage deficit in excess of 50%.

> Socio-religious feeling and deeply ingrained beliefs toward animal life often override prudence, and the connected rituals add to the deteriora-

tion of already meager available resources. Thus culling, or killing and eradicating of old and useless cattle is regarded as a most strict taboo, and more often than not it was observed that in different villages the useless cattle were an added burden on the grazing and feed resources of the region. Such cattle are fed until they meet a natural death, in spite of forage dearth and poor economic conditions. (3, p.20)

"Subjugated,, superstitious, . . . laden with innumerable taboos." These are not the comments of a culture-bound Victorian anthropologist describing distant natives to a rapt Sunday audience amidst the mohair and antimacassars of the Explorers Club. These are Indians discussing fellow citizens. They are expressing a view of peasant communities that is not uncommon among the most modern observers, including scientists and specialists.

In odd contrast to this uncomplimentary opinion is the case study's portrayal of these same peasants as exploiting a harsh and ungenerous environment to the maximum through a set of ingenious strategies termed "age-old and proven" through which the world's most dense arid-land populations have in the past been supported. The use of the word "proven" is instructive as indicating that these practices have been tested in the natural laboratory of inductive demonstration. Part of the "traditionalist" element among the farmers of Luni Block is a tradition that can only be called science. That, of course, is not the element to which the scientists of CAZRI make their objection. What they are complaining about is plainly the peasants' system of values. Here, to be sure, they are outside their competence, since values are precisely what science is not concerned with, just as scientific method can be viewed as a set of techniques designed to eliminate value judgments from a complex of purely rational assertions. Values, beyond the rational, move systematic thought into slippery ground. The same scientists who deplore a practice that permits cows to reach their natural end are not heard to criticize their colleagues who refuse to have their dogs put away as soon as they become too old to watch or hunt. It was Bhaskar Menon of the Conference Secretariat (and of the United Nations Centre for Economic and Social Information) who suggested that Indian peasants are averse to killing their aged cows for the same reasons that prevent Englishmen—and Indian scientists—from applying euthanasia to senile canines. Yet the failure to send old cows to their happy grazing ground is condemned as lacking in judiciousness.

> A judicious use of limited resources and a check on irrational human exploitation are necessary to improve the desert ecosystem. (3, p.60)

That statement contains the essence of what passes for a solution to desertification problems in Luni Block, as the case study sees it. What was once eminently rational has become irrational, not because practices have changed into something different than they were before, but because their context has altered as a result of population growth loading an ingenious system beyond its capacities. Changes in old land-use practices are required if the altered situation is to be confronted rationally. And changes keep coming to Luni Block, although not necessarily good ones.

> The old practice of keeping the land fallow and the use of the animal-drawn plow, which provides the favorable minimum of tillage, are rapidly disappearing with increasing tractorization in the Indian Desert. This is obviously accentuating the erosion hazards. Similarly, modern irrigation techniques have yet to reach the farmers' fields. (3, p.60)

And not merely modern irrigation techniques—CAZRI scientists have developed and field-tested a range of interesting innovations that would enormously improve productivity in Luni Block and remove many current risks. A better selection of crops and varieties would lead to greater efficiency in the use of scarce moisture and would provide ways of dealing with a delayed monsoon or other climatic aberrations. More flexibility should be shown in setting the time of sowing. Improvements can be made in tillage practices, weed control, and the use of fertilizer. Water harvesting and moisture-conservation techniques could greatly stretch limited water supplies (54, p.215ff). Many innovative techniques, developed specifically with the Luni farmer in mind, would require no monetary input.

> The importance of non-monetary inputs for a small farmer engaged in dryland agriculture needs no emphasis. For instance, simple practices, e.g. the soaking of seeds in water and growing crops in paired-row system, have been found to result in good crop establishment and higher yields. (54, p.223)

There is no reason to doubt the achievements of the CAZRI researchers. Indian thinkers are no longer conceived only as fixed in ecstasy on the dance of Siva, not at least since Ramanujan startled mathematics with his precocities. CAZRI is a distinguished arid-zone research institute, its standards as good as any. The grounds for frustration at CAZRI do not lie in the quality of its scientific effort.

> It has been found that a subsurface barrier of clay 1 cm thick at a depth of 60 cm in sandy soil can significantly increase the yield of pearl millet as in certain vegetable crops like tinda (*Citrullus vulgaris* var. *fistulossus*). Water harvesting coupled with such a subsurface barrier increased the yield by about 200%. Desilting of village tanks (located mostly in depressional areas), which is essential to maintain tank capacity, may yield sufficient silt to implement these technologies, at least in limited areas. The recharge of these village tanks can again be improved by lining the runoff channels with emulsion. (3, p.60)

No, it is not the quality of their work. It is something else.

> It is appreciated that simple rather than sophisticated methods stand a chance of quick adoption in the arid areas. But the success of such operations pivots around the motivation and will of the people. (3, p.60)

With regard to man-made microwatersheds,

> with a ratio of catchment to cultivated area in sandy flat lands of 0.5, ... [they] give remunerative yields in pearl millet, sesamum, moong, grain sorghum, etc., avoiding the risks of crop failure in a drought year. . . . Although the state government has adopted this technique in many places, local inhabitants have not shown much interest in the technologies involved. (3, p.60)

Now the issue has become clear. CAZRI has developed a handsome gamut of technologies capable of restoring prosperity to Luni Block—or at least that prospect is in the air—but the peasants who work the land cannot be persuaded to adopt them. Why is that?

> The widespread illiteracy, coupled with the caste, faction-ridden, orthodox, and tradition-bound nature of the population has not led to the adoption of innovations to any substantial extent. (3, p.16)

There they go again, slipping, alas, into an attitude all too common among development analysts. It is called "blaming the victim." CAZRI researchers can propose a marvelous range of innovations capable of revitalizing Luni Block, restoring its productivity, even despite the increase in population density. But when all is said and done, it is the people who work the land who determine whether or not innovations will ever be applied, and the peasants of Luni Block seem to be uninterested in what CAZRI has to tell them. The situation is not quite like that of Greater Mussayeb. There, extension services were merely absent. Here, however, people have been told. But *the message does not get through to them*. Frustration at CAZRI is thus easy to understand. One can even sympathize with it. How can these farmers be so blind to what is essentially in their own self-interest? To suggest that "superstition" is the barrier seems almost an obvious movement of thought.

Yet it must be admitted that the farmers of Luni Block are not the only peasants in the world to turn a deaf ear to proposals for the improvement of their situations, of their very lives. This curious phenomenon is in fact so commonplace that an explanation has been developed to account for it, the same explanation that can be seen shimmering in the Rajasthan desert by the friction given off in the encounter between two ways of life. The problem with the Luni farmer is to be found, indeed, in the fact that he is "traditionalist." He is, in short, not "modern."

Although much has been made of the distinction between traditionalist and modern, the latter a frame of mind that provides a basis for "progress' and "improvement," in precisely what ways these two outlooks differ from one another is a question whose answers remain somewhat nebulous, still a subject of persistent research. What it is to be modern has been specified in definitions containing such criteria as openness to new experience, readiness for social change, an orientation toward long-term planning, a sense of personal worth, a belief that man can master his environment. Extended tests to determine modernity have been developed by Alex Inkeles and David H. Smith and administered by them in at least six countries around the world, as they relate in their book, *Becoming Modern* (Harvard University Press, 1974). Such tests show that the difference between the two attitudes is one of value orientation. Some modern values are, to say the least, equivocal—they include rampant consumerism and disrespect for old people. It is a field that must struggle to avoid tautology—that the reason, for example, people do not improve their lot is because they lack improve-their-lot attitudes, and what these are is determined by checking the attitudes of people who do not improve their lot. Sometimes it seems to be a way in which Europeans accuse others of being insufficiently European. Yet in the end, it all comes to this conclusion in one way or another—that poverty is a state of mind. And part of "thinking poor" is to be found in a lack of receptiveness to learning. And if there is anything to that, the managers of Greater Mussayeb are going to discover that when they have implanted an efficient extension service in Iraq, it is still not going to be enough. Instruction will have to be supplemented by other techniques, whatever they could possibly be, that will "open" the minds of prospective students so that they can hear what someone is trying to teach them.

All sorts of reasons can be put forward as to why people might not be receptive to a message, and in particular to the message of modernity. Since being modern involves a value system, the obvious reason suggests that the message of modernity introduces a conflict in values. It has been said of Indian peasants that they are not concerned about this world, that their attention is fixed on transcendental realms. Bhaskar Menon points out, on the other hand, that the ordinary Indian is a very practical person, whose concern about the things of this world is displayed vigorously whenever the opportunity is given to him, as it is, for example, in those emigré Indian colonies in East Africa, Singapore, and the Caribbean. This is a question difficult to decide, as are in fact most social questions, as one weighs the possibility that the act of emigration may be sufficient to break the spell of transcendence.

And then again people may not be quick to listen because their established practices are not only "age-old," as the case study describes the agricultural system in Luni Block, but also "proven." It is perhaps natural even for "modern" people to cling to what has assayed as gold in the crucible of experience, and to be suspicious of the unfamiliar. Besides being natural, such suspicions might be a demonstration of intelligence, which, if it had been applied in time, would have prevented the disaster of the boreholes in the Azawak, the emergence of schistosomiasis from the reservoir behind the Kariba Dam, all the many examples of technological blundering to be found in Third World development programs.

Or, still again, an innovation may involve no investment of money, but it may demand more work. Peasants who balk at increased labor confirm opinions of them as "shiftless," an attribute that goes with not being modern. Observed whiling away long African afternoons in conversation under the baobab tree, or occupying the cafes at the entrance gate to Greater Mussayeb, they reinforce that stereotype of the poor as lazy, certainly as unmotivated, a crime almost as serious. Yet some peasants, a blessed number, may resist the message of efficiency because they do not regard productivity as the end of existence. If desertification is to be halted in all settings, adjustments might have to be made to quite different values and choices. The peasant experience has all too often demonstrated that efficiency provides increased opportunities for exploitation. Getting through to ravaged traditionalists may require a study of local history. There is nothing unusual in the forced separation of powerless people, legally or illegally, from whatever scanty possessions they may have managed to accumulate. Peasants are indeed suspicious—and with good reason. They may need a special kind of convincing before they can be led to believe that an innovation is genuinely intended for their benefit.

Careful examination of specific situations would undoubtedly lead to still other suggestions as to why "tradition-bound" people are slow to respond to development campaigns, hesitating even to undertake actions that seem almost to guarantee improvements in the material conditions of their lives. The CAZRI specialists have developed a detailed list of such actions. Where they get nowhere is in convincing peasants to adopt them. That is where they have no technique. And too bad, too, because in addition to specific actions, they would like to see the acceptance of a number of general proposals in Luni Block whose benefits appear incontrovertible.

> At least 21-24% of the lands now being cropped should be converted [back into] pastures and other silvo-pastoral purposes to assure sustained production and resource conservation.
>
> About 58% of the area is occupied by loose sandy soil, the stabilization of which is important for the production of grass and [for] afforestation. Techniques of sand-dune stabilization by the use of proper mulching, silvicultural nursery techniques and grass establishment are fortunately available.
>
> . . . the establishment of shelterbelts and windbreaks to provide mechanical obstacles to the free sweep of wind . . . is very necessary. An earlier recommendation for the creation of a greenbelt approximately 400 miles long and 5 miles wide (644 x 8 km) needs urgently to be taken up.
>
> To provide the inhabitants with an alternative source of energy and to protect the woody biomass of the desert, harnessing solar energy is essential . . . wind-speed data are encouraging for the introduction of windmills, which can operate . . . nine months a year. (3, pp.52-53)

If only, if only. Dictatorial powers, unlimited funding (are these what we shall see applied to Golodnaya Steppe?)—how much development experts must sometimes long for them. If only the inhabitants of Luni Block could be persuaded to do what Chinese peasants are already accomplishing in Turfan and Wushenchao.

> It is . . . essential to formulate and execute on a mass scale an educational program stressing the fullest possible participation of communities in the programs of family planning and the adoption of the newer developmental technologies. (3, p.51)

No other solution was found by the case study to the problems it describes in Luni Block. "Participation of communities" means that they should do what others tell them to do "on a mass scale." Once again, academically oriented specialists can think of no way out of their frustrations except to teach somebody something. Hope, such as it is, seems placed in the possibility that "mass scale" education might succeed where more limited, more personal approaches have failed. This is really quite unscientific, to call for education despite the inductive experience of its past failure to penetrate the selected audience. Perhaps this is another illustration of how physical scientists sometimes flounder when they intrude into the social domain, abandoning their own high standards, tentatively groping their way through mysterious regions they seem required to penetrate because social science, supposedly familiar with this *terra incognita*, has yet to come through with anything in the way of assistance to them. Oddly, their appeals to social science have gone as unheeded as the messages they have directed at Luni Block. A social science that could somehow be persuaded to respond might be brought to investigate why it is that Chinese peasants can be activated into doing what Indian peasants continue to resist. But perhaps social specialists, in turn, resist this question in the belief that it is partisan and ideological. Is that where the question is located? Will something as boring as politics be found to contain the ultimate answer to the problem of desertification?

11
MONA

"Gradually the farmers began to realize ..."

For slightly more than half of its 2,900-km length, the Indus River runs swift through the canyons of the Himalayas to emerge at last onto the plateau centered on Rawalpindi, where dry farming is practiced. Farther on, at Kalabagh, where the Jinnah barrage was constructed, the river slides out into a flat alluvial plain over which it moves through skeins of channels to enter the sea in a wide delta below Karachi, 1,200 km south and west of Kalabagh. This is an arid plain, with rainfall diminishing from an annual average of 375 mm in the north to only 75 mm in the south. We are still here in this easternmost part of the subtropical subsidence zone which ends on the other side of the border with India, in Rajasthan and the Luni Block. In its sluggish course over this final minimal gradient, the Indus receives the waters of the Kabul River from the west, and the "five waters" (*Punj-ab*) from east. Three of these five waters—the Ravi, Beas, and Sutlej—were assigned to India in the Indus Waters Treaty of 1960, after partition, while Pakistan received two, the Jhelum and the Chenab. These waters assigned to Pakistan have been developed together with those of the Indus and the Kabul into an irrigation system embracing 13.3 million hectares, which, if regarded as a single project, would be the largest in the world, one which has converted the arid Indus plain into what has been called "the granary of Asia."

The size of this development places Pakistan fourth in the world in the amount of land under irrigation, exceeded only by China and India, with their wet rice cultivation that brings irrigation even into humid regions, and by the United States, although the Soviet Union,

THE MONA RECLAMATION EXPERIMENTAL PROJECT

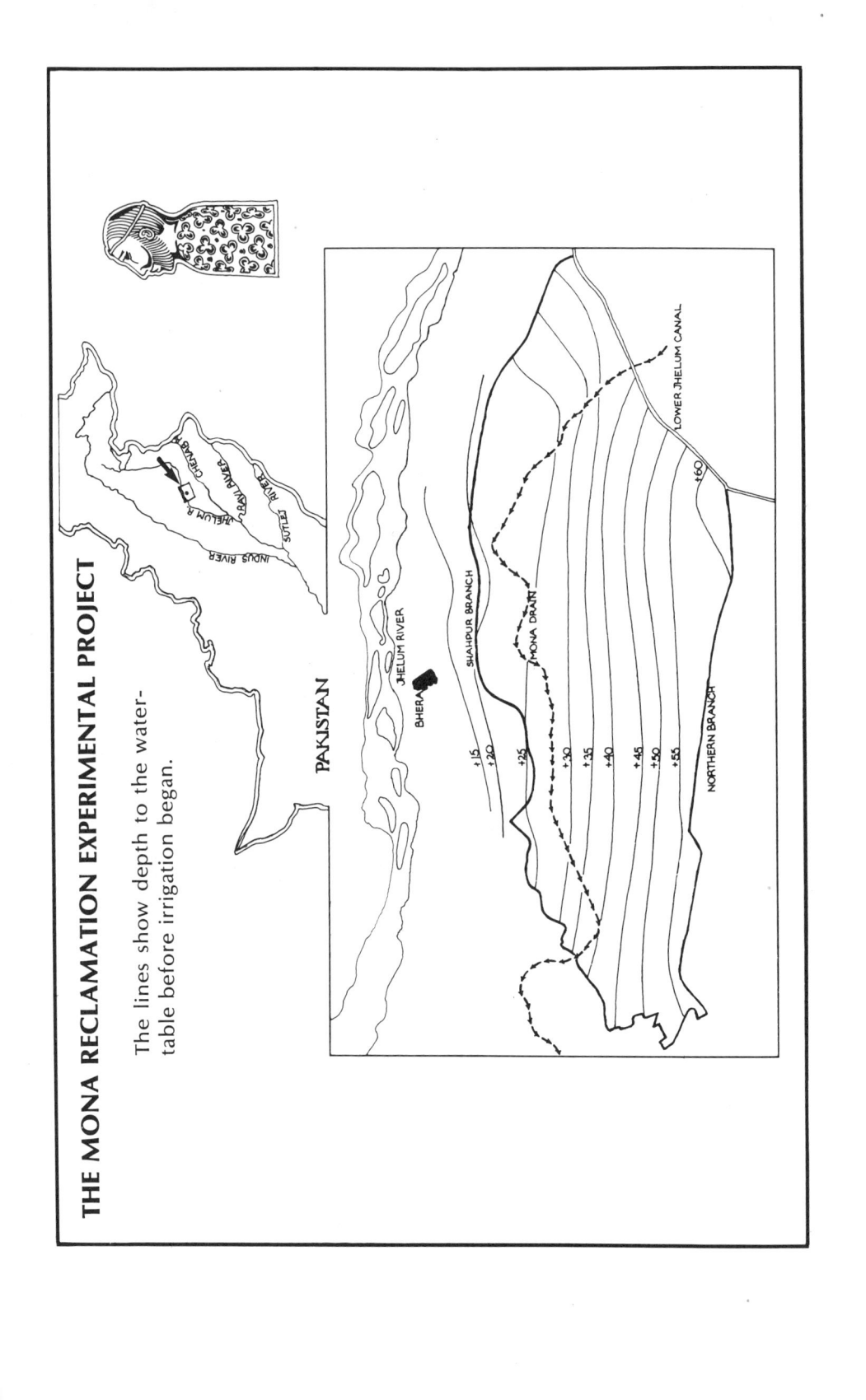

The lines show depth to the water-table before irrigation began.

with huge new irrigation schemes on the drawing board, will soon replace Pakistan in fourth place if it has not done so already. The 14% of the world's croplands that are irrigated produce more than a quarter of all crops, but even a productivity about double that of nonirrigated land fails to express the full potentialities of irrigated cropping. New techniques for allocating water to growing plants—spray, drip, trickle, and pitcher irrigation, among others—stretch the application of available moisture to degrees of efficiency hitherto unknown.

To realize this potential, irrigation systems must be carefully designed and irrigation practices expertly managed, a point emphasized in the management failures in Greater Mussayeb. But it has not been only in Iraq that these requirements have been lacking. Their absence has been so general in the modern world that irrigation had come to be regarded in many places as a technique that automatically seals its own doom. Without proper design and management, irrigation projects become infected with waterlogging or salination, or, what is more likely, with both. Many irrigation systems built in recent centuries have not been properly designed. Bad examples were engineered, often with great care, to bring water where it was needed while insufficient attention was paid to the other major requirement, getting rid of the water once it has been brought to the fields.

In any case, irrigation is an ancient practice in what is today Pakistan, perhaps as ancient as it is in Mesopotamia.

> Irrigation has been practiced . . . from the earliest times. In recorded history, river flow irrigation . . . can be traced as far back as the 8th century AD, when the Arab conquerors differentiated between the irrigated and non-irrigated lands for the purpose of levying land taxes. The oldest form of river flow irrigation is the *sailaba* or "overflow," which is still practiced on a substantial scale within the active flood plains along the rivers. This form of irrigation, though most primitive, has made an important contribution to the agricultural economy. Its inherent advantages of maintaining soils relatively salt-free and high in fertility result from the periodic flooding of the riverain areas. (5, p.9)

Inundation canals were the next development, drawing water out of the rivers flooded by the monsoon. They were inefficient, subject to rapid silting, and a cause of flooding through breaches in their banks. Yet they, too, helped to produce crops on the arid Indus plain, and the Moghuls improved them, adding control structures.

The most spectacular achievement in the utilization of river water took place from about the middle of the 19th century with the development of an intricate system of water control and distribution which has led to one of the largest irrigation systems in the world. A permanent barrage was constructed in 1859 on the river Ravi. (5, pp.9-10)

The Ravi Dam, now supplying irrigation to India, was the first monument in what became a huge system for transporting water on both sides of the international border. In Pakistan, this system came to consist of 17 major barrages and canal diversion works, linked to 63,230 km of conveyance channels in 42 principal canal systems, all with a combined diversion capacity of 250,000 m^3/sec, with individual capacities up to 15,500 m^3/sec. This massive scheme makes agricultural use of 123 billion m^3 in the Indus, Kabul, Jhelum, and Chenab. In addition, irrigated areas get another 7.4 billion m^3 in rain each year while 24.6 billion m^3 of groundwater is available for agricultural use, needing only to be drawn up from the extensive aquifer underlying the alluvial plain. It is a most impressive development, and yet:

Crop yields in Pakistan are among the lowest in the world. The principal reasons for this are the shortage of irrigation water (particularly during the critical period of crop growth), the saline-alkaline quality of the soils, the lack of effective drainage on irrigated lands, the impurity of the seed used, the low level of fertilizer input, the use of antiquated farm implements, inadequate use of plant protection measures, the use of unsatisfactory agricultural and irrigation practices. (5, p.8)

A list so extensive would seem to indicate that very little is right with Pakistani agriculture. In their attack on this set of problems, Pakistani scientists have adopted a strategy that focuses on two key elements. One seeks the improvement of extension services to transmit superior land-use practices to ordinary farmers. The other concentrates on that nemesis of large-scale irrigation systems, drainage, and the difficulties, even disasters, that ensue when drainage is impeded, or not properly designed into the system.

Prior to the introduction of the present system of canal irrigation in Pakistan, the watertable depths over most of the irrigated area were from 24.4 meters to 27.4 meters below the surface. As the extensive network of canals and water courses was unlined, large quantities of water were lost in seepage. Over the years this continuous seepage raised the watertable . . . almost to the ground surface, causing waterlogging and widespread soil salinization. (5, p.11)

The salination is a natural consequence of the waterlogging. All irrigation water contains some dissolved salts, and those in Pakistan range from 100 parts per million in the north to 350 parts per million in the south. These ratios mean that the salt content is low, that the problem does not lie in the quality of the water. Evaporation from persistently high watertables is the process that, given sufficient time, will deposit salts in the soil's topmost horizons. By 1958, when the Salinity Control and Reclamation Projects (SCARP) were established to combat these problems, 31.23% of the soils in the Punjab were affected by waterlogging and 25.63% by salination, while the situation in the Sind, in the southern Indus plain, was even worse. The SCARP program was assigned to the Water and Power Development Authority. This authority organized the Mona Reclamation Experimental Project to carry out research on agricultural development and to encourage an effective use of land and water that would reclaim saline soils. The research was planned so that both physical and social aspects of land and water use would come under consideration.

The Jhelum is the northernmost of the "five waters." The Macedonians called the river Hydaspes, and it was on its banks that Alexander met the army of the Punjab under King Porus, there where the soldiers from afar chopped the legs of war elephants as if they were trees in a forest. Upstream from the battle, after it was over, the Macedonian army toppled real trees to build the boats in which Alexander's forces sailed down that same Jhelum River in the direction of home. A hundred kilometers or so downstream from the battle scene, the Macedonians could look to the south of the river and see beyond the left bank a paramecium-shaped piece of land that today is the site of the Mona Reclamation Experimental Project. Containing 44,500 hectares, of which 41,300 hectares are potentially arable, this site was selected both for reclamation and for the case study because it is representative of conditions to be found in the waterlogged and salinized areas in the north Indus plain. Rainfall here averages 380 mm per year. Soils are inherently fertile despite a relatively low nutrient content with limited availability of nitrogen and phosphate. A low ratio of sodium to calcium keeps the soil open, permitting water to percolate downward so that salinized land can be reclaimed by leaching.

The Rasul barrage was completed on the Jhelum River in 1891, and the Lower Jhelum Canal, which draws on water impounded by the Rasul dam, was opened in 1903 to bring canal irrigation to the Mona district. Before that time, the watertable in the district fluctuated with seasonal recharge, varying from six meters to 18 meters below the surface, with groundwater movement toward the south, away from the river which recharged it. The study zone is bounded by the Shahpur Canal on the north, which has water only seasonally, and the Lower Jhelum Canal and its northern branch on the south, which carry water in all seasons of the year.

> Water distribution to farmers on each outlet is made through a system called *warabandi*. Each farmer gets his share of water for a fixed period during each week or ten-day period as may be the prevalent practice. His time . . . is in direct proportion to his farm area. The farmer diverts water to his field by making a cut in the water course at the beginning of his land holdings. When his stipulated time is over, he closes the earthen cut and allows the water to flow downstream to the . . . next farmer. The practice suffers from the inherent defect that a farmer is obliged to turn water on his field whether he needs it or not, and at critical times of his crop requirements, he may have to wait for his turn. (5, p.31)

Seepage from unlined canals in this somewhat crude system worked together with the barriers thrown by the canals across the natural flow of runoff to begin raising the watertable from the moment the canal system went into operation. A drainage network designed to empty the district toward the west proved unable to keep groundwater at depth. Where the watertable was lowest, it rose the most, so that by 1965, when reclamation by tubewells began in the Mona district, the watertable was close to the surface everywhere and the entire district was affected by waterlogging. Its noxious accompaniment, salination, had deposited sodium and other salts on one-sixth of Mona's arable lands.

These salts are, of course, chemical substances brought down by the Jhelum from up above. They are minute fragments of the Himalayan range out of which the Jhelum springs and which, given enough time, will be worn down to sleepy rounded hills by the microscopic but persistent losses of their mineral substance to the Jhelum, the Ganges, the Indus, and all those other springs and seeps that unceasingly gnaw on them. Bits and pieces of the mountains are temporarily grounded in the soil at Mona where they concentrate locally in such dense quantities that they kill the productivity of the soil. On the other hand, many of these substances transported by water are needed by plants and are used by them after they have been dissolved, changed to ionic form. Carbon and oxygen, two of the 16 elements required by plants, are obtained almost entirely from the carbon dioxide that forms a constituent of air. The other 14 necessities move from being parts of rocks to new positions as parts of plants in a transformation that sometimes requires a time span of geological epochs to complete. Some very common elements are not on the list of those needed by plants, as given on page 99. Sodium for example, although required by animal life, is an element that plants do very well without and one that in fact can be toxic to vegetation. This implies, incidentally, that herbivores cannot get the sodium they need from grazing, and salt licks must be available to them.

The identification of the elements essential to plants is one of the accomplishments of the modern science of botany. It is a part of knowledge that could not have been worked out before chemistry had unveiled the elemental construction of matter, and therefore not before the nineteenth century. Only after that was it possible for a science of agriculture to develop in its modern lineaments. Armed with retort and test tube, the new agriculture has pursued these 14 chemical elements as they penetrate and compose fertile soil. It has tracked them as they are converted into the ionic forms in which they can be ingested by plants, and it has watched, amazed, the dance of their ions, one replacing another on cation exchange sites on clay and humus particles. They have followed each of them through the transformations that deliver them at last into a kind of soil soup from which plants drink by capillary action and osmotic pressure. The movement of essential elements has been located in a grand design, the ecology of soil, which teems with life in a multitude of forms, including the living roots of plants probing downward and outward, questing for water, for the essential moisture that brings them the food they need in solution.

When the Harappans applied gypsum to sodic soils, they, too, were practicing science since the value of gypsum had been established empirically, by experience. Nor can one say that they did this without theory, although the paradigm through which they rationalized this action—whatever it may have been—would doubtless be regarded today as a stange kind of science, perhaps involving concepts of will, even emotion. The modern attitude prefers to see only mechanical cycles, a never-ending rhythm without mind or consciousness, as balances are maintained or altered in energy, moisture, nitrogen, phosphorus, all the other essential elements. Even in its childhood, a stage of existence that it may not yet have left, the new agriculture discovered how cycles and equilibria can be changed purposefully, how soil can be transformed in almost any desired direction, actions whose possibilities are confined only by the dismal realities of economics. Crops are produced through techniques that more and more resemble cuisine. Ingredients are added or removed from soil, which is soaked or drained, mulched, burned over, mixed in tillage of various types, left to rest in fallow, like loaves sitting on a windowsill. The new agriculture does not yet know everything. It does not know, just as an example, how chlorine functions to promote growth in roots, where this essential element evidently does its work, but it will undoubtedly find this out before long.

It does know why a few crops, such as paddy rice, are so peculiar that they thrive in soaked conditions that would kill most plants. Without going into that, even though it is a peculiarity that feeds most of Asia, it can be said of waterlogging in general that it fills the pores in soil with liquid, bringing about an anaerobic condition of oxygen deficiency that hinders the respiration of roots and depletes the soil of its nitrogen supply by converting nitrogen into a gas that bubbles back into the atmosphere. Waterlogging also means that water evaporates from the soil surface leaving behind the salts previously held in solution to form incrustations—or ever more concentrated solutions in the moisture that remains. Extremely salty water behaves as if it were thirsty. Seeking to dilute itself, it exerts a reverse osmotic effect, preventing plants from absorbing moisture, moving moisture in the wrong direction, even pulling it out of roots. Harappans knew that salty water is bad for plants, but a concept such as reverse osmotic effect would have been outside their usual paths of thought just as it is foreign to the pastoralists of Mussayeb or the farmers of Luni Block, this and all the rest that the new science would love to tell those old peasants if only they could be persuaded to listen.

Salts also make the soil more alkaline, moving it away from that ideal pH of 5.5 for organic soils or 6.5 for mineral soils, the former a state of ever so slight acidity wherein essential nutrients are most richly available to plants. A soil should not be too acid, as soils tend to be in regions of heavy rainfall, and a pH below 5.5 will ask for applications of lime to move it toward the alkaline side. Dryland soils rarely have problems of excess acidity. Low rainfall means a lack of leaching, leaving alkalizing salts to linger in upper horizons. Under very alkaline conditions, several of the essential substances form insoluble compounds and cease to be available to plants. Phosphates, in particular, form the insoluble tricalcium phosphate denying plants the phosphorus atoms required in the nucleus of every plant cell.

Among all the salts, common table salt is the worst offender. As it goes into solution in the soil, forming a broth sometimes more concentrated than seawater, its sodium cations become active, pushing the pH to an extreme of alkalinity beyond nine or ten. Sodium then attacks soil structure, disintegrating those clods and peds that provide easy channels for the percolation of moisture. A proportion as low as 20% of exchangeable sodium cations can work this damage in coarse, sandy soils, while only 10% is enough to start the process in fine-textured clays. Dispersed particles clog the soil's pores, and horizons become impermeable to both air and water. A hard crust can form on sodic soils, blinding white where sodium chloride has precipitated on the surface and put the soil to bed, whose white sheets are stained with black slimy pools where dispersed colloids that once were humus are extruded from the soil to signal the destruction of fertility. Sodic soils need special treatment before any other rehabilitation can be applied to them. Gypsum replaces sodium cations with those of calcium, that constituent of cement and bones that is also needed by plants. Only after the sodium ions have been so replaced, the pathways in the soil thereby unblocked, can other excesses of other salts be dealt with.

Soils affected by salts are reclaimed by leaching, which is to say, water is poured on them to dissolve the salts and carry them away downward and outward, away from the root zone. Roughly 300 mm of water low in salt, such as the comparatively clear waters of the Jhelum River, will leach up to 80% of the soil salts, which is why regions with more than 380 to 400 mm of annual rainfall will tend to have few salty problems. In many situations, rainfall plus irrigation water, applied in amounts calculated so as just to supply plants what they need, is sufficient moisture to keep the soil automatically leached of salts. Sometimes, however, in certain very arid situations, plant needs do not add up to enough water to carry out leaching as well, and additional water, termed the leaching requirement, must be added if salt concentrations are to be avoided and salts effectively washed away. Leaching requirements have sometimes been ignored in irrigation systems, as has proper drainage, made all the more important by the leaching requirement. These oversights constitute the principal reason why irrigated lands end up progressively damaged through waterlogging, salination, and sodium concentration, a destruction apparent in 5,000 years of historical record in which the effects of this form of desertification extend to the crusting and decay of entire civilizations. Conversely, the unmatched endurance of ancient Egypt was at least partly due to the fact that irrigation supplied by the annual flooding of the Nile automatically leached and drained the soils to be planted, so that only today, with the construction of the Aswan high dam, which has brought an end to the annual inundation by the river, is this granary of the ancient world for the first time confronting problems with salination.

In the reclamation effort applied to the Indus plain, directed by SCARP, waterlogging was the problem that had to be dealt with first. Elevated watertables had to be lowered so that leaching could take effect. One approach would be to line the entire system of canals and water conduits to prevent the seepage through which 25% of irrigation water was lost en route to the farmer's field. The new Rajasthan canal in neighboring India carries water across the Indian Punjab on a bed lined with burnt clay tiles. A future can be envisioned so desperate for fresh water that all irrigation, regardless of expense, would be carried through pipes to prevent evaporation as well as seepage. In the present-day Indus plain, in a country with a per capita gross product (in 1973) of only $121 per year (79, p.696), even the least expensive lining methods—plastic sheets or bitumen coating—would involve prohibitive outlays, not to mention the inconvenience of interrupting a working system in order to line it. In any case, lining the canals would merely cut off a principal source of groundwater without eliminating the present excess. SCARP decided on another approach. Tubewells would be installed and the water pumped out of the soaked earth. This method had the advantage that the water thus sucked out of drenched soil would be an extra amount for irrigation, as affluent farmers had already found out by their installation of private tubewells. By the time of the case study, 11,000 tubewells had been put in place by the Water and Power Authority to supplement the 146,000 tubewells of smaller capacity installed by landowners. In the study area, 138 deep tubewells were sunk, each with a pumping capacity of 0.11–0.6 m^3/sec. Another reason why Mona was designated as a study area was because previous investigations in the district provided baselines on which comparisons could be drawn. For the Mona Reclamation Experimental Project was established, among other purposes, to carry out precise monitoring of all aspects of tubewell performance, including groundwater level and quality, state of the soils, effects on agriculture, and beyond—to monitor the social and economic conditions of the people whose lives would be affected by what was going on at Mona.

> The project tubewells started pumping in 1965 to control waterlogging and to supply additional irrigation water. This imposition of a new discharge source on the groundwater reservoir changed the [then] existing hydrologic balance and the watertable began declining gradually. As a result of continuous tubewell operation over the past eleven years, the watertable has gone down by 0.9 to 1.8 meters and has now stabilized over most of the area. (5, p.74)

So far, so good. Even if the watertable had been brought down to nowhere near its pristine depth, it had at least been lowered below the root zone. As for the salinized sections of land, eleven years of gypsum and leaching increased the salt-free portion of the study area from 80.6% to 84.5%. Mona had succeeded in demonstrating what had become apparent in some other parts of Pakistan, that salinized soils can be reclaimed if leaching water is available that is low in salts, demonstrating at the same time that this cleansing operation advances with hideous slowness, as was evident from the prospect that the reclamation of Mona will require more than a generation to complete, a process as tedious as it is essential to the ultimate prosperity of the country.

And what of the people of Mona and their social and economic condition, this to be monitored along with the state of the soil? Unlike their neighbors in Luni Block, these are warrior peasants, suppliers of manpower to the armed forces, dwellers in the gateway to invasion of the subcontinent, whose fierceness has been refreshed throughout history by the intermittent arrival of invading armies. Many of these farmers had received their land in 20-hectare grants on condition that they maintain a mare for the cavalry. Islamic inheritance practices have worked to fragment most holdings since they dictate that all sons must receive equal shares. Almost half of the farmers in Mona own their own land, and while half of these again have holdings too small for even subsistence, they demonstrate their independence by refusing to rent additional land, preferring to get by somehow on what their own land provides, in the process undoubtedly overworking it. The maintainers of mares are spared this inexorable disintegration since on horse-breeding grants, succession was established by primogeniture—undoubtedly the reason why the other half of the local landholders still have farms sufficient for subsistence.

> In traditional rural communities, where instead of scientific rationality, folklore and superstitions dominate, the introduction and adoption of agricultural innovations is an intricate problem. (5, p.83)

Once again, a scientist elite expresses its opinion of the peasant mind. Although this lofty attitude is commonplace in the world, taking no account of the invincibly empirical attitudes of peasants, blinkered as it is in the narrow view that only science is "rational," its grounds for believing that peasants are incapable of systematic thought have apparently even less justification in Mona than they do in the Luni Block.

> The adoption of agricultural innovations was slow in the case study area in the post-irrigation period. . . . The use of synthetic fertilizers in the area was introduced as late as the fifties. Initially the fertilizers were distributed free of charge, and farmers were induced to make use of this important input through demonstration plots. In the beginning, the farmers were reluctant to use chemical fertilizers and change their centuries-old system, mainly due to illiteracy. Gradually, however, the farmers began to realize the benefits of the use of improved inputs, as, through demonstration, they themselves saw the advantages of the change in increased yields and consequently higher income. (5, p.67)

That a reluctance to abandon an age-old and proven system should not be attributed simply to common sense arises out of a need on the part of "modern" people to find something to blame in the traditionalist complex, something that will explain why visiting consultants are not automatically regarded as the benefactors that they consider themselves to be. Here, the villain is found in "illiteracy," as though even an illiterate peasant doesn't understand that the official approach is in some ways like that of a dope pusher—get the peasants hooked on fertilizers provided "initially . . . free of charge"—the next thing anyone knows these additives, mysteriously converted into essentials, will have become the major expense in their operations. In any case, these warrior farmers in Mona were not too difficult to convince. Unlike their frustrated colleagues just across the border in the Luni Block, Pakistani peasants seemed to be well on the road to becoming "modern" in 1965, the year when tubewells first began to pump groundwater out of the Mona district.

> In a survey conducted in 1965–66 it was found that there was an emerging consciousness on the part of the rural people that productivity and

prosperity go hand in hand, and that the traditional belief that all that happens in life is predetermined and that man has to accept it as a *fait accompli* considerably weakened. Over two-thirds of the farmers were willing to leave their traditional agricultural practices in favor of the improved techniques, and to borrow money to invest in agricultural operations. Almost three-fourths of the farmers thought that only hard work could change their fate. An element of rationality could be observed from the fact that 87% of the respondents in the rural communities were of the opinion that it was better to send a sick person to a hospital. (5, pp.63-64)

Less a scientific assessment than a bouquet of "modern" biases, that statement offers something of amusement in its saturation with unconscious value assertions. A reluctance to go to the hospital may display one of the more rational aspects of the peasant outlook. It would be a view shared by the middle class in the United States, where rocketing medical costs combined with a nagging persistence of iatrogenic disorders have converted going to the hospital to an utter last resort. The common opinion that traditional peoples are hopelessly fatalist was acquired from the observation of ethnic groups subjugated in colonial systems which made observation of them possible in the first place, and in which they had, in fact, lost control of their lives. The view that this outlook characterized their mental life through all of time helps to reinforce an image of traditional peoples as essentially children among whom it is always a pleasant surprise to find even one element of "rationality" and who therefore stand in ardent need of the course of instruction that the benevolent and paternalistic consultant so longs to convey to them.

Peasants may be victims of folklore and superstition, but in many ways they seem to be much like other people. They want assurances before they will abandon practices that have had centuries of success. Demonstrations are therefore essential in the "intricate problem" of how to introduce innovations.

> Agricultural extension . . . [has] long-term objectives [which] are the establishment of confidence among farmers in market-oriented production as a means for increased satisfaction of wants, bringing farm leadership to bear on local problems, providing media for concerted action by villagers in the interest of agricultural reformation and improved living conditions. Various extension approaches are being followed and these will be evaluated, and a study carried out of the personal and situational factors impeding the adoption of improved agricultural practices. (5, p.72)

What could be more directly to the point, as that point was shaped, for one example, by the overexploited, exhausted soil of Luni Block? And yet the statement comes close to saying that people are going to be examined, their personal and situational factors studied, in order to find out how they can most easily be manipulated, brought to adopt agricultural practices that, because they involve "improved living conditions," no further justification is required to go ahead with human manipulation. Or is that "market-oriented production" so ardently sought, not necessarily because it is good for people—or whether or not it is good for people—but rather because it is perceived by some distant officeholder as good for the problems that bother him, such as an international balance of payments? To solve the problems that markets themselves generate, peasant leisure must be annihilated, the rhythm broken of lives once lived close to nature, and for this must be substituted the "hard work" that three-quarters of the farmers in the Mona district—and here the bureaucrat sighs with relief—have already been manipulated into accepting. In this perspective, extension services are particularly valued as a continuing instrument whereby manipulation, disguised as teaching—and isn't that anyway what a lot of teaching is all about?—can be indefinitely pursued into the future. Now, once such conceivable purposes and attitudes have been brought into the light, and the point made that this bureaucratic underhandedness might even exist in some situations, no one has to insist that this sort of thing prevails universally, and one might even retreat to a less condemnatory and not so hostile a position by suggesting that a principal purpose in making such dreadful charges is merely to illustrate that there are indeed unconscious value positions in what appear to be even the most progressive and upward-looking proposals. Sometimes, it is even possible, such value positions may be other than entirely unconscious.

As portrayed in this case study, extension services, "the bridge . . . between provincial departments of agriculture, research organizations and the farmers" (5, p.94), are a second essential to be combined with demonstrations in a process that has been fraught with such difficulties, tinged with such mystery, in places like Luni Block. Yet in the past, in the Mona project, extension services were poor.

> Many farmers who were keen to accept new ideas and advice could seldom get an opportunity of meeting with extension workers. . . . Considering that the output of research was of no practical benefit unless

transmitted to the farmers, special attention was given to the constitution of an effective extension service in the Mona project. . . . Different techniques and approaches are being tried in the project. Some of the most effective techniques adopted are seventh-day schools, periodic farmers' gatherings, model farms and field demonstrations, libraries, agricultural competition, farm guide clubs and seed bank schemes. To evaluate the effectiveness of extension activities and the impediments to the adoption of improved agricultural practices, a special study has also been initiated. (5, p.94)

This strong focus on information and extension programs, assisted, as the case study declares, by the spread of that ubiquitous innovation, the transistor radio, has shown the desired results.

A decade ago, less than one third (31%) of the farmers were using chemical fertilizer and more than two-thirds of them did not know about the availability of improved seeds. In 1976, 95% of farmers were using chemical fertilizer and over 90% improved seeds of wheat. A critical difference has been made by extra irrigation water and proper drainage conditions, as all dwarf and early maturing varieties need more water besides other inputs. (5, p.83)

Heavy applications of fertilizer are largely what is meant by "other inputs." These new dwarf and early maturing varieties of wheat are the remarkably productive hybrids, bred in Chapingo's fields, for which Normal Borlaug received the Nobel Prize. Together with the "miracle maize" developed in Colombia and the super rice emerging from research in the Philippines, the superior wheat that has come to dominate Pakistan's irrigated agriculture lies at the heart of the so-called Green Revolution, with its prime examples of how the world's increasing food requirements are being met—to the extent that they are being met—by enhancing production on land already in cultivation rather than by the more hazardous expedient of attempting to bring new land into cultivation. The Green Revolution demonstrates the importance of protecting the land that is now in agriculture, to reiterate a central conclusion, a treasure worth any effort to keep it free of that scabrous disease called desertification.

The rehabilitation project had the desired impact on the economy of the case study area. With the installation of tubewells, the problem of waterlogging and salinization has been arrested. The additional water provided by the tubewells encouraged crops which require more water.

> The area under wheat, rice, maize, sugarcane and orchards has proportionally increased, while the area under cotton and bajra [millet] has decreased. The land utilization pattern has improved. In 1965-66, the area sown more than once for both summer and winter crops was 14% of the total farm area, rising to 30% in 1970-71. The cropping intensity increased from about 100% to nearly 130% The rotation of crops has become more pragmatic. Now wheat does not follow year after year but is rotated with crops such as sugarcane, cotton and rice. Marketing facilities have improved. The value of livestock increased from 10 million rupees in 1965 to about 17 million rupees in 1975-76. The value of crops rose about twofold in the same period. (5, p.77)

Pakistan clearly expects agricultural productivity to continue rising until the Indus plain matches the output of the best irrigated lands in the world. Productivity will continue to go up within the Mona project, and Mona, in turn, will lead the way for other parts of the lower Indus valley. Optimism is possible because Mona seems to have found channels of communication, more important than those other channels carrying water, through which contact has been cemented with the people who work the soil. Since communication is possible, the authorities are making every effort to communicate, expanding and improving extension services, testing and evaluating a variety of extension techniques. Yet behind all this busy activity lies something clouded, hidden, a kind of gift given to the nation's agricultural experts without which their efforts might have been useless. In the mysterious heart of the modernization process lies something which the Pakistan experience has exhibited but has not solved. The Pakistani farmer had all by himself somehow already surmounted those barriers to modernization before rehabilitation ever began in the Mona Rehabilitation Experimental District. He was already open to innovation. There he was, demanding instruction, complaining that the extension worker was not to be found. How did he get that way? What made him so different from his superstitious colleague, the farmer in Luni Block, not much farther than a long day's drive away by road.

12
GOLODNAYA STEPPE

"In accordance with the government decision"

IT WAS ON THE BANKS of the Jaxartes that Alexander of Macedon, complaining that he had no more worlds to conquer, turned about to lead his forces in the direction of the Punjab, of King Porus and of his view of what was to be the Mona Reclamation Experimental Project. There at the edge of the world he had set out to conquer, the farthest boundary of the Persian Empire, there on that Persian frontier, he founded the city of Alexandria-the-Farthest. After turning away from that ultimate point, marching back toward India and Babylon along the north-facing slope of the Turkestan Mountains, Alexander could turn his gaze north toward Siberia across the nearer view of what must have struck him as a huge and desolate basin. Today, that same river, flowing from the T'ien Shan to the Aral Sea, linking China to Soviet Central Asia, no longer bears its Greek name. It is called Syr Darya, in the language of the Turks who made Turfan their capital, and Alexandria-the-Farthest is now called Leninabad in honor of a later master of Central Asia who also came from far away. The desolate basin is no longer desolate, consisting as it does today of cotton fields irrigated by Syr Darya waters. In its former condition, as Alexander would have seen it, this basin was described by one N. F. Ulyanov in 1876, in the days before irrigation had been brought to it.

> In summertime, the Golodnaya (Hungry) Steppe looks like a burned-out yellow-gray plain which, being completely lifeless under the scorching sun, quite vindicates its name.... Already in May, grass seed becomes yellow and withered, birds fly away, tortoises look for hiding places, and the Steppe again turns into a lifeless, torrid area, and on the horizon distant snow-capped peaks are barely discernible through the

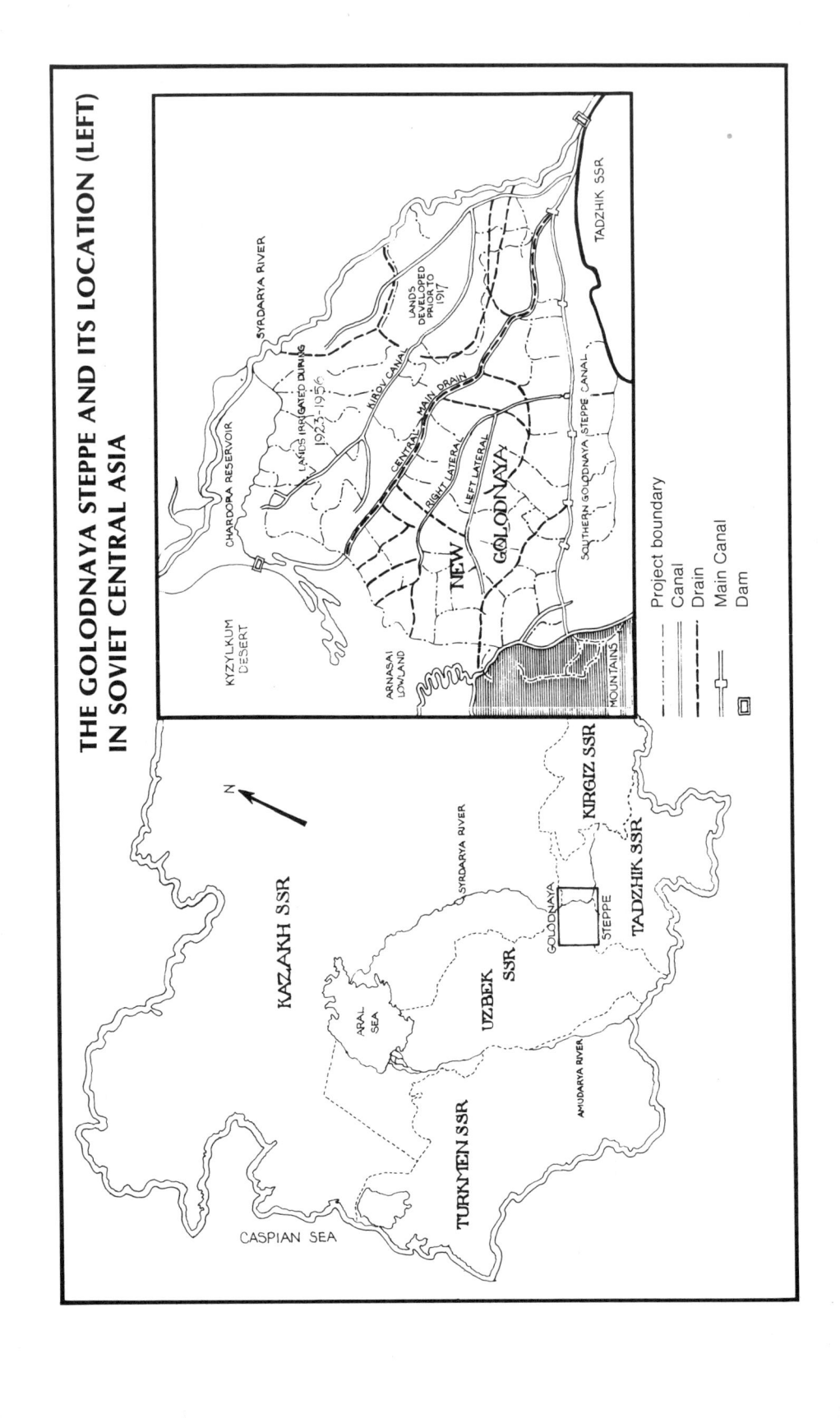

THE GOLODNAYA STEPPE AND ITS LOCATION (LEFT) IN SOVIET CENTRAL ASIA

overheated air. The bones of camels and horses scattered here and there and the stalks of umbels, resembling bones, and dispersed by the wind add to the oppressive impression of the Golodnaya Steppe. (15, p.2)

Now it is green and inviting there, a land transformed, where cotton nods in Siberian blasts that once dispersed umbels. Yet the poor performance of Soviet agriculture has been much publicized in the fecund West, where it has served as a basis for self-congratulation and where little sympathy has been shown to the distinctive cropping problems of this most extensive of all nations, one that has cultivated its territories, for all their extent, under the dilemma that where it rains, it is too cold, and where growing seasons are long, rain is lacking, arid conditions prevail, and the land is vulnerable to desertification.

During the Khrushchev years, the Soviet government attempted to resolve some of its agricultural problems through an enormous extension of cereal cropping by rainfed or dry farming techniques. Plows broke the plains of Kazakhstan, a Soviet Saskatchewan, to treat the world to the interesting lesson that a government that celebrates long-term planning could make the same mistake as private American farmers motivated, as some insisted, by short-term greed. Like the American high plains in the thirties, the soil of Kazakhstan blew away in dust storms in the sixties. It was a disaster that had the same domestic effect as the American dust bowl and thus performed the ameliorative function of disaster, that of awakening people to needs—in these examples, to the ecological needs of arid-land systems. There was an additional reaction in both countries, a swing toward irrigation agriculture, perhaps only coincidentally in the United States, where the dust bowl happened to occur at a time when a number of large hydroelectric power dams were under construction as public works projects to combat the great depression. Some of these dams, Grand Coulee in Washington State, for example, were designed also to back up large amounts of irrigation water. In the Soviet Union, the shift toward irrigation was more abrupt, more clearly the expression of a policy shift, as it became clear that the USSR had turned to irrigation in the hope that controlled watering would finally resolve the nation's never-ending problems with agriculture.

Currently in the Aral Sea basin in Central Asia and south Kazakhstan, 6.2 million hectares of irrigated lands account for 92% of agricultural output and provide employment to 95% of the agricultural population in this region. . . . The irrigation potential amounts to 52 million hectares. . . . In order to increase the output of such products as cotton, rice, fruits and grapes in the Aral Sea basin, it is planned to accelerate irrigation development. . . . The five-year plan 1976-80 assumes to add annually 180,000 to 200,000 hectares of irrigated lands. By 1990, the total area will reach 9 million hectares. This will result in nearly full utilization of the available water resources—Syr Darya, Amu Darya, Zarafshan, Talas, Assy and other rivers. Further development of irrigation is planned based on the use of Siberian river flow (Ob and Irtysh). Ambitious plans for the transfer of their flow southward are formulated for execution during 1990-95. (15, p.1)

"Ambitious" is perhaps too thin a word for projects that would take the waters of huge Siberian rivers, now discharging far from active agriculture into the distant Arctic Ocean, and turn them southward into the drylands of Kazakhstan and Central Asia. Questions have been asked about the ecological effects of this Arctic loss of large amounts of fresh water. Soviet authorities have issued statements saying that polar ecosystems would suffer only minor disturbance, implicitly denying that the diversion of the rivers might result in the melting of the ice covering the Arctic sea. If the world remains at peace, it will undoubtedly have a chance to see for itself what the effects will be, since there is no reason to disbelieve that the Soviet government intends to go ahead with this fantastic proposal.

In looking to such a future, the Golodnaya Steppe, bits of which have been watered for almost a century, provides a preview of what is possible. Located in the wasp waist of Uzbekistan, where the Syr Darya leaves the Tadzhik border, the steppe contains 600,000 hectares of potentially arable lands. At nearby Dzhizak, once the region's sole and only town, average annual precipitation is 366 mm while open pan evaporation adds up to 1,390 mm. Salty solonchak soils occur in light sierozems showing various degrees of alkalinity, all overlying salty groundwater. The tsarist regime began irrigation works close to the river as a lure to attract Russians into a region populated by peoples of Turkic and Iranian stock, and thus to tighten a permanent grasp on the region by St. Petersburg. Construction was applied to intake only—the besetting sin of irrigation works—supplying water to 23,000 hectares farmed by Russians who were, in addition, given a bonus for migrating to this remote, isolated terrain but who were not correspondingly given any instruction in the mysteries of irrigation. Drainage facilities continued to be ignored despite an early scientific assessment that they were essential. By 1914, secondary salination had turned the irrigated portions of Golodnaya Steppe into "an abomination of desolation . . . a nightmare of malaria, typhus and other diseases" (15, p.19). When the steppe fell under the scrutiny of the new Soviet regime in 1922, 61.8% of its irrigated lands had become salinized.

Between 1923 and 1956, irrigation was brought to 250,000 hectares, comprising a broad strip to the west of the river, on which cotton was planted. Golodnaya became one of several key sites on which Soviet specialists taught themselves the science of irrigation agriculture.

> By 1958 in the old zone of Golodnaya Steppe, some 12 meters of open main drains and field drains had been furnished per hectare. Although this did not fully eliminate the problem of salinity, it contributed to reducing the area of solonchaks from 35.3% of irrigated areas to 9.1%, while heavily saline soils decreased from 22.5% to 18.8%.
>
> Investigations carried out . . . in 1964 revealed that effective soil desalinization on most lands irrigated up to 1956 might be achieved through leaching in association with vertical drainage. . . . It was only due to the construction of over 250 wells of vertical drainage scattered over the whole territory . . . that made possible the reduction of solonchaks to 1,000 hectares and almost totally eliminated heavily saline soils. This raised the cotton yield over the whole territory from 17 quintals per hectare in 1963 to 32 quintals per hectare. (15, p.19)

But long before such wells were even considered, Soviet authorities had decided to try out what is called, in bureaucratic formula, often so empty, "an integrated approach" to bringing irrigation to an additional 262,000 hectares in the southwestern part of the roughly triangular Golodnaya Steppe. Yet this turned into an approach in which integration, surprisingly—of all the key elements of settled life—became its outstanding characteristic, a massive operation reminiscent of the almost military way in which an attack was mounted, say, on North Slope oil. One wonders about ideological differences when reviewing Soviet calculations on "reimbursable capital expenses," "turnover tax shares," "discount rates," and how long it would take the project to turn a profit. Here one remembers that even Lenin said, "Socialism is accounting" (74, p.115n). There are differences, to be sure, coming to light in the way the project functioned, or in the blunt techniques through which its labor was recruited. By 1973, capital investments in the New Zone of Golodnaya Steppe had added up to 1,458.9 million rubles (about $2 billion), which might strike the onlooker as an enormous amount of money to spend on a "burned-out plain." It is a figure that shows not only the high capital requirements of complex, mechanized irrigation schemes, but also the amount of investment required when all of life is paid for, embracing much more than the irrigation system itself. It represents the amount of money needed to convert a desolate wasteland into a productive, self-contained economic entity in which modern people lead modern lives.

The project was inaugurated in 1956 with a five-year preparatory period in which an industrial and transportation infrastructure was built on the steppe: five plants for manufacturing reinforced concrete, two gravel-sorting mills for non-ore materials, a plant for manufacturing tile drainage pipes, another for making bricks, two plants for manufacturing silicate-concrete items for housing, four repair shops for mechanical equipment also capable of fabricating nonstandard items, 93 km of railway, 1,746 km of paved roads, 1,805 km of power transmission lines, 187 km of water-supply conduits, 510 km of communication lines, 324 km of gas mains, one million square meters of dwelling space for 40,000 construction and industrial workers, their housing organized into five communities equipped with service and cultural amenities. This and a huge irrigation system—$2 billion pays for many things. All construction was laid out on a timetable so that each stage would follow in a natural sequence, each element appearing coincidentally with the need for it.

In that same preparatory period, the first section of Southern Golodnaya Steppe Canal, the main intake for the project, was also constructed, to be dedicated in December, 1960. The main canal was sealed against seepage with river silt, the particles of which are smaller than the sands through which the main channel was excavated. The extension of the main canals continued through the following five years—the southern canal, with eight check structures, completed to 117 km, beyond which it joins the Tokursai River, the central branch with its right lateral to 246 km, its left lateral to 214 km, the second stage of the central main drain. Upstream from the Farkhad headworks, the southern canal is supplied with an intake of 300 m^3/sec. The central branch, designed to irrigate 146,000 hectares, has a head discharge of 164 m^3/sec, with the right and left laterals at 55 m³/sec and 60 m³/sec, respectively. The Kurgantepa branch irrigates 16,000 hectares with a head discharge of 20.3 m³/sec.

Parallel with the system for supplying water, a preplanned on-the-farm network was also scratched into the soil in conformance with what everyone already realized—that the Soviet government would make no tsarist mistakes. The Central Golodnaya Steppe main drain, 57 km long, was reconstructed with a discharge capacity of 90 m³/sec, while other principal collectors were built to a length of 470 km. As canals and drains reached out prying fingers across the wasteland, *sovkhozes*, state farms, were organized at the rate of three to five a year, then set to constructing the on-farm intake and drainage networks and eventually to do the actual farming. These fully mechanized *sovkhozes* are agricultural factories.

> *Sovkhozes* in the Golodnaya Steppe are mainly specialized in cotton growing, their areas under irrigation averaging 6,000–7,000 hectares. Experience gained in land development has demonstrated that such a size is to be preferred since it assures optimum operation of the farm. A *sovkhoz* includes a central village where all dwellings, cultural and service utilities and the main production base are concentrated. The territory of the *sovkhoz* was divided into agroproduction divisions, each covering 1,500–1,800 irrigated hectares. Each division has a production-utilities center with facilities for storing and maintaining machinery and implements. Workers are brought by car from the central village to the centers. The basic production unit is a team responsible for serving an area of 100–150 hectares. A field camp provided with shower rooms and a shed for small quantities of fertilizer is built for each team. Workers can take their rest there. (15, p.55)

Each *sovkhoz* is a replica of the entire project in miniature, its various elements, including the construction of dwellings and amenities, of industrial projects, and the bringing of land into cultivation, carried out in accordance with a timetable.

> It takes four to five years to establish a *sovkhoz*, including all the components such as: irrigation and drainage networks, land levelling, construction of industrial and civil engineering projects. . . . On average, each farm built 150–200 km of canals, either concrete-lined or converted into flumes and pipelines, 500–600 km of subsurface horizontal drainage, 50–100 km of collectors, 40–50 km of farm roads, all in addition to . . . the leaching of saline lands. (15, p.50)

Devoted to raising cotton, the Golodnaya Steppe was made self-sufficient to the extent that part of the project was assigned to food and fodder crops. While the size of the livestock population was not stated, each *sovkhoz* directed a sizeable expenditure toward the construction of cattle sheds. Specialized enterprises were developed for poultry raising and the fattening of young livestock, while communities came to be graced with butter factories, cold storage facilities, and canneries. Auxiliary services came to include the repair and maintenance of farm machinery, as well as supply depots from which farms were issued with agricultural chemicals, fertilizers, spare parts, oil, and fuels. Processing enterprises were set up to treat cotton fibers and seeds. Cotton production was mechanized from sowing to picking, thence to processing. Golodnaya Steppe, in the heart of Central Asia, became a capital-intensive operation, in which one worker tilled on the average six irrigated hectares, with individual output reaching as high as 19 tons of raw cotton per harvest.

Data on the output of the project began in 1961, at the end of the preparatory period, when the first cotton was planted and harvested. As salt went down, leached into the depths of the earth, cotton came up, increasing in quantity up to 1973, the latest date supplied by the case study, when 309,000 tons were ginned. Calculations are provided to show that by 1972, 11 years after production began, the huge amount of capital invested in irrigation and general development had been paid back.

> Subsequently [to 1972], the Golodnaya Steppe provides the State with an income the annual rate of which is 60–100 million rubles. The income is ever increasing despite the yet growing investments. (15, p.66)

All this sounds too good to be true. Planning to cover every contingency, investments attuned to deliver cotton and profits, a desolation transformed, the rustle of wind blowing through green fields, a soft background to the happy hammering of cotton gins and factories. Yet an outside observer can find few grounds for doubting this smooth flow of events. Between 1961 and 1972, cotton production in the Soviet Union rose from 1,701 million to 2,356 million metric tons, an increase of 655,000 metric tons, of which Golodnaya Steppe could well have provided almost half (79, p.123). A setback occurred in 1968 in Golodnaya, the one year in which a decline in cotton production, accompanied by the departure of 600 workers, interrupted an otherwise unmarred picture of progress on the steppe. The figures are there to read in the case study, which neglects to say what happened in that year, which was, in any case, only a dip in an otherwise unblemished advance in which average production per worker rose from 7.4 tons of cotton in 1961 to 18.1 tons in 1971.

Only a few minor questions remain. An estimate of the size of the steppe's predevelopment population, for instance, leads to what is doubtless unfruitful speculation. By 1974, 36,486 workers were "engaged in development," which presumably means that this number manned the 52 *sovkhozes* and the various factories established in the Golodnaya Steppe New Zone. Service workers and family members composed a total 3.1 times this large for an entire population of 113,000. If that is the final total, a reasonable figure, it is 56 times as large as the population of the entire Golodnaya Steppe, New Zoné and old, before its development. For it was said that in 1878, a total of only 2,000 people lived there.

> In the pre-irrigation period, the Golodnaya Steppe was a typical waterless desert where, on a vast area, the only water sources were isolated wells with saline water used by nomads and caravans crossing the steppe. . . . To find means of survival . . . from the end of May to the beginning of October was quite impossible. That is why in the period before irrigation this territory was almost unpopulated. The local people (Uzbeks, Kirghiz, Tadzhik) were confined mainly to piedmont and mountainous areas rimming the steppe. They lived in rural settlements, their main occupation being cattle raising in distant pastures, sowing small plots to grain crops, growing fruit trees and vines on the banks of mountain rivers and streams, almost all of which dried up in July. (15, pp.2–3)

This description, accepted by the case study, is typical of those accounts of drylands made by observers who, having never seen such terrain before, are shocked by their apparent desolation into a misunderstanding of their possibilities. Far from being a "waterless desert," the Golodnaya Steppe receives almost enough rainfall for cropping. Harvests are taken in the Azawak—unwisely, it is true—under conditions of less rain than in Golodnaya, although there in the Sahel, the rain falls during the growing season and winters are not so cold. Along with the general depreciation of the area provided by nineteenth-century observers from Russia, one suspects that the population, too, was underestimated, since the nomadic fraction remaining after the subtraction of 2,000 persons settled in villages would give the steppe a density of herdsmen lower even than the Sahelian subdesert, that strip at the Sahara's very edge. But 2,000 or 10,000, whatever the number may have been, the case study provides not one word as to what happened to them. Rapt and absorbed by the astounding possibilities of Golodnaya Steppe under irrigation, the authors were oblivious to the ingenious and romantic adaptability of low-intensity agricultural and pastoral systems. An earlier way of life seems to have been wiped out with scarcely a passing thought, in contrast to the French in the Sahel, who annihilated the life of the Kel Tamasheq while giving it a good deal of attention. The veiled Tuareg made a permanent penetration into the Gallic psyche, riding their camels endlessly over the dunes of French literature. They became in a way the Cossacks of the French.

The elimination of a culture is, of course, one way of handling the problem of communication, the difficulties of which were made so evident in Luni Block. Mandan Indians no longer need be asked if wheat should be grown in North Dakota, or encouraged to use "rational" methods of cultivation. This is a tricky matter since if the culture is destroyed while the people remain, demoralized and deculturated, the effect can be disastrous to the land. Yet the destruction of subsistence ways of life, styles and patterns once universal, has happened everywhere, benignly in one region, viciously in another. The very word "subsistence" has taken on gritty connotations, summoning up a picture of illiterate peasants struggling to wrest a meager living out of tiny holdings. The word no longer means what it once meant—the control of one's own life in conditions of amply leisure, a rich diet, ritual and celebration, gatherings around the fires at night to recite the epics of the culture. In their old life as subsistence farmers, Colombian peasants examined by Michael Taussig expended 1,700 calories a day; as plantation laborers, a condition into which they were subsequently driven, they were required to expend 3,500 calories per day. As Taussig said, "Lower-class people are well aware that wage labor on the plantations is an enormous energy drain in comparison with peasant labor. They fetishize the cane as a plant 'which dries one up' " (75, pp.107–108). No doubt about it—modern life, for all its labor-saving devices, really makes people work. It is what is meant by the Book of Genesis when God told Adam, as he expelled him from his subsistence Eden, that henceforth he would earn his bread by the sweat of his brow.

The nomads of Golodnaya Steppe have gone with the wind. What happened to 2,000 or more subsistence farmers and herdsmen may perhaps seem a trivial question when weighed against the modern life of more than 100,000 people engaged in an integrated program that produces annual profits of 60 to 100 million rubles. Unless the case study's silence on this subject conceals a dark significance, the children of former nomads might even be sharing this new life. They might have been enrolled in one of the many training programs which are provided as essential for generating the variety of skills needed in a genuinely integrated program. As the irrigation network extended outward, people were imported to establish and work the *sovkhozes*, and they arrived throughout the development period at the rate of 6,000 to 10,000 a year. A certain proportion of the new arrivals were specialists, fresh graduates of machine schools assigned to Golodnaya. Most of the others, new to Golodnaya and unfamiliar, all but a few of them, with irrigation agriculture, had to be trained on the spot.

> *Sovkhoz* workers arriving to be engaged in development are either insufficiently experienced in agricultural jobs, or their knowledge can be but partly employed in modern farms. In the newly established *sovkhozes*, irrigation, drainage and the construction of industrial projects are accomplished in conformance with the latest advances in science and technology. For proper operation and maintenance of state farm engineering structures, the new personnel must master new skills. (15, p.54)

Where did the new arrivals come from? The project made an effort to attract employment on a volunteer basis. The productivity of the mechanized cotton farms was such that wages could be set at 2.5-3 thousand rubles per year, twice the average earnings in the rest of the Uzbek SSR, and to this a 15% bonus was added during the development period when life was more rugged. The houses provided to workers, set on 0.08-hectare plots, were said to be the best in the Uzbek Republic.

At the same time, the project was seen as a mechanism whereby labor surpluses in nearby portions of Central Asia could be reduced. So most of the incoming workers were not volunteers, however attractive the salaries and housing may have been. They were ordered to go to Golodnaya Steppe, a process referred to as the "organized resettlement of people from densely populated regions and districts in accordance with the government decision" (15, p.53).

> The Golodnaya Steppe absorbs manpower from the Fergana and Zarafshan Valleys, from the mountain regions of the Syr Darya and other districts known for abundant labor resources and low output per worker. (15, p.54)

This much criticized Soviet practice of telling people where they will live and work seems, on reflection, to add another element to the many similarities between Soviet operations and those of, say, a large multinational corporation. So do bonuses and incentives, used in both systems to encourage workers to their best efforts after they are installed and established.

> Compared to other regions, the virgin lands are provided with greater quantities of scarce commodities—cars, motorcycles, etc.—to be sold to the best machine operators and workers. This is to be decided by appropriate organizations and the region's authorities. (15, p.54)

So the oppressiveness of the Soviet establishment, the only employer in the vicinity, deciding even who can have a motorcycle, not to mention "etc.," provides a foretaste of what life under capitalism would be like if that system should complete its evolution into one gigantic corporation, since it is clear that the principal concern of both institutions, corporation and Soviet, is that measure of efficiency—output per worker. One doesn't wish to say that workers whose output is so measured have become converted into mere cogs in the machine. No, they are the new people who have replaced the tradition-bound, superstitious peasants who are so difficult to convince. They were lured to the steppe—or ordered there—instead of permitting such a resource as Golodnaya to be developed privately by the sort of crusty ranchers or lessees whose assent must be obtained before anything can proceed. The mistakes made in Greater Mussayeb—that sort of situation is avoided, too, by means of training programs that convert newcomers into skilled irrigationists. The point is, too, that these people are trainable. They are mobile, conditioned to move, as people are in all industrial countries, open to new ideas, eager to learn. They are, in short, "modern," the kind of people whom one would expect to find in a developed country like the Soviet Union.

Can we say, then, that the Soviet Union has solved the problem of desertification? Is that all it takes? There is an enormous convenience to be found in the ability to move people around at will, including the original inhabitants, those hard-to-reach nomads and peasants, so difficult to convince. Then new people are ordered in, modern people, easy to convince. Heights of efficiency are drawn from these new people through the medium of incentives—good salary and a bonus, the best housing in the Republic, a chance to buy a motorcycle, even a car.

13

TURKMENIA

". . . shifting cubic kilometers of water"

THE SOVIET ATTITUDE toward nomads, undefined in the discussion of that former habitat of nomads, the Golodnaya Steppe, is made clearer in a second case study prepared by the USSR. Here, the case under consideration is an entire Soviet republic. Almost as large as Spain, Turkmenia is the most arid of the constituents of the Soviet Union, with portions of its 488,000 km² thirsting on the dry side of the 100-mm isohyet—the northern part of the Kara Kum Desert and the environs of the Kara Bogaz Gol, that salt-caked evaporation basin into which the Caspian Sea dumps its waters. The speakers of Turkish who inhabit Turkmenia have been pastoral nomads since they first appeared in history, more than 2,000 years ago, from somewhere out of northeast Asia. They brought their herds and flocks to Turkmenia in the twelfth century as part of a larger movement of Turkic peoples out of Central Asia, the same movement that carried the Turks for the first time into Turkey. In 1065, one year before William the Conqueror put an end to Saxon rule in England, the Byzantines drove the Turkish Uzes out of the Balkans. Six years later, Byzantium lost eastern Anatolia to Alp Arslan, a Seljuk cousin of the Uzes. Trailing far behind in the wake of these raiders were the rest of the Uzes (Ghuzz) peoples, mounted horsemen who migrated with their animals, passing the Amu Darya after 1153, when they defeated their Seljuk cousins, gone soft in the luxury of Iran, and fixed a boundary between Turki and Irani which has lasted into the present day. What had been northern Khorasan, an Iranian land of deserts and far-sweeping pastures, became Turkmenia.

In the pre-revolutionary period, pastures were utilized by the nomadic technique. The local population bred karakul and fat-tailed sheep, a lo-

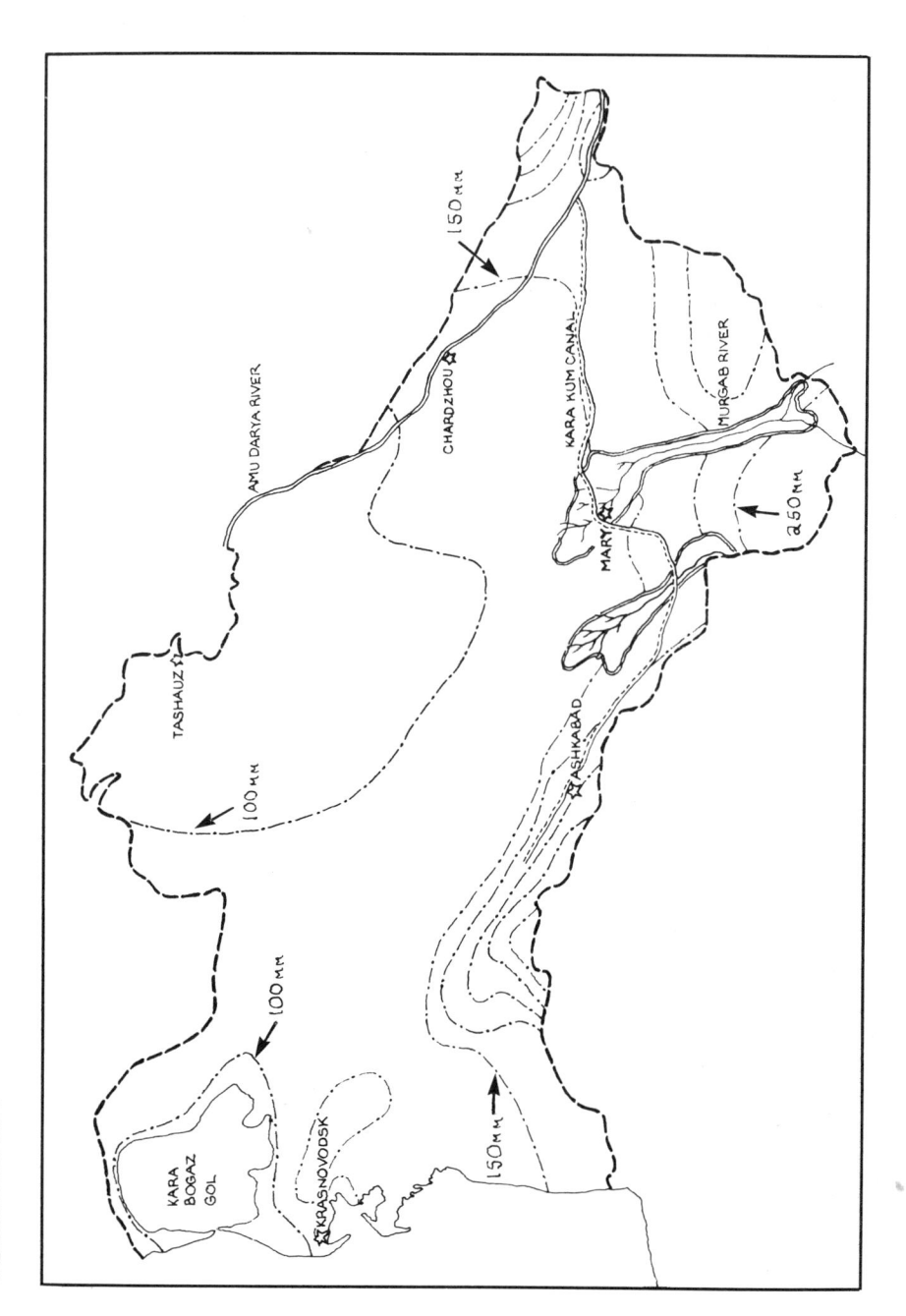

TURKMENIA

cal coarse-wool breed of goats, and dromedaries. Karakul sheep grazed on sandy pastures in the southeastern parts, while the fat-tailed sheep and coarse-wool goats prevailed in Turkmenistan's western part. People engaged in camel breeding in central Kara Kum and in Turkmenistan's northwest. (14, p.25)

Rotational grazing of pastures around water wells was a technique developed by nomadic pastoralists which was recognized as efficient and adopted by subsequent Soviet pastoralists. On the whole, however, the new Soviet experts saw nomadic practices as leading to desertification. This was primarily because of poor development of water resources, leaving much of the pasture unused, while those parts of it near to wells and reservoirs were overgrazed and subject to excessive woodcutting. The remedy was found not merely in developing new watering points so that the full pasture could be brought into use, but also in abolishing nomadism. In the old days,

> there was no strict distribution of pastures among farms and planned management of pastures was therefore impossible. (14, p.26)

Apparently, the natural communism of the nomadic life style was annoying to Soviet authorities since it goes against concepts of order and system characterizing the "modern" world. Perhaps Soviet attitudes seem mechanical and heartless, framed in exclusive pursuit of the bitch goddess efficiency. Yet the destruction of the old Turkmen life style can find its parallel in many places in western Europe, where private property and the enclosure movement have long since eliminated old nomadisms, all except for the embattled Gypsies and those bands of Lapps who lead reindeer across northern Scandinavia and—yes—the Soviet Union. The Lapps, and the nomads who still direct flocks in the most hidden parts of Siberia, will last only until progress catches up with them, along with their fellow wanderers in Iran and the Kalahari, in the Sahel, on the shores of the Arctic seas. Nomadism may be an intelligent response to extreme conditions, of which one is aridity, but there is little to indicate that it will survive much longer anywhere in a crowded world where the need for intensive production will allow no more room for peoples who go their own way, out of control, as it were.

The principles and character of pasture management have been changed. Small nomadic privately-owned farms have been amalgamated into large collective and state-farming enterprises. . . . The establishment of large-scale sheep-breeding and camel-breeding farms made possible planned utilization of pastures on a fixed territory. This improved the state of watering and care of grazing grounds, ensured more rational pasture use and prevented the development of desertification. (14, p.26)

Except for two camel-breeding *sovkhozes*, the new Turkmenia with its huge sheep stations—22 *sovkhozes* dividing up 30 million hectares—might be a larger Gascoyne if big government were not there, as in Vale, to make investments on a scale far surpassing the possibilities of private Australian lessees. Water, for instance—5,200 wells, 54 drill holes, 336 springs, and more than 600 catchment structures have opened up two-thirds of the vast Turkmenian rangelands to grazing, with another five million hectares to be opened up in the tenth five-year plan. Most of this water is from underground, moderately to strongly mineralized. As in Vale, pastures have been improved by plowing and seeding, with special attention paid to the planting of shrubs found palatable by sheep.

Pasture improvement techniques vary in different natural districts. In foothill deserts where rainfall ranges from 160 mm to 280 mm, autumn–winter shrubs and semi-shrubs are planted in accordance with the strip system of plowing—the width of rows being 10-15 meters, the intervals 10-50 meters. Pastures on barkhan sands close to wells are improved by sowing a mixture of shrubs and semi-shrubs. Good pastures are created in proximity to watering points, and the improvement of approximately 20% of the pasture of every farm in the foothill zone will meet the demands of autumn–winter grazing. Special techniques for restoring vegetation by sowing shrubs on sands close to wells have been recommended for the Kara Kum desert where rainfall ranges from 120 mm to 140 mm. Methods of pasture improvement have been worked out by strip plowing on low-ridge sands and on takyr [clay] plains by planting shrubs and semi-shrubs and building moisture accumulating strips. (14, pp.29-30)

Emergency stocks of fodder have been established with which to confront the inevitable appearance of drought, and sheep are provided with supplementary feed in certain seasons. Such measures have expanded the sheep population by 2½ times, bringing it to 4,256,000 head (1974), of which 70% are karakul sheep producing an annual one million pelts and 15,000 tons of wool. The nomads are gone, but those of their techniques that are still used, developed "through centuries of knowledge of desert conditions" (14, p.9), enable wool to be produced on inexpensive natural (but improved) pastures at a cost one-quarter to one-half as high as elsewhere in the Soviet Union.

The crowning achievement in Turkmenistan is, however, the development of irrigation agriculture. The slope and topography of southern Turkmenistan made possible the construction of what the case study contends is "the largest irrigation hydrotechnical project in the deserts of the world" (14, p.17).

> Even 100% application of Turkmenia's water supplies could not resolve its desertification problems nor develop more than a small part of the deserts in the Republic. At the same time, the biggest river of Soviet Middle Asia, the Amu Darya, with an annual discharge exceeding 62.4 km^3, flows along the northeastern boundary of Turkmenistan. A great part of that water used to flow into the Aral Sea and get lost eventually in evaporation. For ages the people of Turkmenistan dreamt of making use of that water for the development of a part of the deserts, for irrigated agriculture, and to control desertification. However, this called for shifting tens of cubic kilometers of water to populated desert places remote from the Amu Darya, where the land was particularly suitable for development. (14, p.16)

These cubic kilometers of water have since been shifted. They have become an artificial river, directed more than 900 km across fixed and shifting sands, alluvial and submontane plains, to Ashkabad, the capital of the Republic.

> The length of the first section (to Mary) was 400 km of which 300 km pass over sandy desert. . . . The construction was carried out between 1954 and 1959. The "pioneer canal" method was used in which water follows the builders as they progress ensuring water supply and transport links. This also accelerated the wetting of the canal and stabilized subsequent seepage losses. The "pioneer canal" was built . . . using bulldozers and excavators and its widening was carried out by suction dredges. (14, p.17)

By 1975, this man-made river had a head discharge of 400 m^3/sec with a total annual intake exceeding 9 km^3, or one-seventh of the Amu Darya's total flow. It provided irrigation water to 506,000 hectares on which 55 *sovkhozes* had been established—nine for cotton, 21 for sheep breeding, six for poultry, nine for fruits and grapes, one for melons, one for beef and dairy products, one for swine breeding, and one for camel breeding.

The Kara Kum Canal also provides a preview of what the diversion of north-flowing Siberian rivers will be like. It is a testing ground in the techniques of transporting large amounts of water over long distances.

> Further development of the Kara Kum Canal is planned. It will reach western industrial districts, and a new cotton-growing area with an irrigated territory exceeding 100,000 hectares will be established in the southwestern [corner of the Republic]. The total length of the canal will exceed 1,500 km; it will irrigate one million hectares. The upper section will have reservoirs with a capacity of 3.5 km^3 for partial seasonal regulation of the discharge. This is where a considerable part of the silt from the Amu Darya will settle. It is intended to build two more reservoirs at the canal's ending, . . . their total capacity exceeding 1 km^3. The annual water intake of the Kara Kum Canal is expected to add up to 17.1 km^3. (14, p.18)

Early in its development, the irrigation system encountered a problem with weeds. This was solved by the introduction of plant-eating fish (*Ctenopharungodon idella, Hypophthalmichthus molitrix*). Vegetation has sprouted out of the reach of fish, on the banks along the length of the canal, whose waters are used also for the trees, shrubs, and flowers that make life amenable in dryland communities. Like natural rivers, the canal provides transport and recreation.

Oil that comes from fields in western Turkmenia is refined at Krasnovodsk on the Caspian, with another refinery recently constructed in the eastern Kara Kum. Oil is the basis of a petrochemical industry. Large deposits of natural gas have been tied into the Middle Asia system of gas mains and pipes. Sulfur, bromine, and iodine are mined, together with Bentonite clay, mineral salts, and potassium for fertilizer.

As easily damaged as they are by agricultural misuse, drylands are equally susceptible to ill treatment from mining and industry. The disposal of waste products, including urban wastes, is a particular problem in arid environments where natural processes of biodegradation are slow to work. Roads, power lines, gaslines, and oil pipelines must be sited and maintained with care if they are not to trigger erosive processes. Roads and surface works, in their turn, often need protection from shifting sand. Sowing and planting must accompany excavations if buried pipelines are not to persist as permanent slashes across arid landscapes. Near Oglat Merteba, tank tracks still visible from the maneuvers of World War II indicate that the resilience of drylands can require generations to repair damages brought on by disturbance unrelated to agriculture.

Turkmenia provided a rare opportunity for advance planning on a republic-wide scale. Timid developmental efforts of tsarist days had left this huge region almost untouched. Turkmen pastoralists still took their herds along routes established in previous centuries. Overflow irrigation was practiced along the Amu Darya and Murgab rivers and along the north-face slopes of the Kopet Dag, the mountains separating Turks from Iranis, just as it had been practiced when Darius the Great ruled this distant part of the Persian Empire. Such old ways persisted because they were successful. They made productive use of the land without degrading it except, as the study testily pointed out, around watering points and places where livestock tended to concentrate.

That planning could embrace the soil of an entire republic was another tribute to nascent agricultural sciences, in which Russian experimentalists had been in the forefront since 1883, when Vinogradsky first isolated the soil's nitrifying bacteria, and 1886, when Dokuchaiev developed the first scientific classification of soils. These dates, contemporary with the pioneering work of that unsung American, E. W. Hilgard, mark the parturition of a science of agriculture, then struggling to be born. An empirical agriculture, a catalogue of the hit-and-miss findings of observation and experience, had been feeding some or much of mankind for up to ten millennia. A scientific agriculture not only had to wait for the emergence of other sciences on whose backs it rode, but also had to rise above the scorn of researchers for the mere dirt beneath their feet. Man's gaze had heretofore been fixed on the stars. Dokuchaiev's ideas did not penetrate America until 1927, when an English translation was made of a German version of his writings. The present U.S. system of soil classification, the one in which most dryland soils are categorized as aridisols, was not adopted until 1965.

Developed in an era when learning was becoming ever more specialized, the new scientific agriculture was at first afflicted with ecological myopia. The science of the "home," *oikos* in Greek, has in the end turned out to be something quite different from carpentry and masonry. It has become the science of that ultimate home consisting of the earth itself, its soil, atmosphere, liquids and life forms, their chemical constituents, and their permeation with energy and moisture. The perspective that is oikological recognizes distant ramifications, the penetration of effects into remote and unexpected corners. Who could have foreseen that the Aswan Dam, erected far down in the desert of Nubia, would destroy fisheries in the eastern Mediterranean? Yet this was foreseen, predicted by precocious ecologists of whom Mohammed Kassas was one, who were told that the dam was so important to the life of Egypt that Mediterranean fish—and fishermen—would have to get along without the nourishing silt that had immemorially been carried seaward by the Nile. Failure to take an ecological attitude, to view land use as always an intrusion into a network of interacting systems, including social systems, has resulted in those misapplications of technology that have strengthened resistance to innovation on the part of traditional peoples. On the other hand, the recognition that blunders have been made, as chronicled by Farvar and Milton (44), has strengthened ecological awareness, making the ecological attitude the dominant perspective among the sciences concerned with land use. It has resulted in an approach to projects that is increasingly interdisciplinary, an effort to break out of the straitjacket of specialization.

Soviet interest in arid lands now centers in the Institute of Deserts located in Ashkabad, the capital of the Turkmen SSR, and scientists from this institute were the authors of the case study. That land-use planning could embrace an entire republic was made possible also by an ecological attitude which sees the interrelationships that link into systems and that link systems one to another, such as the system of pastures—and in Turkmenia, livestock routes circle out and back in loops festooning most of the Republic's land surface—or the elements of an entire watershed, in this case that of the artificial river, the Kara Kum Canal, whose waters must be drained harmlessly away after they have nourished the lawns and trees of Ashkabad and Mary and more than an annual million tons of cotton. River oases are linked to pastures via the fodder concentrates—cotton cake, oil-seed meal, mixed feeds, barley—which supplement those produced directly from pastures to keep sheep from losing weight and from overattacking depleted pasture in slack growing seasons or in years of drought. Both irrigation and pasture have myriad links with industry and with the power network that connects to pumps on wells and to the structures that regulate the dispersal of the Kara Kum waters.

Just as an entire republic can be viewed as an ecological unit, so the entire earth is mankind's ultimate *oikos*, the final ecological unit, provided, of course, that the solar constant is really constant. If not, then the ultimate ecological unit may be the solar system, the galaxy, the universe. For most practical purposes, however, the earth is a unit beyond which there is only the rarest need to look. And the earth, researchers have been arguing, needs much more understanding as a unit. A knowledge of the whole would not only specify the causal location of such terrestrial elements as an ozone layer, it would also bring precision to the educated guesses appearing on the table on page 14. To understand the earth, one must first look at it, monitor its shifts in time.

Two large-scale schemes for monitoring—one for the Andean drylands of South America, the other for the arid regions of south Asia—were proposed as transnational projects to be developed as part of the preparations for the Conference on Desertification. If all went well, these would serve as the first step toward the installation of a global system of monitoring based on remote sensing of the kind provided by the LANDSAT system. Satellite imagery would be supplemented by aerial photography and land traverses, like those carried out in the Gascoyne, to establish "ground truth." The perfection of ground truth was a principal goal of a Seminar on Desertification sponsored by six scientific associations, including the American Association for the Advancement of Science, held in Nairobi immediately following the world conference. What the scientists present wanted to do was to define a set of "critical indicators" that would help them to "assess vulnerability to desertification" and to "predict the onset of desertification before it starts" (66, p.4).

In contrast to the urge toward global monitoring, one turns to the conclusion of these same scientists, as well as of other colleagues not present at the Nairobi seminar, that desertification, as it is occurring in the contemporary world, is the work of man. It follows that its occurrence is always known, since men must be present where it is happening. The Sahelian nomad, the desert bedouin, the Gascoyne sheepherder, and the Vale rancher know very well, as the case studies indicate, when desertification is affecting their land. When, in the richer countries, the witnesses of the process have also happened to have been its agents, they have in the past tended to place the blame elsewhere, especially on climate. The more traditional farmer or pastoralist has not shown himself to be quite so quick to rationalize, realizing that he himself is to blame, but asking fatalistically what he can do. He has to cook his food. He must raise the money to pay his taxes. In either case, regardless of where the blame is placed, the fact of desertification is known—to someone. What then is added by monitoring the vanishing shrubbery *en masse*, instead of continuing to stare in despair at the separate, uprooted bushes?

Global monitoring might seem more useful if a global program to combat desertification were in fact an imminent prospect. A more accurate assessment of global data might then lead to a more intelligent allocation of resources for combating the problem. To be sure, the Plan of Action to Combat Desertification, as reviewed and approved by the 500 delegates from 94 countries who were present at the Conference, outlined through its 28 recommendations just such an integrated worldwide campaign against what it declared to be a global threat to one of humanity's fundamental resources. But when the moment came to supply financing to the kind of global effort involved in the Plan of Action, the Conference hesitated. The chasm between rich and poor nations that had yawned in the United Nations General Assembly when a Conference on Desertification was first proposed was found, at that moment in the Conference itself, to be gaping still. The poor countries made a plea for a special fund, then settled for a special account (32, p.37), with no guarantee that any funds would ever be placed in that account. Donor countries announced that they would continue to finance projects on their merits, leaving the situation much as it was before the Conference took place. By this attitude, the donor countries made an expendable luxury out of the global monitoring of desertification and took the critical importance out of those "critical indicators" that would reveal the onset of desertification more promptly, with less chance of error.

Or is that too abrupt an opinion? There is always a temptation to say that pure research is a luxury, and it is a temptation that is the harder to resist the shorter is the supply of financing. One falls into the trap of believing that these little bits of interesting data have been obtained with money that could have improved human lives and have therefore been purchased at a human cost. One hears the packs of philistines shouting that all available funds should be spent on projects, each to be reviewed and financed on its merits. If these shouts had always prevailed, there would be no new sciences of agriculture—and there would be a corresponding dearth of technical solutions to apply to projects reviewed on their merits.

An integrated global approach as requested in the Plan of Action to Combat Desertification might be the only way to halt the process before the end of this century, something the Plan proposes as an admirable target, but an attack developed through individual projects will probably be the pattern in the immediate future, and that is not an approach likely to halt the process before the century's end. Implicit in the case studies is a standard procedure for dealing with the separate situations in which projects will come to be undertaken. Nothing smaller than some kind of ecological unit—an entire watershed, a coherent rangeland, an irrigation district—should be selected for rehabilitation if unwanted effects are not to spill in from outside. The Gascoyne basin, both a watershed and a coherent rangeland, is a proper object of rehabilitation, although it should probably be bounded so as to include also the small district around Carnarvon irrigated by Gascoyne water. Sheer extent makes rehabilitation effective in Vale and Turkmenia, or could make it effective in the Azawak and Eghazer, all complexes of distinct ecosystems.

Systems which should be treated as coherent units are conveniently divisible into *eco-units*, characterized by distinctive but uniform vegetation. As the irreducible elements of the environment, eco-units join together to form *facets*, each typified by a distinctive combination of soil, slope, hydrology, and vegetation. The Chinese case studies place particular emphasis on the use to be made of each separate facet and the distinctive measures required for their separate rehabilitation. Facets interlock to form the ecosystem, and a change in one facet will affect others. As it is analyzed into its constituents, the ecosystem to be rehabilitated becomes first of all an object for study. It is the kind of study that the case studies have all carried out. It is here that the case studies are at their best, in this physical domain where the authors are at home.

Geometrical units selected for study—the square, almost, of Oglat Merteba, the tilted rectangle of Combarbalá—are not proper objects for rehabilitation. Yet they provide guidance as to what should be done with them if they were. Like the other study zones, they are analyzed into facets and eco-units by identifying their different soils and slopes, vegetation and hydrology, and the location of groundwater and the determination of its condition. Climate is assessed and its history examined to the extent that data are available from the past. Interconnections among facets and eco-units are determined.

Identification is made of the processes through which desertification is taking place—wind and water erosion, sheeting, scalding and gullying, the disappearance of palatable pasture and its replacement by species less palatable but better adapted to worsened conditions, deterioration in the quality of the soil, its structure and texture, its nutrient supply. Reconstruction of the climax vegetation and of successive disclimaxes traces the route that degradation has taken and provides clues as to how rehabilitation might best proceed. The physical causes of degradation are established, a goal that is sometimes elusive. As Warren reported in the component review on *Ecological Change and Desertification*:

> An example of a glib conclusion can be taken from Arizona where many observers blamed over-use of the range for the appearance of gullies at the turn of the century. A close examination of the evidence led Cooke and Reeves to a much more complicated explanation. They found that there had been little gullying during the period of heaviest stocking levels, and the gullies had only begun to develop well after the numbers of cattle had fallen. In search of another explanation, they first looked to the rainfall and found, with earlier workers, that although there had been little sustained change in annual amounts during the period of gullying, there had been a consistent increase in intensity at some seasons. Nevertheless this alone had probably not been enough to form the gullies, for the history of each particular case showed that there had almost always been some local disturbance of the surface such as the cutting of a roadside ditch or the insertion of a culvert.... Driven by enthusiasm and a sense of impending crisis, observers of dryland condition seldom have the time for such niceties. (22, p.6)

The case studies show that the common physical causes of desertification in drylands are overgrazing complicated by trampling associated with local concentrations of stock around feedlots and watering points, the unwise extension of cultivation into regions climatically unsuited to it, and the destructive consumption of woody vegetation. To those causes, widespread and of common occurrence, can be added damage by rodents or insects. Other physical causes make occasional appearance—the improper siting of roads and construction projects, for example, or the uninhibited use of off-the-road vehicles. All physical factors in desertification can be exacerbated by drought, which is at least a temporary change of climate, shifting isohyets away from desert cores if deserts are nearby, so that livestock whose numbers are adapted to normal conditions are suddenly too many, the unwisdom of rainfed cultivation is stretched by nature rather than man, and the germination of replacement vegetation is interrupted, sometimes for years on end. And to all these can be added the waterlogging and salination that spell the death of irrigated lands when the systems that water them are improperly designed or inefficiently managed.

From this sort of analysis, explicit in the case studies, a physical solution to degradation emerges that is technologically appropriate and economically feasible. If such a solution cannot be proposed, and there are no such examples in the case studies, then it is said that the case is irreversibly desertified. This means, as has been indicated, that careful management will not result in noticeable improvement within 25 years, one human generation. In this sense, the assertion so often made at the Conference and during the preparations for it that no matter what form degradation has taken, a physical solution can be found for it unless it has been "irreversibly" desertified amounts to little more than a tautology. Cases are called "irreversible" when no solution can be proposed for them that would return the costs of rehabilitation. The term is thus seen to be economic in nature rather than technological, a part of the social rather than the physical sciences. Fortunately, even in accordance with such financial criteria, little of the planet's degraded land, stripped and exposed to the ravages of wind and water under climates that provide them protection when man does not intrude, can be regarded as "irreversibly" desertified.

The causes and course of desertification in Turkmenia have been ascertained by Soviet investigators, and their findings were summarized in the Turkmenia case study. Stock concentrations had created degraded piospheres around the formerly limited number of watering points while vast extents of pasture went unused for want of water. Woody vegetation had undergone destruction. Landscapes had been damaged by industrial development—by roads, mines, and pipelines, and by seismic techniques for oil and mineral exploration. Salination was an unremitting threat to irrigated cropping. The destruction of vegetation had laid large areas open to the particular problems of an arid landscape under a strong wind regime—wind erosion and the mobilization of marching sand dunes. Such was the situation to be encountered in the Republic before a rehabilitation program got under way.

Salination has since been dealt with by the application of drainage, including vertical drainage via tubewells. The possibilities of sprinkle and drip irrigation have recently come under investigation.

> It has been experimentally proven that the near-to-oasis aeolian sands can be developed for the cultivation of forage crops if sprinkling irrigation is used. The introduction ... of organic and mineral fertilizers on the irrigated gray-meadow soils with an irrigation rate of 5,500–6,500 m^3 per hectare on sands may yield from 500 to 1,000 centners [one centner = 100 kg] of green corn or sorghum per hectare. (14, p.33)

Plans for the future include green zones around towns, parks, and truck gardens on the maritime shell sands on the Caspian and Aral Sea coasts and plantings on salinized sands in the west.

> Research into salinized sands of western Turkmenistan has been completed and recommendations have been compiled for their fixing and afforestation. A detailed investigation of the salt resistance of psammophytic shrubs made it possible to select a promising range of plants for the afforestation of salinized sands. (14, p.33)

The destruction of woody vegetation has been counteracted by linking dwellings to natural gas, deposits of which occur so extensively in the Republic.

Pasture improvement has involved the replacement of nomadism by the territorial imperatives of fixed *sovkhozes*. Unused pasture has been opened up by the construction of additional watering facilities, even to the extent of bringing water in by pipe where local natural sources do not occur. Karakul sheep, which together with camels are the subject of selective breeding experiments, can be spread more thinly over far wider pastures even though their numbers have mounted.

A major assault was launched against the problem of wind erosion and shifting sands, now monitored by remote sensing.

> To work out scientific principles of deflation control, the lowland territory of Turkmenistan was analyzed into regions in terms of the extent of wind erosion. A wind erosion map was prepared. ... Sand-fixing operations were conducted on an area of 140,000 hectares from 1951 to 1968. Approximately 300,000 hectares were covered by this work from 1971 to 1975. The plan for 1976–80 covers an area of 330,000 hectares. (14, p.34)

The attack on sand involved the proper siting of communities and industrial projects, the fixing of shifting sand along the routes of gas mains, electric transmission lines, and motor roads, and around industrial and farming facilities. Stabilization was carried out through plantings, afforestation, and the use of binding substances.

As in Vale, in another of those countries where money can be found for the active improvement of rangeland, investments made in the plowing and seeding of pastures were repaid, the case study declares, within two to four years. Special techniques for restoring vegetation were recommended for even the arid Kara Kum where rainfall is less than an annual average of from 120 mm to 140 mm.

> Local shrubs . . . and perennial grasses develop quickly, yield lavish fruit and much more production of pasture forage, ensuring thereby adequate year-round feeding of sheep. Fit for utilization in the second and third year, they continue to flourish for not less than 12 to 30 years. (14, p.29)

The Ashkabad Deserts Institute continues to pursue research in all aspects of dryland improvement—drainage and management of irrigation projects, the stabilization of moving sand, the cultivation of pastures, afforestation, rodent control, conservation of natural fauna, the siting of industrial and transportation facilities, the location and management of dryland parks and recreation areas.

> With the growth of population, the recreational role of arid regions will be much greater. More tourists will be attracted to the desert by its unique beauty, the peculiarities of its flora and fauna, and the undisturbed quiet. The application of warm and dry desert climates for medical purposes will be increased, and the present health establishments for the treatment of kidney disorders (Bairam Ali) will be supplemented with many others. (14, p.39)

The development of physical solutions to the physical problems of Turkmenia involved that interweaving of improved environments that constituted the integrated Turkmenistan program, with its culmination in the spectacular Kara Kum Canal. There is just one hint in the case study that the development of Turkmenia was not a totally smooth process, and that whereas physical solutions were forthcoming, solutions to the social problems related to desertification have not been so readily achieved.

> The psychological aspect is another important factor in environmental protection. Thus far, the understanding of the problem is insufficient, not only by the bulk of the population, but by many local executives. (14, p.39)

The point is not elaborated, nor is the reader informed about the ways in which psychological problems manifested themselves. Did the Turkmen nomads balk at being organized into *sovkhozes*? What happened to the former inhabitants of the areas now being scientifically irrigated, those people who were carrying out more primitive styles of irrigation? In the reference to "executives," there is an indication that directives containing scientifically established procedures were not always efficiently carried out.

> When the population of Turkmenistan was comparatively small, the damage inflicted by man on nature was self-restoring. Now, when the load on desert ecosystems has radically increased, the necessary self-restoration no longer takes place. As a result, we see signs of anthropogenic desertification in many districts. In view of this, it is necessary to conduct regular education of the people, explaining the importance of environmental protection. This will be conducted by the publication of posters and pamphlets, by short films, by sponsoring photo exhibits and lectures. (14, p.39)

Such messages raining down from above are the solution proposed in the case study for dealing with the persistence of poor land-use practices by ordinary people. This is in obvious contrast to the so-called free world in which ordinary people had to take to the streets to persuade their own governments to cease conducting official depredations on an always helpless environment. Other than that, Turkmenia reinforces an impression made by the discussion of the Golodnaya Steppe that ordinary people in the Soviet Union are handled in the same way that a corporation deals with its employees. What are regarded as good performances on the part of workers are rewarded with good salaries, bonuses, better housing, the chance to buy scarce consumer items, and, certainly not least, a role that carries authority over one's fellow men. All that certainly constitutes one way of handling the social problems associated with desertification, and in that sense, looks much like a solution to the desertification problem. As part of this particular solution, failure in the Soviet Union results in being cast into an outer darkness more Stygian than anything within the capacity of even multinational corporations, or so one would presume about a situation in which the one corporation, the very nation itself, admits no competition and provides no place else to go. In such a situation, how fortunate it is, how very lucky, that this nation seems to be conscious of the needs of the environment.

14

CHINA

"Man can conquer heaven"

TO THE WEST, in which a thousand blossoms bloom, the single-minded Chinese predilection for the thoughts of Mao Tse-tung seems childish and naive, if not the rote mouthings of an enslaved people. By their unceasing sloganeering, the Chinese reinforce an impression that they have lost the capacity for independent thought. Even in their materials intended for circulation abroad, such as their case studies in desertification, Chinese authors seem to be addressing, not the world outside, but only themselves.

> Before liberation, the people of China suffered from oppression and exploitation under imperialism, feudalism and bureaucratic capitalism. Its natural resources were subjected to destruction and plunder, and the land to irrational use. Vegetation in the desert areas was destroyed, and wind and sand became a serious menace. Farmland, human dwellings, pastures and roads were often buried under shifting sand. The deserts were constantly advancing. (10, p.5)

To the contemporary man of China, everything finally seems to be politics. The focus is narrow, seeming to deny life's richness and variety, just as China seems to reject the West's strident individualism, producing that gray portrait of the Chinese that their critics liken to life in an ant heap. As Mao himself said, "Politics is the commander, *the soul in everything*" (85, p.85).

> Since the founding of the People's Republic of China, people of all nationalities in the desert areas got organized under the leadership of Chairman Mao and the Chinese Communist Party and, relying on the

strength and wisdom of the masses and using their own hands, they launched an all-out war on the deserts. . . . In the "In agriculture, learn from Tachai" mass movement, they adhered to the principle of class struggle and the basic lines of the Party, and with the heroic spirit of "man can conquer heaven," launched a stubborn struggle against the sand scourge. (10, p.5)

It is curious that Tachai itself was not presented as a case study, offering the Conference a chance, in agriculture, to learn from it. This most famous of all agricultural production brigades would have qualified for the Conference by its location in an area vulnerable to desertification, a semiarid region (average annual rainfall, slightly over 500 mm) in the T'aihang mountains of eastern Shansi. It was in 1964 that Mao first pronounced the slogan, "In agriculture, learn from Tachai," thereby drawing the country's attention to this particular commune as a model for socialist agriculture. Later in the same year, Chou En-lai explained that this honor was not due entirely to Tachai's agricultural achievements. Chou told the Third National People's Congress:

The principle of putting politics in command and placing ideology in the lead, the spirit of self-reliance and hard struggle, and the communist style of loving the country and the collective, in all of which the Tachai Brigade has persevered, should be vigorously promoted. (85, pp.1-2)

The preeminence of ideology is emphasized also in *Tachai—The Red Banner*, the chronicle of the Brigade as recorded by the Chinese in 1977 (85). In that book, it is stated:

Tachai's party branch often sums up the transformations there in these words: "People's thinking has changed. The land has changed; farm techniques and output have changed. The change in thinking is the key to all else." (85, p.51)

"Often" is the word that here oppresses, bringing a picture to the mind of Tachai's party branch directing an exercise in the group chanting of that sentiment. In a politicized society, not even Tiger Head Hill, dominating Tachai's verdant fields, can be left in repose as a mere scenic wonder.

Every day, as school lets out, one can hear the ringing songs of Tachai's children. Here is a favorite one:

> *Standing on Tiger Head Hill,*
> *Facing the rising sun, I sing*
> *In praise of Chairman Mao, our saving star,*
> *In praise of the great Communist Party.* (85, pp.6-7)

If these schoolchild sentiments suggest the possibility that school lets out just as the sun is rising, they also lead one to wonder why the Chinese would bother transmitting them to the West as if they could possibly appeal to the decadent minds who invented the hand-held calculator, a device which will eventually eliminate school. At the same time, if you make a determined effort to penetrate the thickets of Chinese expression, you might end up wondering if there isn't some truth in the way the Tachai Party Branch often sums things up. Isn't a change in thinking precisely what is needed in Luni Block, not to mention Combarbalá, Oglat Merteba, and Greater Mussayeb? Isn't that what the authors of the respective case studies seemed to be saying? Let us review the major findings to emerge thus far from the case studies to see if it is not true, indeed, that a change in thinking is the key to all else. Explicitly or implicitly, the case studies—and there are only a few left to review—have agreed that the following assertions are true:

1. The deserts of the world are where they are because of climate.

2. Climate is variable, always shifting. It has been always shifting in the past—toward warm or cold, wet or dry—as we are told by geology, pollen grains, the spiraling shells of *Neogloboquadrina pachyderma* brought up in cores from the deep-sea bed. But the direction in which climatic change is at present moving has not yet been ascertained. The case studies provide no grounds for saying that climates anywhere are becoming more arid.

3. If a change in climate toward aridity cannot be detected, climatic change cannot be held responsible for desertification in the contemporary world and certainly not for recent accelerations in the process. The cause of desertification must be sought elsewhere.

4. Gerbils and locusts are capable of assisting the process of desertification, as several of the case studies point out. However, the

principal source of this modern plague is another life form, *Homo sapiens sapiens*, which brings on desertification by abusing the land.

5. The physical manifestations of desertification are seen in dust storms, in sheeting, scalding, gullying, and other expressions of wind and water erosion, in the loss of soil fertility, the breakdown of soil structure, the mobilization of sand dunes, the replacement of good forage by undesirable invaders, the thinning and disappearance of vegetation, and the progressive exposure of naked earth or rock. In irrigation projects, desertification appears paradoxically in the form of waterlogging, usually accompanied by salt or alkaline deposits.

6. The ways in which man abuses the land are known. An examination of any specific example of desertification will reveal the precise actions through which the human user reveals that he has lost, or been forced to disavow, his former reverence for the miracle of nature.

7. Since the physical causes of desertification can always be determined, physical solutions can always be proposed. Some land has been degraded "irreversibly," but that is an economic situation, not a technical one. There are very few such cases. As the table on page 000 indicates, it would pay to rehabilitate almost every case of desertification. This is a triumph of the new agricultural sciences, made even more effective by the adoption of an ecological attitude.

To this point, all is well. Our short review provides grounds for believing that desertification can indeed be halted everywhere on the planet. Land already degraded can be returned to a condition of sustained productivity, a review of the case studies goes on to indicate, since the new sciences have stripped practically all situations of those technical mysteries that might have prevented a decent economic return from rehabilitation within the short-term perspective of 25 years.

Nothing in such a review denies that desertification is still raging on at a truly horrendous pace. In the rich countries, damaged land will be rehabilitated—money can be found for that—when economics calls for rehabilitation or when desertification becomes too depressing an eyesore. Here as elsewhere the best defense against desertification is prevention, the adoption of proper land-use practices that prevent land from being ravaged in the first place. This is much the least expensive approach, much less costly than rehabilitation, which demands outlays rising exponentially as the course of degradation proceeds. Fortunately, prevention is being urged along in the rich nations by the emergence of the new environmental consciousness.

In the poor countries, however, the heirs of folk wisdom and experience, the peoples of traditional societies, are damaging their environments, and neither prevention nor rehabilitation seems immediately possible in so many situations in Africa, Latin America, and south Asia. Nor is it that the people of those societies have any illusions about what they are doing—filmed and reported interviews continually testify to their realization that they are damaging the land. They say they have no choice, a pathetic assertion that testifies to the pressures they are under. These are not *physical* pressures. Broadly speaking, they are *social*, a category that can be taken to include economic, political, and cultural factors. Thus, the case studies lead on to another conclusion in addition to those listed in the preceding brief review. It is a conclusion that might have been deduced from the finding, if one had thought the matter through when that finding became clear, that desertification in the contemporary world is due to the actions of man.

8. The physical causes of desertification are effects of prior causes, and these, the ultimate causes of desertification, are always social.

The physical symptoms of desertification are always the expression of a social malaise. Despite the wide prevalence of folk wisdom, ignorance can be a cause of desertification as in a situation in which wisdom has not yet had time to evolve as when a strange new environment, an unfamiliar biota, is first encountered. Such was the situation in which the pioneers of the Gascoyne found themselves, as well as the first ranchers in Vale, the bemused Spaniards who mined and ranched the region of Combarbalá. If their failure to pause, to take stock, to approach their unfamiliar environments with caution, can be regarded as an expression of social malaise, the philosopher of desertification, taking a tolerant view of their essentially romantic situations, must be careful about drifting into a new tautology. In any case, their ignorance was quickly replaced by rationalizations that justified overexploitation, and that came to be fueled by the disadvantages characterizing agriculture in its relations with banking, markets, and industry everywhere in a world increasingly dominated by commerce. You can sympathize with the Gascoyner trying to squeeze a little more income out of a flock of sheep too numerous for the sustained productivity of his range. His life is remote and lonely, filled with hard physical labor on a wild frontier, and for all his efforts, he ends up in debt to the commercial houses, the resentful recipient of a net income less than that of a minor clerk in some unimportant business in the distant city. When the Gascoyne sheepman was told to reduce the size of his flocks, he looked beyond the efficient agricultural agent who was delivering him this message, across a thousand kilometers of mulga and atriplex, to that clerk who goes to the movies every night if the whim so moves him.

The social causes of desertification are apparent in the case studies, or readily deducible from them, even if they were not analyzed with the beautiful precision that the authors, physical scientists, brought to their descriptions of physical phenomena. Rampant population growth is one, occurring everywhere in the Third World, saturating landscapes beyond their capacities as worked by traditional technologies. Laws and traditions of inheritance are another, shattering holdings into splinters incapable of providing subsistence to even one family, a process of disintegration that is accelerated when populations are exploding. Other social causes can be drawn from the case studies and other sources—archaic and irrational systems of water rights, damaging systems of land ownership and tenure. In their component review on *Population, Society and Desertification*, Kates, Johnson, and Haring cite the example of the vineyard oasis of Mendoza, Argentina, as a place where an inept tenant system is destroying productive land.

> No factor is more important in contributing to desertification in Mendoza than is the land tenure system. Viticulture is the primary agricultural activity and large numbers of Mendoza farmers work under a sharecropping (*contratista*) system. While the owner of the property supplies the capital equipment and farm land, the *contratista* provides the labor. The contract generally runs for eight years. During this time, the *contratista* must clear the land, plant it in vines, cultivate and harvest the crop, and pay 82% of the yield as rent. At the end of the contract period the land reverts to the owner just as the vines reach maximum production and the sharecropper must look for employment elsewhere. . . .
>
> The *contratista* system contributes to desertification in a number of ways. Because a *contratista* holds the land for only a short time, his ability and willingness to invest in capital improvements is minimal. Yet these capital improvements are often essential to reducing the risk of salinization. . . . It is no accident that the most saline soils in the area

are those in the oldest part of the oasis where the *contratista* system is most pervasive. . . . The *contratista's* unwillingness to put capital into the improvement of a short-term holding is matched by the landowner's reluctance to invest in upgrading land quality. For the landlord, the land primarily represents a long-term hedge against inflation. (23, p.19)

Politics can devastate the land, certainly in its extreme manifestation, in war, in which the use of defoliants is a recent development that makes desertification into a combat weapon. Even in its somewhat milder expressions, politics can exert a devastating impact, as did colonialism when it took a form in which colonists occupied all the best land, forcing native owners to saturate ever more marginal acreage. Such displacements, however, are of minor importance when compared with the permanent and more pervasive effects left behind by the colonial order wherever it functioned, and where even the departure of the Europeans left a rich panoply of agricultural societies still stripped of control over their lives, that control then having been transferred to the capitals of newly independent nations. Ancient subsistence economies were battered or demolished as their peoples and cultures have been inexorably swallowed up by the modern world of money and markets. Colonialism had departed, but in its place, flinging technological thunderbolts, was its natural offspring, the logical, uninterrupted extension of the colonial order, but given a new name, disguising the unceasing destruction of cultures. It had come to be called "socioeconomic development." Peoples everywhere, as they experienced the impact of this grand design—Africans, Asians, Indonesians, Polynesians—were required to look on helplessly as the important decisions affecting their lives came to be made elsewhere, far away, in some national capital newly sprung up amidst the palm trees on the Guinea coast or on the shores of the Indian Ocean, or even farther away, in the most distant metropolises—on Wall Street, on the Paris Bourse, in Zurich where the price of chocolate endlessly fluctuates. Worse, many of these distant decisions made no sense from the local point of view. The natural response was a fatalism that asks, What does it matter? It is a social attitude in which a multitude of social ills take root, a lassitude toward life that germinates the intertwined problems of population and desertification. The few who were energized to meet the new demands of money and markets made the situation even worse, ripping up the sensitive earth to grow their groundnuts everywhere, ignoring sustained productivity for the charms of quick profits. In their way, these energetic people were also victims, another expression of the destruction of antique social orders.

There are anthropologists who would say that powerlessness is the root to which the destruction of ecosystems can be traced. Thus, E. N. Anderson:

> The ecological crisis is largely a result of the political and economic structure, specifically of the balance of power. (33, p.272)

This is a radical view inasmuch as it would find the solution to the problem of desertification in a realignment of power structures. Yet it is a radicalism shared by the United Nations. The materials prepared for the Conference include reference to connections between powerlessness and desertification. Thus, *Desertification: An Overview*:

> Increasingly over the past 50 to 100 years, pastoral nomadism has found itself at bay. The political status of the nomads has declined, and with it, their control of grazing rights, their relations vis-a-vis adjacent crop-based systems, and their role in desert transport and commerce. . . . That nomadic pastoralism is in trouble is evident in increasing desertification associated with such systems. (16, p.35)

In making the point with reference only to pastoral nomads, the *Overview* did not go far enough. All sorts of people exercising all the variety of dryland livelihoods live far from centers of power in both a geographical and a political sense, a circumstance that has brought their lives into ever closer association with desertification, both as agents and victims. The countries most severely affected are far from the world's major centers of wealth and power. The disadvantages such countries experience would be rectified by a global realignment of power structures if the United Nations were to have its way and the New International Economic Order should come to pass. Such, at least, is the hope of the United Nations Third World majority.

As a subject, a science, desertification remains the property of the physical scientists who developed it, who did the best they could to direct the world's attention to the damage being inflicted on productive land, and who performed the incalculable service of providing physical solutions to the problem as it reveals itself in all its physical manifestations. These distinguished researchers can hardly be said to merit censure for their reluctance, so evident in the case studies, to move outside their own areas of competence and provide intricate social analysis to what turns out to be ultimately a social problem. On the contrary, they are to be commended for their early recognition that social and economic factors play fundamental roles in the problem of desertification. They are certainly not to be blamed when the calls they have been issuing for at least a decade that an appropriate contribution to the problem be made by the social sciences have elicited no particular response. It was a lack of response that had to be faced also by the Conference Secretariat as it attempted to carry out the directive of the General Assembly to collect and assess all available knowledge on the subject. The knowledge available from the social sciences turned out to be notable for its absence. Recourse was had at last to geographers, whose subject has experienced a renaissance by turning to the examination of the relations between social systems and physical ecosystems. As those geographers Kates, Johnson, and Haring said:

> Desertification is a human phenomenon, more a social, economic and political problem than a technical one. [Its] complexity is the major finding of our review. (23, p.48)

Complexity is an outcome of the very fact that all cases of improper land use can be attributed to social causes, often to a complex interweave of social causes. This is the first conclusion that might have been expected from the social sciences if they had deigned to turn to this question. The social factors underlying specific cases of desertification can always be detected through a scrupulous examination of the social situations in which such cases are embedded. An analysis of that kind is analogous to the careful physical examination required to determine the precise physical causes of desertification, always expressive as they are of social maladjustment. Just as on the physical side, when an underlying social cause is identified, a social solution can be proposed. As an agronomist might suggest contour plowing as a remedy for excessive water erosion on slopes, so the social scientist might suggest reform of the inheritance laws, the rationalization of archaic systems of water rights, even a national program of land reform. The social scientist will project an emigration rate defining the expected flow of country people to the city and will propose measures to ease the transition for the migrant and to speed the process whereby this traveler becomes a productive member of society in his new setting. Where population growth has generated too many people for the land to support, the social scientist may suggest the introduction of family planning programs to be coordinated with the establishment of alternative livelihood systems, such as industry or mining or the development of crafts, just the sort of thing that was suggested for the assistance of the depressed *comuneros* of Combarbalá.

Contributions of this kind, however, never seem enough. A feeling persists that with no more than that social science would be doing only half its job. Something is still missing, perhaps to be remedied by the inclusion of anthropologists on the interdisciplinary teams, a presence increasingly requested. For it is one thing to suggest that water rights or land ownership be rationalized and quite another and more difficult thing to get them rationalized. This seems not at all to be an action of the same order as getting a farmer to switch to contour plowing. Social action seems somehow qualitatively different from mere physical action. Since it always affects relationships among people, power relationships included, social action always seems to contain a political element. But since social action is what is directed to social problems, isn't it true that social action, its techniques and procedures, is a part of social science? What is being dealt with here if it is not culture?

Perhaps there is another kind of ignorance, capable of intruding even into old and rich traditions, arising when old conditions change and ancient knowledge becomes less and less applicable to them. Luni Block might provide an example of such a process at work. There, population growth has supersaturated an already densely worked environment. This growth has transformed the old condition so that agriculture carried out in accordance with the old precepts now destroys the resource base. Specialists from CAZRI have come to Luni Block and carried out investigations there which have yielded a set of new precepts capable, these specialists say, of supporting the denser populations without further damage to the land. Some of these improved practices do not even require money, just more labor. In short, a physical solution to the problem of desertification in Luni Block has been proposed. The only thing still missing seems to be the social solution. An integral element in such a social solution would be a proven technique whereby the farmers of Luni Block could be persuaded to adopt the physical solution. While awaiting this social solution, the CAZRI researchers fidget in a state of understandable frustration. They have proposed also a massive educational program, as if they could think of nothing else one could do, although they have no way to guarantee that the local farmers will listen to what someone is trying to teach them, or that they would act on those teachings if they should happen to penetrate their resisting intellects.

Agricultural extension services were proposed—by hope untinged with reflection, it would seem, as the solution to the problems of Greater Mussayeb. The case studies set in Combarbalá and in Oglat Merteba contain lists of the physical measures required to bring desertification to a halt in those regions. Both also suggest social measures that might be undertaken, some of them rather vague. Extension services themselves are one kind of social measure, and among those situations seeking solutions, only the Chile case study, preferring demonstration plots, hesitates to suggest the establishment of an educational program. But whether the measures suggested are physical or social, the problem in the problem, so to speak, always lies in how to get them carried out. Even in richer settings—in Vale and in the Gascoyne—the willing collaboration of those who actually use the land had to be obtained before rehabilitative measures could be applied. In Turkmenia and the Golodnaya Steppe, willing collaboration is obtained by means of incentives, or so the Soviet case studies declare. Willing collaboration—which is, to be sure, something social, even mental, rather than physical—keeps popping up as if insisting on presenting itself as the key to programmatic success. Well, then, since it is social, one naturally anticipates that social science will have developed theory and procedures for arousing it.

Extension, education, communication—the issue is how to make effective contact with those who use the land, those who, when all is said and done, will care for it or abuse it. Rural people, peasants, "superstitious" people, as some say of them, traditionalist, conservative, remote, they compose that vast population least affected by modernity, least touched by development, the most difficult to reach with that nonformal education that is increasingly being summoned to the service of development. It is "nonformal," so-called because its recipients are too old for school. According to its supporters, many of whom are ardent, it is the key and trigger to community action. Yet it is poorly understood, not well analyzed, lacking deep roots in the soil of social science. "Nonformal education, though not a recent phenomenon, has received little systematic study," said Philip Coombs (38, p.xv). One observes a lack of agreement as to how it should be carried out. Few would claim to know exactly how nonformal education should be delivered, or how it should be applied to gain the collaboration that is its goal. Or is that its goal?

The community development movement that has flowered as former colonies have become independent nations has taken the form of a quest for collaboration, and community development theory is an elaboration of methods of how local participation and enthusiasm can be aroused. Reacting against the blundering of certain "experts" with their misapplied technology, one current of community development has come to view the failure of efforts to improve life in the Third World as a natural result of the scorn of the rich for the poor and the failure of those who possess science to appreciate the skills, adaptations, and even the profound knowledge exercised by peasants and paupers. This stream of community development has become loaded with a certain emotional freight, a crusading zeal, sometimes appearing almost as a call to social revolution. To this extent it has moved beyond the domain of science while yet being indicative of the dilemmas that haunt social science. While natural science is usually able to don a cloak of emotional neutrality, to appear superior to contending forces, social action always takes place in the midst of the battle, in the center of life. It must develop an "involvement" which, at the same time, strips it of its scientific wrappings. Yet what could be more rational than what has come to be an axiom of community development? This is that collaboration is obtained by collaborating. The solution to problems of social action is to be found in the principle of popular participation.

The draft Plan of Action to Combat Desertification, submitted to the Conference for review and amendment by the delegates, passed through this process of examination and debate with comparatively few alterations. One of the principal changes made by the delegates emerged from the unanimous approval given to an entirely new recommendation which was inserted in the final version of the Plan to appear as Recommendation 3:

> It is recommended that public participation be made an integral element of the prevention and combating of desertification and that account be thus taken of the needs, wisdom and aspirations of the people. (32, p.13)

Naturally, one would expect such a recommendation to be approved by the Third World majority at the Conference. To them it might serve almost as a battle cry through which the poor nations could reassert the dignity of their peoples, so recently humiliated by colonialism. Nor does it matter whether the wisdom of the people is a resource frequently utilized by the officials who are even now busily building the new nations that make up much of the Third World or who exercise a talent, so highly developed in much of Latin America, for keeping the *campesinos* in their place. What matters is that the wisdom is there. Some day the occasion might arise for utilizing it.

Recommendation 3 was also supported by the delegates from the rich countries—and why not? It costs them nothing, while making them seem open-minded, no longer the arrogant colonial masters. They would remind us of the Peace Corps, the *Deutsche Entwicklungsdienst*, all those volunteers from the richer nations who have gone out into the world to work and create good will without the expense—and the ecological blunders—involved in constructing, say, hydroelectric projects. Popular participation sometimes seems more a set of precepts than a science. When he sees how easily those precepts are recited, the observer becomes cynical and jaded and finds himself drifting into polemic.

If physical action is in question, the new enlightenment dictates that an ecological approach be taken. If social action is at issue, the present orthodoxy requires popular participation. In the former case, the concept is clear and its application difficult, requiring as it does the determination of what are functional ecosystems and foresight regarding the most distant secondary effects of action. In the latter case, no one knows precisely what is meant, but the community development worker seems to be doing it when he engages in nothing more than a visit to the local *cantina* to listen to what the other customers happen to be complaining about.

Yet, to give them their due, it is probably true to say that the delegates to the Conference on Desertification voted in favor of Recommendation 3 because they believe that popular participation is effective—whatever it may happen to be. This is a belief that is widely expressed, but it may be supported as much by sentiment as by any final demonstration that the principle constitutes effective practice. Like a mob scene, popular participation is a heuristic around which everyone has gathered, but where all is confusion in both theory and practice.

It will be recalled that CAZRI's summons for a mass educational program stressed "the fullest possible participation of communities in . . . family planning and the adoption of newer developmental technologies" (3, p.51). Here it is evident that by "participation" is meant something that consideration shows to be really far less than "the fullest possible." What is wanted is that people should sit quietly and listen to what they are being told. They should participate, yes, but in what has been proposed by others, by CAZRI, by the Ministry of Health, Family Planning, and Urban Development. No indication appears that their own desires are to be consulted, and the principal reference to ancient wisdom is a comment that old skills should be examined via ethno-agricultural studies before being jettisoned in favor of "newer developmental technologies" (3, p.51). This might be designated as the conservative view of popular participation, what Louis XIV might have meant by the term. People participate by making an appearance, at which they receive their marching orders, although this is a point of view that can be stretched to include all sorts of irrelevancies, games, and festivals—for example, Roman circuses that have no other purpose than to catch the popular ear for the message that someone else wants to implant in it.

Moving away from that extreme toward an appreciation of native lore and intelligence, a spectrum of attitudes can be distinguished among which would appear the injunctions of the Diocesan Community-Based Programs of the Rural Missionaries of the Philippines. "Go to the people!" the missionaries exhort the readers of their fund-raising brochure (65, p.1). "Live with them. Learn from them. Love them. Start with what they know. Build on what they have." The Inter-American Foundation would start and also end with "what they know," as expressed in the Foundation's statements, *They Know How*, a title reversing the foreign-aid fatigue expressed in *We Don't Know How*, an account by William and Paul Paddock of U.S. assistance failures resulting from a discredited "expert" approach. More than a science—indeed, not a science—the attitudes of the Inter-American Foundation constitute a philosophy. What this philosophy involves is stated by the Foundation in its own brochure (49, p.1):

- Human beings have value and dignity, not merely needs and uses;
- commoners have the right and capacity to promote their own well-being, manage their own affairs, and make accountable their own institutions;

- people everywhere manifestly know their own world better than any outsider and their lives should not be controlled, manipulated, or engineered by others;
- the ideals of justice, respect, equity, compassion and the commonwealth are basic to human existence. The aspirations may have varying veneers in different societies but they must be understood and respected.

Popular participation is more than a principle and a technique; it is an ethical attitude, and while the Foundation is subsequently clear in its conviction that this ethical perspective will yield practical success—that it is, in the Foundation's view, the *only* route to practical success—the impression is strong that this is an attitude that should prevail whether it is successful or not. The goals of life are not production goals. Yet it seems an interesting coincidence that production goals, the transformation of harsh material realities, can be achieved, as the Foundation perceives it, only through this refined spiritual attitude. Wheat quotas are to be met by the recognition of the human dignity in even the least of us. Desertification is to be halted by exalting humanity, smashing oppression, and returning to people control over their lives. The manifesto of the Inter-American Foundation is thus seen to be a restatement of the view that desertification accompanies powerlessness and the loss of control by people over their own lives.

Popular participation as a radical attitude has attracted its widest audience through the writings and pedagogical practice of Paulo Freire, a Brazilian lawyer turned educator, who developed his distinctive approach in attempting to bring literacy to adults in those desolate, poverty-stricken backlands, *os sertões*, where Euclides da Cunha reported his epic drama of struggle and fanaticism in the literary classic of Brazil. Among competing theories of community development, Freire's views have moved to preeminence because he provides a detailed, coherent perspective that conforms with a wide contemporary and humanitarian attitude toward peasant populations and the victims of underdevelopment. Condemning the sloganeering of both right and left, he has the advantage of avoiding precise political classification, of eluding the old political categories, even though he speaks of the evolution of communication between a community and a community development worker as a "dialectical process," but one that is in practice more Socratic than Marxist or Hegelian. His impact undoubtedly stems from elements in his outlook that are enormously appealing, his insistence that dignity and humanity are proper to all persons, his notion that oppression is a theft of humanity. This and his development of a detailed pedagogical method for making contact with the disadvantaged peasant and for returning to him what he says has been stolen.

For Freire, too, production goals, projects aimed at material targets, are entirely secondary, but he would also say that material results will follow when the poor break out of the system that oppresses them and keeps them poor.

> [The] struggle . . . to life-affirming humanization . . . does not lie simply in having more to eat (although it does involve having more to eat and cannot fail to include this aspect). (45, p.55)

The focus of the Freirean community worker is not centered on knowledge, traditional or otherwise, or on what he has to teach, but on attitudes. He serves not as a teacher at all in the traditional sense, but as a catalyst, stimulating and exciting the community in a dialogue in which the teacher is also a student and the students are teachers. Even to absorb a message, much less to act on it, the community must adopt an open and willing attitude arising out of a "critical consciousness"—*conscientização*, in Freire's Portuguese terminology—through which its members become critical of the world, aware of their unique place in the world. They are led to see that by their work they transform the world, which, because of their activities, by the fact that they are in the world, is not the same as it was before. In coming to understand these things, they extirpate the oppressor who had taken up residence inside their very psyches, so that previously, they had found their self-identity in their relationship with the "boss," the *patron*, agreeing with that person's opinion that they themselves are lazy, shiftless, and stupid. How can people learn anything, we find Freire asking, when they are convinced of their own stupidity? And yet catalyzing them away from that conviction can be dangerous business. While the oppressor still lives within them, the people of a community can be induced even to kill the community development worker, and Freire reports such a case (45, p.130).

It is also political business—like all social action. After the 1964 coup established a military government in Brazil, the new regime jailed Freire, accusing him of "bolshevizing" the peasants. The catalyst of Pernambuco subsequently agreed to go into exile, the fate of all those who endeavor to shake the torpor out of the Latin American *campesino*. In time, he went to work for the World Council of Churches in Geneva, whence he was to be found taking his pedagogy to illiterates in the new African nation of Guinea-Bissau. His acceptance in that Marxist nation increases the tendency to identify him with the extreme left, as does his use of such an "old left" term as "oppressor," which clangs archaically on the contemporary ear. Or he has found himself ever leftward because that is where the right would drive him even though his work in Pernambuco evaded the conventional labels of ideology.

In any case, Freire's history illustrates the sort of thing that social action runs up against. For all his broad impact on community development theory, the political overtones to his approach made the undiluted application of his technique impossible in his own country. A nutrition education project was attempted in northeast Brazil in 1974 using a modified form of the Freirean pedagogy. "The political situation was such," however, "as to prevent any encouragement of critical consciousness," said Dr. Therese Drummond, then working out of Cornell University. A program that is fully Freire "could only be considered in a favorable political situation," she concluded (42, p.17). This discouraging statement could imply a fatal limitation to the method, since the "oppressor" can hardly be expected voluntarily to consign himself to extinction. Drummond thus gives expression to one of the great dilemmas confronting social action programs—their theory may be superb and their application impossible. Yet even a partial application of the Freire method was "of value as an initial exploration," said Drummond, suggesting that "a larger and longer effort is justified" (42, p.17).

The United Nations Declaration of Social Progress and Development, General Assembly Resolution 2542 (XXIV) of 11 December, 1969, stated that "social progress and development require the full utilization of human resources." This was terminology, the ubiquitous "human resources" especially, a phrase much in current vogue, that seems to view people as things, objects to be "utilized," rather than as subjects in which autonomous attitudes should be encouraged. But it happened merely to be the United Nations and its way of talking: no "oppressive" implication was intended. The declaration went on to say that social progress and development require "the active participation of all elements of society, individually or through associations, in defining and achieving the common goals of development." Scarcely a dissenting voice can be heard today to come out against the concept of popular participation, although there might be some dissension about whether just anybody should be asked to help define the common goals of development. This and other disagreements about how the theory of popular participation should be interpreted have arisen because the approach is said to have had inconclusive results. A quarter of a century has passed since India's Community Development Program, based on principles of self-help enunciated by Gandhi and Rabindranath Tagore, was inaugurated in "a great surge of hope and enthusiasm."

> All over India, community schools and village halls were constructed, roads built and paved, water wells dug and protected, compost pits filled, school gardens and backyard vegetable patches planted, sewing classes and youth clubs opened. Moreover, a new image of the government as a source of help and service was created and the villagers began to see that for the first time the agents of government were there to help them, not simply to demand taxes and enforce regulations. . . . It must also be said that . . . the Community Development Program had not significantly altered the basic conditions of life in rural India. Abject poverty, malnutrition and ill health, indebtedness, and above all, India's worsening food crisis had but one remedy—a large production of wealth from the land. (38, pp.70-71)

And so with the *Animation Rurale* movement in former French Africa, seeking the "awakening of rural people and their energies."

> There is little doubt that *animation rurale*, like the Indian CD movement, achieved considerable success in its first objective of stimulating rural people in behalf of development and creating a greater awareness of their own interests and capacity. . . . But, as in India, inspiring villagers was not enough; sophisticated technical advice and more practical material help were necessary follow-ups. (38, p.73)

It might even be concluded that the popular participation movement is so much inspiring nonsense. The most effective approach, this debunking might go on to say, is that of the profit-seeking corporation, or that of the Soviet Union when it set out to transform the Golodnaya Steppe. People should be told what to do and then motivated to do it through a system of rewards and punishments. Yet a closer look at its internal workings indicates that the Soviet Union may embody a relationship between government and people that is somewhat more complex than its case studies revealed it to be. The United Nations described the planning process developed by the Soviet Union, taking the information from Soviet sources.

> On the basis of societal preferences, general priorities are established and written into a draft national plan. This is widely disseminated and discussed by all segments of the population. Through their representatives, the people's reaction to this tentative definition of alternatives is taken into account in formulating the definitive plan which, in turn, is ratified by popular representatives. (80, p.5)

If that is the way planning proceeds in the Soviet Union now, it may not always have been thus. In his memoirs, Khrushchev asked:

> Why did our agriculture lag so far behind our industry? Why were we so at the mercy of the capriciousness of nature and the fluctuation of harvests. . . . ? Stalin deserves much of the blame. . . . For Stalin, peasants were scum. (74, p.112)

His own attitude, Khrushchev reported, was quite different.

> The main thing in the struggle for socialism is the productivity of labor. For socialism to be victorious, a country must get the most out of every worker. And when I say, "get the most," I don't mean by force. (74, p.115)

What he does mean is by incentives.

> I realize that by publicly advocating material incentives I'm opening myself up to those know-it-alls who will say our people should be motivated not by money but by ideological considerations. (74, p.114)

Seen in that light, material incentives might almost have some remote connection with popular participation. Still, national referendums are worlds away from the dynamic, intimate dialogue proposed by Paulo Freire, whose method, after all, is directed not at those forward-looking citizens of developed nations but toward those ravaged nobodies whom the Inter-American Foundation quaintly calls "commoners." Yet referendums and material incentives represent aspects of the principle of popular participation to which even the Soviet Union makes philosophical obeisance. Whether or not Soviet citizens participate in the decisions that control their lives, the Soviet Union asserts in principle that those who work the land should be consulted. They should not be forced.

The outlook of that other socialist empire, China, is more immediately akin to that of Freire.

> Our cultural workers must serve the people with great enthusiasm and devotion, and they must link themselves with the masses, not divorce themselves from the masses. In order to do so, they must act in accordance with the needs and wishes of the masses. All work done for the masses must start from their needs and not from the desire of any individual, however well-intentioned. (45, p.83)

This statement by Mao Tse-tung, cited by Freire, is linked by him to his own philosophy. As the story of Tachai is presented, this model commune comes close to being a model also of the Freire method, its outward achievements arising from a change in the inner life. The peasants experienced *conscientização*, awakened to the place that they occupy in the world, to the fact that in working they transform the world, they became like "the foolish old man who removed the mountains," and their self-esteem restored, they were capable of anything. The change in thinking was the key to all else.

Even accepting the propagandistic account of the commune contained in *Tachai—The Red Banner*, questions arise out of what is presented as a utopian progress. Tachai grew from its own roots, but depended on a flow of ideas from above. "We can't go wrong as long as we follow the party," said Chen Yung-kuei, himself a peasant, but the one who played the role of community development worker in Tachai. Freire wants the relation between teacher and community members to be symmetrical, a street of two-way communication, but it can never be entirely so. From the community development worker, the students—peasants or workers—get something distinctive. The community must be activated, galvanized, as the peasants of Tachai were said to be by the thoughts of Mao as presented to them by Chen. Not just in the opening moments but for an extended period of time, flagging spirits must be boosted again and again with fresh stimulation. A national hero today, a member of the Politburo, Chen Yung-kuei experienced his moments of denunciation. Even in propaganda, demons lurk between the lines, where there are hints of the kinds of excesses described in the stories of Chen Jo-hsi (37).

It is impossible to discuss Tachai in an atmosphere purged of politics. How could it be otherwise? This "iron-clad proof of the superiority of the socialist system" (85, p.12), "this shining red standard of heroism" (85, p.2), is presented as the living expression of contemporary Chinese purpose, a microcosm of the nation. Here, in miniature, was played out the struggle against capitalism and revisionism, the defeat of the "renegade" Liu Shao-chi, the violent drama of the Red Guards. But then all of China's successes against desertification, Turfan and Wushenchao as well, and the others listed in the present case study, which is not a case study unless the entire nation be accepted as the case, all are presented as specific triumphs of the socialist order. In contrast, the Soviet Union is not quite so youthfully exuberant in the third generation after Potemkin. Still the Soviet case studies do not omit all words of praise for that nation's political order.

> The activities of the tsarist government resulted in the complete degradation of newly developed lands. After the victory of the Great October Socialist Revolution, the young Soviet state showed much concern over the condition of irrigated farming in Central Asia. (15, p.15)

That on Goldonaya. And on Turkmenia:

> Vast territories which were desertified owing to the irrational use of natural resources in the pre-revolutionary epoch were inherited by the Turkmenian SSR.... (14, p.4) With the establishment of Soviet power and the incorporation of Turkmenistan into the Union of Soviet Socialist Republics, the principles of the economy were changed.... Agriculture and industry were improved on the basis of modern scientific achievements (14, p.3). Planned socialist economy gave the possibility of applying powerful technical facilities. (14, p.36)

Why, one wonders, cannot the rehabilitation of the Vale rangelands be similarly credited to government in a capitalist regime? The American Revolution is now, of course, a very old order, too diffident to say more than that Vale

> would be a practical demonstration of the government's ability . . . to solve a critical national problem. (13, p.36)

Although China and the Soviet Union both term themselves "socialist" and credit their successes to their socialist system, it is evident that the political and social approaches to problems within the two nations are as night and day, yin and yang, the Soviet Union bringing massive planning and technical applications down from above, counting on material incentives to gain local cooperation, China seeking to change ways of thinking below so that local people, technically unaided, will work out their own solutions. Approaches so contrary to one another should end up demonstrating that if one succeeds, the other will fail, and yet they both, in their way, succeed. Socialism can then be given credit for procedures that are opposed even in their ideology.

Socialism itself, whatever that is, cannot then constitute a political formula that guarantees an end to desertification through the efforts of an awakened peasantry. If doubt lingers over that statement, it is ultimately dispelled by the languid cultivators of Tanzania, where rural socialism, *ujamaa vijijini*, proclaimed by President Julius Nyerere in accordance with Freire-like principles, has failed to interrupt the African enjoyment of long afternoon conversations or the pleasures of resting beneath the trees. "The duty of the party is not to urge people to implement plans which have been decided upon by a few experts or leaders" was the 1971 declaration *Mwongozo— The TANU Guidelines*. "The duty of our party is to ensure that the leaders and experts implement the plans which have been agreed on by the people themselves." (35, p.249) What is there in the African environment that vitiates such sterling principles? Is that what Freire himself is going to encounter in Guinea-Bissau? The explication of such African mysteries seems an obvious task for social science, one whose pursuit has already yielded a generous bibliography but no conclusive results. And so it seems that for all the enthusiasms of the Lanchow Institute of Glaciology, Cryopedology and Deserts, to which the present case study is credited, the world is so decadent a scene that neither proper land use nor the drive toward rehabilitation can be linked to any one political order, however it may be infused with youthful enthusiasm. And yet, paradoxically, it would also seem that proper land use is inseparably political, since the intimate connection between abuse of the land and failings in the social and political order force the investigator in search of causes that always go beyond mere physical disciplines. Unfortunately, and as already indicated, not a great deal of going beyond has thus far taken place.

> Both the social scientists and the natural and physical scientists are at fault for their past reluctance to work together, but there has more often been ignorance or naiveté than hostility. (86, p.187)

That was a comment made to arid-lands researchers in a UNESCO–AAAS conference held in 1969 at the University of Arizona by Richard B. Woodbury, chairman of the anthropology department at the University of Massachusetts. Woodbury also had this to say:

> Social science is scarcely past its embryonic stage in contrast to centuries of growth by physics, botany, engineering and many other fields of endeavor. But the past few decades have seen a rapid advance in our understanding of the nature of human behavior, and prediction of the outcome of a specific course of action is becoming possible to a degree that can have significance to planners and administrators. We can no longer afford to exclude the human factor in our manipulations of the environment, nor is it appropriate to separate "hard" sciences from "soft" sciences in planning the best use of the arid third of the earth. (86, p.187)

Now that technological answers to the physical problems of arid lands have been worked out, these remarks seem to suggest, the "soft" sciences must now be admitted into a field reluctant to welcome them. There is indeed perhaps something "soft" in the failure of those sciences to hear the appeals that the physical sciences had been making to them for at least the preceding decade. In any case, the implication is that with physical answers in the cupboard, the social sciences should now come along and provide in much the same way social answers to the social side of the problem of desertification. That even in their embryonic stage the soft sciences can make contributions of "significance to planners and administrators" reflects an optimism that anticipates complete social solutions from the later, mature social sciences. That their present condition is allegedly callow is an excuse often brandished as the reason why the social sciences so rarely yield triumphs on the scale of those produced almost daily by the physical sciences. Disguised as science, social thought may indeed be younger than physics or engineering although it is not all that young, the effort to wangle hard sciences out of the arcana of human behavior going back more than a century and a half to Saint Simon and French positivism. If it should turn out that the dilemmas of social science cannot be palmed off on its innocent childhood, then something else must be interfering with the application of what social science says it already commands—predictions that have significance for planners.

Or is there something fundamentally askew in the presumption that the natural sciences and the social sciences are the same sort of thing, the latter merely an embryonic or inchoate version of the former? This is an old question recently revived, one that is undergoing a good deal of contemporary debate. It leads immediately to other questions, those concerned with social action, through which the problem of desertification will or will not be solved in a way that is not a catastrophe for man. Social action is carried out in the pursuit of social ends, and ends constitute value systems discovered neither by science nor by reason, as the eminent American sociologist, Talcott Parsons, has pointed out (59, p.250ff). Technological action is a form of social action, and it is directed to human purposes, and to that extent it becomes clothed in political wrappings for all that it may persist in pretending that it is a mere expression of neutral science. Even an apparently innocuous decision—to change, say, a pattern of contour plowing—arises out of the social milieu and can have social effects and overtones. As rational as any procedure may be, action always contains nonrational elements expressive of values and to that extent transcends the purely technological, even if transcendence is sometimes trivial.

When action, however, is aimed at social matters, the things that social science deals with, its nonscientific, nonrational elements, are rarely trivial. Modifying inheritance procedures, systems of water rights, land tenure or ownership, writing or enforcing laws, even when concerned with such physical questions as the size of herds, in what locations cultivation is to be practiced and where excluded, how the collection of woody vegetation is to be regulated—all these actions modify power relationships and contain therefore a political element. Physical solutions sometimes require nothing more for their application than the perception that they are correct. Such is rarely the case with social solutions, whose application always seems to involve conflicts of values and of human interests and whose achievement seems to require public consent.

In the industrial countries, an "industry" has been created out of the conviction that public consent can be engineered by the arts of public relations. Governments have taken naturally to public relations practices, some governments consisting of little more than public relations stances, but then this is something that governments have always done and long before such arts were elaborated into a systematic methodology. Even though public relations has become an accepted part of political campaigning, as in some sense it has always been, something about it when it is too obviously pursued is considered to be raffish and disreputable, just as any open attempt to manipulate people is placed in low repute. At the Conference in Nairobi, no government proposed that public relations should be employed to resolve the social aspects of the problem of desertification. No, the governments represented in Nairobi allied themselves with contemporary community development theory by proposing that consent be obtained not by manipulation, but by popular participation. This, after all, is the ethical art and a position beyond reproach, yet a position still so vague that who knows what nuances were clinging to it in the minds of all those who voted for it at the Conference? Some undoubtedly supported the principle on metaphysical grounds, seeing it as an embodiment of a contemporary system of values which should be brought to life in society whether or not the animation of those values happens to result in the solution of the problem for which popular participation was originally summoned forth. Something that is good in itself, this frame of mind declares, popular participation should reign even if it does nothing toward improving the productivity of degraded land.

The nonlogical elements embedded in social action are the reason why human problems remain problems—no matter that they have technological or physical solutions. As to the problem of desertification, the solutions to it conveyed by the natural sciences will undoubtedly become even more effective, easier to apply, demolishing still more of those obstacles raised against rehabilitation by economics. Yet the solutions provided by the natural sciences are already adequate, which is to say that the amount of funding reasonably to be anticipated will never exhaust the possibilities of successful application. But then almost every human problem has a technological solution. In the few that do not, a technological solution is felt to be imminent or inevitable and merely undiscovered. In a way, a problem does not even become a problem until a technological solution to it is at least anticipated. Before that, it is, like death, the expression of fate, an act of God. If a technological solution to death should be found, then death would become the most poisonous of human problems. Natural science has become the wonder of the world by repeatedly demonstrating its capacity to convert anticipated technological solutions into real ones. In so doing, it changes scientific problems into social ones. And all the advances of social science have served only to demonstrate that social problems do not have scientific solutions. It is here, rather than in its "youth," that social science exposes a nature which, when compared in its effectiveness to physics, will remain forever immature. To expect an effectiveness of that kind is asking social science for something it is incapable of giving. And, at that, at the prospect that social engineering will never become an exact science, humanity can heave a sigh of relief and continue on its tortuous, unpredictable and lamentably human course.

If every human problem, each ultimately social, lacks a rational solution, the question then becomes: Do the important problems have any solution? A first conclusion would be that they do not, since all human problems are at best only partly solved, just as desertification will remain a problem for as long as mankind uses the land. There is another sense, too, in which human problems seem to lack the possibility of solution. They all interact in a tangle in which each affects all in the ecological unity that embraces the planet. Implicit in many proposals for social action is an attitude that solutions will not ultimately be possible until, say, war is banished from the earth, or social justice is everywhere achieved. It is a way of saying that no human problems will be finally solved until the ultimate goals of all social action are realized. On that outcome, of course, humanity will wait indefinitely. A catalytic approach, such as that of Freire, seems to be focused on ultimate goals. "This then is the great humanistic and historical task of the oppressed to liberate themselves," he says, "and their oppressors as well" (45, p.28). Yet Drummond appears to declare that a partial application of the catalytic method makes partial solutions possible. What conditions make partial solutions likely? Since social action is not a science, answers to that question seem elusive.

A social and political revolution may help, as in China or the Soviet Union, as long ago in France and the United States, when a turbulent break with the past shatters traditions that have become oppressive and opens minds to novel and unexpected possibilities. Emigration may constitute a personal revolution whose fruits are enjoyed, for example, by the rich Indian merchants of Nairobi, who can ponder from their mansions the fate of the relatives they left behind to continue living in shacks. The achievements of Vale, the Gascoyne, the Mona project—all can be said to follow rude awakenings, revolutions in miniature. They are the fruits of disaster that transformed a previous cavalier attitude toward the land, just as the disaster of drought in the Sahel uprooted public complacency over desertification as a global problem. Revolutions, turbulence, disaster— these seem to constitute for societies the catalyst that the community development worker tries to make of himself in the catalytic approach to community action. But then what? Successes achieved in campaigns against desertification all share certain characteristics. What has been catalyzed in all cases is a firm political will on the part of governments to undertake action in quest of solutions. Yet the history of Greater Mussayeb shows that such political will is not enough; that while a necessary condition, it is not sufficient, that something more is needed. That something more, as Luni Block has indicated only too tediously, is popular participation, public consent, the approval of the action proposed among those whom that action will most intimately affect. If political will be taken as an expression of sovereignty, of the workings of society at its highest level, then popular participation will be seen as its converse, a manifestation of will at society's lowest levels, at the grass roots.

The appeals that Sahelian countries made at the Conference on Desertification would seem to indicate that financing is also a necessary condition for success in combating the degradation of the land. On the contrary—to return to China—the experience of Turfan and Wushenchao proves that financing is not essential.

The Chinese experience seems to go directly against that received wisdom that declares that "inspiring villagers is not enough," as Coombs and Ahmed suggested, that development also requires "sophisticated technical advice" and "practical material help." In China, where financing was not available for very much in the way of public works projects, a firm political will was at first expressed in no other way than by "inspiring villagers." The Chinese case studies attribute success in combating desertification to this firm political will joined to a model of popular participation in which the members of communes not only consented to proposals, they originated and devised them as active expressions of local value systems. Recent Chinese history seems to show that when a catalytic style of popular participation can be realized, then outside financing is not needed, and foreign aid, whether coming from abroad or from a distant national capital, can be dispensed with along with visiting technicians and their "sophisticated technical advice."

The case studies implicitly converge toward a tacit agreement on at least this assertion—that the essential elements for success in programs to combat desertification consist of political will joined to local consent. The case studies other than those prepared by China show that programmatic success almost always involved infusions of outside funding. Even in the Gascoyne, where the lessees themselves were asked to finance rehabilitation by accepting postponement of income, the program began with provincial expenditures on surveying and on convincing lessees, and it was obvious that rehabilitation of the Gascoyne would have proceeded much more rapidly if land treatment had been applied, at government expense, as on the Vale rangelands. What makes China so different that its capital-deficient communes can rehabilitate their lands all by themselves? Is there some answer to desertification to be found in that elusive quantity, national character? The suggestion has been made that, rather than be credited to socialism, Chinese achievements should be charged to whatever it is in the Chinese character that gives that nation's peasants their reputation for diligence and sobriety, a national temperament needing only political stability for the release of its energies. Although Chinese agriculture is slowly becoming mechanized, the first campaigns against desertification in north China were conducted with pick and shovel, by carting water in buckets slung from poles across the shoulders to dibble moisture onto maize in years of drought, as was done in Tachai. Freire would claim that his catalytic approach works as effectively among *sertanejos* in Brazil as anything revealed in China. But on whatever basis, whether or not the Chinese peasant possesses some mysterious secret, the China case study reports an impressive list of accomplishments.

> A protective forest belt has been built that runs across the western parts of the three provinces of Liaoning, Kirin and Heilungkiang [through the center of old Manchuria]. . . . It is more than 800 km long, 500 km wide and provides protection to more than 45 million mu [3 million hectares] of farmland. It is China's largest farmland protection forest area and it has proved its efficiency in protecting farmland against the wind–sand scourge. . . . In the Yuling area in Shensi Province in the southern part of the Maowusu sandy land, 3.5 million mu [233,000 hectares] of prevent-wind-stabilize-sand forests and farmland protective forests have been built since liberation, effectively blocking the southward onslaught of sand storms. Meanwhile, water resources were utilized to rehabilitate sandy land, and 350,000 mu [23,000 hectares] of farmland have been created in the depth of the desert. The Yanchiaopan Production Brigade in Chingpien county leveled . . . sand dunes and created over 11,000 mu [750 hectares] of fertile farmland, and every year since 1971, the grain yield per mu has exceeded the "Yellow River Record." (10, p.6)

The case study goes on to list other projects and accomplishments stretching across the full width of China's arid northlands.

The case studies on Turfan and Wushenchao described many of the techniques employed in the stabilization and planting of moving sand dunes, the establishment of protective forest belts or strips or grid patterns of trees. The methods used have included the use of "guest" soil, the massive use of groundwater for irrigation and the construction of *kulun*, the careful selection and establishment of a vegetation cover planted not only to stabilize soil but to rehabilitate soil quality. Nowhere is there greater irrigation experience than in China which, with its wet rice culture extended well into humid areas, cultivated (in 1970) 43% of all the irrigated acreage on earth.

Political will conjoined with peasant diligence has made possible the realization of China's avowed aim of providing every citizen an adequate diet, an astounding accomplishment with a population estimated in 1970 at not less than 800 million. It is a policy that perforce directed the government's attention to that neglected north in which the Southeast Asia Monsoon begins to run out of rain, but where precipitation, even on a desolation like the Maowusu sandy land, averages up to 450 mm per year, while the dunes of Ke-erh-hsin are favored with an annual rainfall of as much as 600 mm. Such places are typical of man-made deserts, sandy wastes which, from a climatic point of view, should not exist as such. The Chinese are correct when they attribute the condition of such places to "the abuse of the land and its vegetation," whether carried out under "generations of feudalistic rulers," "the Kuomintang," or whomever. René Grousset gave a false impression when he said that the deserts of Asia "are like cancerous patches" as if their spread were a natural phenomenon. The Chinese, who see correctly that what has happened is the work of man, may end up rehabilitating all such neglected regions from the Pamirs to the Pacific.

15

THE NEGEV

"A garden has been planted at Sodom on the shores of the Dead Sea"

IN THEIR VARIATIONS, the scholasticisms of popular participation call for respectful attention to stores of traditional wisdom as an element in the procedure and as a way of giving traditional peoples a feeling of participation. This procedure may be more than mere window dressing for hopes; there may actually be something of value in what peasants know. Their lore may be irreplaceable in its intimate familiarity with the eccentricities of local environments. At the Conference, a high official of a Sahelian country was overheard to say, "These experts come around with all their instruments and equipment. They go out and take all these measurements, run all these analyses. Then they come back and tell my father what he already knows."

Then, too, the injunction to listen serves as a prescription against the elitism that would hinder true communication. Nor is there anything surprising in the fact that genuine instruction is often to be found in precepts that have experienced up to ten millennia of development. Yet to recognize this sometimes requires a change of attitude on the part of visiting consultants as profound as anything they ever may ask of those who are coming to have no choice but to adapt to the demands and discontents of the modern world.

One ancient and long-forgotten technique uses only rainfall to grow fruits and vegetables in a region that receives an annual average of no more than 100 mm of precipitation, seated astride the line that marks the edge of the true desert, usually considered suitable—if for any agricultural purpose at all—only to the thinnest pastoralism. The technique, now revived, was developed by the Nabataeans, an Arab people who ruled the Negev from their rock-cut capital at Petra and who brought this desert region an extended period of

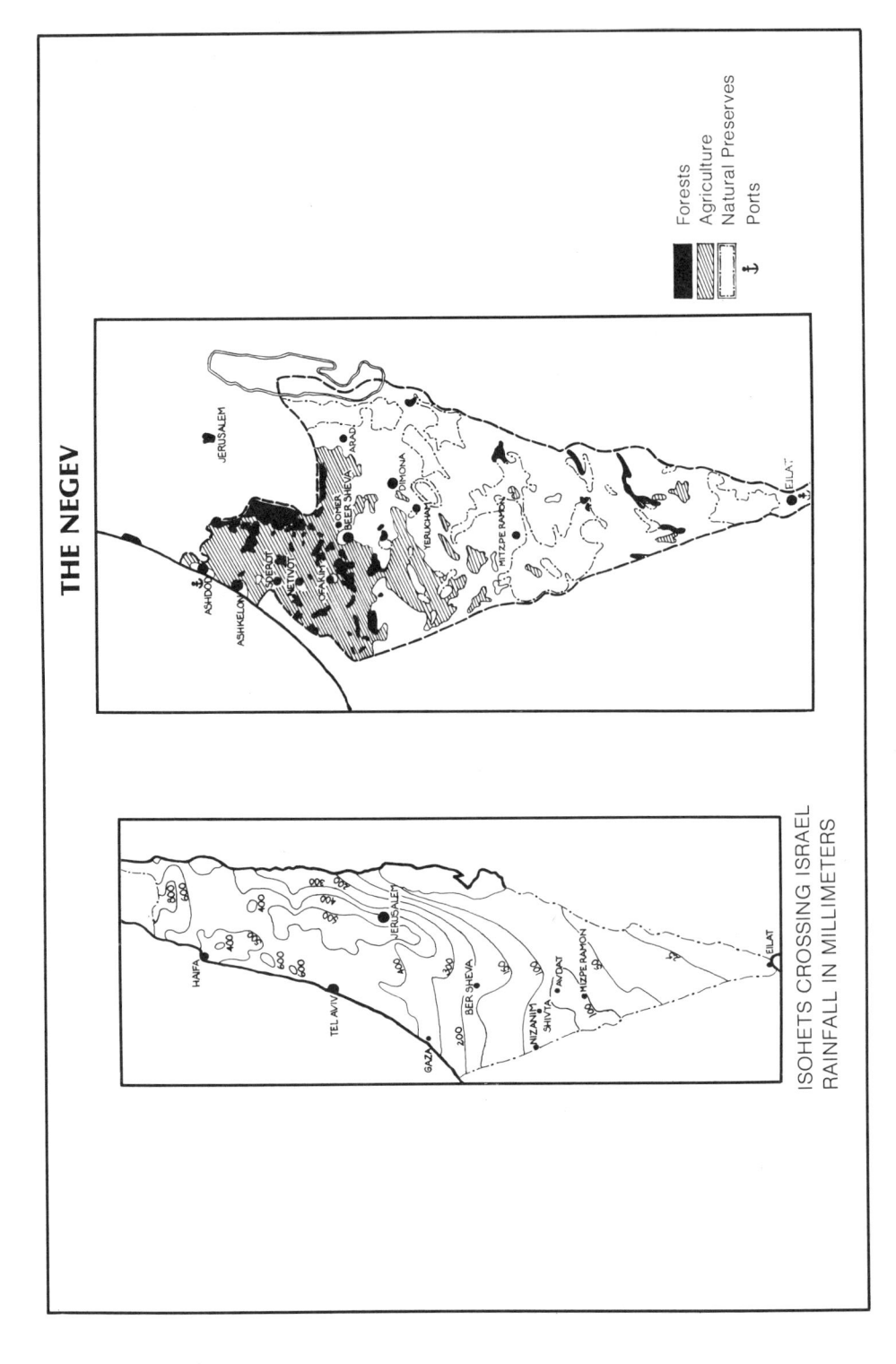

ISOHETS CROSSING ISRAEL
RAINFALL IN MILLIMETERS

prosperity. It was the Nabataeans, in that millennium before they were engulfed in the tide of Islam, who lived in a land rich in aromas, according to Diodorus, whence they exported to the world "myrrh and the frankincense which is most dear to the gods" (69, II, p.47). At Avdat, one of their caravansaries in the Negev, Michael Evenari examined the ruins of their terraced fields and set out to reconstruct the Nabataean system of runoff agriculture.

> This site represents the remains of an ancient Nabataean town whose inhabitants cultivated the wadis from about 200 BC to 400 AD. The wadis are terraced, and rainfall falling on the hillsides was collected by a series of long channels, each channel bringing water to a specific part of the wadi terraces. Although the region's total annual precipitation amounts to only 100 mm, this usually includes at least one rainfall heavy enough to result in a flood that will wet the wadi soil sufficiently to yield a good crop. The Nabataeans were skilled hydraulic engineers and succeeded in constructing thousands of these farms with efficient water collection and distribution systems. (12, pp.33-34)

It takes 50 hectares of runoff area to water one hectare of crops, making investment costs too high—today, at least—to yield an adequate return. Unperturbed by the dictates of modern economics, the Nabataeans also found erosion to be a blessing, as the runoff washed fertile silt into their wadi catchments. The Evenari team has also experimented with individual microcatchments, graded and planted with one bush or tree, seeking to determine the optimal catchment size for different species. The work at Avdat, advanced and at the same time ancient, is an exercise in how to make the most of a scanty supply of water. But then the entire nation of Israel, as the case study shows, is a laboratory in advanced techniques of water conservation.

> All water in Israel is derived from rainfall, which occurs only during the winter season. A large proportion of this precipitation simply runs off into the Mediterranean or the Dead Sea, or evaporates from the soil. The remainder seeps into underground aquifers or drains into Lake Kinneret [the Sea of Galilee] and is stored (minus evaporation loss) until needed, which is generally during the long, dry summer season. These storage basins are relatively far from the arid Negev, which has no reservoirs of good quality water. (12, p.23)

All its water supplied by rainfall, Israel is thinly favored with natural precipitation, as the map on page 276 indicates. In a small, densely populated, semiarid to desert country seeking both industrialization and self-sufficiency in agriculture, water would prove to be the limiting factor and would have to be treated as a "scarce and precious natural resource" (12, p.25).

> Shortly after the establishment of the State, it was realized that water would have to become a nationalized commodity, owned and regulated by the government in accordance with a centralized plan for its distribution and use. The government needed to be legally empowered to transport water on an interregional basis, despite possible objections of vested interest groups. Hence the Israel Water Law was legislated in 1959, stating: "Israel's water sources are public property controlled by the State, and devoted to the needs of its residents and the country's development. . . . A person's right in land does not grant him rights in water sources located on that land or passing through it or within its boundaries." (12, p.26)

Even before the passage of that law, the government had begun the construction of a centrally managed water-supply system consisting of a network of canals, reservoirs, pipes, and pumping stations to carry 300 million m^3 per year from Lake Kinneret and the more humid north to the more arid agricultural lands in the south. In 1977 it could be said:

> Israel uses today over 95% of its potential water supply. This amounts to only about 1,600 million m^3 per year, which is the annual rate of replenishment of all water sources. (12, p.24)

Expressed another way, Israel's total annual water supply is only one-fifth of the present intake of the Kara Kum Canal in Soviet Turkmenia and less than one-tenth of that canal's planned annual intake. By 1985, Israel's projected water needs will come to 2,000–2,100 million m^3 annually or 25% more water than the country receives. Where is the extra water to come from?

> It is intended to eliminate this deficit by the treatment and use of municipal and industrial waste effluents, the use of saline water resources and possibly, in the future, by desalination of ocean water. (12, p.24)

To conserve water, sprinkler irrigation is sprayed on plants in a simulation of rainfall. Brought to the nozzle head through pipes, water is no longer lost in evaporation from canals and open ditches, and those no longer, in turn, take up space in which plants can flourish. Land no longer needs to be precisely leveled to accommodate gravity flow while applications by spray are more uniform, increasing water efficiency, factors that balance the high cost of sprinkler equipment.

Drip or trickle irrigation, even more efficient in its use of water, is an Israeli invention developed in the early 1960s. Water drips in a constant flow from plastic hoses, a drop at a time, directly onto the soil beside the plants, placing this "scarce and precious natural resource" precisely where it is most needed. The trickle method proved to be a breakthrough technique for irrigation with brackish water typical of the few aquifers in the Negev, the arid-to-desert Israeli south which constitutes most of the country. The constant dripping provides excellent leaching in the tiny area around the plant while salts accumulate away from the plants and between the rows. Many plants that do poorly in brackish water—onions, green peppers, cucumbers, citrus fruits—do well when irrigated by the trickle system even when the water contains 2,000 to 3,000 parts per million of soluble salts. Salty water can be used even with conventional irrigation, as Israeli farmers have discovered, if irrigation techniques are altered.

> To prevent salt accumulation around the germinating seed, salts must be leached continuously out of this zone. This has been achieved by changing the irrigation practice. No pre-irrigation is given, but very large quantities of water are applied during the sowing-to-emergence period, exploiting the water which was "saved" from pre-irrigation together with the water normally applied at post-sowing irrigation. Results achieved with this method are very favorable compared with those of the conventional method. (12, p.42)

Since groundwater is saline under both the Negev and the Arava Valley, which occupies the Great Rift in its brief course between the Dead Sea and the port of Eilat on the Gulf of Aqaba, much experimentation has gone into the development of salt-resistant plant varieties, such as cotton, wheat, sugar beets, and fodder plants. This work is carried out at Ben-Gurion University in Beer Sheva, the metropolis of the Negev.

> Suitable seeds are collected from deserts all over the world, and sown in the nursery. Those which germinate and grow well for at least one season are transferred to experimental fields. Plants which grow success-

fully in the field are selected for repropagation in the nursery. New seedlings are distributed to various locations, representing different climatic regions, and their progress is recorded. Plants can now be recommended for all regions of the Negev. A garden has been planted at Sodom on the shores of the Dead Sea, irrigated with local underground saline water, and landscaping is being developed in the town of Eilat and along the Red Sea shore under similar irrigation. (12, pp.45-46)

Paulo Freire has described the sort of peasant attitudes with which he seeks to generate dialogue, which he strives to penetrate with his distinctive techniques. In so doing, he explains why some users of the land are so difficult to reach with the message of modernization.

Magic thought is neither illogical nor pre-logical. It possesses its own internal logical structure and opposes as much as possible any new forms mechanically superimposed. Like any other manner of thinking, it is unquestionably bound not only to a way of acting but to a language and a structure. To superimpose on it another form of thought, implying another language, another structure, another manner of acting, stimulates a natural reaction: a defensive reaction in the face of the "invader" who threatens its internal equilibrium. (46, p.184)

In 1975, the latest year for which the case study supplied figures, there were 33 *kibbutzim* or communal settlements in the Negev plus 37 *moshavim* or small-holders cooperatives. Arava contained six *kibbutzim* and six *moshavim*, for a total of 82 agricultural settlements in Israel's arid south. The great majority of settlements were located in the northern and western Negev, where

many of the *moshavim* . . . were settled in the early years of statehood by planned direction of new immigrants from Asian and North African countries with no previous experience in agriculture. . . . These settlements utilize water brought from the north . . . and have some rainfall which enables them to grow winter grains. The outstanding irrigated crop is cotton. Deep loessial soils are prevalent. (12, p.76)

These *moshavim* were not settled then by immigrants from industrial nations. Coming from traditional cultures and unpracticed in agriculture, such immigrants might seem, at first glance, to be comparable to the untutored pastoralists of Great Mussayeb. In the unsettled domain of social action, one can never say for sure, but a community development worker might be forgiven for supposing that a Freirean or catalytic approach might have a stimulating impact in a situation so apparently like that of Greater Mussayeb. The Israel case study makes it clear, however, that a technique which reaches to the roots of the spirit was not needed in the Negev, where the Yemeni and Algerian Jews who operate the *moshavim* could scarcely restrain their eagerness to apply the next technological breakthrough to emerge from the nurseries of Ben-Gurion University. On arrival, however, these new immigrants were subjected to a process of social action.

> Efficient agricultural research organization, closely linked with a wide-ranging extension service, converted new immigrants with no previous agricultural experience into modern farmers within a few years. To do this it was necessary to control the main factors of production and income so that the new farmers rapidly learned that industrious effort resulted in profit. In such a manner the farmer has been encouraged to invest maximum effort, and in so doing, has not only overcome the adverse conditions of his environment but has utilized them to his advantage. (12, p.79)

The fact of immigration again, itself involving a revolution in outlook, may account for the readiness of these newcomers to accept new messages. Upon arriving in Israel, they were absorbed into a culture that has shown not the least hesitation in changing practices whenever something apparently better came along. This is graphically illustrated by the history of wheat cultivation in Israel.

> Originally, all local wheats were hard wheats (*Triticum durum*), the main cultivars being Nouris and Ettit. During the early thirties, selection from local varieties was introduced, but the main elements in increasing yields were improved agrotechnical practice, crop rotation and chemical fertilization. From 1930 to 1945 the yields in the new agricultural system increased from 700 to 1,200 kg per hectare, with occasional record yields of 3,500 kg per hectare. At that time, new varieties of *T. aestivum* were introduced and began replacing *T. durum*, mainly because of better baking quality and higher yield potential. The cultivar Florence was introduced from Morocco in 1937, but because of its sensitivity to rust, was replaced by Florence/Aurora (F/A) from Algeria. Under good conditions F/A yielded as much as 5,000 kg per hectare. (12, p.48)

At this point, enter the Green Revolution.

In 1957/58, the new Mexican dwarf cultivars were introduced. These were high-yielding but had poor baking quality. In 1962/63, new dwarf and semi-dwarf cultivars were introduced, also with high-yielding potential, but with better baking quality. Trials at Lakhish Experimental Station with 380 mm mean annual precipitation reached 7,000 kg per hectare. The dwarf and semi-dwarf cultivars rapidly replaced F/A, which accounted for only 10% of the total area in 1972 and was not sown at all after 1973. (12, pp.50-51)

This chronicle illustrates the rapid shifts that agricultural practice can take to adapt itself to the outpouring of discoveries and developments flowing from the new agricultural sciences. Here in Israel, these sciences increased wheat yields by an astounding factor of 10. To keep abreast of things would seem to require an attitude opened not just once but permanently, a mind that is constantly receptive, always on the prowl, having shifted, along with agricultural practices, 180 degrees away from the conservatism of tradition. Freire insists that extension services that provide no more than extension, which is to say instruction, will have little impact on traditionalist peasant societies. Some method, his or another's, must be employed that is capable of transforming the paths of thought, which will then welcome the "invader" come to destroy old equilibriums. Modernization arises from a new outlook on life, not from instruction in any particular technique. And the traditionalist world is wide, as anthropology has revealed—there is not just one traditional attitude but thousands, embracing an inexhaustible variety of outlooks. You wonder sometimes why they cannot simply be left alone, like the wild ancestor of *Triticum durum*, whose extinction would remove from the world a precious genetic resource, a defense against frailties that might come to afflict domesticated varieties. Traditional societies, in all their enormous panoply, undoubtedly contain cultural resources which the modern world might one day need to revitalize an outlook that has become corrupted in novelty or stunted in an atomic standoff. Still, it seems vaporous and utopian to expect many of the old cultural values to be preserved in a world where the modern outlook is apparently irresistible as it pursues its single-minded goal of creating poverty in even the most remote backwaters. Even now, for example, the Indians of the Amazon basin are undergoing an inevitable transformation from members of culturally rich and independent societies into the urban and *lumpen* proletarians they will be when their metamorphosis is completed.

In this situation, instead of bewailing the inevitable, community development workers must provide societies under the invincible assault of modernity with some means of self-defense, not a defense against irresistible modernity itself, but a defense against being converted into poor people. This is in some respects what community development is all about. The question arises, in the pursuit of this task, if any one approach is suitable to the great variety of communities under attack. The differences among traditional communities and their situations in a changing world—as between Greater Mussayeb, for example, and the Negev with its nomadic bedouins, now in the process of being sedentarized—might indicate that different community development approaches should be tested. What may be needed are Ben-Gurion universities with nurseries in which social techniques can be given a trial in order to see if they germinate and are worth a full field test.

It seems likely that a society would have to be given a scrupulous examination, in analogue to the minute scrutiny that physical scientists apply to physical matters, before an approach could be designed that would exactly suit local attitudes and conditions. Some traditionalist societies might unexpectedly turn out to be like those of the *moshavim* of the Negev, or of the irrigators of Mona, needing no transformations in their basic attitudes to absorb a Green Revolution. Others would probably have to have confidence restored, the stultifying mental patterns of oppression exorcised, before they would be capable of opening themselves, like withered wheat brought back to life.

Trickle irrigation might be called a Green Revolution, one of many, but what the phrase originally referred to was a triumph of plant genetics that produced not only high-yielding dwarf wheats, but other new and remarkable cereals as well. The new varieties demand heavy applications of fertilizer and are thus expensive in energy, as much energy as it takes to manufacture the synthetic fertilizers that are customarily applied to them. To the extent that the new varieties can be installed in a particular setting, they might provide an example of how desertification can be ameliorated by a purely technological act. By feeding more people while using less land, the Green Revolution automatically helps to limit unwise extensions of cultivation. However, as the fertilizer requirement indicates, even this act is not exclusively technological.

When technology, almost alone, can lead to positive results, a possibility that softens human prospects, it may seem odd that scientists should step back from their earlier assessment, made during the conference preparations, that mankind is now in possession of sufficient technical knowledge to combat desertification in all its manifestations. "There is an implicit overconfidence in the adequacy and feasibility of existing technology" (66, p.1), researchers from six scientific associations stated at the post-conference seminar held in Nairobi. Since "feasibility" is in doubt because of social factors, these paladins of the natural sciences are of course correct. "Although knowledge, technology and expertise are available for the treatment of each of the acknowledged causes of desertification," they go on to say, "it is rare that treatment is successfully carried out. Failure can be due to a number of factors, the most obvious being tardy diagnosis and the fact that problems are treated piecemeal with inadequate integration of all factors involved" (66, pp.3-4). Integration of all factors would of course require the presence of the social sciences. "Attention to social processes is particularly important. For if people are largely responsible for desertification, desertification is most efficiently combated by diagnosing and arresting the social and economic processes that lead to it." (66, p.3)

After thus driving straight toward the heart of the matter, the seminar then drifted backward on the tangent of tardy diagnosis. This is to be remedied by the development and field testing of those desertification "indicators," alarm bells that would promptly signal the onset of the unhoped-for process. Besides physical indicators, social indicators would also be included, and the working party "to undertake field adaptations of the newly identified set of indicators" (66, p.10) would include social scientists—anthropologists, sociologists, economists. Despite this attention to social factors, that a focus should be placed on "indicators" at all seems misplaced in the absence of a global commitment to halt desertification everywhere. The upshot of the matter, project by project financing, means that desertification will not be halted simply because its presence is detected, whether sooner or later. The donor countries have committed themselves to no initiatives. There is nothing in their agreement to review projects for financing that would prevent them from looking on impassively while desertification races through countries too poor or too disorganized to do anything about it. That this will not be their stand, however, is indicated by the fact that projects against desertification are indeed being financed, even while an integrated, global assault on the problem is no more than a mirage visible on the dryland horizon.

The establishment of "critical indicators," and the global monitoring in which such indicators would occupy a revered and respected place, might be justified if a global attack on desertification were actually in prospect, as requested in the Plan of Action to Combat Desertification. In such an event, all examples of desertification would be assigned courses of treatment, and prompt diagnosis would underlie thrift since delay puffs up the cost of rehabilitation in a progressive disease such as this one. Alas, the Plan of Action will not be carried out as written—but then such plans never are, and it is idle dreaming to expect that of them. They constitute guides to what should be done—and to what would be done in a world perfect enough never to have allowed the problem to arise in the first place. For plans of action, detailed and rational as they are, inevitably scant that nonrational side to earthly improvement where unanalyzed, perhaps unanalyzable, currents of will prevail. The Conference, like all such conferences, generates publicity, helping to create a broad public opinion in favor of taking action. It brings people together who return home afterward to make the problem at issue more of a current issue within the counsels of their respective governments. And it turns out that more projects and programs, reviewed on their merits—and the nonrational elements in social action conspire against any other course—are approved for financing than would otherwise have been approved, and the world looks up one day from mourning a "rejected" Plan of Action to discover that much of the problem has been dealt with, piece by piece. Very likely, this is the way that the drylands will eventually be rescued from desertification, in a multiplication of approved projects, the involvement of more disciplines, the stimulation of community action under the benign gaze of the eye of LANDSAT, whose findings will undoubtedly be supplemented and explicated by an occasional traverse on the ground.

Interchange among disciplines is essential to producing prescriptions—mixing the physical with the social—for the treatment of all problems that require an ecological perspective. The Conference and its preparations constituted a clearing house of knowledge *de luxe*. Yet the application of the prescription is not something in which knowledge any longer matters. As to "diagnosing and arresting the social and economic processes" that lead to desertification, the social scientist might be able to diagnose them, but he cannot arrest them. That requires something else—the emergence of political will, which, everywhere except in China, it seems, will sooner or later take the form of financing, plus the enthusiastic and intelligent participation of the people who will actually do the work, an expression of local, parochial will. What is required here is not social science but social action. Unfailingly political, awash in values, social action has been the missing ingredient, the exhortative, nonscientific, and essential last stage in the achievement of solutions.

The world thus seen as will and idea, in Schopenhauer's formulation, represents the conjunction that characterizes these world conferences that have been held under the auspices of the United Nations, and this despite Schopenhauer's pessimism and his opinion that reform is futile. Nor would the United Nations give complete primacy to will, as Schopenhauer does, preferring to think that in a world conference, will and idea, politics and science, will be given a unique opportunity to meet on terms of equality. Even so, it occasionally happens, even at these conferences, that will demonstrates its primacy over idea, and an example of such an occurrence took place at the Conference on Desertification, stimulated by the Israel case study, which happens to include this statement:

> After the Moslem conquest in 640 AD, there began a rapid decline of agriculture and apart from a few hundred nomadic Bedouins, no settlement henceforth existed in this area [the Negev]. Wars and internal instability, as well as increased pastoral nomadism, led to the destruction of terracing with resultant erosion and depopulation. The breakdown of central authority institutionalized land-use systems whereby land was exploited without regard for conservation. The result was a rapid deterioration of this sensitive ecosystem. (12, p.22)

This description of the end of Nabataea is, on the whole, no more than what might be expected when an agricultural civilization is overrun by nomadic pastoralists. But the comment goes too far since, in implying that desert pastoralists in the pursuit of their own land-use system have no regard for conservation, Arabs of old were charged with a greater sin than indifference to terrace agriculture, and their modern descendants may not have been entirely unjustified in showing a certain pique. Together with their African allies, the Arabs were able to round up the votes needed to pass Resolution 7, which, approved over the objections of the United States, "denounces" the associated case study, *The Negev, A Desert Reclaimed*, declaring that "it expresses religious fanaticism and contains elements which are historically inaccurate" (32, p.41).

If battered by will, the idea persists and demands development, and to say that physical solutions to desertification are at present adequate does not imply that further research should not be undertaken to make such solutions even more effective. "Adequate" may be far from "ideal," as sometimes it is distant even from "good." One can compose a list of findings that would vastly simplify the task of halting desertification. Certain successes in the physical sciences would almost certainly redound to the benefit of social action and, like some possibilities opened by the Green Revolution, almost automatically lead to improved land use. Long-range weather forecasting is in that category, enabling the land user to adjust in advance the intensity of his land use to conform with shifts in weather, especially there where it matters most, in vulnerable drylands that come close to the edge of biological productivity. It almost seems as if the drylands might singlehandedly be saved by the development of a cheap, portable, efficient, and acceptable solar cooker that would eliminate the ceaseless demand for firewood. Solar energy, and its form transmuted into wind, should find ideal application in the drylands where the sun shines almost every day, and where the *harmattan*, the *sirocco*, the trades, or some other river of air is always on the move, to create the wind–sand scourge the Chinese complain of, to give rise to the *khamsin* which blasts hot out of Arabia to dry the orchards of the Negev.

Like asparagus after a healthy rain, indications are springing up everywhere that recent green revolutions are only a foretaste of what the new agricultural sciences are capable of. With slight exceptions, the exploitation of plant and animal life has continued to be confined to those species whose utility was detected by peoples whom the Victorians would have termed savages. Certain recent discoveries, however, open a vista of almost unlimited possibilities.

The seed of the jojoba (*Simmondsia chinensis*), a dweller in the drylands, yields about 45% liquid wax that requires little or no refining for use as a lubricant. Jojoba oil is superior to that other lubricant that has passed a death sentence on the mighty sperm whale, who might now experience a reprieve thanks to this humble bit of dryland vegetation, whose secretions have the added advantage that they don't smell fishy. Jojoba was described in a report prepared for the Conference by the United Nations Institute for Training and Research (UNITAR).

It has the important industrial qualities of a very high viscosity index and very high flash and fire points; it will take up about 25% more sulfur than will sperm whale or lard oil; it darkens less than other oils on sulfurization and remains liquid. Perhaps most important, it is undamaged by repeated heating. . . . Potential uses appear almost limitless. (31, p.8)

Out of the guayule plant (*Parthenium argentatum*), another inhabitant of the drylands, a high-quality variety of rubber has been found to flow. Commercial interest has been shown in both jojoba and guayule, revived in the case of the latter and both varieties stand on the edge of intense commercial production.

But then there are thousands of dryland plants, not to mention species adapted to other climatic regimes, whose present potential has never so much as been considered, at least by "modern" people—for food, alcohol production, fibers, gums, oils, waxes, medicines, dyes, tannins, perfumes, or fuels—much less those potential possibilities that might be released by genetic manipulaton. Animals, too, are rich in possibilities, especially those dryland herbivores that are more efficient users of natural pasture than are domestic bovines, also being immune to the sting of the tsetse fly. Even though game ranching has thus far shown mixed results where it has been attempted—and experiments continue in Africa—there is nothing in nature dictating that bovines can be domesticated and elands cannot. The critical problem in game ranching may not concern the mysterious process of domestication at all, but may rather involve the even more complicated matter of getting consumers accustomed to another species of meat.

In the agricultural laboratory that is the State of Israel, less attention has been paid to livestock than to cropping. Dairy cattle and a sheep industry—fat-tailed Aawassi for milking, German Meat Merino for mutton—are both based on imported feed concentrates. Beef cattle are maintained on Negev rangelands under 200 mm of annual rainfall. Inconclusive attempts have been made to improve Negev pastures with plantings. Opinion has recently veered to *Atriplex nummuluria* and *Cassia sturtii* as superior to the *Atriplex halimus* that was planted and then discontinued.

Meanwhile the bedouins of the Negev rangelands, those dwellers within the ruins of Nabataea, are slowly but inevitably abandoning the nomadic life.

> Negev bedouins . . . are undergoing a process of economic transition common to many Bedouin in the Middle East (and to pastoral tribes in Africa). In the traditional phase their livelihood was based on animals and access to pasture land, with a balance between population and land resources. After 1870, access to land was limited by the various administrations, and population pressures increased so that an imbalance was created. The last decade has seen the increasing influence of proximity to modern society. (12, p.97)

Here once again can be seen the fateful connection between excessive population growth, the destruction of an ancient demographic equilibrium, and the poking interference by outside power, those "various administrations" that carried their busybody intrusions into the Negev to show the Bedouin how someone else had decided to control their lives for them. Israel confronts the end of nomadism without regret, seeing its passing as a historical inevitability, and helping the process along by a

> policy of encouraging Bedouin to settle in planned government villages and work for wages, with land cultivated only for subsistence. (12, p.97)

And thus the proud and fierce dweller in the desert is remodeled into an urban proletarian at the bottom of the social scale of those whose lives are regulated by installment plans. There is no longer room for the wild, romantic nomad in a country whose every square inch is subject to planning. Even the stark Negev is all plotted out in prospective settlements, mines, quarries, processing plants, tourist and recreation areas, industries, cropping areas, and rangeland. A half million hectares of "unique desert landscape" have been assigned to nature preserves and parks, all the more reason for getting the Bedouin a job sweeping the streets or taking out the garbage since that unique desert landscape was what he once called home. In the Negev, population growth and movement are also planned items. The region's 1974 population of 232,716 is expected to become 615,000 by the year 2000.

Israel's thirst for water led the nation to carry out two prolonged experiments in rainfall enhancement through cloud seeding. The second of these conducted from 1969 to 1975, was designed to increase rainfall in the Lake Kinneret catchment, the source of the National

Water Carrier System that transports water to the Negev. The experiment managed to increase rainfall in that watershed by 17%.

The intention to bring every technology to its assistance appears in Israel's experiments with the desalination of water.

> Saline water rich in chlorides is best desalinated with electrodialysis methods, while water rich in sulfates responds best to reverse osmosis (12, p.36). It is more difficult to desalinate seawater, which is more saline than brackish water and often has a higher organic matter content which can cause fouling of desalination equipment. The use of vapor-compression methods . . . has been successful in Eilat although the price of desalination is still too high for normal agricultural use. . . . Recently, with the development of new distillation processes . . . which can utilize lower temperatures, interest in a combined water/electricity plant has been revived. Undoubtedly, as agriculture becomes more sophisticated and as the price of desalinated water is reduced, these methods will become economical for producing water for irrigation. This development might take place sometime toward the end of the next decade. (12, pp.37-38)

An example of this more sophisticated agriculture can be found on the other side of the Arabian Peninsula in the sheikhdom of Abu Dhabi, where a two-hectare desalination-greenhouse complex, planted directly on desert sands, shipped out 230 tons of vegetables in its first six months in operation. Israel, too, is interested in such advanced complexes, practically food factories, settings in which the use of desalinated water will first become economically feasible for irrigation. This is because such greenhouses take advantage of the thrift in water exercised by trickle irrigation which is added to the conservation of water that is characteristic of any closed environment, where evaporation stays within. In such "controlled environment agriculture," the "return per unit of water applied is three to four times higher than the return for conventional agriculture" (12, p.69). To irrigate one hectare of greenhouses requires the application of only 7,500 m^3 of water per year. Other advantages can be found in a controlled environment, utilizing the desert's advantages—high radiation, clear winter days, warm winter nights—and the particular advantages possessed by Israel. These are: farmers with advanced skills and advanced farm services, research institutes, extension services, efficient packing houses, effective marketing services. Israel's advantages are thus all human. They are not the gift of nature, which is here penurious.

If greenhouses could be sealed during the daylight hours without resultant excess overheating, then evapotranspiration losses would be markedly reduced. This would result in drastic economy in irrigation water. A system is being developed which will economically collect excess solar radiation during the daylight hours, store it in the greenhouse soil and release it during the cold hours of the night. In principle a "closed system," this could bring about . . . the efficient utilization of desalinated seawater. (12, pp.69-70)

The first of the Negev's greenhouses was build in the western section in 1971. By 1977, 16 hectares of greenhouses were producing tomatoes, watered from conventional sources, at yields up to 250 tons per hectare. Some planners were talking about as many as 100 new settlements to be established in the Negev before the turn of the century and to be based on greenhouse agriculture. Could this be a glimpse of a technological future in which the bulk of mankind's foodstuffs will issue from controlled environments? U.S. Department of Agriculture specialists have suggested that even beef cattle might be raised in a controlled environment of colossal glass towers, skyscraper ranches, oversize versions of the way in which chickens are raised today. This is a vision of a brave new world that would first require a solution to the world's energy problems. But that is not impossible. If the civilization survives, prying physicists will sooner or later undoubtedly succeed in harnessing the unlimited capacities of fusion power, and we will all receive another lesson in how technology is capable of transforming our lives. In such a world, there would be no more peasants with their rich varieties of custom and tradition, no more need for philosophies like that of Paulo Freire. The technicians who once advised peasants would themselves be producing humanity's food, seated at the consoles that govern the computers that in turn control food production. Perhaps only space-demanding cereal grains would still be grown outside under the sun, shining down on pastures no longer needed by confined herbivores. The first of the domesticated plants would then also be the last to be grown in natural conditions. As for desertification, that problem would have become irrelevant.

16

TURAN

"Often authoritarian, always technocratic"

THE SILK ROAD, said Ptolemy, began at Antioch, then the metropolis of the Levant (48, p.40). On its way to Ecbatana (Hamadan), the capital of the Medes, it passed a little to the south of the cave of Shanidar, where the earliest remains of a domesticated sheep were uncovered. Beyond Rae, near modern Tehran, the road skirted the rampart of the Alborz. Then, rounding the lofty cone of Demavand, the highest mountain in western Asia, it passed under the present village of Sangsar, whose shepherds summer their flocks today in the high pastures of the Alborz. Then on beyond Hecatompylos, through the later Naishapur, where Omar would compose his couplets, the road passed what was to be Meshed, the holy city of Shi'a, surmounted the Kopet Dag, and entered Central Asia, in which the first important stop was Mary, a city then as it is today, but now perched across the Kara Kum Canal.

If the traveler had continued with the caravan, he could eventually climb to the roof of the world, the "hills of Komedai," as Ptolemy called the mighty Pamirs, in which he would encounter a stone tower. It was at this spot that the merchants of Rome exchanged wine and oil for the silks of Serica. If this were not the end of the road for the traveler from the west, if instead he had gone on, he would have entered Serica itself. There the road split into two branches, one passing to the south, the other to the north of the empty Takla-makan, its giant dunes, as high as skyscrapers, migrating slowly over its mountain-rimmed basin. The northern branch carried the traveler to Turfan, the prosperous city of the Tokharians, the Yueh-chih, as the Chinese called them, occupying their verdant oasis on the route that later was to lure the Uighur Turks from the east and bring Buddhism from the west to far Cathay, a belief that placed in the temples of Turfan statues of bodhisattvas who looked

TURAN AND
THE TURAN BIOSPHERE RESERVE

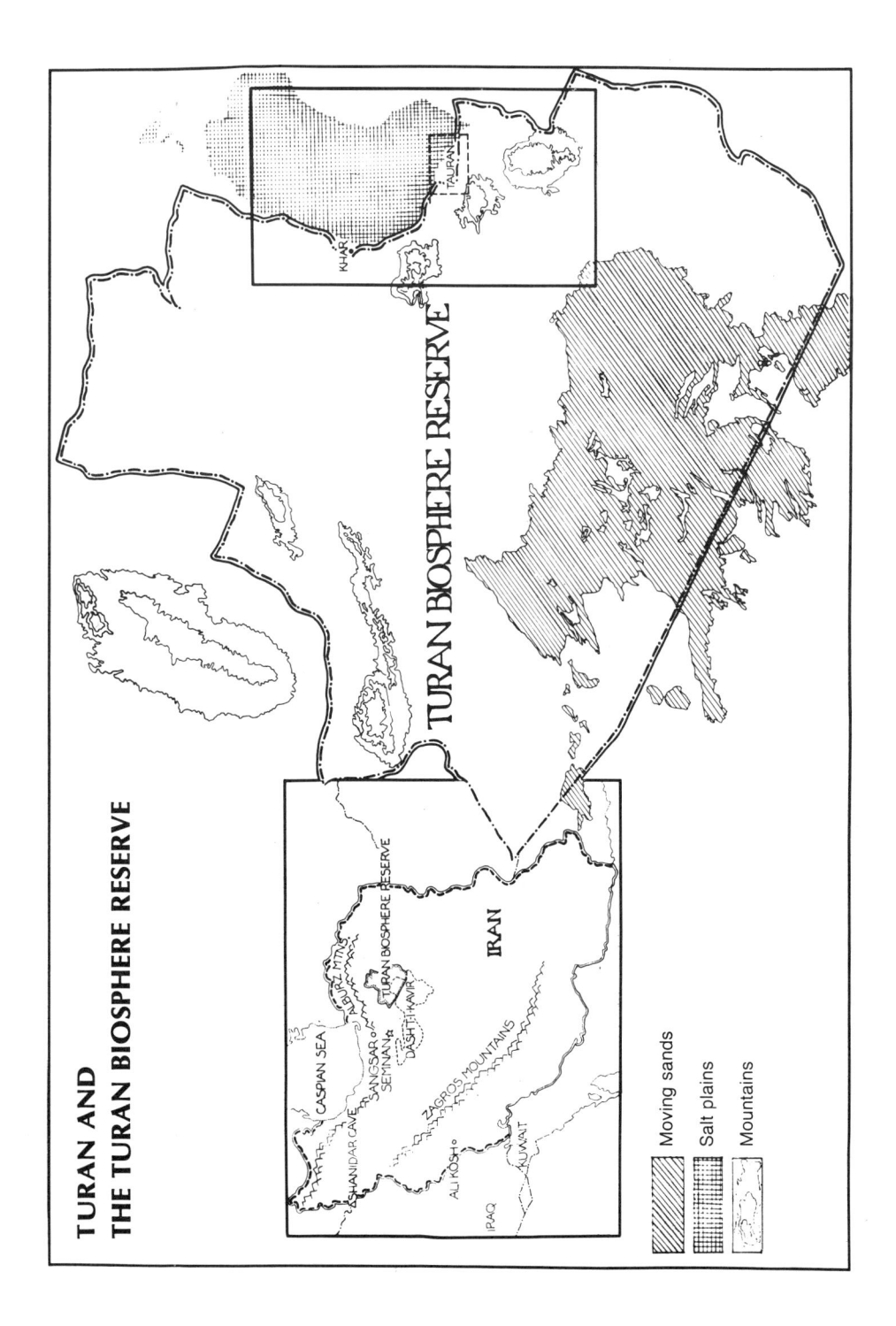

like Apollo. This road can still be followed, although Serica is now called the People's Republic of China. The northern branch still leads to Turfan, where today one can see that the Five-Star Commune has established five-ditch forest belts as part of its stop-wind-block-sand campaign. This road is the world linked then and now, more or less.

What would the agents of the merchant Maes Titonius have been thinking as they moved on beyond Hecatompylos, capital of Parthia, to skirt the northern edge of the ghastly salt desert, Dasht-i-kavir, a preface to that farther place where the road would follow the grim border of the Takla-makan? All those empty wastelands. The agents of the merchant from whom Ptolemy got his information—would they have thought that the world itself was empty? No, strangely, men have never thought that, even when it was true. "The world is already full," St. Jerome complained in *Against Helvidius*, "and the earth does not hold us" (57). In those days, Scyths and Sacae, wild horsemen, wheeled their ponies over endless landscapes today assigned by the Soviet Union to cotton. The plants are watered by artificial rivers that are carried over the drylands so that accountants in distant Moscow, busily auditing the books on the Golodnaya Steppe, will find shirts for sale in the stores. What would the agents of Titonius, of Jerome himself, have thought of today's world, so crowded that wild horsemen no longer have anywhere to ride, where the nomad in all his variety is doomed, where even the subsistence farmer is everywhere forced to abandon his gruff and classic independence to become a tenant, a ranch hand, a wage earner working for somebody else, or if not that, nor a laborer in the city, then a member of a *moshav*, a commune, a *sovkhoz*? In a world of "modern" attitudes, one of whose pillars is the cause and sanctity of the individual, the end draws near for the most ancient forms of individualism. Relationships that old individualists had formed with the land, pacts and treaties drawn up 10,000 years ago when every spring and freshet was the haunt of its tutelary spirit, are no longer possible to tractor drivers or combine operators directing their complex machines through the tedium of commercial monocultures, and even less possible for the people seated at the consoles that will regulate production in the beef or pork factories of the future. After three million years of evolution, adapting to the demands of the land, can this plastic species adapt to this as well, to the end of all personal and spiritual relationships to the land, without paying a subtle price? Or is mankind, the adolescent, merely leaving the nursery?

It was wretched country around Hecatompylos, the modern Shahrud, when the agents checked it out. The geographer Strabo said that it was "poverty-stricken, so that on this account the kings send their own throngs through it in great haste, since the country is unable to support them even for a short time" (71,V, p.273). This may have been a slight exaggeration. There were pockets of prosperity in Parthia, and so had been since around 750 B.C. when a technological revolution, the invention of the *qanat*, permitted the first great cosmopolitan empire, that of the Achaemenids, to develop on the immense and arid Iranian plateau. The *qanat* is a tunnel bringing water, usually from ready access at the foot of hills, to where it is wanted for crops or gardens. Construction of the *qanat* and subsequent entry to it is made through regularly spaced wells or shafts, so many of them today evident on the plateau of Iran that it looks as though Mithra had machine-gunned it. These irrigation tunnels, making possible the great oases of Isfahan and Shiraz, established a pattern of life on the plateau that remained much the same until the next great technological revolution, the introduction of machinery, which the government of Iran dated at around 1960, in the middle of a siege of drought years.

> The long drought at the end of the fifties and the beginning of the sixties ensured that desertification would receive comprehensive attention in the future. It was at this time that Iran began to embark on a program of intensive economic development. . . . In 1962, a program of land reform was begun; in 1963 all forests and rangelands were nationalized, and in 1967 the nationalization program was extended to the country's water resources. These administrative and legislative measures . . . had far-reaching effects on man–land relationships throughout those parts of Iran vulnerable to desertification. (11, pp.13–14)

"Vulnerable to desertification"—that means practically the entire country.

> Of Iran's 1.65 million km² all but the Caspian littoral and parts of the northwest fall into Meigs' semi-arid, arid or extremely arid classification, and most of this area, outside the small proportion (5%) that is cultivated, is considered desert by Iranians. (11, p.7)

Almost 20% of the national territory is extremely arid, consisting of the two deserts Dasht-i-lut and the "salt plain," Dasht-i-kavir, both to be ranked among the most desolate landscapes on earth.

What is neither cultivated nor desert, all the rest—125 million hectares—is considered to be rangeland. Iran is speckled with villages as it is with *qanats*, 65,000 of them, most provided with *qanats*, two-thirds of them with less than 250 people, almost one-third with less than 50 people. Roaming this rangeland are an estimated 700,000 tent-dwelling nomads, guiding their flocks and herds to seasonal pastures in patterns of transhumant movement. Most of the people living in the rangelands are villagers, and most of them, about half of Iran's total population, do both—cultivate the soil and tend livestock. In its avowed concern with development, Iran has been wondering what to do about its rangeland, so much of it, and good only for thin pasture and *qanat* irrigation.

But to return to poor Parthia. If the king had been rushing his throngs eastward on the Silk Road, they would have raced past the salt marshes of the river Kal-i-shur about 150 km beyond Shahrud, Hecatompylos. There, fanning out to the south, an area of 1.8 million hectares has today been set aside as a Biosphere Reserve, one of nine such, portions of the Iranian landscape participating in the program called "Man and the Biosphere" carried out under United Nations auspices. The Turan Biosphere Reserve, on both sides of the skimpy but perennial Kal-i-shur, extends southward over rugged country until it drops down at last into the naked, glistening playas of the Dasht-i-kavir.

> The Reserve presents a variety of habitats, including three extensive plains at different altitudes, varying from 700 meters to 1400 meters, a saline river system, three mountain systems rising to a maximum of 2200 meters, large areas of broken country, some 200,000 hectares of sand, including moving dunes, and a vast expanse of barren playa. Climatological data is incomplete [but shows] the 200 mm isohyet passing through the northern part of the area. The southern plain probably received less than 100 mm. . . . Rainfall of several millimeters at a time generates sheet runoff and wadi flooding. . . . Soils are generally light and sandy except for solonchak in the playas. Vegetation varies according to land form and . . . human activity. Woody shrubs predominate with ephemerals and annuals growing largely in their protection. Perennial cover on the plains varies between 5% and 40%. Flora and mammalian fauna generally show great affinity to the Kara Kum in Soviet Turkmenistan to the north. (11, p.16)

In short, an arid region, not brilliantly favored. Although Zawi Chemi and Shanidar, containing some of the earliest evidence of agriculture, are not far away, man did not take root in Turan until much later, not until Achaemenid or early Macedonian times when thin, pre-*qanat* populations began supporting themselves there probably by runoff irrigation. The period of greatest investment, represented by heavy *qanat* construction, occurred during the Sassanid period (224-637 A.D.) and the subsequent epoch of early Islam. Like much of western Asia, Turan never recovered its old prosperity after the devastation of the Mongol invasions. The people of Turan—with their *qanats* and cattle, their sheep, goats, and camels, relicts of Sassanid practices—were to be the focus and interest of the case study rather than just the land itself. To get a close look at the people, a 1000 km^2 rectangle on the eastern edge of the Biosphere Reserve was designated for concentrated study. This geometry includes the Plain of Tauran, containing 18 tiny villages, typical of Iranian rangelands and not to be confused with the Turan Reserve in which it lies, and the Plain of Khar, recently forsaken by its former inhabitants. People of a backwater, so isolated and lost that their past has vanished except for scraps to be gleaned from tales by travelers, all foreigners.

> Towrone (Tauran) is a small fortified village, situate in the districts of Ismael Khan, an independent chief who also claimed the desert [George Forster reported in 1783], nor is it probable that the property will ever be disputed. Many travelers, it is said, have perished in this track from the intense heats and scarcity of water, which, in the course of the first stage, is procured but in one spot, by digging small wells. (11, pp.40-41)

And yet not so isolated, as the case study was quick to reveal. Every year, the transhumant herdsmen of Sangsar trek their sheep and goats down from the Alborz to find winter pasture in Turan. The people of Turan are accustomed to supplementing their incomes through services provided to these nomadic pastoralists and their 125,000 animals. Nor is the Plain of Tauran unaffected by mechanization, the irresistible infection of the modern world. That is in the time of today, of course, when lorries are replacing camels and mechanical pumps hold out the false lure of leisure from the backbreaking labor of maintaining *qanats*. Pumps and trucks require fuel and therefore money, and holes are thereby torn in once closed social ecosystems. Or almost closed—as far removed as Tauran is from the beaten track, its social ecosystem has rarely been completely closed. From their capital in distant Ctesiphon, where Mesopotamia's two rivers approach each other in that neighborhood of Greater Mussayeb that has never lacked a capital city, the Sassanid Persians provided political stability to Tauran and a stimulus that generated an episode of *qanat* construction. Then the passage of invaders, one after the other—Arab, Mongol, Timurid, Turkman—kept the social system open to a world of limitless danger. The fortified villages then prevalent in Tauran would not have typified a closed system. And now the case study, from which action will arise that will not finish until the traditional life of Tauran has vanished utterly. For this is a continuing, long-term study, part of a larger exercise through which Iran hopes to make critical choices, determining the future of all its rangelands.

> The Turan Program sought to bring together representatives of all the academic disciplines that could be brought to bear on the history of the interaction of human activity and the natural resources of the area, and formulate a theoretical framework or set of criteria that would integrate their work and lead them to focus on problems of long-term management. (11, p.15)

A dialogue would be generated among the physical, biological, and social sciences, out of which the criteria integrating their work would arise, and did arise, to be stated in fact at the end of the study. What should be integrated are:

> (a) the theoretical and field orientations of the physical, biological and social sciences; (b) the functions of research, experimentation and management; (c) the participation of the research team, the local population and relevant decision makers. (11, p.9)

This bow to popular participation is more than perfunctory, as the text goes on to state.

> Careful attention should be given to building on existing technologies, supporting innovation within existing traditions, and introducing modern or exotic technologies only where the payoff and risk are well defined. (11, p.9; 11, p.58)

Later on, the case study would say:

> Government intervention is often characterized by a tendency toward solutions with a patronizing or charitable flavor. They are often author-

itarian, and always technocratic. This is above all the result of distrust for the traditional rural world. It is also due to a certain ignorance of this rural world (11, p.57)

Precepts from the modern testament of social action—these begin to have the flavor of Freire, almost of Mao Tse-tung. Yet early in the study, it is made clear that for all these fine statements, the ultimate decisions have already been made. By whom? By "decision makers," no doubt, those ever present but elusive entities who dominate twentieth-century life. Iran proceeded to fund the research team to insure that these prior decisions were carried out.

> It is recognized that evaluation of conditions and trends in these complex and interlocking ecosystems and human-use systems can be made only according to certain criteria, not according to absolute standards. The criteria implicit in this study derive from the view that since Iran can cultivate only 10% of its 165 million hectares in order to support a population of 35 million presently growing at 2.8–3.0% per year, and counts 100 million hectares as arid rangelands [a figure not quite consistent with others in the study], it must plan for maximum sustainable productivity from the natural resources throughout its total territory. (11, p.17)

The Iran case study is simply frank enough to admit openly what is tacit and concealed in other case studies, wherein an overt appeal is made to the principle of popular participation. That is, that the ultimate goal of agricultural action has already been decided without the trouble and inconvenience of asking herdsmen and farmers what they think. "Maximum sustainable productivity" is an eminently reasonable goal, coupled as it is with a powerful feeling—not quite a demonstrated theorem—that in a world of exploding populations, the inevitable accompaniment of any other policy would be malnutrition and death by starvation. It also happens to be the declared goal of the Plan of Action to Combat Desertification if "optimum" can be taken as synonymous with "maximum."

> The immediate goal of the Plan of Action to Combat Desertification is to prevent and to arrest the advance of desertification and, where possible, to reclaim desertified land for productive use. The ultimate objective is to sustain and promote, within ecological limits, the productivity of arid, semi-arid, subhumid and other areas vulnerable to desertification in order to improve the quality of life of their inhabitants. A cam-

paign against desertification should take its place as a priority among efforts to achieve optimum and sustained productivity. (32, p.7)

Certainly, in specific situations, "maximum sustainable productivity" presents unlimited possibilities for conflict with local goals and attitudes. The case study contains no hint that such conflicts are possible. Its authors, identified only as The Department of the Environment, Tehran, see maximum sustainable productivity as presenting a difficulty, but this

> is how to achieve this aim while also developing the highest possible standard of living for the total population (11, p.17).

But, again, is this what the local people want, to be swept up into the consumer culture implied by the phrase "the highest possible standard of living"? Undoubtedly some of them do, although it is clear that none have been asked. Undoubtedly also, some do not, and the quality of local desires, centered on dreams quite different from a highest possible standard of living, can be found in the resistance of nomadic groups in Iran to government efforts to sedentarize them.

Sustainable productivity looks like one of those policies with which even the most remote peasant would agree, were he to be asked. Sustainable productivity, as referred to in the Plan of Action, was accepted by the Conference as the ultimate purpose of all action to halt the progress of desertification. The difficulty that crops up here is not so much with the concept "sustainable" as it is with that other notion, "maximum."

> An example of alternative methods would be strategies to concentrate the population into settlement centers large enough to support the full range of services and facilities recognized necessary to civilized life, *versus* relatively homogenous distribution of the rural population in order to facilitate the most efficient use of resources. A second example lies in the alternatives of maximum diversification of land use *versus* zoning of specialized land-use patterns. (11, p.17)

Still other patterns, not suggested here, might ease alleged tensions between proposed alternatives. Conflict may be illusory between on the one hand, civilized services, the movie house and the bowling alley—and, to be sure, the public library and the health post—and, on the other, the most effective use of resources. It is as though the Department of the Environment, Tehran, had never heard of the *sovkhozes* just to the north, in the Kara Kum where the fauna and flora are so similar to those of Tauran. In a nation dedicated to Islamic capitalism, such establishments would certainly not be called *"sovkhozes,"* not even "commune" or *"kibbutz."* "Agricultural cooperative" is the term that would be used for something that might, in the end, amount to more or less the same thing. But whatever the term that will come to name organizational structures, whatever the "alternative method" that is eventually chosen, "maximum" sustainable productivity implies that ultimate decisions will be made far from the arena of popular participation. For it is the members of the research team who are uniquely positioned to determine what way of life will yield maximum sustainable productivity. To obtain it, they will decide matters so crucial to the flavor of local living as whether people should be spread out or bunched together into communities. Whatever they decide, the support of the people will then be sought afterward, by "public education" (11, p.58), that familiar solution, by means of some curriculum or other through which people will be told what is good for them.

If popular participation, as a principle of social action, receives an inconsistent formulation in the Iran case study, so the incorporation of social science into the research effort seems little more than a gesture. Or so it appears, for example, in the story of the abandonment of Khar and the death of two villages in Tauran.

> The most conspicuous feature of the landscape around Khar and Tauran is the sand. Khar was abandoned in 1940 because the labor required to keep the *qanat* free of sand from year to year was leading more and more people to migrate, until the point was reached where the whole population decided to cut their losses and leave. The cause for the abandonment about 1960 of Baba Kuh, a much smaller settlement on the Hojjaj River, appears to have been similar. Another small settlement, Yaka Rig, also on the Hojjaj River at the southern edge of the high sand, was abandoned in 1973. However, although the abandonment of Yaka Rig is generally said to have been due to sand, further investigation suggests that an unusually severe flood in the river damaged the *qanat*, and the sand was simply a factor making it more than usually difficult to organize the investment needed to repair it. (11, p.44)

Thus the case study finds for the abandonments physical causes, shifting sands, complicated in one case, as "further investigation" showed, by a flood. This was further *physical* investigation, to be sure, indicative of the physical orientation of the Department of the Environment, Tehran. Thus limited in its perspectives, the investigation answered none of the interesting questions about *social* events as traumatic as the abandonment of a home occupied for a thousand years. How could it be presumed that the inhabitants of Khar, whose villages existed for more than a millennium at the edge of shifting sands, knew no method of sand stabilization? In fact, they would have seen—if nothing else—the modern action of *Goebelia pachycarpa* as it stabilized moving sands in the vicinity of Tauran (11, p.28). Ignorance would have been a profoundly indicative social trait. But then the inhabitants of Khar are also charged by the case study with a mistaken strategy.

> Since the prohibition of charcoal production finally became effective in the late sixties, there has been a significant increase in vegetation on the margins of the sand and decrease in sand movement. In this context [a] traveler's report that the people of Khar had outlawed camel grazing in their territory is interesting. They were after all continuing to produce charcoal—a practice that may have been more lucrative but was probably a more serious threat to the environment. (11, p.44)

While precision is brought to the analysis of physical cause, now found in the destruction of woody vegetation, the social background remains amorphous and shadowy. In the social sphere, speculation is asserted as fact, such as the reason proposed for overgrazing by the traditional pastoralist.

> The primary concern of the traditional pastoralist appears always to be in the condition of his animals, which he considers to be his basic capital, not the vegetation which he believes will always recover. (11, p.34)

An allegation often heard as an explanation for overgrazing, you wonder, when you think about it, if it isn't just one of those conclusions with a "patronizing and charitable flavor." It seems unlikely that scientific agriculture could learn in 50 years that the pasture is the basic resource, and not the animals, while herdsmen, always observant, could not absorb this simple instruction in 10,000 years of traditional pastoralism. The herdsman's animals are indeed his liquid capital, capable of being bought and sold, borrowed or exchanged, a circumstance that has little to say about the pastoralist attitude toward pastures. To charge the traditional pastoralist with an attitude of unconcern toward pasture performs two functions for the modern expert—it sidesteps the need to investigate the real reasons for overgrazing, complex social questions, and it justifies his yearnings to teach the pastoralist something, justifies in fact his position as an "expert." While discussing pastoralism, the case study had this to say of the Chubdari, pastoralists sedentarized in Turan, where their flocks were recently reduced by drought:

> During the recent succession of good years, the Chubdari flocks have finally grown again to the point where they are forced to challenge the Sangsari for rights to their old grazing areas. In order to make their challenge effective, they are forced to overgraze as a calculated risk. (11, p.34)

Reminiscent of the competition between Tuareg and invading Fulani around the newly constructed water holes in the Azawak, this situation is much more to the point than vapid statements that pastoralists do not understand the role of pasture. At the same time, it is a thin description that shrieks for elaboration, as did those comments on the abandonment of Khar. Where, you wonder, did the people go when they abandoned their villages? To another village? To the distant city? Was their departure caused by the push of sand or by the pull of the metropolis? Why, just now, after a thousand years, did the people of Khar find the maintenance of their *qanat* to be too much for them? Some of the migrants from Khar should still be alive and capable of giving interviews. Did the people of Yaka Rig never suffer a flood before? Why just now was it "more than usually difficult to organize the investment needed" to repair their *qanat*? What you suspect when such questions arise in the mind is that profound changes in social attitudes have been covered over by shifting sands, which may have provided the excuse for leaving Yaka Rig but not the reason for it.

To be fair, some effort was made by the case study to answer such questions. Interviews carried out in Tauran show a people demoralized by the crushing impact of modern life, which has intruded so intensively, even here, in the last two decades. Young people in Tauran have turned against their ancient home. They show their demoralization by their dissatisfaction with their lives.

> Appraisals of the quality of life in Turan today are . . . invariably unfavorable, but the opinions of local residents tend to vary with their age. Many young people, especially youths who have served their statutory

term in the armed forces and therefore traveled extensively outside the area, tend to seek ways of moving to the city permanently. The reasons they give fall under the headings of variety of social life and economic opportunities. Other age groups often argue for the advantages of life in Turan. Many of their reasons are negative, deriving from general conservatism, and fear of failure in a new social and economic niche, but positive reasons are also voiced. Freedom to organize their own work and lives, even though the work may be arduous, obviously carries weight, as well as the knowledge that so long as they have land and water they need never depend on others for a livelihood. . . . But however definite an informant might be about advantages of life in Turan, he is likely to complain about the lack of medical facilities and . . . the lack of good roads and public transport. (11, pp.55-56)

A fascinating melange of hints and innuendo, it is also clear that this summary of discussions with local people wears the blinders of city life. It is culture-bound in a way that is common among metropolitan researchers, people who have "a certain ignorance of this rural world." For example, a "fear of failure in a new social and economic niche" by older people, skilled in the handling of a different and difficult environment, would seem more an expression of intelligence than of negative conservatism. And this while the unfortunate youth having been jabbed by the heroin lure of city life with its movies, excitement, variety, are now determined to convert themselves into members of the lowest urban classes, wage laborers dependent on the beneficence of others. Is there the least doubt that any other fate awaits the bumpkins from Tauran in the great city of Tehran? But to return to the old people, who in continuing to see the value of an independent life are not quite so demoralized as the interviewers would imply with their comment about "invariably unfavorable" assessments, you wonder also about their complaints concerning the lack of modern transport and the absence of medical facilities. These are novel discontents, very modern. In their youth, the older people would not have known that such things existed. By coincidence, they also happen to be the things that the modern-minded development worker wants to bring them.

The principal changes that have come about in Turan since the early fifties are the establishment of basic security, the cessation of charcoal production, the change from camels to motorized transport and the resulting commercialization of pastoralism and agriculture. It is noteworthy that these are all exogenous changes. (11, p.56)

It is also noteworthy that, except for the cessation of charcoal production, an industry that no longer characterizes the plain of Khar, possibly because there are no longer people there, including charcoal makers, all these changes work to demolish the independence of Turan and give control of local lives over to people who are far away. Among those distant decision makers are those who have reached into this once almost lost world to take its young men away for their statutory term in the armed forces from which they come back home again with their old values shattered. Like taxes, military service is an instrument of the modern state that performs functions that go far beyond merely national security. And on that subject, the case study having brought up the issue of "basic security" in Turan:

> Villages used to be fortified, and the area was controlled by leaders who sought to concentrate the ownership of resources in their own hands. At certain periods . . . security was very poor, which further enabled local leaders to expand their power, usurp official authority and exploit local populations. Turan took on the character of a "refuge area" attracting refugees from the effects of economic decline in more fertile parts of the country. . . . The most wealthy and influential members of the population of Tauran in the fifties had been exiled from the southwestern province of Fars in the last century. A rival group were outlaws from the same area. (11, p.45)

People who bring to others the gift of "security" like to point out the oppressions of the past even when they are contradicted by influxes of refugees. In any case, Tauran has lost its leaders, oppressive or otherwise.

> Another fundamental change that is less often noticed has occurred in the structure of society. The families that provided the leaders of the society up to the sixties no longer fulfill that function, and have either migrated, become impoverished, or are now scarcely distinguishable from the average family. (11, p.56)

How did that happen? Since this crucial social event is not explained, you are left to wonder if it could have anything to do with that gift of security, which seems to have been imposed at the same time that two villages were abandoned in Tauran. The arrival of security in Turan precisely when the society there becomes no longer viable, as the abandonments, the interviews, and the collapse of the old social hierarchy all indicate, might be no more than an odd coincidence, but it would be interesting if social science would tell us if that is all it is. The "principal" change that has come about in Turan since the early fifties is not among those listed above. It is rather the loss of viability in an ancient culture, the destruction of a way of life. Khar had already gone under, and while life will probably continue in Tauran, it will no longer be what it was. The old people who still have some feeling for independence will soon be gone, while the young people cannot wait to chuck this independence and pay whatever price is demanded by the "social and economic opportunities" of the city. Turan, meaning a way of life, an expression of the inexhaustible ingenuity of the human spirit, becomes just another name on the long list of places that have succumbed to the overwhelming monotony of modernity. Here as in so many other places, and soon, not even a nod will any longer be needed in the direction of popular participation. The "relevant decision makers" will simply have come in to tell the demoralized survivors, castaways on the poverty-soaked shores of the modern world but now referred to as "human resources," what has been decided by the research team in the interests of maximum sustainable productivity.

Grim speculation, arising from the social science deficiencies of the Iran case study, is paradoxically elicited precisely because the Iran case study has made some effort, unlike most of the others, to carry out a more than superficial social analysis, an intention that should be commended even if the effort did not succeed. This particular case study provides a foothold for social speculation that is missing from Chinese sloganeering or from the tacit social analysis—or social blank—that characterizes the other case studies. Rather than criticize the Department of the Environment, Tehran, for devoting, as it did, the final third of its essay to a detailed description of the physical elements of Turan—plants, animals, soils, and ecosystems—the authors should be congratulated for their attempt to reconstruct the economic situation of a Sangsari shepherd and a Taurani farmer-stockbreeder, and for coming to the conclusion that the survival of these two ways of life will ultimately depend on social issues.

> Economic review suggests that the outlook for transhumant pastoralism in Turan is uncertain unless productivity can be increased and shepherding be made more attractive. Economically, the self-employed resi-

dent mixed farmer does relatively well. However, the viability of this latter adaptation during the coming decades will depend on the interest of the younger generation and the rate of migration to the cities. Apart, therefore, from arguments concerning the ecological efficiency of these two adaptations, there is room for serious doubt about the survival of either unless they are included and encouraged in long-term management and development programs. (11, p.55)

While thus concurring with grim speculation, the case study then drifts into one of those modern ways of talking, so beloved of development specialists, that presents only an illusion of meaning. For if traditional adaptations can survive many vicissitudes, the one thing they cannot survive is their inclusion "in long-term management and development programs." Something survives, it is true, but it is not the old way of life, whatever precious values it may have embodied, however many outlaws from Fars it may have harbored.

So again the Iran case study exposes itself to comment for its virtue in daring to discuss society. Of all the case studies, this one alone gives any clear indication of the possibilities in social science for determining the specifics in social situations that bring about desertification rather than the broad generalities that are elsewhere deducible. For desertification is a problem, not on Mars, where the process is rampant, but on the planet earth, where it affects human life. Agent and victim, man himself is the creator of desertification, fouling his only nest as he applies stress to sensitive ecosystems beyond their capacity to absorb his intrusions. The case studies, products of physical science, concentrate their attention on what happens to land when its resiliency fails. The causes of desertification, which are social, elude them—but not entirely. With their hints and implications, the case studies permit a loose grasp of social causation to be reconstructed, which, if not as reliable as reconstructions of climax vegetation, is more central to the problem of desertification.

No doubt this is all because the subject itself is at that certain gawky stage in its development. The physical scientists were the first to encounter the problem only because their branches of learning have attained to such an advanced condition that they were prepared to make something out of the encounter and certainly not because social issues come later into view. That physical science should have brought the problem to public attention, assisted by disaster, is the way the world operates in the present era. Physical science is sure of itself; its statements are believed. Physical scientists speak forth from the triumphs of agronomy, their comments buoyed up by the Green Revolution. They will, of course, continue their research, and new triumphs will emerge from it, altering the face of agriculture, incorporating more stunning improvements into the technological solutions to desertification. While they are so occupied, the problem itself must be assigned elsewhere—to the social scientists perhaps. Then again, perhaps not. The appropriate assignment may be to those who have some clue as to how to generate social action while respecting the values and attitudes of the people being prodded into movement. And that is not a scientific matter at all. It is, rather, metaphysical. It is something that demands not social science, but social therapy.

Still, after reading the case studies, one yearns to see societies examined as carefully as plant communities. One longs to see changes in attitudes traced as scrupulously as those tracks through which botanists pursue the successions of disclimaxes through historic time. The social impact of technological change is what we think we need to know. The inheritance of land and its ownership, rights to water, salt, and pasture, demographic patterns among land users, the connections of land users with markets, agencies of finance, centers of power, urban life, social services, amenities and entertainments, how and how much they are taxed, educated, treated for illness and disease, chronicles of social disintegration, the loss of self-confidence, of the ability to make the decisions that matter—these are the things that now await an investigation as meticulous as that which CAZRI has applied to the depredations of gerbils in Luni Block.

A program of social science research might do much to clarify the connections between desertification and its ultimate causes, of which overgrazing, the destruction of woody vegetation, the unwise extension of cropping, and waterlogging and salinization of irrigated lands are but symptoms. Much might be accomplished despite inherent dilemmas from which natural science seems mercifully to be spared. For the dilemmas of social science lie not only in the fateful circumstance that its dénouement always unfolds in contexts of political action but that it also begins its drama enshrouded in values. "The myth of a 'value-free' social science is now thoroughly dead," said E.N. Anderson (33, p.266), which is to say that social science is social. Max Weber said something similar despite Talcott Parsons' subsequent objections (59, p.592ff). The values lurking in the social analysis contained in the Iran case study might almost pass unperceived since they are the common value assumptions of the modern world. As such, they are expressed as maxima—maximum sustainable productivity, the highest possible standard of living. The social analysis of an example of desertification might lead to a recommendation for land reform, but not unless the researcher is politically capable of reaching that recommendation. Social science shares that attribute with natural science—that what it finds is something it has been looking for. The Iran case study pries into questions, and expresses values thereby, that find only fleeting reference in the others.

> Desertification processes in vulnerable arid and semi-arid areas have been inseparable from social and economic processes in neighboring, more fertile areas. (11, p.57) . . . in order to prepare for and plan human exploitation of vulnerable areas in the future and reduce the risk of desertification to the minimum, it is necessary to reduce the basis of cultural discrimination between urban and rural living. (11, p.58)

To say that desertification is a physical outcome of cultural discrimination, an assessment not inconsistent with the views of Freire, is to embark on a radical analysis of the problem, an unexpected position to be taken by a government headed by a King of Kings. To pursue that assessment is to move toward the conclusion that land is abused because people have been abused. Such people wreck the productivity of the land they use, fully aware that their actions are damaging, because they find the pressures on them to be so overwhelming that in their powerlessness they become fatalistic. Land is degraded because people have been degraded. Social science might reach such a conclusion if researchers were psychologically and culturally prepared to reach it. Investigators would carry out their interviews, measure societies according to the social indicators that this particular search entails, draw up their tables and diagrams, and arrive at the conclusion that desertification will be brought to a halt when social justice prevails. As long as it is hopelessly chained to value systems, social science might as well fetter itself to liberation. It is a connection that it often claims anyway, just as anthropologists are heard continually declaring their sympathy for their objects of study. Yet whatever social justice may be, its pursuit is admitted by all but the last retreating troops of broken millennial armies to be, alas, eternal. It is a shimmering vision beyond all programs, leading social action ever onward, while desertification, should its conquest be linked to the millennium, would by that time be crossing the Mississippi in its inexorable advance.

But then, on the other hand,

> the most important theme that issues from this study and from the experience of the Turan Program so far is the importance of investment (11, p.58).

The term "investment" brings leaping to mind the $10 million or so invested in the Vale rangelands, or the billions of rubles that the Soviet Union has sown in Central Asia. But this sort of injection of heavy financing by an outside agency—whether the U.S. Bureau of Land Management or the Central Soviet in far-off Moscow—is not exactly what the Iran case study is referring to. That something is more personal, more local. That such is intended is apparent in the one example of administrative action given in the study.

> In order to provide an element of personal investment in the human use systems of arid rangelands in Iran, and induce the population generally to recognize the value of these renewable natural resources, it has recently been decided at Government level to embark on a program of long-term leasing of the country's rangelands to individual pastoralists. It is hoped that the introduction of an element of personal investment and responsibility in this way will play an important part in Iran's struggle against desertification. (11, p.58)

Although some irony can be found in the fact that the government is now selling pastoralists what used to belong to them by right, cleverly combining the struggle against desertification with increased government income, nonetheless, the sort of personal investment here in question implies the improvement of conditions by people acting on their own. It is the same sort of investment to which the case study refers when it says that the greatest investment in Tauran was made during the Sassanid era, when the people, working for no one but themselves, constructed the area's *qanats*. It is the self-help that refurbishes the oasis of Turfan, creates grass *kulun* in Wushenchao, reforests Kenya by planting a billion seedlings (as the Kenyans have announced it is their intention to do), and reclaims the Negev as, a few generations ago, it cleared and planted the American wilderness. It is that goal of social action attainable by various avenues according to various theorists. It comes about by political change, say the Chinese, that changes also the way people think. It follows the exorcism of the oppressor, says Paulo Freire, whose presence within corrupts the natural drive and ingenuity of peasant peoples. It follows the urge toward "investment" in the opinion of oil-rich Iran, which seeks to generate such through economic incentives. And so it is pursued in different ways—by means of revolution, subversion, or through respectable capitalist channels—this attitude, this state of mind, what is it exactly? It seems to be a kind of confidence, self-respect, hope for the future, that once it is present, changes the world and without which the world cannot be changed regardless of the *outside* investment that may be poured in from coffers across the seas. Or isn't that what the tangled problems of Third World development have been teaching us?

In any case, it is a course of instruction that seems to have been taken to heart by the donor nations, providing them with whatever rationalizations they needed to evade financing a global Plan of Action to Combat Desertification. Supporters of the Plan have seen in this evasion more sinister motives—selfishness, malevolence, an alliance among oppressors to guarantee the flow of primary commodities—typical of politicians who always refuse to implement these grand designs drawn up by selfless science to solve the problems of the world. Theoreticians, however, rarely give credit to the perspectives of practical wisdom. To review projects, each on its merits, as donor countries announced at the Conference that they would continue to do, is a course of action that follows from the bitterly learned lesson that financing, all by itself, is never enough. Representatives of governments showed that they had learned that lesson by their unanimous insistence at the Conference that the Plan contain a special recommendation on popular participation. When this issue came to a vote, no objection was heard from Brazil, but there is no reason to think that this lapse signifies a change of heart that would allow Freire to return to the task of catalyzing a sense of human dignity among his fellow countrymen. As already made evident, popular participation can receive universal approbation only because there is no agreement as to what it is. Yet all interpretations concur in what it is supposed to achieve. It is expected to instill in people the drive and ambition that equip them to solve their own problems. It endows them with an attitude from which will flow an essential *personal* investment.

Desertification is more or less kept in control in countries rich enough to plow and seed their rangelands. Wealth is the grease that gives industrial societies that blessed suppleness in which few are trapped into abusing the land against their better judgment or despite their rationalizations. Universal literacy rings consent to goals such as sustained productivity, even though ignorance, arising from new environments and the annihilation of peasant wisdom, creates those dust bowl disasters that industrial societies have a habit of repeating. When they set out to repair blunders made, as in Vale or the Gascoyne, industrial societies must gain the willing collaboration of their own peasants. It is a term misapplied to gruff and independent stockmen and ranchers, not because they are heroes of the cinema, but because, for good and ill, they lack the peasant mentality, which is, however, not totally absent from industrial societies, as evidenced by Appalachia, or by those urban slums in which a catalytic approach, developed by the late Saul Alinsky, was applied with some measure of success. It would seem ludicrous to approach American or Australian ranchers using catalytic methods. Nonetheless, they are people whose human dignity requires respect, whose advice must be sought, and with whom patient negotiations will shape the design that programs will have to take. So, too, the cotton-growing *sovkhoznik* has to be consulted, or so the Soviet Union insists. Shadowing such consultations and negotiations are the material incentives which industrial societies, capitalist or communist, pull out to secure consent, collaboration, and even efficiency.

The social ambience is quite different in those traditional societies in which material incentives are applied with dubious success. Such societies will usually have been desertified by poverty and its spiritual corollaries—hopelessness, fatalism, and lack of self-esteem. In such situations, it seems that the Chinese are quite right in insisting that a change in thinking is the key to all else. And this whatever "else" may be—whether it is to become "modern" or to revitalize a traditional culture.

In their insistence on the inclusion in the Plan of Action of Recommendation 3, the nations present in Nairobi gave the world's endorsement to the principle that the road to defeating desertification passes through the human mind. This is the critical connection which, if sealed, enables the rest of the Plan of Action to be dispensed with. After all, all those many recommendations concerned with the *physical* repair of degraded landscapes can be found by consulting Anaya Garduño (21) and other such references and need not be repeated. What is needed is the impulse to look them up. And then to apply the prescription arising from a scrupulous examination of the desertified situation, as known by the agronomist or as located in the References. The Plan of Action needed perhaps no more than two recommendations: (1) Do whatever is needed to inspire people with confidence that they can solve their own problems and fire them with the determination to do so; (2) provide them with whatever technical or financial aid that they, local people, thereupon ask for. But a Plan of Action so simplified applies to any problem, and not just to the problem of desertification.

Desertification has other obvious connections with all those other problems confronting mankind—food, water, energy, population, pollution, cities, disarmament, social justice, the rights of women and minorities, the exhaustion of natural resources, Third World development. The rights of women? Women are the major users of land in some places and slaves to the gathering of cooking fuel in others. The interlocks that hook one problem to another give rise to the concept of one *problématique*, one vast, complex, and tangled problem that contains them all. Each can then be viewed as an aspect of the overarching *problématique* and the question then becomes: Which of them constitute the most strategic entrées, the solution to which will most powerfully echo through the entire tangle? The catalytic approach would find the key in social justice. Speaking at the recent World's Fair in Spokane, Washington, former AAAS President Athelstan Spilhaus suggested that population and energy were the key entry points, whose solution would most readily facilitate the solution of all.

The problem of desertification has also been proposed as a key point of entry. Not because its physical solutions are known—technological solutions, as has been said, are known to all the problems listed. Rather because the technological solutions to desertification seem more acceptable, less controversial, than the solutions to many other problems. A solution to desertification would ramify benefits quickly through the tangled *problématique*. Its effects on the problems of food, water, poverty, and the state of natural resources are obvious. Its effects on other elements of the tangle are less immediately evident but clear upon reflection. It is said to have the great advantage of being easier to solve than other problems. And yet one wonders if this is really true, if all problems, all really social in nature, are not all equally hard to solve. Since they have all arisen out of ways of thought, nothing but changes in ways of thinking—and feeling—will resolve any of them. The Turan program would equalize "rates of socioeconomic change in city and desert," which is to say, get remote drylands people to think like city people. Difficulties which the authors reveal about themselves would seem to call for another kind of equalization—that city people who carry out desertification studies should begin to think more like the people who live in the drylands. That may be so, and yet what they propose may not be too different from the subversive idealism of the catalytic approach.

So we arrive at last to the conclusion that to improve the conditions of human existence, we must first improve the conditions of human existence. In the ecosystem of earth, it is as though nature herself reacts harshly to the rules of a game that perpetuates poverty and degradation among such a large proportion of the dominant species, a game which if permitted to continue much longer will find the fun gone from playing it for everyone. Relevant decision makers must take note of this hitherto obscure rule of the game. When social justice is refused, nature herself ultimately exacts a revenge. It is a rule that is apparent when societies are viewed as ecosystems. When part of the social ecosystem is ravaged—and in the present world, it is a large part—the effects will be felt by all. The nature of the threat to humanity must be grasped and old definitions of subversion abandoned. It is not the poor who are everywhere, threatening to invade "society's favorite places," in the image drawn by Ortega y Gasset (58, p.36). It is poverty itself that is the intruder. The present outcry for popular participation may signify that the true nature of the *problématique* entangling twentieth-century mankind is indeed coming to be grasped. If that is so, community development workers need not after all begin their work by trying to change the way people think in Washington, Moscow, and Brasilia in order to reestablish sustained productivity on the harsh plain of the Azawak. And in all those other places.

No matter what happens, whether the problem, the *problématique*, is finally resolved or not, life in Tauran will never again be the same, although it is difficult to say precisely what the future holds for this district now that Iran has apparently entered an epoch of sharp and occasionally violent political transition. Yet whatever now comes to pass, this cluster of old, self-sufficient villages has been spotted by the modern world, just as the prying eyes of national bureaucracies eventually peek into every last hidden corner. The villagers no longer supply themselves with what they want and need. Now they are partially dependent on an outside, wider world. They turn their new, unpleasant feelings of dependency against their old home, that peculiar little place that occupies a square of high ground between the marching sands beyond the intermittent Hojjaj River and, far below like a white hell, the glittering playas of the great salt desert. In a few years, the old people will be dead and the young people gone off to get menial jobs in the cities, and someone entirely different, an employee of some kind, will be growing food and pasturing livestock in this far corner of poor Parthia. Tauran will have become secure, its shifting sands stabilized, desertification halted everywhere in the vicinity, for Iran has the oil wealth to do that easily. Tauran will have become modern, the pattern of its new existence determined by which way that decision went—whether to spread the people out or bunch them together. Fortunately, in the end, no decision makers, relevant or otherwise, will establish all the flavor of the new life that will have replaced the old life in Tauran. Ordinary people will decide the little things, just as they always have. It is their only revenge.

REFERENCES

Documents of the United Nations Conference on Desertification

The Case Studies

1. A/CONF.74/9. *Case Study on Desertification. Region of Combarbalá, Chile*, Instituto de Investigaciones Agropecuarias, Chile, 1977.
2. A/CONF.74/10. *Case Study on Desertification. Greater Mussayeb Project, Iraq.* Foundation for Scientific Research, Iraq, 1977.
3. A/CONF.74/11. *Case Study on Desertification. Luni Development Block, India.* Central Arid Zone Research Institute, Jodhpur, 1977.
4. A/CONF.74/12. *Case Study on Desertification. Oglat Merteba Region, Tunisia.* Tunisian National Institute for Agronomic Research, 1977.
5. A/CONF.74/13. *Case Study on Desertification. Mona Reclamation Experimental Project, Pakistan.* A/CONF.74/13Add.1. *Mona Reclamation Experimental Project: Synoptic Map of Desertification Hazards.* Planning and Coordination Cell, Irrigation, Drainage, and Flood Control Research Council, Pakistan, 1977.
6. A/CONF.74/14. *Case Study on Desertification. The Eghazer and Azawak Region, Niger.* A/CONF.74/14/Add.1. *The Eghazer and Azawak Region, Synoptic Map of Desertification.* Institut de Recherches en Sciences Humaines, University of Niamey, Niger, 1977.
7. A/CONF.74/15. *Australia. Gascoyne Basin. An Associated Case Study.* Department of Ariculture, Western Australia, 9 May, 1977.
8. A/CONF.74/16. *China. Tame the Wind, Harness the Sand and Transform the Gobi. An Associated Case Study.* Office of Environmental Protection. Sinkiang Uighur Autonomous Republic, People's Republic of China, 6 June, 1977.
9. A/CONF.74/17. *China. Control the Desert and Create Pastures. An Associated Case Study.* Wushenchao Commune, Wushenchao Banner, Inner Mongolia Autonomous Region. People's Republic of China, 6 June, 1977.
10. A/CONF.74/18. *China. Combating Desertification in China. An Associated Case Study.* Lanchow Institute of Glaciology, Cryopedology and Deserts, Chinese Academy of Sciences, Lanchow, People's Republic of China, 6 June, 1977.
11. A/CONF.74/19. *Iran. The Turan Programme. An Associated Case Study.* A/CONF.74/19/Add.1. *The Turan Programme. Maps.* Department of the Environment, Tehran, 6 June, 1977.

12. A/CONF. 74/20. *Israel. The Negev: A Desert Reclaimed. An Associated Case Study.* Environmental Protection Service, Ministry of the Interior, Israel, 9 May, 1977.
13. A/CONF.74/21. *The Vale Rangeland Rehabilitation Program: The Desert Repaired in Southeastern Oregon.* U.S. Department of Agriculture Forest Service Resource Bulletin PNW-70, 1977.
14. A/CONF.74/22. *USSR. Integrated Desert Development and Desertification Control in the Turkmenian SSR. An Associated Case Study.* A/CONF. 74/22/Add.1. *Integrated Desert Development and Desertification Control in the Turkmenian SSR. Maps.* Institute of Deserts, Academy of Sciences of the Turkmenian SSR, Ashkabad, 2 June, 1977.
15. A/CONF.74/23. *USSR. Golodnaya Steppe. An Associated Case Study.* USSR Ministry for Reclamation and Water Management, Moscow, 27 May, 1977.

Other Conference Documents

16. A/CONF.74/1/Rev.1. *Desertification: An Overview.* Conference Secretariat, Nairobi, 1977.
17. A/CONF.74/2. *World Map of Desertification with Explanatory Note.* UNESCO, FAO, WMO, Geneva, 1977.
18. A/CONF.74/3. *Draft Plan of Action to Combat Desertification.* Conference Secretariat, Nairobi, 1977.
19. A/CONF.74/3/Add.2. *Economic and Financial Aspects of the Plan of Action to Combat Desertification.* Conference Secretariat, Nairobi, 1977.
20. A/CONF.74/5. *Climate and Desertification.* By F. Kenneth Hare. Nairobi, 1977.
21. A/CONF.74/6. *Technology and Desertification.* By Manuel Anaya Garduño. Nairobi, 1977.
22. A/CONF.74/7. *Ecological Change and Desertification.* By Andrew Warren and J.K. Maizels. Nairobi, 1977.
23. A/CONF.74/8. *Population, Society and Desertification.* By Robert W. Kates, D.L. Johnson, and K. Johnson Haring. Nairobi, 1977.
24. A/CONF.74/24. *Transnational Project: The Management of Major Regional Aquifers in Northeast Africa and the Arabian Peninsula.* Conference Secretariat, Nairobi, 1977.
25. A/CONF.74/25. *Transnational Greenbelt in North Africa.* Conference Secretariat, Nairobi, 1977.
26. A/CONF.74/26. *Transnational Project on Management of Livestock and Rangelands to Combat Desertification in the Sudano–Sahelian Regions (SOLAR).* Conference Secretariat, Nairobi, 1977.
27. A/CONF.74/27. *Transnational Project to Monitor Desertification Processes and Related Natural Resources in Arid and Semi-Arid Areas of South America.* Conference Secretariat, Nairobi, 1977.
28. A/CONF.74/28. *Transnational Project to Monitor Desertification Processes and Related Natural Resources in Arid and Semi-Arid Areas of Southwest Asia.* Conference Secretariat, Nairobi, 1977.
29. A/CONF.74/29. *Sahel Greenbelt Transnational Project.* Conference Secretariat, Nairobi, 1977.
30. A/CONF.74/31. *Status of Desertification in the Hot Arid Regions. Climate Aridity Index Map. Experimental World Scheme of Aridity and Drought Probability.* (Maps) UNESCO, FAO, WMO, Geneva, 1977.
31. A/CONF.74/34. *Study of Alternative Economic Strategies for the Development of Arid and Semi-Arid Lands.* A summary report on a conference jointly

organized by the United Nations Institute for Training and Research and the California Department of Water Resources, Sacramento, California, and Nairobi, Kenya, 1977.
32. United Nations Center for Economic and Social Information (CESI): *United Nations Conference on Desertification: Round-Up, Plan of Action and Resolutions*. New York, United Nations, 1978.

Other References

33. E.N. Anderson, Jr.: "The Life and Culture of Ecotopia" in Dell Hymes, editor: *Reinventing Anthropology*. New York, Vintage Books, 1974.
34. Aristotle: *Politics*. Cambridge, Massachusetts, Harvard-Heinemann, Loeb Classical Library, 1967.
35. Giovanni Arrighi and John S. Saul: *Essays on the Political Economy of Africa*. New York, Monthly Review Press, 1973.
36. John C. Caldwell: *The Sahelian Drought and Its Demographic Implications*. Overseas Liaison Committee, American Council on Education, OLC Paper No. 8, December, 1975.
37. Chen Jo-hsi: *The Execution of Mayor Yin and Other Stories from the Great Proletarian Cultural Revolution*. Translated by Nancy Ing and Howard Goldblatt. Bloomington, Indiana University Press, 1978.
38. Philip H. Coombs with Manzoor Ahmed: *Attacking Rural Poverty*. Baltimore, Johns Hopkins University Press, 1974.
39. Roy L. Donahue, Raymond W. Miller, and John Shickluna: *Soils. An Introduction to Soils and Plant Growth*, fourth edition. Englewood Cliffs, N.J., Prentice-Hall, 1977.
40. Harold E. Dregne, editor: *Arid Lands in Transition*. Washington, D.C., Publication No. 90 of the American Association for the Advancement of Science, 1970.
41. Harold E. Dregne: "The Changing Scene" in Harold E. Dregne, editor: *Arid Lands in Transition*. Washington, D.C., Publication No. 90 of the American Association for the Advancement of Science, 1970.
42. Therese Drummond: *Using the Method of Paulo Freire in Nutrition Education: An Experimental Plan for Community Action in Northeast Brazil*. Ithaca, N.Y., Cornell International Nutrition Monograph Series No. 3, 1975.
43. Erik P. Eckholm: *Losing Ground*. New York, W.W. Norton, 1976.
44. M. Taghi Farvar and John P. Milton, editors: *The Careless Technology*. Garden City, New York, Natural History Press, 1972.
45. Paulo Freire: *Pedagogy of the Oppressed*. Translated by Myra Bergman Ramos. New York, Seabury Press, 1970.
46. Paulo Freire: *Education for Critical Consciousness*. New York, Seabury Press, 1973.
47. M.H. Glantz: "Dealing with a Global Problem" in M.H. Glantz, editor: *Desertification*. Boulder, Colorado, Westview Press, 1977.
48. René Grousset: *The Empire of the Steppes*. Translated by Naomi Walford. New Brunswick, New Jersey, Rutgers University Press, 1970.
49. The Inter-American Foundation: *They Know How*. Chicago, 1977.
50. P.L. Jaiswal, editor: *Desertification and Its Control*. New Delhi, Model Press, 1977.
51. R.W. Katz and M.H. Glantz: "Rainfall Statistics in the Sahel" in M.H. Glantz, editor: *Desertification*. Boulder, Colorado, Westview Press, 1977.
52. H.N. Le Houérou: "The Nature and Causes of Desertization" in M.H. Glantz, editor: *Desertification*. Boulder, Colorado, Westview Press, 1977.

53. André Malraux: *Antimemoires*. Paris, Collection Soleil, 1967.
54. H.S. Mann and R.P. Singh: "Crop Production in the Indian Arid Zone" in P.L. Jaiswal, editor: *Desertification and Its Control*. New Delhi, Model Press, 1977.
55. Mao Tse-tung: *Five Articles by Mao Tsetung*. Peking, Foreign Languages Press, 1972.
56. John R. Mather: *Climatology. Fundamentals and Applications*. New York, McGraw-Hill, 1974.
57. John T. Noonan: *Contraception. A History of Its Treatment by the Catholic Theologians and Canonists*. Cambridge, Massachusetts, Harvard University Press, 1966.
58. José Ortega y Gasset: *La Rebelion de las Masas*. Colección Austral, No. 1. Madrid, Espasa-Calpe, 19th edition, 1972.
59. Talcott Parsons: *The Structure of Social Action*. New York, Macmillan, 1968.
60. Marco Polo: *The Travels*. New York, Penguin Books, 1974.
61. President's Science Advisory Committee: *The World Food Problem*. Washington, D.C., May, 1967.
62. Anders Rapp, H.N. Le Houérou, and B. Lundholm, editors: *Can Desert Encroachment Be Stopped?* Ecological Bulletin No. 24, Swedish Natural Science Research Council, 1976.
63. Anders Rapp: *A Review of Desertification in Africa—Water, Vegetation and Man*. Stockholm, Secretariat for International Ecology, Sweden (SIES), 1974.
64. Joan Robinson: *Economic Management in China*. Modern China Series No. 4, Anglo-Chinese Educational Institute, 1976.
65. Rural Missionaries of the Philippines: *Diocesan Community Based Health Programs*. A brochure.
66. Science Association's Nairobi Seminar on Desertification: *Statement*. Nairobi, August, 1977, mimeographed.
67. Bob Scholte: "Toward a Reflective and Critical Anthropology" in Dell Hymes, editor: *Reinventing Anthropology*. New York, Vintage Books, 1974.
68. Mahmoud Seklani: *La Population de la Tunisie*. Paris, Comité International de Coordination des Recherches Nationales de Démographie, 1974.
69. Diodorus Siculus: *Diodorus of Sicily*. Translated by C.H. Oldfather. Cambridge, Massachusetts, Harvard University Press, Loeb Classical Library, 1961.
70. Aurel Stein: *On Ancient Central-Asian Tracks* New York, Pantheon Books, 1964.
71. Strabo: *The Geography*. Translated by Horace Leonard Jones. Cambridge, Massachusetts, Harvard University Press, Loeb Classical Library, 1960.
72. Minze Stuiver: "Atmospheric Carbon Dioxide and Carbon Reservoir Changes" in *Science*, Vol. 199, 20 January, 1978.
73. Jeremy Swift: *Desertization in the Sahel*. Institute for the Study of International Organization, Sussex University, Brighton, England. Mimeographed.
74. Strobe Talbott, translator and editor: *Khrushchev Remembers*. Boston, Little, Brown, 1974.
75. Michael Taussig: "Nutrition, Development and Foreign Aid: A Case Study of U.S. Directed Health Care in a Colombian Plantation Zone" in *International Journal of Health Services*, Vol. 8, No, 1, 1978.
76. Arnold Toynbee: *A Study of History*, Vol. 4, The Breakdowns of Civilization. New York, Oxford University Press, 1962.
77. Peter J. Ucko and G.W. Dimbleby: *The Domestication and Exploitation of Plants and Animals*. Chicago, Aldine-Atherton, 1969.

78. United Nations Environment Programme: *Overviews in the Priority Subject Area—Land, Water and Desertification*. UNEP/PROG.2 Nairobi, February, 1975.
79. *United Nations Statistical Yearbook 1975*. New York, United Nations, 1976.
80. United Nations: *Popular Participation in Decision Making for Development*. Sales No. E.75.IV.10. New York, 1975.
81. United Nations: *Resolution Adopted by the General Assembly*, 29th Session, Agenda Item 12, 5 February, 1975. A/RES/3337 (XXIX).
82. United Nations: *1636th Meeting of the Second Committee of the General Assembly*, 22 November, 1974. A/C.2/L.1370/Rev.1.
83. United States Bureau of the Census: *Population of Tunisia, Estimates and Projections, 1967-2000*. Washington, D.C., U.S. Department of Commerce, Series P-96, No. 3, March, 1971.
84. K.A. Wittfogel: "The Hydraulic Civilizations" in W.L. Thomas, Jr., editor: *Man's Role in Changing the Face of the Earth*. Chicago, University of Chicago Press, 1955.
85. Wen Yin and Liang Hua: *Tachai. The Red Banner*. Peking, Foreign Languages Press, 1977.

INDEX

Abadan, 30
Abalak, 126, 141, 142
Abbasid Caliphate, 23, 33, 34
Abu Dhabi, 290
Acacia aneura (mulga), 61
Acacia spp., 95, 136, 185
Achaemenid (Empire), 30, 296, 298
Ader Mountains, 124
adiabatic lapse rate, 64
Advisory Committee on Arid Zone Research (UNESCO), 5
aerial spraying of rangeland, 176
Afghanistan, 13, 49
Africa, 3, 13, 15, 49, 152, 194, 261, 266
  case studies in, 91, 117
Afro-Asian dryland belt, 49, 66, 179
Agadès, 120, 122, 123, 127, 129, 131, 132–133, 135, 141, 178
agricultural cooperatives, 36, 39, 302
agricultural productivity (maximum sustainable, optimum), 300–302, 310, 313
agriculture, 39
  future possibilities of, 287
  origins of, 28
Agropyron cristatum, desertorum (crested wheatgrass), 173, 176
Agropyron spicatum (bluebunch wheatgrass), 171
Ahmed, Manzoor, 271
Aïr (Mountains), 117, 120, 122, 124
Akkad, 32
albedo (or earth, moon), 65
Alborz (mountains), 293, 298
Albuquerque, N.M., 17
Alexander (of Macedon), 201, 213
Alexandria-the-Farthest, 213
Algeria, 7, 13, 136, 281

Alhagi canescens, 55
Ali Kosh, 28, 30
Alinsky, Saul, 313
alkalinity (of soil), 204
al-Musta'sim, 34
Alp Arslan, 227
alternative livelihoods, 159, 254
Amazon (river, basin), 52, 65, 282
American Association for the Advancement of Science (AAAS), 17, 235, 267, 314
Amu Darya (river), 216, 227, 231, 233
Anarrhinum brevifolium, 107
Anaya Garduño, Manuel, 11, 12, 156, 313
Anderson, E.N., 252, 309
Andes (mountains), 49, 67, 147, 148
Andropogon gayanus, 136
Animation Rurale, 262
Anogeissus pendula, 185
Antioch, 53, 293
Appalachia, 313
aquifer, 13, 100, 128
Arab(s), 126, 141, 167, 199, 275, 286, 299
Arabia (Arabian peninsula), 7, 13, 28, 33, 34, 48, 49, 66, 290
Arabian Sea, 77
Aral Sea (and basin), 213, 215, 216, 231, 240
Arava Valley, 279, 280
Aravalli Hills, 179, 186
arboriculture, 96, 168
Arctic Ocean, 150, 216
Argentina, 7, 13, 67, 153
arid (regions, conditions), 52, 53, 78, 85, 168, 187, 295; *see also* rangelands
  definition of, 83–84

origins of aridity, 66-67
aridosols, 100
Arid Zone Research Programme (UNESCO), 5, 15
Aristida mutabilis, 129, 136, 141
Aristida pungens, 95
Aristida spp., 185
Aristotle, 23
Arizona, 238
Aroga moth, 126
Artemisia arbuscula (low sagebrush), 177
Artemisia herba-alba (wormwood), 95
Artemisia ordosica, 85
Artemisia tridentata (big sagebrush), 171
Arthrophytum scoparium, 95
Ashkabad, 234
Asia, 13, 20, 28, 45, 47, 52, 147, 153, 156, 167, 179, 204, 235, 293
  case studies in, 23, 45, 77, 179, 197, 213, 227, 245, 275, 293
Assam, 186
associated case studies, 19, 20, 21
Aswan dam, 206, 234
Assy (river), 216
Atacama (desert), 49, 66, 67, 145
Atlantic Ocean, 131
Atlas (mountains), 91
atmospheric circulation, 64
Atriplex spp., 62, 115, 288
Australia, 7, 19, 78, 81, 84, 153, 313
  case study in, 59
Australian dryland complex, 50, 83
Australocedrus chilensis, 149
Avdat (Israel), 277

Baba Kuh (Iran), 312
Babylon, 23, 25, 28, 33, 213
Bagdad, 26, 33, 34
Bahamas, 153
Balanites aegyptiaca, 136
bamboo(s), 184
barley, 28, 32, 53, 95, 106, 184
Batisse, Michel, 18
Beas (river), 197
Beaufort scale, 48, 53
Beau Geste, 120

Beer-Sheva, 279
Benguela current, 67
Ben-Gurion University, 279
Benizit tribe, 96
Berbers, 91, 111, 126
Beringia, 153
Bermuda High, 131-133, 151
Bidgemia (Gascoyne), 62
Bio Bio (river), 145
Blepharis linariifolia, 136, 141
Boise, Idaho, 163
Bolivia, 13, 49
borehole program (Niger), 120, 125, 128-130, 158, 194
Borlaug, Norman, 211
Botswana, 49
bouzou, the, 120
Brazil, 7, 50, 259-260, 312
Bromus tectorum (cheatgrass), 171
Bronze Age, 33
brousse tigrée, 2
Bryson, Reid, 132
Buchloë dactyloides (buffalo grass), 170
Budyko, M.I., 82, 83
Bully Creek (Oregon), 163
Bureau of Land Management (U.S.), 163, 170-174, 311
Burns, Oregon, 173
Burundi, 7
Bus Mordeh, 28
Byzantium, 227

Cabo Verde, 1
Cairo, 53
Calama, Chile, 145
Caldwell, John C., 131, 135
California, 66
Calligonum spp., 107, 185
Calotropis procera, 186
camels, 2, 79, 84, 122, 124, 125, 215, 230, 232, 303
Cameroon, 7, 122
canal lining, 206, 219
Capparis decidua, 185
carbon dioxide in the atmosphere, 153-155
Caribbean (sea, region), 50, 194

Carnarvon (Western Australia), 59, 63, 67, 71, 76
carrying capacity (stocking rates), 72-73, 128
Carthage (Carthaginians), 91, 96
Cascade Mountains, 66, 163
Case studies on desertification, 16
Caspian Sea, 227, 232, 240, 296
Cassia sturtii, 288
cattle, 62, 79, 84, 87, 121-122, 124, 125, 134, 155, 165, 220, 221, 238, 288, 291
cattle taboo (India), 189-190
Cenchrus spp., 75, 136, 185
Central Arid Zone Research Institute (CAZRI), 181, 182, 190-195, 254, 257-258, 309
cereals, 28, 53, 84, 106, 109, 115
Cerro Tololo, 147
Chad, 3, 13, 15, 135
Chapingo (*Colegio de Posgraduados*), 156, 211
chemical elements required by plants, 99, 203-204
Chenab (river), 197, 200
Chen Jo-hsi, 264
Chen Yung-kuei, 264
chicken farming (poultry), 158, 231
Chile, 7, 13, 18, 49
  case study in, 145
China (and The People's Republic of), 19, 20, 26, 29, 67, 149, 156, 157, 168, 197, 237, 264-266, 286, 293, 294, 307, 312, 313
  case studies in, 45, 77, 245
  map of, 46
Ch'in Shih Huang-ti, 77
Chott Djerid, 91
Chou En-lai, 246
Chrysothamnus spp. (including rabbit brush), 176
Chubdari, 304
Chuquicamata (Chile), 145
Citrullus lanatus, 129
Citrullus vulgaris (tinda), 192
climate(s), classification of, 79
  changes in, 3-4, 149-156, 167, 181, 247

prediction of, 133, 287
climax (vegetation), 75, 101-103, 147, 184-185
CNRS (National Center for Scientific Research, France), 94
Colombia, 7, 50, 211, 222
colonialism, 109-111, 117, 120, 126-127, 251
Combarbalá, Chile, 18, 167, 172, 175, 237, 247, 249, 254, 255
  case study in, 145
  map of, 146
Committee on Arid Lands (AAAS), 17
community development, 256, 259, 262, 270, 280-281
Community Development Program (India), 262
component reviews, 11, 250
comunero(s), 156-161, 254
Concepcion, Chile, 145
Conference on Arid Lands in Changing World (1969), 17
Congo (river, basin), 49, 52, 65, 153
Congress (of the United States), 173-174
contratista, 250-251
controlled environment agriculture, 290-291
Coombs, Philip, 255, 271
Coquimbo District (Chile), 145
Coriolis force, 66
Corispermum hyssopifolium, 86
Cornell University, 261
costs and benefits of combating desertification, 13, 72
  table on, 14
cotton, 84, 212, 215, 231, 279
critical indicators, 235-236, 284-285
Ctenopharungodon idella, 232
Ctesiphon, 33, 298
cultivation, limit of, exceeding proper limits of, 84, 104-105, 113, 115, 126, 138, 139, 142, 169, 187, 189, 238-239
cultivation of new lands, 51-52
cumin seed, 156, 158
Curaçao, 50
Cyamopsis tetragonoloba, 185

cycles (of nitrogen, nutrients, etc.) 103, 104
  diagram of, 93
Cymbogon spp., 129, 136
Cynodon dactylon, 95
Cyperus conglomeratus, 136
Cyrenaica, 168

Dahomey (now Benin), 7
Dakar, 135, 179
Dakoro, 141
Dakotas, the, 50
Danube (river), 78
Darius, 233
Dasht-i-Kavir, 179, 295, 296, 297
Dasht-i-Lut, 296
date (fruit), 115
Davis, Raymond, 151
Dead Sea, 277, 279, 280
Death Valley, 50, 83
Delhi, 179
Demavand, 293
Department of the Environment (Iran), 301-303, 307
desalination (of sea water), 290
desert, 2, 34, 47, 48, 49, 51, 53, 76, 167, 247
  amount of, on earth, 50, 168
  climatic causes of, 63
  definition of, 82-83
  man-made, amount of, 168
desertification, 6-7, 26, 33, 72, 74, 76, 103, 134, 138, 140, 141, 142, 168-169, 175, 225, 229-230, 238-239, 252-253, 284-285, 296, 307-312
  annual rate of, 169
  causes of, 94, 104-106, 156, 251
  and climate, 155
  definition of, 11, 12, 17, 97-98
  monitoring of, 235-236
  nature of the subject, 10
  relation to other problems, 314-315
  review of causes and manifestations of, 247-249
Desertification: An Overview, 11, 252
desertization, 10
Deutsche Entwicklungsdienst, 257

development (social, economic), 108-110, 194-195, 261, 312, 314
Diaguita (Indians), 155
Diallo, H.A., 7
Digdiga (Niger), 128
Diodorus (Siculus), 276
disclimax (vegetation), 102
Djerba, island of, 91
Dokuchaev, V.V., 233
domestication (of plants, animals), 28-29
Dregne, Harold, 17
drip (trickle) irrigation, 240, 279, 283
drought, 155, 192, 296
  in Coquimbo, 153
  in Gascoyne basin, 70-71
  in the Sahel, 3-7, 120-123, 130, 169
Drummond, Therese, 261
"dry" farming, *see* rainfed farming
dryland complexes, 49, 66-67
drylands, 52-53
  extent of, 84
dryness ratio
  in Gascoyne, 63
  at Mussayeb, 34
  at Turfan, 48
  at Wushenchao, 78
dunes, sand, 85, 169
  fixing of, 86, 240-241, 273, 303
  invasion by, 79
"dust bowl," 170, 215
Dzhizak (Uzbek), 216

Easter Island, 145
Ecbatana (Hamadan), 293
Echinochlos colomum, 185
ecological viewpoint, approach, 137, 158, 174, 175, 233, 248, 257, 285
ecosystem, 29, 102-103, 148, 155, 158, 237, 315
eco-unit(s), 237
Ecuador, 7, 49
education programs, 114
Eghazer and Azawak (Niger), 18, 156, 178, 188
  case study in, 117
Egypt, 7, 13, 27, 30, 206

Eilat, 279, 280
Elaeagnus angustifolia, 55
Elam, 30
Eleusine compresa, 185
El Hamma oasis, 96
England, 153
erg, 2, 91, 94
erosion, 61, 72, 104, 115, 147, 177, 187, 189, 191, 240, 253
Ethiopia, 7
Ethiopian highlands, 49, 84
Euphrates (river), 23, 25, 26, 28, 32, 34, 35, 40
Europe, 149, 153, 155
evapotranspiration, 34, 80, 82
Evenari, Michael, 277
extension services, 41, 42, 43, 158, 193, 209-212, 255, 282

facet(s), 237
family planning, 96, 112, 187, 189, 196, 254, 258
Farvar, M. Taghi, 234
fatalism, 251, 310, 313
Fatimids, 111
Fergana (valley), 224
Fiji, 7
five-ditch system of wind protection, 55
Five-Star Commune, 55, 295
Florence (wheat), 281
fodder crop(s), 85, 115, 230, 240-241, 279
Food and Agriculture Organization of the United Nations (FAO), 15, 19, 168
Foolish Old Man (who removed mountains), 88
Ford Foundation, 112
Forster, George, 298
Foss, P.O., 171
France, 7, 8, 9, 142, 150, 270
Freire, Paulo, 259-261, 263-264, 266, 270, 272, 280, 281, 282, 291, 300, 310, 312
Fulani (Peul, Bororo), 121-122, 124, 129, 137, 304

game ranching, 288
Gandhi, M.K., 262
Ganges (river, basin), 186, 202
Gao (Mali), 2
Gascoyne Basin, 6, 78, 79, 81, 84, 130, 134, 149, 156, 160, 165, 167, 169, 172, 230, 235, 249-250, 255, 270, 271, 313
  case study in, 59
  map of, 60
Gascoyne Junction, 74
Gascoyne River, 59
Gaya Region (Niger), 121
Geneva, Switzerland, 17, 19, 261
Geraldton (Western Australia), 59
Germany, Federal Republic of, 7
Ghana, 3, 7
Gibson Desert, 50
Gigiri (Kenya), 9
Gilgamesh, 30
Globigerina pachyderma, 150
goats, 79, 91, 95, 106, 109, 122, 124, 156, 157, 182, 187
Gobi Desert, 49, 53
gobi land, 53, 56
Goebelia pachycarpa, 303
Golodnaya Steppe, 195, 227, 242, 255, 262, 265, 295
  case study in, 19, 213
  map of, 214
Goose Lake (Oregon), 166
Gramineae, 183
grasses, 183-185
Great American Desert, 67
Great Basin, 163
Greater Mussayeb (Mussayib), 18, 57, 89, 116, 156, 158, 165, 193, 194, 199, 224, 247, 254, 271, 280, 283, 299
  case study in, 23
  map of, 24
Great Wall (of China), 77, 78, 85
Greece, 94
greenhouse(s), 290-291
greenhouse effect, 154
Green Revolution, 52, 211, 281-282, 283, 287, 309
groundnuts, 84

"ground truth," 71, 235
groundwater, 47, 85, 87, 100, 279
Grousset, René, 48-49, 167, 273
"guest soil," 56-57
Guinea (coast), 3, 7, 49, 84, 91, 124, 126, 135
Guinea-Bissau, 261, 266
Gulf Coast (U.S.), 78
Gulf of Aqaba, 279
Gulf of Guinea, 2, 132
Gulf Stream, 149
gullying, 238
Guti, 32
Gypsies, 229

Haiti, 7
Halostachys belangeviana, 55
hammada, 94
Han (Dynasty), 47, 79
Hare, F. Kenneth, 82
Haring, K. Johnson, 11, 250, 252
harmattan, 287
Hassain al-Bakr, Ahmed, 40
Havana, 8
Heady, Harold F., 19
heat equator, 65, 66
Hecatompylos, 293, 295, 296, 297
Hedin, Sven, 45
Hedysarm mongolicum, 86
Heilungkiang (Province, China), 272
hijuela, 157
Hilgard, E.W., 233
Hillah (Iraq), 23, 26
Himalaya, 66, 202
Hindiya Barrage, 26, 27
Hojjaj (river), 302, 316
Holland, 152
Homestead Gold Mine, 151
Honan (Province, China), 53
horizon (in soil structure), 98, 99, 101
horses, 78-79, 178, 215
housing, rural, 38-39
Hulagu, 34
"human volcano," 132
Humboldt Current, 67
humus, 56, 100, 101, 103
  total energy in, 99
Huns (Hsiung-nu), 47, 77, 79, 85

Hydaspes (river), 201
hydraulic hypothesis, 27
hydrological cycle, 99-100
hyperarid (very arid), 296
  amount of, 168
  definition of, 82-83
Hypophthalmichthus molitrix, 232

Ibadan, 135
Inca (civilization), 147
India, 7, 13, 18, 49, 78, 197, 200, 206
  case study in, 179
Indian Council of Agricultural Research, 188
Indian Desert, 179, 180, 189
Indian Ocean, 1, 49, 59
Indonesia, 65
Indus (river, basin), 186, 197
Indus Valley civilization (Harappa), 27, 203
Indus Waters Treaty, 197
In Gall (Niger), 122, 125, 141
inheritance (of land), 157, 207, 250, 309
Inkeles, Alex, 193
Institute of Deserts (Turkmen SSR), 234, 241
insurance strategy, 125
Inter-American Development Bank, 18n, 147
Inter-American Foundation, 258-259, 263
investment (in land), 14, 311-312
Ioullemden basin (Niger), 122
Iran, 7, 13, 19, 20, 28, 49, 66, 179, 227, 229
  case study in, 293
Iraq, 7, 18, 116, 199
  case study in, 23
irreversible degradation (of soil), 97-98, 239, 248
irrigation, 23, 53, 59, 116, 141-142, 156-157, 163-164, 197, 215, 223, 273, 278
  drainage in, 26, 31, 32, 36, 37-38, 40, 200, 202, 205-207
  origins of, 30
  productivity of, 199

Index

by qanat, 296
Isfahan, 296
Ismael Khan, 298
isohyet(s), 84–85, 133
   definition of, 83
Israel
   case study in, 275
   map of, 276
Israel Water Law, 278
Italy, 7, 94
Ivan the Terrible, 79

Jagatai, Khanata of, 53
Jamdat Nasr, 30, 34, 35
Japan, 7
Jaxartes (river), 213
Jenghiz Khan, 53
Jerome, Saint, 295
jessour, 94, 106, 109
Jhelum (river, canal), 197, 200, 201, 202
Jinnah Barrage, 197
Jodhpur (India), 181
Johnson, Douglas L., 11, 250, 252
Jordan, 7
Jordan, Michael, 165
Jordan Valley (Oregon), 165
Juan Fernandez islands, 145
Juniperus Phoenicia L., 95

Kabul (river), 197, 200
Kairouan, 111
Kajiado, 1
Kalabagh (Pakistan), 197
Kalahari (desert), 49, 63, 153, 229
Kal-i-Shur (river), 297
Kano (Nigeria), 135
Kansu (Province, China), 77
Kara Bogaz.Gol, 227
Karachi, 197
Kara-khoja, 45, 47
karakul (sheep), 229–230, 240
Kara Kum Canal, 231–232, 234, 241, 278
Kara Kum Desert, 227, 229, 230, 241, 297
Karelinia caspica, 55
karez system, 47

Kariba dam, 194
Karun (river), 28
Kassas, Mohammed, 16, 168
Kates, Robert W., 11, 250, 252
Kazakhstan, 215, 216
Kel Dinnik, 117
Kel Tamasheq: *see* Tuareg
Kenya, 1
Kenyatta Conference Center, 1, 9
khamsin, 287
Khar, Plain of, 298, 302, 303, 307
Khartoum, 168
Khorasan, 227
Khrushchev, Nikita, 215, 263
Khuzistan, 26, 28, 30
kibbutz(im), 280, 302
Kirghiz, 221
Kirin (Province, China), 272
Kopet Dag, 233
Krasnovodsk, 232
Kublai Khan, 53
kulun, 85–87, 89, 273, 311
K'un-lun, 45.
Kuomintang, 156, 273
Kurban-Tungut Desert, 87
Kuruk-tagh, 47
Kuwait, 7

Lagos, 135
Lake Aidin, 47
Lake Chad, 135
Lake Kinneret (Sea of Galilee), 277, 278, 289
Lake McLeod (Western Australia), 59
Lakeview, Oregon, 166
Lakhish Experimental Station, 282
Lanchow, 77
Lanchow Institute of Glaciology, Cryopedology and Deserts, 77, 266
land areas by climate and soil, 50–53
   estimated cropland, 51
LANDSAT, 235, 285
land values in arid regions, 14
Lapps, 229
La Serena (Chile), 149
Latin America, 7, 20, 261
lateritic soils, 52

leaching (and requirement), 27, 31, 35, 40, 205-207
Lead, S.D., 151
least developed countries, UN list of, 3, 135
legumes (nitrogen fixation), 31, 56
Le Houérou, H.N., 10, 84
Lenin, V.I., 217
Leninabad, 213
Leptadenia pyrotechna, 186
Liaoning (Province, China), 272
Libya, 7, 13, 49
Lima (Peru), 67
Little Ice Age, 152
Liu Shao-chi, 265
locusts, 120-121, 188, 247
Lop Desert, 50
Los Angeles, 53
Luni Development Block, 208, 210, 212, 247, 254, 309
  case study in, 18, 179
  map of, 180
Lygeum spartum, 95

Macedonians, 201, 298
Madagascar, 7
Maes Titonius, 295
Maghrib, 91
maize, 52, 53, 211, 212
Maizels, J.K., 11
Malheur County, 163
Malheur Lake, 166
Malheur River, 164
Mali, 3, 15, 122, 127, 135
Malraux, André, 89
Man and the Biosphere Conference (Sfax), 16
Man and the Biosphere Programma (MAB), 297
Manchuria, 49, 78, 272
Mann, H.S., 188
Mao Tse-tung, 54, 88, 89, 245-247, 264, 300
Maowusu, 85, 272
Maradi, 141
Mareotis, 168
Marsh Arabs, 32

Marx, Karl (Marxism), 88, 261
Mary (Turkmenia), 231, 234
Masai, 1
Mauritania, 4, 135
Mayatta, well of, 117, 121, 139, 143
meat (and hides), 53, 115, 124
Mediterranean (sea, climate), 49, 91, 94, 145, 234, 277
Meekatharra (Western Australia), 63
Meigs, Peverell, 15, 81, 82, 168, 296
melons, 56, 232
Mendez, Ruben, 13
Mendoza (Argentina), 250-251
Mendoza Center for Scientific and Technical Research (Argentina), 16
Menon, Bhaskar, 190, 194
Merino sheep, 62
Meriones hurrianae (gerbils), 188, 247
Mesopotamia, 25, 26, 28, 30, 31, 33, 34, 35, 116, 168, 199, 298
Mesozoic, 150
Mexico, 7, 50, 66
Mexico (City), 53, 154-155
Milankovitch, Milutin (Milankovitch Hypothesis), 132, 151-154
millet, 53, 84, 121, 124, 183, 184, 185, 192, 212
Milton, John P., 236
mining, 147, 159, 232, 239
mist desert, 84
mixed farming, 182-183
"modern" vs. "traditional," 193-195, 209, 224, 229, 282-283, 295, 304-305, 307, 310, 313
Modoc County, 166
Moghul(s), 179, 199
moisture index, 80-82
Mona Reclamation Experimental Project, 270, 283
  case study in, 18, 197
  map of, 198
Mongol(s), 33-34, 40, 67, 79, 298, 299
Mongolia, 49, 77, 179
monitoring of drylands, 235-236
monsoon, 3, 77-78, 152, 155, 156, 199, 273
Morocco, 7, 13, 281

Morse, Wayne, 174
Morus alba, 55
moshav(im), 280, 281, 283, 295
Murgab (river), 233
Mussayeb: see Greater Mussayeb
Mwongozo—The TANU Guidelines, 266

Nabataeans, 275, 277, 286, 288
nadi, 183
Nairobi, 1, 8, 235, 270, 284, 313
Namibia (Namibian Desert), 49, 66, 67, 84
National Water Carrier System (Israel), 289-290
nebka, 94
Negev, 311
  case study in, 19, 275
  map of, 276
Neogloboquadrina pachyderma, 247
neolithic (man, developments), 29, 69
New International Economic Order, 252
Niamey, 120, 137
Niger, 3, 15, 18
  case study in, 117
Nigeria, 7, 134, 135
Niger River, 2, 122, 135
Nile (river), 27, 206
Nineveh, 33
Ninurta, 31
nirin irrigation, 23, 26, 34, 35
nomads, nomadism, 23, 33, 39, 41, 68-69, 78, 84, 107-108, 117, 221, 227, 229, 240, 252, 283, 286, 288-289, 297, 298, 303-304
nonformal education, 255-256
North America, 153
North American dryland complex, 50, 83
Nyerere, Julius, 266

oats, 184
Ob and Irtysh (rivers), 216
Oglat Merteba, 123, 156, 167, 178, 237, 247, 254
  case study in, 18, 91
  map of, 92

oikos, 233, 235
olive(s), 115, 158, 175
Ordos Plateau, 77
Oregon, 66
  case study in, 19, 163
Oregon Trail, 165
Organization of African Unity, 3
ORSTROM (French Office for Scientific and Technical Research), 94
Ortega y Gasset, José, 315
Ottoman Empire, 25, 110
Ovalle (Chile), 149
overgrazing, 73, 79, 104-105, 115, 139, 141, 166, 169, 187, 238
Ovis orientalis, 28
Owyhee River, 163
ozone layer, 154, 235

Pacific Ocean, 66, 273
Paddock, William and Paul, 258
Paiute Indians, 165
Pakistan, 7, 13, 49, 66, 179, 186
  case study in, 18, 197
paleolithic (man, ways of life), 29
Pamirs, 45, 273, 293
Panama, 149
pan evaporation, 80
Panicum spp., 185
Paraguay, 153
Paris, 97, 120
Parsons, Talcott, 268, 309
Parthenium argentatum (guayule), 288
Parthia, 295, 297, 316
participation, popular, 196, 256, 271, 275, 299, 302, 312
pastoralism, 29, 33-34, 68-69, 84, 124-125, 130, 133, 222, 230, 233, 240, 303-304, 311
Patagonia, 49, 67, 153
Peace Corps, 157
ped(s), 100
Peiyang River, 48
Penman, H.L. (Penman method), 34, 82
Pennisetum typhoideum (pearl millet), 185
Persian Empire, 213
Persian wheel, 27

Perth (Western Australia), 59
Peru, 7, 13, 27, 49, 67, 84
Petra, 275
pH (of soils), 204-205
Phaseolus aconitifolius, 185
Philippines, 7, 211, 258
Phragmites communis, 55
Pinus halepensis L., 95
piosphere (and trampling), 129, 139, 239
pipelines (in arid lands), 232-233, 239
Plan of Action to Combat Desertification, 11, 12, 16, 17, 20, 236-237, 256-257, 285, 300-301, 312, 313, 314
Pleistocene (glaciation), 53, 132, 150-152
Pliocene, 152
plowing rangelands, 176-177, 230, 241
Poa secunda (Sandberg bluegrass), 171
political will, 271-273, 286
Polo, Marco, 45, 53
population (human), 4-5, 169-170, 250, 254
　of drylands, 53, 84-85
　of Eghazer and Azawak, 125-126
　of the Gascoyne Basin, 62
　of Golodnaya Steppe, 221-223
　of the Indian Desert, 179
　of Iran, 300
　of Luni Block, 181-182
　of the Negev, 289
　of the Tuareg, the Fulani, 139
　of Tunisia, 96, 97, 108, 110-112
　of Western Australia, 59
Population Council, The, 112
Populus bollean, 55
Populus simonii, 86
Portugal, 126
Porus, King, 201, 213
powerlessness, 252
problématique, the, 314-315
profile (of soil), 98
Prosopis cineraria, juliflora, 185, 186
Ptolemy, 293, 295
public relations, 269-270
pulse(s), 185, 189

Punjab, 197, 201, 206, 213
Punta Burros, 148

qanat, 296-299, 302, 304, 311

radiational index of dryness, 82
Rae (Iran), 293
rain (rainfall), 145, 290
　causes of, 64-67
　in Coquimbo, 148-149
　as defining climates, 84
　in Eghazer and Azawak, 123, 130-131
　in the Gascoyne, 59, 61, 63, 68, 70
　in Golodnaya Steppe, 216
　in Israel, 277-278
　in the Kara Kum, 230
　in Luni Block, 182
　in Mona, 201
　at Mussayeb, 34
　in North China, 273
　precipitation cycle, 99-100
　problems with, 31
　total annual amount, 64
　in Turan, 297
　at Turfan, 47
　in Vale District, 165
　at Wushenchao, 78, 85
rain beat seal, 104
rainfed farming, 28, 53, 85, 102, 182-185, 239
　under desert conditions, 275-276
rain shadow, 66
Rajasthan, 49, 181, 206
rangelands
　Gascoyne monitoring, 75
　Gascoyne survey, 61, 71-73
　Vale survey, rehabilitation, 172-178
Rannof Cutch, 179
Rapp, Anders, 10, 11, 134
Rasul Barrage, 202
Ravi (river, dam), 197, 200
Rawalpindi, 197
recreational use of drylands, 177-178, 241
Red Sea, 49, 280
reg, 94

resilience, 102, 233
Resolution 3337 (XXIX) (UN General Assembly), 8, 15, 18
Retama raetum, 107
Rhantherium suavolens, 95, 106, 107
rice, 51, 52, 183, 184, 197, 204, 211, 212
Rift Valley, 279
roads (in arid lands), 232–233, 238, 239
rodent depradation, 188, 238
Rome (Roman times), 2, 91, 96, 111, 168
Rural Missionaries of the Philippines, 258
Russia, 79
Rwanda, 7
rye, 184

Sahara (Desert), 1, 2, 13, 49, 50, 66, 83, 91, 94, 95, 97, 123, 145, 147, 149, 152, 178
Sahel, the, 2, 26, 49, 61, 63, 77, 84, 99, 148, 149, 155, 156, 169, 221, 222, 229, 270
  case study in, 117
  earlier droughts in, 3
  relief efforts in, 4
  transnational project in, 13
sailaba, 199
Saint-Simon, C.H. de R., 267
salinity (salination, salinization), 25, 32, 33, 35, 56, 156, 189, 200–205, 207, 216–217, 239–240, 279, 309
Salinity Control and Reclamation Projects (SCARP), 201, 206
Salix michrostachya, 86
Samawah (Iraq), 23
sand, 48, 169, 239, 302; *see also* dunes
Sangsar(i), 298, 304, 307
Santiago (Chile), 145, 157
Saraswati River, 181
Sargon of Akkad, 32, 33
Saskatchewan, 50
Sassanid (Persia), 298, 299
satellite imagery, 235
Scandinavian countries, 7

schistosomiasis, 194
Schoenefeldia gracilis, 136, 141
Schopenhauer, Arthur, 286
Schouwia thebaica (alwat), 124
Science Advisory Committee to the President of the United States, 51–52
Scorzonera divaricata, 55
Secretariat of the United Nations Conference on Desertification, 9, 10, 15, 190
Secretary General of the Conference on Desertification, 12, 113
seeding rangeland, 173–177, 230, 241
Seljuk (Turks), 227
semiarid (regions, conditions), 52, 66–67, 168, 296
  definition of, 83–84
Seminar on Desertification (Nairobi), 235, 284–285
Senegal, 4, 15, 135
Senegal River, 135
Serica, 293
sesamum, 192
Sfax (Tunisia), 16, 18
shadoof, 27
Shahpur Canal, 202
Shanidar (cave), 28, 293, 297
Shansi (Province, China), 246
sheep, 28, 59ff, 79, 84, 91, 95, 106, 109, 120, 122, 124, 165, 182, 229–231, 288
Shensi (Province, China), 272
Shiraz, 296
Siberia, 45, 49, 216, 229, 232
sierozems, 101, 109, 216
Silk Road, 29, 45, 48, 53, 55, 293, 295, 297
Simmondsia chinensis (jojoba), 287–288
Simpson Desert, 50
Sinai (peninsula), 49
Sind, the, 201
Singapore, 194
Sinkiang-Uighur Autonomous Region (China), 48
sirocco, 94, 287

slash-and-burn, 102
Smith, David H., 193
Snake (river), 163, 165
social (and cultural) factors in desertification (in problems of arid lands), 17, 37, 39, 42, 239, 249, 284
   in Combarbalá, 156-161
   in Eghazer and Azawak, 116-122, 124-125, 126-127, 142-143
   in the Gascoyne, 73-74
   in Luni Block, 186-187, 189-190, 192-196
   in Mona District, 206-212
   in Mussayeb, 39-42
   in Oglat Merteba, 107-116
   in Turan, 303
   in Turkmenia, 241-243
   in the Vale District, 166
social science, contributions of, 266-267, 308-310
Socorro, N.M., 17
sodic soils, 203, 205
Sodom (Israel), 280
soil(s), 95
   degradation of, 14, 83
   in Gascoyne Basin, 68
   in Luni Block, 185
   in Mona District, 201
   nutrients in, 31, 72
   processes in, 98
   properties (qualities) of, 40, 50-51, 56
   sciences of, 175, 233
solar constant, 65
solar cooker, 287
solar energy, 65, 151, 287
solar neutrinos, 181
Soldier Creek (battle of), 171
solonchaks, 216
Somalia, 1, 49
Sonora (desert), 50, 66
Songhai Empire, 2, 3
sorghum, 53, 84, 124, 183, 184, 192
soudure, 3, 124
South African dryland complex, 49, 66
South America, 13, 15, 145ff

South American dryland complex, 49-50, 66, 235
Southeast Asia monsoon, 78
South Pole, 149, 151
Soviet Central Asia, 49
   case studies in, 213, 227
sovkhoz(nik), 219-221, 223, 230, 231, 240, 242, 295, 307, 313
Spain, 94, 145, 155
Spilhaus, Athelstan, 314
Spokane, Wash., 314
sprinkle irrigation, 240, 278-279
Squaw Butte Experimental Station, 173, 176
Steens Mountains, 166
Stein, Sir Aurel, 45, 47, 50
Stipa Tenacissima (halfa, esparto), 95, 107
Stockholm Conference (on the environment), 8, 16
Strabo, 296
subdesert (very arid), 34, 53, 84, 91, 168
subhumid (regions, conditions), 52
   definition of, 83-84
Sudan (climatic zone), 49, 84, 123
Sudan (country), 7, 13, 15, 168-169
Sudano-Sahelian transition zone, 84
sugar beets, 279
sugarcane, 184, 212
Sumeria (Sumerians), 30, 78
Sutlej (river), 197
Swift, Jeremy, 127-128
swine, 232
Syr Darya (river), 213, 216, 224

tabia, 94
Tachai (commune), 54, 88-89, 246-247, 264-265, 272
T'achang Mountains, 246
Tadzhiks, 216, 221
Tagore, Rabindranath, 262
Tahoua (Niger), 117, 123, 129, 131, 133, 138, 141
Takla-makan (desert), 49, 50, 53, 67, 293, 295
Talas (river), 216

Tamarix ramosissima, 55
Tanezrouft, 2
Tanzania, 1, 7, 49, 266
Tarim basin, 45, 48
Tauran, 298-299, 302-303, 311, 316
Taussig, Michael, 222
Taylor Grazing Act, 170, 171
Tchin Tabaraden, 121, 122, 125, 138, 141
technological solutions, 269, 283-284, 287
tectonic movement, 149-150
Teguidda-n-tesemt, 125
Tehran, 243, 303, 305, 307
teleconnections, 133
Tepe Sabz, 30
Texada saltworks, 59
Texas Tech University, 17
Thar Desert, 63
Third World, 5, 7, 96, 110, 112, 194, 250, 252, 256-257, 312, 319
Thornthwaite, C.W., 81, 82
Thornthwaite Tank, 81
Three Rivers Station, 63
Tibesti mountains, 152
Tibet, 77
T'ien-shan range, 45, 47, 48, 213
Tigris (river), 25, 26, 28, 30, 34
Timurid(s), 299
Tofamanir (Niger), 141
Tokharia (Tokharians), 53, 293
Tokursai (river), 218
Tolba, Mostafa K., 12, 13, 16, 17, 21, 113
tourism, 177-178
Townley, Ralph, 10, 11, 16, 188
trade winds, 66
Transnational Projects, 13-14
Tribulus terrestris, 129
Tripolitania, 168
Triticum spp., 28, 281-282
trypanosomiasis, 124
tsetse fly, 124, 288
Tsinghai, 77
Tuareg (Kel Tamasheq), 3, 117, 167, 178, 222, 304
tubewells, 206-207, 211, 240

Tunisia, 7, 13, 16, 18, 84, 158
  case study in, 91
Turan, 19
  case study in, 293
  map of, 294
Turan Biosphere Reserve, 297, 298
Turfan, 19, 67, 85, 196, 213, 271, 273, 293, 295, 311
  case study in, 45
Turkestan, Chinese, 48
Turkestan Mountains, 213
Turkmenia (Turkmenistan), 255, 265, 278, 297
  case study in, 19, 227
  map of, 228
Turks (Turkmen), 47, 48, 216, 227, 229, 233, 242, 299

Uganda, 7
Uighur Turks, 47, 293
ujamaa vijijini, 266
Ukraine, 78
Ullman, Al, 174
Ulmus pumila, 55
Ulyanov, N.F., 213
UNESCO (United Nations Educational, Scientific and Cultural Organization), 5, 15, 16, 17, 18, 19, 34, 94, 97, 147, 168, 267
Union of Soviet Socialist Republics (USSR, Soviet Union), 19, 52, 197, 262-266, 270, 311, 313
  case studies in, 213, 227
United Arab Emirates, 7
United Nations, 3, 9, 15, 61, 84, 121, 188, 252, 263, 297
United Nations Centre for Economic and Social Information (CESI), 190
United Nations Conference on Desertification, 1, 6, 8, 11, 12, 13, 16, 20, 50, 97, 121, 140, 147, 236, 239, 256-257, 269, 271, 275, 285, 286-287, 312
United Nations Conference on Trade and Tariffs (1947), 8

United Nations conferences, 8, 167, 286
United Nations Declaration of Social Progress and Development, 261
United Nations Development Programme (UNDP), 18
United Nations Environment Programme (UNEP), 9, 15, 16, 167, 168
United Nations General Assembly, 6, 8, 9, 10, 15, 18, 236
United Nations Institute for Training and Research (UNITAR), 287
United States, 17, 197, 209, 215, 270, 286
  case study in, 163
United States Agency for International Development (AID), 4
University of Arizona, 17, 267
University of Cairo, 16, 168
University of California (Berkeley), 19
University of Massachusetts, 267
Upper Volta, 3, 135
Urumchi, 48
Uzbekistan (SSR), 216, 221, 223
Uze(s) (Ghuzz), 227

Vale District, 230, 235, 241, 249, 255, 265, 270, 313
  case study in, 163
  map of, 164
Vale Rehabilitation Program, 172
Venezuela, 7, 50
Vigna radiata, 185
Vinogradsky (S.N.), 233
Vitus vinifera L., 56

wadi, 94
Wakhan, the, 49
warabandi, 202
Ward, Barbara, 9
Warka (Erech), 30
Warren, Andrew, 10, 238

Washington (State), 66
Water and Power Development Authority (Pakistan), 201, 206
waterlogging, 27, 32, 33, 38, 202, 205-207, 309
Weber, Max, 309
West Africa, 13, 78, 84, 85
Western Australia, 59
wheat, 28, 52, 53, 95, 106, 155, 156, 183, 184, 211, 212, 279, 281-282
Willamette Valley, 165
wind, 239
  in Luni Block, 189
  in Turfan, 48, 56
  in Turkmenia, 240
  at Wushenchao, 86-87
Woodbury, Richard B., 267
woodcutting, 79, 104-107, 109, 137, 138-139, 142, 169, 185, 187, 238, 239, 240, 303
World Council of Churches, 261
World Map of Desertification, 15, 34, 50, 52, 82, 83, 100, 168; *see also* endpapers
World Meteorological Organization (WMO), 15, 19, 168
Wushenchao (commune), 196, 271, 273, 311
  case study in, 19, 77

Yaka Rig (Iran), 302, 304
Yellow River, 27, 54, 77
Yemen, 7
Yucatan, 27, 50
Yugoslavia, 7

Zagros-Taurus mountains, 28, 30, 32
Zaire, 7
Zarafshan (river), 216, 224
Zawi Chemi, 28, 297
Ziziphus lotus, 95
Ziziphus nummularia (jujube), 185, 186